KU-529-675

International Study Centre
Queen Margaret University College
Edinburgh EH12 8TS

Grammar Express

with answers

For self study or the classroom

Property of
Effective Learning Services
Queen Margaret University

Marjorie Fuchs & Margaret Bonner

with Kenna Bourke

Pearson Education Limited
Edinburgh Gate
Harlow
Essex CM20 2JE
England
and Associated Companies throughout the world.

www.longman.com

© Pearson Education Limited 2003

The right of Marjorie Fuchs and Margaret Bonner to be identified as authors of this Work has been asserted by them in accordance with the Copyright, Designs and Patents Act 1988.

Authorised adaptation from the American English language edition, entitled *Grammar Express*, First Edition by Marjorie Fuchs and Margaret Bonner published by Pearson Education, Inc, publishing as Addison Wesley Longman, Inc., Copyright © Addison Wesley Longman, Inc. 2001.

This edition published by Pearson Education Limited © Pearson Education Limited 2003.

All rights reserved; no part of this publication may be reproduced, stored in a retrieval system, or transmitted in any form or by any means, electronic, mechanical, photocopying, recording, or otherwise without the prior written permission of the Publishers.

ISBN 0 582 77645 7

Printed in Malaysia, PJB

Acknowledgements
The authors would like to thank Françoise Leffler, Senior Development Editor, and Christine Lauricella, Senior Production Editor, for their commitment and support.

The publishers and authors would like to thank the following people and institutions for their feedback and comments on the material:
Andrea McMahon - St Giles College, London; Pippa Sutcliffe - ILA Cambridge; Diane Naughton - Centro de Lenguas Modernas, Universidad de Granada; Sinforoso Fernández-Camuñas - Opening English School, Madrid.

Parts of *Grammar Express* are adapted from the intermediate and high intermediate levels of *Focus on Grammar, Second Edition* © 2000.

We are grateful to the following for permission to reproduce copyright material:

Photographs
Ace Photo Agency pages 132, 176; AP/Wide World page 268; Courtesy of Beth Boyd page 175; CORBIS pages 26 top (© Asian Art & Archeology, Inc), 26 bottom, 28 (© Bettmann), 48 (© S Carmona), 88 (© Jenny Woodcock/Reflections Photo Library); 166 (© Peter Guttman), 169 (© Kevin Schafer), 195 (© Kevin R Morris), 210 (© Tom Steward), 218 (Steven Chenn), 290 (© John Springer Collection), 304 (© Hulton-Deutsch Collection); Greg Evans International page 306 bottom; Mary Evans Picture Library page 238; Exposure New York/Stephen Danelian page 18; Katz/FSP pages 62, 235; © The New Yorker Collection, 1988 Charles Adams page 124; © The New Yorker Collection, 1989 Tom Cheney from cartoonbank.com.All Rights Reserved page 214; © The New Yorker Collection 1964 Frank Modell from cartoonbank.com. All Rights Reserved page 258; Courtesy of the New York State Governor's Traffic Safety Committee page 142; PA Photos/EPA page 192; PEANUTS© UFS page 286; PhotoDisc page 66(Jack Hollingsworth), 206(Bronwyn Kidd), 226(PhotoLink), 244(PhotoLink); Tony Freeman/PhotoEdit page 324; Powerstock/Superstock pages 162, 202; Reprinted with permission from Reader's Digest. Copyright © The Reader's Digest Assn.Inc pages 264, 266; Rex Features pages 70, 76; Bob Sacha page 110; © Michael Dwyer /Stock Boston Inc page 256; Neil Turner/Times Educational Supplements page 306 top.

Illustrations
Ronald Chironna pages 27, 34, 35, 65, 160, 191; Brian Hughes pages 20, 188; Jock MacRae pages 53, 180; Paul McCusker pages 38, 98, 294; Andy Myer pages 10, 32, 46, 54, 80, 82, 88, 102, 112, 116, 158, 192, 222, 232, 246, 254, 272, 282, 314, 322, 326; Dusan Petricic pages 2, 6, 8, 14, 16, 17, 18, 21, 36, 40, 50, 58, 60, 66, 74, 84, 92, 96, 106, 120, 128, 150, 184, 198, 236, 250, 278, 308, 318, 330; Steve Pleydell-Pearce pages 106, 142, 146, 172, 190, 300.

Text
Information on page 136 is based on the Roper Reports Worldwide 1998 Global Consumer Study

Cover by Raven Design

Contents

PART VII: Modals (II)

PART VIII: Adjectives and Adverbs

PART IX: Gerunds and Infinitives

Appendices

About the Book

Welcome to *Grammar Express*

Grammar Express features

- Short, easy-to-use **four-page units**
- **Grammar points** presented and **contextualised** through cartoons, photos and other illustrations
- Clear **Grammar Charts** showing the forms of the grammar point
- **Chart Checks** to help you use the grammar charts
- Clear **Grammar Explanations** and **Examples**
- **Usage Notes** telling you how English speakers use the grammar point
- **Be careful! Notes** showing typical mistakes students make
- **Pronunciation Notes** to help you pronounce words correctly
- A **variety of exercise types** to practise the grammar points
- **SelfTests** to check your progress
- **Appendices** with helpful lists and information
- An **Answer Key** so you can check your answers
- An **Index** to help you find grammar points quickly

UNITS

Grammar Express has 76 units. Each unit has four pages – two pages of grammar presentation and two pages of practice. This is how a typical unit works:

Presentation

The grammar point is presented in three steps.

1. **Illustration**

   Each unit begins with an illustration – a cartoon, comic strip, photo with speech bubbles or a newspaper headline – which introduces the grammar point in context. It also introduces the topic of the unit. (For example, in Unit 8 the cartoon introduces the grammar point *used to,* and the unit topic, fashion.)

   A **Check Point** helps you think about the meaning of the grammar point in the illustration.

2. **Charts**

Grammar Charts show the forms of the grammar point. (In Unit 8 you can see *used to* in statements, questions, and short answers.)

Chart Checks ask questions about the grammar charts. They help you notice important information about the forms and uses of the grammar point you are studying.

An **Express Check** follows the Grammar Charts. This is a quick and easy way for you to try out the forms in the charts.

3. **Notes**

Grammar Notes present **Grammar Explanations** on the left and **Examples** on the right. Timelines show the meaning of verb forms. (For example, in Unit 8 the timeline for *used to* shows that you can use it only for the past.)

Usage Notes tell you how English speakers use the grammar point. (In Unit 8 the Usage Note for *used to* explains that this form is more common in affirmative statements than in negative statements or questions.)

Be careful! Notes point out typical mistakes that students make. (One of the Be careful! Notes in Unit 8 warns you not to confuse *used to* with *be used to* or *get used to.*)

Pronunciation Notes tell you how to pronounce the grammar point correctly in everyday speech. These notes use easy pronunciation spellings.

Check it out! tells you where to look in the book (appendices or other units) to find more information about the grammar point.

Practice

Two pages of exercises give you practice in understanding and using the grammar point. A typical unit has four exercises.

Exercise 1

The first exercise is always a 'for recognition only' exercise. This means that you will have to find or understand the grammar point but you will not have to use it yet. (For example, in Unit 8 you will read a short magazine article about fashion, and find and underline all the examples of *used to* which refer to past habits.)

Exercises 2 and 3

In these exercises, you actively practise the grammar point. There are a variety of exercise types, including multiple choice, fill-in-the-blanks, describing pictures, sentence combining, and asking and answering questions. The exercises always show the grammar point in a context that is related to the unit topic. (In Unit 8, Exercise 2, you will complete sentences about fashion in the past while you describe pictures

Exercise 4

This is always an **editing** exercise. In this exercise, you will have to find and correct typical mistakes that students make when they use the grammar point.

TESTS

The 76 units of ***Grammar Express*** are divided into 15 parts. After each part you will find a **SelfTest**. These tests will help you review and see how well you have learnt the material in the part. The **SelfTests** have multiple-choice questions similar to questions found in a variety of international examinations.

APPENDICES

At the back of the book, you will find 32 **Appendices** with useful information, such as lists of common irregular verbs, verbs followed by the gerund, verbs followed by the infinitive, spelling and pronunciation rules and differences between British and American English.

An **Appendix Quiz** practises elements from the Appendices.

ANSWER KEY

The **Answer Key** provides answers to the Check Points, Charts Checks, Express Checks, all the practice exercises and the SelfTests.

Grammar Express can be used for self study or in the classroom. You can either start with Unit 1 and work through the entire book, or choose the units you want to focus on. We hope you enjoy learning grammar with ***Grammar Express***.

Good luck!

UNIT 1 Present Continuous

Hundreds of fans **are waiting** for the Airheads to arrive.
AIRHEADS
Wow! The Airheads **are dropping** from the sky!

CHECK POINT

Tick the best advertisement for this TV news programme.

❒ It's happening now!

❒ It happens every day!

CHART CHECK 1

Tick the correct answer.

The present continuous is made up of two parts:

❒ ***be*** + base form of verb

❒ ***be*** + base form of verb + ***-ing***

Which part changes with different subjects?

❒ ***be***

❒ base form of verb + ***-ing***

AFFIRMATIVE STATEMENTS		
Subject	***Be***	**Base Form of Verb + *-ing***
I	**am** **'m**	**waiting**.
He/She/It	**is** **'s**	
We/You*/They	**are** **'re**	

*You is both singular and plural.

NEGATIVE STATEMENTS			
Subject	***Be***	***Not***	**Base Form of Verb + *-ing***
I	**am** **'m**	**not**	**waiting**.
He/She/It	**is** **'s**	**n't** **not**	
We/You/They	**are** **'re**	**n't** **not**	

CHART CHECK 2

Circle T (True) or F (False).

T F In questions, ***be*** comes after the subject.

***YES/NO* QUESTIONS**		
BE	**SUBJECT**	**BASE FORM + -ING**
Am	I	**standing**?
Is	she	
Are	you	

SHORT ANSWERS					
AFFIRMATIVE			**NEGATIVE**		
Yes,	you	**are.**	**No,**	you	**aren't.**
	she	**is.**		she	**isn't.**
	I	**am.**		I	**'m not.**

***WH-* QUESTIONS**			
WH- WORD	**BE**	**SUBJECT**	**BASE FORM + -ING**
Why Where	**am**	I	**standing**?
	is	she	
	are	you	

EXPRESS CHECK

Complete these sentences with the present continuous form of the verbs in brackets.

Why ______________ you ______________ (leave)? They ______________ still ______________ (perform).

Grammar Explanations	Examples
1. Use the **present continuous** to describe something that is happening now.  	■ I'**m standing** outside the Theatre Royal ***right now***. ■ As I'**m talking** to you, the fans **are gathering** in front of the theatre.
2. Use the **present continuous** to describe something that is happening these days, even if it's not happening right now. 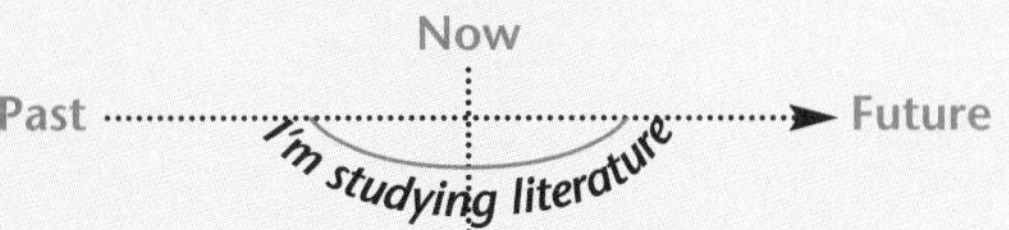 	■ The Airheads **are playing** at the Theatre Royal ***this week***. ■ I'**m studying** literature ***this term***.
3. USAGE NOTE: The **contracted form** is usually used in speech and in informal writing.	**A:** Bye, Jack, we'**re leaving** now. **B:** Wait! I'**m coming** with you.

Check it out!

For different forms of negative contractions with *be,* see Appendix 24 on page 345.
For spelling rules for the present continuous, see Appendix 19 on page 343.

1 ***IDENTIFY*** • *Read this letter. Underline the present continuous verbs that describe something happening now. Circle the present continuous verbs that describe things that are happening these days.*

Dear Steve,

I'm working very hard these days, but I have some good news. Right now, I'm sitting at a desk in the Entertainment Section of the *Tribune*! Of course I'm still taking journalism classes at night as well. The job is temporary – Joe Sims, the regular reporter, is taking this month off to write a book. This week we're preparing to interview your favourite group, the Airheads. In fact, at this very moment they're flying into town by helicopter. They're performing at the Theatre Royal all week. How are you getting on? Are you still writing music? Oops! The crew are calling me. We're leaving for the theatre now. Write soon!

Steph

2 ***COMPLETE*** • *Read this conversation. Complete it with the present continuous form of the verbs in brackets. Use contractions whenever possible.*

BEV: Bye, Joe, I __'m leaving__ (1. leave) now.

JOE: Where ________ you ________ (2. go)?

BEV: I ________ (3. go) running. Ann ________ (4. wait) downstairs.

JOE: Great! Why don't you take the dog out with you?

BEV: Why don't *you* take him? It's your turn.

JOE: I can't. I ________ (5. work) on my book.

BEV: But you ________ (6. not do) anything right now. You ________ just ________ (7. sit) there.

JOE: That's not true. I ________ (8. sit) here but I ________ also ________ (9. think) about my work. Can't the dog go with you?

BEV: No, because afterwards we want to go to the Plaza. The Airheads ________ (10. stay) there this week and Ann wants to get their autographs. You know she's a big fan of theirs.

ASK & ANSWER • *Steph is interviewing Paul, the lead singer of the Airheads. Write questions using the words in brackets. Give short answers.*

STEPH: Paul, are you introducing any new songs on this tour?
1. (introduce / any new songs on this tour?)

PAUL: Yes, we are. We're introducing some songs from our new album, *In the Air.*
2. (Yes / we)

STEPH: Your fans are so excited to see you after such a long time.
____
3. (Why / tour / again?)

PAUL: We want to play for live audiences. We enjoy that.

STEPH: ____________________
4. (What / work on / these days?)

PAUL: Some exciting new material. But we aren't talking about it yet.

STEPH: ____________________
5. (Who / sing / now?)

PAUL: Sylvia is singing some of the songs from the album.

STEPH: ____________________
6. (she / replace / Tina?)

PAUL: ____________________. Tina has just had a new baby but she'll be back in a few months.
7. (No / she)

EDIT • *Read this letter. Find and correct six mistakes in the use of the present continuous. The first mistake has already been corrected.*

I ~~write~~ 'm writing to you from my hotel room. Everyone else is sleep but I sitting here, looking at the sea. We're staying at the Plaza in Atlantic Beach and the view is beautiful. The tour is goes well. The audience is crazy about the new songs but the fans is always asking for you. How's the baby? Has she got a good voice? Do you teaching her to sing yet? Maybe both of you will come along for the next tour!

Sylvia

UNIT 2 Present Simple

John **is** always in a hurry and he **does** everything at once.

He **works** all the time – he never **relaxes**.

CHECK POINT

Tick the best caption for the cartoons.

❒ John At Work This Week

❒ John's Typical Working Week

CHART CHECK

Circle T (True) or F (False).

T F The form for ***he/she/it*** ends in ***-s***.

T F Negative statements have ***do not*** or ***does not*** before the base form.

T F Questions have ***do*** or ***does*** after the subject.

AFFIRMATIVE STATEMENTS

Subject	Verb
I/We/You*/They	**work.**
He/She/It	**works.**

**You* is both singular and plural.

NEGATIVE STATEMENTS

Subject	Do not	Base Form
I/We/You/They	**do not** **don't**	**work.**
He/She/It	**does not** **doesn't**	

***YES/NO* QUESTIONS**

Do	Subject	Base Form
Do	you	**work?**
Does	he	

SHORT ANSWERS

Affirmative			Negative		
Yes,	I	**do.**	**No,**	I	**don't.**
	he	**does.**		he	**doesn't.**

WH- QUESTIONS			
***WH-* WORD**	***DO***	**SUBJECT**	**BASE FORM**
Where When	**do**	you	**work**?
	does	he	

EXPRESS CHECK

Unscramble these words to complete the question.

work • Why • he • does ______________________________ all the time?

Grammar Explanations	Examples
1. Use the **present simple** to talk about what happens regularly. 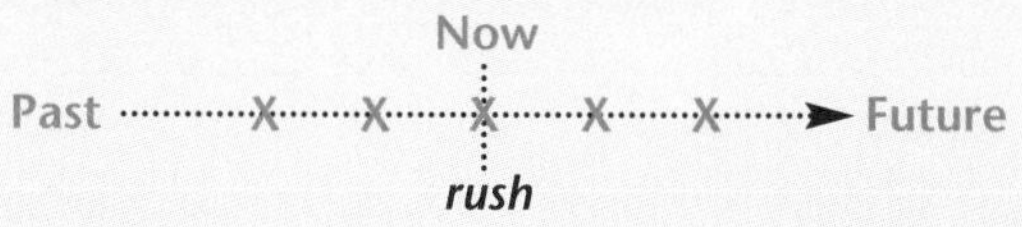	■ Some people **rush** through life. ■ They **don't relax**. ■ Other people **are** calm. ■ They **don't feel** tense.
2. Use **adverbs of frequency** with the present simple to express how often something happens. 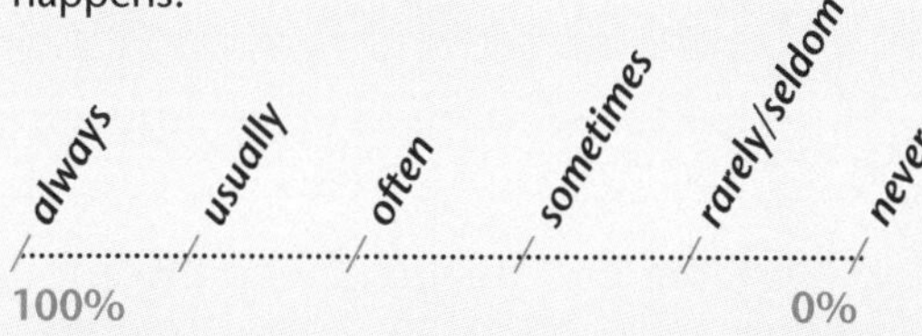	■ She ***never* relaxes**. ■ You ***usually* take** life easier. ■ We ***sometimes* sleep** late. ■ They ***rarely* go** on holiday.
▶ **BE CAREFUL!** Adverbs of frequency usually come before the main verb but they go after the verb ***be***.	■ We ***usually* rush** around too much. ■ We**'re *often*** stressed out.
3. Use the **present simple** to talk about scientific facts.	■ Stress **causes** high blood pressure. ■ Water **freezes** at 0°C.

Check it out!

For spelling rules for the third person singular *(he / she / it)* of the present simple, see Appendix 20 on page 343.

For pronunciation rules for the third person singular *(he / she / it)* of the present simple, see Appendix 27 on page 348.

IDENTIFY • *Read this extract from a book review. Underline the present simple verbs. Circle the adverbs of frequency.*

Books Section 10

CALM DOWN! By Dr Sara Roads

In today's fast-paced world, we (never) escape stress. Stress always affects us psychologically but according to Dr Roads, author of the new bestseller, *Calm Down!*, it also affects us physically. For example, stress causes high blood pressure. Doctors often prescribe medication for stress-related illnesses. Medicine usually lowers a patient's blood pressure. But, Dr Roads claims, 'You don't always need pills. Relaxation exercises are sometimes as effective as pills. For example, breathing exercises relax you and lower your blood pressure at the same time – and it only takes a few minutes!'

COMPLETE • *Megan and Greg have completely different types of personality. Read about one and write about the other.*

Megan	Greg
1. Megan **doesn't relax** easily.	• Greg ___relaxes___ easily.
2. She ___doesn't take___ time to enjoy herself.	• He **takes** time to enjoy himself.
3. Megan and her boyfriend never **go** on holiday.	• Greg and his girlfriend often ______________ on holiday.
4. She ______________ through the day.	• He **doesn't rush** through the day.
5. She **is** nervous.	• He ______________ nervous.
6. She **is** always in a hurry.	• He ______________ never in a hurry.
7. She **finishes** other people's sentences for them.	• He ______________ other people's sentences for them.
8. She ______________ a lot.	• He **doesn't worry** much.
9. She ______________ enough time to finish things.	• He**'s got** enough time to finish things.
10. Megan**'s got** high blood pressure due to stress.	• Greg ______________ high blood pressure due to stress.

ASK & ANSWER • *Peter is an accountant. Look at his schedule. Write questions and answers about his day.*

MONDAY NOVEMBER 18

6:00–7:00	get up, exercise	**12:00–12:30**	lunch
8:00–9:00	work on reports	**12:30–5:00**	return phone calls
9:00–12:00	see clients	**5:30–7:00**	go to evening class

1. When / get up?
   When does he get up? ______ He gets up at 6:00. ______
2. exercise in the morning?
   Does he exercise in the morning? ______ Yes, he does. ______
3. work on reports in the afternoon?
   ______ ______
4. When / see clients?
   ______ ______
5. have a lunch break?
   ______ ______
6. What / do / from 12:30 to 5:00?
   ______ ______
7. Where / go / at 5:30?
   ______ ______

EDIT • *Read Peter's diary entry. Find and correct ten mistakes in the use of the present simple. The first mistake has already been corrected.*

I'm so tired. I ~~have never~~ [never have] time to relax. I work all day and studies all night. My boss tell me that I need a holiday. I agree but I afraid to take one. Does my boss thinks that the office can function without me? I dont want them to think I'm not necessary. But my wife is unhappy, too. She complain that she never sees me any more. My schedule are crazy. I don't think I can keep this up much longer. I don't wants to give up evening classes, though. I think often that there has got to be a better way.

UNIT 3 Stative Verbs

CHECK POINT

Tick the correct answer.

According to the fish, the worm

❐ has the flavour of chicken.

❐ behaves like a chicken.

CHART CHECK

Circle T (True) or F (False).

T F Some verbs have both a stative and an active meaning.

T F A verb used with a stative meaning is not used in the continuous.

VERBS WITH STATIVE MEANINGS
I **want** to go fishing.
He **owns** a big boat.
The weather **seems** fine.
They **hate** fish.

VERBS WITH BOTH STATIVE AND ACTIVE MEANINGS	
NON-ACTION	**ACTION**
The fish **weighs** five pounds.	He**'s weighing** the fish now.
We **think** it's a good day for fishing.	We**'re thinking** about going.
This fish **tastes** delicious.	I**'m tasting** the fish now.
This food **smells** good.	The cook **is smelling** the food.

EXPRESS CHECK

Complete these sentences with the correct form of the verb **weigh.**

I _______________ the fish now. It _______________ five kilos.

Grammar Explanations	Examples
1. Many verbs describe states or situations instead of actions. These verbs are called **stative verbs**.	■ John **owns** a boat. *(The verb **own** describes John's situation, not something he is doing.)*
Most stative verbs are not usually used in the present continuous even when they describe a situation that is happening now.	■ He **wants** fish for dinner. NOT ~~He is wanting fish for dinner.~~
2. Stative verbs are usually verbs that:	
a. describe a **state of being** *(be, feel)*	■ Jane **is** tired but happy. ■ She **feels** good.
b. express **emotions** *(hate, like, love)*	**A:** Do you **like** my new dress? **B:** I **love** it!
c. describe **mental states** *(know, remember, believe, think [= believe], suppose, understand)*	■ I **know** a lot of good recipes. ■ Ali **remembers** your number. ■ I **think** you're right.
d. show **possession** *(have, have got, own, possess, belong)*	■ This bike **belongs** to Sam. ■ Some students **own** microwaves.
e. describe **perceptions** and **senses** *(hear, see, smell, taste, feel, notice, seem, look [= seem], appear, sound)*	■ I **feel** relaxed. ■ David **seems** tired.
f. describe **needs** and **preferences** *(need, want, prefer)*	■ I **need** a pen.
g. describe **measurements** *(weigh, cost, contain)*	■ How much **does** it **cost**?
3. **Can** is often used with verbs of perception. We do not usually use the continuous form.	■ I **can hear** the telephone. NOT ~~I hear the telephone.~~ NOT ~~I'm hearing the telephone.~~ ■ **Can** you **smell** gas? NOT ~~Are you smelling gas?~~
4. **BE CAREFUL!** Some verbs can have stative and active meanings ***(taste, smell, feel, look, think, have, weigh)***.	STATIVE ■ I **can taste** garlic. Did you put some in? *(I notice garlic.)* ■ The soup **tastes** good. Try some. *(The soup is good.)* ACTION ■ I'**m tasting** the soup to see if it needs more salt. *(I'm trying the soup.)*

Check it out!

For a list of common stative verbs, see Appendix 2 on page 337.

IDENTIFY • *Read this conversation. Underline all the stative verbs that describe a situation that is in progress. Circle all the stative verbs that describe a situation that is generally true.*

ANNA: This steak tastes delicious. Your salmon looks good, too.

BEN: Here, I'm putting some on your plate. I think you'll like it.

ANNA: Mmm. I do like it! Funny, I usually don't like fish.

BEN: Red has that effect on people.

ANNA: I have no idea what you're talking about. What do you mean?

BEN: Well, colours can change the way we feel. For example, people often feel hungrier in a red room. I notice that you're looking at the red wallpaper.

ANNA: And I certainly feel hungry. I'm eating half your salmon.

BEN: That's OK. I'm tasting your steak. It's delicious!

CHOOSE • *Complete this magazine article with the correct form of the verbs in brackets.*

John Bints is in a sports shop. The flowers ____smell____ (1. smell / are smelling) nice but he isn't really paying attention to the scent because he ________ (2. looks / is looking) at a pair of running shoes. They ________ (3. cost / are costing) a lot more than he usually pays but John really, really ________ (4. wants / is wanting) those shoes. He's the victim of 'smart scents', aromas that shops use to make customers buy more.

The other side of the town, John's daughter Myra is doing a history test in a classroom that was recently painted yellow. Although Myra ________ (5. hates / is hating) history, she ________ (6. seems / is seeming) to be doing well on this test. She ________ (7. likes / is liking) the new colour of her classroom. She ________ (8. doesn't suspect / isn't suspecting) that it's helping her with the test, but it is. Scientists have shown that yellow improves both memory and concentration.

We now ________ (9. know / are knowing) that smells, colours and sounds affect our moods and even our health. In fact, right now John's wife, Cindy, ________ (10. thinks / is thinking) about John and Myra. She's sure that John is spending too much on shoes and that Myra is failing another history test. Cindy suffers from migraines but she ________ (11. hasn't got / isn't having) a headache today. She's in the garden and she ________ (12. listens / is listening) to bird and insect sounds. They always calm her down.

COMPLETE • *Read this conversation. Complete it with the correct form of the verbs in brackets. Use the present continuous or the present simple.*

A: Hi, Ali. Mmm. Something ___smells___ (1. smell) good! What's cooking?

B: Fish soup. I ______________ (2. taste) it to see if it ______________ (3. need) more garlic. ______________ you ______________ (4. want) to try it?

A: Mmmm. It ______________ (5. taste) good but I ______________ (6. think) it needs salt.

B: OK. I ______________ (7. think) of adding some tomatoes, even though it ______________ (8. not be) in the recipe.

A: That ______________ (9. sound) like a good idea. But wait a minute. I ______________ (10. look) at the recipe and it says you can add milk. How about that?

B: I ______________ (11. not know) if the milk ______________ (12. be) fresh.

A: I'll check. Hmm. I ______________ (13. smell) it but I ______________ (14. not be) sure. Let's add the tomatoes instead.

B: OK. I ______________ (15. love) cooking! The whole house ______________ (16. smell) great when you cook. And it always puts me in a good mood.

A: I ______________ (17. know) what you ______________ (18. mean). I ______________ (19. feel) the same way.

EDIT • *Read this diary entry. There are eight mistakes in the use of active and stative verbs. Find and correct them. The first mistake has already been corrected.*

16 March

Not a good day! I feel depressed and I've got a headache. ~~I'm needing~~ need to do something to change my mood and get rid of this pain. Last week, I'm reading an article about how smells can affect mood and even health, so at the moment I smell an orange (for the depression) and a green apple (for the headache). They smell nice but I'm not thinking that I notice a difference in how I feel! I think I'm preferring to eat something when I feel down. But I worry that I'm weighing too much. So, at the moment I have a cup of peppermint tea with lemon. The article says that the peppermint smell helps you eat less. Well, I don't know about that! A chocolate ice cream sounds pretty good right now! It's seeming that there are no easy solutions.

UNIT 4 Present Continuous and Present Simple

Cross-Cultural Confusion

Friends from different cultures often **have** different ideas about time.

Sometimes they **don't agree** about social distance, either.

CHECK POINT

Circle T (True) or F (False).

T F Karl is arriving late tonight.

T F In Sam's culture, people rarely stand close to each other.

CHART CHECK

Tick the correct answers.

The present continuous has:

❒ one part

❒ two parts

The present simple has:

❒ one form

❒ two forms

PRESENT CONTINUOUS			
Subject	***Be***	**Base Form + *-ing***	
I	**am**	**arriving**	now.
We/You*/They	**are**		
He/She/It	**is**		

*You is both singular and plural.

PRESENT SIMPLE			
Subject		**Verb**	
I/We/You/They	never always	**arrive**	on time.
He/She/It		**arrives**	

EXPRESS CHECK

*Complete the following charts with the verb **buy**.*

PRESENT CONTINUOUS			
SUBJECT	BE	BASE FORM + -ING	
I			flowers now.
You			
He			

PRESENT SIMPLE			
SUBJECT		VERB	
I	usually		chocolates.
You			
He			

Grammar Explanations

Examples

1. Use the **present continuous** for things that are happening now.

- Sam **is talking** to Taro.
- At the moment, Taro **is speaking** English.

Use the **present simple** to describe what happens regularly.

- Sam **talks** to Taro every day.
- Taro **speaks** Japanese at home.

2. Use the **present continuous** for things happening these days.

Now
Past
Future
We're studying.

- We**'re studying** in the US ***this month***.
- Laura**'s studying** in France ***this year***.
- **Are** you **studying** hard ***these days***?

3. **REMEMBER!** Most **stative verbs*** are not usually used in the present continuous even when they describe a situation that exists at the moment of speaking.

- Jane **wants** to go home right now.
  NOT ~~Jane is wanting to go home right now.~~

4. Use the **present simple** to talk about scientific facts and physical laws.

- Stress **causes** high blood pressure.
- Water **boils** at 100°C.

Check it out!

*For a list of common stative verbs, see Appendix 2 on page 337.

IDENTIFY • *Read these diary entries written by Brian, a student studying in Argentina. Circle all the verbs that describe what is happening now. Underline the verbs that describe what usually happens.*

28 June: (I'm sitting) in a seat 3,000 metres above the earth en route to Argentina! I usually <u>have</u> dinner at this time but right now I've got a headache from the excitement. The person next to me is eating my food. She looks happy.

30 June: It's 7:30. My host's parents are still working. Carlos, the father, works at home. The youngest son, Ricardo, is sweet. He looks (and behaves) a lot like Bobby. Right now, he's looking over my shoulder and trying to read my diary.

4 July: The weather is cold now. I usually spend the first weekend of July at the beach but today I'm walking around in a heavy sweater.

6 August: I feel so tired tonight. Everyone else feels great in the evening because they have long naps in the afternoon.

2

COMPLETE • *Some students are talking outside a classroom. Complete their conversations with the present continuous or the present simple form of the verbs in brackets.*

1. **LI-WU:** Hi, Paulo. What ___are___ you ___doing___ ? (**a.** (do))

   PAULO: Oh, I ________ (**b.** (wait)) for the class to start.

   LI-WU: How are you? You ________ (**c.** (look)) tired.

   PAULO: I *am* a little tired. I ________ (**d.** (work)) a lot in the evenings this term. Hey, is that your teacher over there?

   LI-WU: Yes. She ________ (**e.** (talk)) to one of my classmates.

   PAULO: I wonder what's wrong. He ________ (**f.** (not look)) at her. He ________ (**g.** (look)) embarrassed.

   LI-WU: Oh. That ________ (**h.** (not mean)) anything. In Taiwan it's not respectful to look directly at your teacher.

2. **MORIKO:** Look, there's Miguel. He ________ (**a.** (talk)) to Luisa.

   NINA: Yes. They ________ (**b.** (do)) a class together this term.

Moriko: They ______ (c. stand) very close to each other. ______ you ______ (d. think) they ______ (e. go out) together?

Nina: No. I ______ (f. not think) it ______ (g. mean) anything special. I ______ (h. come) from Costa Rica, and people there normally ______ (i. stand) that close to each other.

3. **Rasha:** There's Hans. Why ______ he ______ (a. walk) so fast? The lesson ______ (b. not start) until 9:00. He ______ still ______ (c. have got) ten minutes!

Claude: He always ______ (d. walk) fast. People from Switzerland often ______ (e. seem) to be in a hurry.

4. **Yoko:** Isn't that Sergio and Luis? Why ______ they ______ (a. shake) hands? They ______ (b. know) each other.

Jing: In Brazil, men ______ (c. shake) hands every time they ______ (d. meet).

EDIT • *Read this student's diary. Find and correct eleven mistakes in the use of the present continuous or present simple. The first mistake has already been corrected.*

It's 12:30 and ~~I sit~~ I'm sitting in the library. My classmates are eating lunch together but I'm not hungry yet. At home, we eat never this early. Today our homework topic is 'culture shock'. It's a good topic for me right now because I'm being pretty homesick. I miss my old routine. At home we always are having a big meal at 2:00 in the afternoon. Then we rest. But here in Toronto I'm having a conversation class at 3:00. Every day, I almost fall asleep in class, and my teacher ask me, 'Are you bored?' Of course I'm not bored. I just need my afternoon rest! This class always is fun. This term, we work on a project with video cameras. My team is filming groups of people from different cultures. We are analyse 'social distance'. That means how close to each other people stand. According to my new watch, it's 12:55, so I leave now for my one o'clock class. Teachers here really aren't liking it when you are late!

Unit 5 Imperative

To do this exercise, **bend** your knees and **place** your right foot in front, like this. **Punch** with your right fist.

CHECK POINT

Check the correct answer.

The woman in the photo is

❒ giving instructions on how to do an exercise.

❒ ordering someone to do an exercise.

CHART CHECK

Tick the correct answer.

Imperative sentences

❒ include a subject.

❒ don't include a subject.

AFFIRMATIVE	
BASE FORM OF VERB	
Bend	your knees.
Punch	with your fist.

NEGATIVE		
DON'T	**BASE FORM OF VERB**	
Don't	bend	your knees.
	punch	with your fist.

EXPRESS CHECK

Use these verbs to complete the charts.

touch listen stand up

AFFIRMATIVE	
Base Form of Verb	
	to the music.
	your toes.
	straight.

NEGATIVE		
Don't	**Base Form of Verb**	
		to the music.
		your toes.
		straight.

Grammar Explanations	Examples
1. The **imperative** form of the verb is always the base form. It is the same whether it is directed at one or several people.	■ Mary, please **get** ready. ■ **Get** ready, guys!
2. The **subject** of an imperative statement is ***you***. However, we do not say or write *you* in imperative sentences.	■ **Stand up** straight. Not ~~You stand up straight~~.
3. The imperative form has a number of **uses**. Use the imperative to:	
a. give **directions** and **instructions**	■ **Turn** left at the traffic lights.
b. give **orders** or **commands**	■ **Don't move!**
c. make **requests** (Use *please* in addition to the imperative form.)	■ ***Please* read** this article. ■ **Read** this article, ***please***.
d. give **advice** or make **suggestions**	■ **Don't exercise** if you feel unwell.
e. give **warnings**	■ **Be** careful! **Don't trip over** that mat!
f. invite someone	■ **Come** to the gym with us tomorrow.

MATCH • *Match each imperative with the correct situation.*

	Imperative		Situation
g	1. Don't touch that!	a.	Someone is visiting a friend.
____	2. Look both ways.	b.	Someone is going out into the cold.
____	3. Dress warmly!	c.	Someone is crossing a street.
____	4. Don't bend your knees.	d.	Someone is taking an exam.
____	5. Mark each answer true or false.	e.	Someone is exercising.
____	6. Come in. Make yourself at home.	f.	Someone is tasting some food.
____	7. Add a little more pepper.	g.	Something is hot.

2

MATCH • *You're going to give instructions for making a banana-strawberry shake. Match a verb from column A with a phrase from column B.*

Column A	Column B
Add	the ingredients until smooth.
Slice	six strawberries.
Wash	a banana.
Cut	orange juice into the blender.
Blend	the strawberries in half.
Pour	the fruit to the orange juice.

LABEL • *Now write the sentences in order under the correct pictures.*

1. Slice a banana.
2. ____________________
3. ____________________

4. ____________________
5. ____________________
6. ____________________

CHOOSE & COMPLETE • *Read this advertisement for a martial arts school. Complete it using the affirmative or negative imperative form of the verbs in the box.*

get	choose	reduce	improve	learn
miss	register	take	~~think~~	delay

MARTIAL ARTS ACADEMY

Don't think (1.) that martial arts is only about physical training. A good martial arts programme offers many other benefits as well. ________ (2.) self-defence and more at the Martial Arts Academy:

- ________ (3.) stress. Martial arts training helps you relax.
- ________ (4.) your concentration. Martial arts students focus better.
- ________ (5.) fit. Strength and flexibility improve as you learn.

We are offering an introductory trial membership. ________ (6.) this special opportunity. ________ (7.) lessons with Master Lorenzo Gibbons, a ninth-level Black Belt Master. ________ (8.) classes from our convenient timetable.

________ (9.)! ________ (10.) now for a two-week trial.

ONLY £20. ◆ UNIFORM INCLUDED.

EDIT • *Read part of a martial arts student's essay. Find and correct five mistakes in the use of the imperative. The first mistake has already been corrected.*

For the Black Belt essay, Master Gibbons gave us this assignment: ~~You write~~ Write about something important to you. My topic is *The Right Way*, the rules of life for the martial arts. First, respects other people – treat them the way you want them to treat you. Second, helped people in need. In other words, use your strength for others, not to use it just for your own good. Third, no lie or steal. These are the most important rules to me.

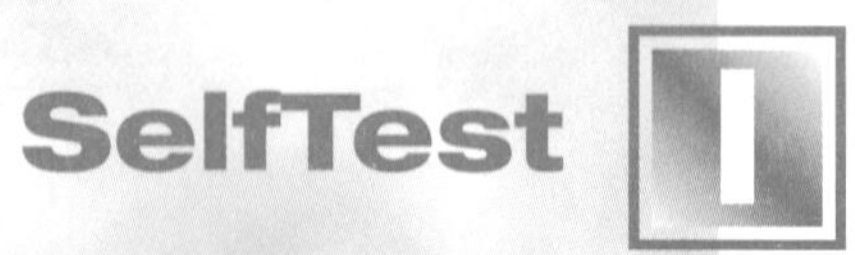

SECTION ONE

Circle the letter of the correct answer to complete each sentence.

EXAMPLE:

Jennifer never _______ coffee. A (B) C D

(A) drink (C) is drinking

(B) drinks (D) was drinking

1. _______ ready for school? It's already 7:00. A B C D
   (A) Do you get (C) You get
   (B) Are you getting (D) You are getting

2. Nick _______ to Greece every year to visit his family. A B C D
   (A) is going (C) go
   (B) he goes (D) goes

3. Why _______? The lesson isn't over yet. A B C D
   (A) are you leaving (C) do you leave
   (B) you are leaving (D) you leaving

4. Something _______ good. Is that fresh bread in the oven? A B C D
   (A) smells (C) smell
   (B) is smelling (D) smelling

5. Which class _______ best? A B C D
   (A) are you liking (C) you like
   (B) you are liking (D) do you like

6. _______ loose clothes to exercise. You'll be more comfortable. A B C D
   (A) Wear (C) Wears
   (B) Wearing (D) You wear

7. Please _______ to class on time. We start at exactly 9:00. A B C D
   (A) we come (C) you're coming
   (B) come (D) comes

8. I _______ something outside. Are the doors locked? A B C D
   (A) 'm hearing (C) hearing
   (B) can hear (D) hears

9. Walk! _______ run! A B C D
   (A) Not (C) Don't
   (B) No (D) You don't

10. —Do you like fish? A B C D
    —Yes, I _______.
    (A) am (C) don't
    (B) do (D) like

11. Harry works all the time. He ________. A B C D
(A) never relaxes
(B) relaxes never
(C) often relaxes
(D) relaxes sometimes

12. What ________ these days? A B C D
(A) are you doing
(B) do you do
(C) you are doing
(D) you do

13. The baby's so big! How much ________ now? A B C D
(A) weigh
(B) she weighs
(C) is she weighing
(D) does she weigh

14. —Are you taking an English class this term? A B C D
—Yes, I ________.
(A) take
(B) am taking
(C) do
(D) am

15. Water ________ at 100°C. A B C D
(A) boil
(B) boils
(C) boiled
(D) is boiling

SECTION TWO

Each sentence has four underlined words or phrases. The four underlined parts of the sentence are marked A, B, C and D. Circle the letter of the one underlined word or phrase that is NOT CORRECT.

EXAMPLE:
Mike usually (A) drives (B) to school but today (C) he walks (D). A B C (D)

16. Fran usually is swimming (A) before work (B) but this morning she's (C) jogging (D). A B C D

17. The wind is blowing (A), it (B) rains (C) and the sky looks (D) grey. A B C D

18. Where (A) you are (B) working (C) these days after school (D)? A B C D

19. The floor is (A) wet so walk (B) slowly and no (C) fall down (D)! A B C D

20. Something (A) is seeming (B) different – are (C) you wearing (D) a new perfume? A B C D

21. We always (A) eat out (B) because we hates (C) cooking (D). A B C D

22. Peter arrives usually (A) early but (B) today (C) he's (D) late. A B C D

23. I need (A) my CD player if you don't (B) using (C) it at the moment (D). A B C D

24. I never (A) have (B) anything to write with because (C) I'm always lose (D) my pens. A B C D

25. Turn (A) left at the lights and you (B) don't (C) forget (D) to signal! A B C D

Past Simple: Affirmative Statements

Oh, Albert! You were a good man but a terrible poet!
I was a poet.
I travelled far and wide.
I lived till I was 80
and then I died.
ALBERT RIMES
1910–1990
RIP

CHECK POINT

Tick the year these sentences appeared in the newspaper.

'Poet Albert Rimes lives in Belgium.'

❐ 1989 ❐ 1999

'Poet Albert Rimes lived in Belgium most of his life.'

❐ 1989 ❐ 1999

CHART CHECK

Tick the correct answer.

How many forms has the past tense of ***be*** got?

❐ one ❐ two

What do you add to the base form of regular verbs to form the past tense?

❐ *-d* or *-ed* ❐ *-t*

THE PAST SIMPLE: *BE*		
SUBJECT	***BE***	
I/He/She/It	**was**	young in 1930.
We/You*/They	**were**	

**You* is both singular and plural.

THE PAST SIMPLE: REGULAR VERBS		
SUBJECT	**VERB**	
I/He/She/It/We/You/They	**moved**	fifty years ago.
	worked	

THE PAST SIMPLE: IRREGULAR VERBS		
SUBJECT	**VERB**	
I/He/She/It/We/You/They	**wrote**	poetry.
	became	famous.
	built	a monument.

EXPRESS CHECK

Complete the chart.

BASE FORM OF VERB	**PAST SIMPLE**
be	____________ and ____________
come	____________
save	____________

Grammar Explanations / Examples

1. Use the **past simple** to talk about things that are now finished.

Past ········X········ Now ········► Future
He was a poet.

- Albert Rimes **lived** in the twentieth century.
- He **was** a poet.
- He **wrote** poetry.

2. You can use the **past simple** with **time expressions** that refer to the past *(last week, by 1980, in the twentieth century, fifty years ago).*

- ***By 1930***, he **was** famous.
- He **died** over ***ten years ago***.

3. The **past simple** of **regular verbs** is formed by adding *-d* or *-ed*.

► **BE CAREFUL!** There are often spelling changes when you add *-ed* to the verb.

Many common verbs are **irregular**. Their past tense is not formed by adding *-d* or *-ed*.

BASE FORM		**PAST SIMPLE**
live	→	live**d**
join	→	join**ed**
play	→	play**ed**
study	→	studi**ed**
hop	→	hop**ped**
be	→	**was/were**
have	→	**had**
get	→	**got**
go	→	**went**

Check it out!

For spelling rules for the past simple of regular verbs, see Appendix 21 on page 344.

For pronunciation rules for the past simple of regular verbs, see Appendix 28 on page 348.

For a list of irregular verbs, see Appendix 1 on pages 336–337.

IDENTIFY • *Read about Japanese poet Matsuo Basho. Underline all the regular past tense verbs. Circle all the irregular past tense verbs.*

Matsuo Basho wrote more than 1,000 three-line poems or 'haiku'. He chose topics from nature, daily life and human emotions. He became one of Japan's most famous poets and his work established haiku as an important art form.

Matsuo Basho was born near Kyoto in 1644. His father wanted him to become a samurai (warrior). Instead, Matsuo moved to Edo (present-day Tokyo) and studied poetry. By 1681, he had many students and admirers.

Basho's home burnt down in 1682. Then, in 1683, his mother died. After these events, Basho felt restless. In 1684, he travelled on foot and on horseback all over Japan. Sometimes his friends joined him and they wrote poetry together. Travel was difficult in the seventeenth century and Basho was often ill. He died in 1694 during a journey to Osaka. At that time he had 2,000 students.

CHOOSE & COMPLETE • *Read this biography of another poet, Emily Dickinson. Complete it using the past simple form of the verbs in the box.*

be	become	lead	leave	~~live~~	see	wear	write

Emily Dickinson, one of the most popular American poets, ___lived___ (1.) from 1830 to 1886. She __________ (2.) about love, nature and time. These __________ (3.) her favourite themes. Dickinson __________ (4.) an unusual life. After just one year of college, she __________ (5.) a recluse – she almost never __________ (6.) her house in Amherst, Massachusetts. At home, she __________ (7.) no one except her family, and she only __________ (8.) white.

address appear happen write

In addition to her poetry, Dickinson __________ (9.) many letters. Other people always __________ (10.) the envelopes for her. During her lifetime only seven of her 1,700 poems __________ (11.) in print – and this __________ (12.) without her knowledge or permission.

Now complete these lines from a poem by Emily Dickinson.

bite ~~come~~ drink eat hop see

A bird ___came___ (13.) down the walk:
He did not know I __________ (14.);
He __________ (15.) an angle-worm in halves
And __________ (16.) the fellow raw.
And then he __________ (17.) a dew
From a convenient grass,
And then __________ (18.) sidewise to the wall
To let a beetle pass.

3 ***EDIT*** • *Read part of a student's diary. Find and correct eight mistakes in the use of the past simple. The first mistake has already been corrected.*

Today in class we read a poem by Robert Frost. I really ~~enjoy~~ enjoyed it. It was about a person who choosed between two roads in a forest. Before he made his decision, he spents a lot of time trying to decide which road to follow. Many people thought the person were Frost. In the end, he take the road that was less travelled on. He decided to be a poet. That decision change his life a lot.

Sometimes I feel a little like Frost. Two years ago I decide to come to this country. That were the biggest decision of my life.

Past Simple: Negative Statements and Questions

THE DAILY NEWS

DID SHE CRASH?

—LAE, NEW GUINEA, JULY 2, 1937. Amelia Earhart's small plane left the island of Lae at exactly 12:00 midnight. She **was not** alone on the flight but she and Fred Noonan, her navigator, were very tired. She reported her last position at 8:14 p.m. After that, she **did not make** radio contact again. Why **did** they **disappear**? **Were** they exhausted? **Did** they **run out** of fuel? The US Coast Guard started its search for the answer at 10:15 p.m.

CHECK POINT

Circle T (True), F (False), or ? (the article doesn't say).

T F ? The plane crashed.

T F ? Earhart made radio contact after 8:14 p.m.

T F ? Earhart had a navigator with her.

PAST SIMPLE: NEGATIVE STATEMENTS

CHART CHECK 1

Tick the correct answers.

What word do you add to *be* to form a negative statement?

❐ *not* ❐ *did not*

What do you add to other verbs to form a negative statement?

❐ *not* ❐ *did not*

BE			
SUBJECT	**BE**	**NOT**	
I/He/She/It	**was**	**not**	here last year.
We/You*/They	**were**	**n't**	

*You is both singular and plural.

CONTRACTIONS
was not = **wasn't**
were not = **weren't**

REGULAR AND IRREGULAR VERBS			
SUBJECT	**DID NOT**	**BASE FORM OF VERB**	
I/He/She/It We/You/They	**did not** **didn't**	**call** **fly**	last night.

CONTRACTIONS
did not = **didn't**

PAST SIMPLE: QUESTIONS

CHART CHECK 2

Tick the correct answer.

Which word(s) can begin *yes/no* questions with *be*?

❐ *was*

❐ *were*

❐ *did*

Which word(s) can begin *yes/no* questions with other verbs?

❐ *was*

❐ *were*

❐ *did*

YES/NO QUESTIONS: BE

BE	SUBJECT	
Was	she	here last year?
Were	they	

SHORT ANSWERS

AFFIRMATIVE			NEGATIVE		
Yes,	she	was.	No,	she	wasn't.
	they	were.		they	weren't.

WH- QUESTIONS: BE

WH- WORD	BE	SUBJECT	
Why	was	she	here last year?
	were	they	

YES/NO QUESTIONS: OTHER VERBS

DID	SUBJECT	BASE FORM	
Did	she	fly	to Mexico?

SHORT ANSWERS

AFFIRMATIVE	NEGATIVE
Yes, she did.	No, she didn't.

WH- QUESTIONS: OTHER VERBS

WH- WORD	DID	SUBJECT	BASE FORM
Why	did	it	disappear?

EXPRESS CHECK

Unscramble these words to form a question and an answer.

navigator • she • have • Did • a ______________________________?

she • didn't • No ______________________________.

Grammar Explanations / Examples

Grammar Explanations	Examples
1. Use the **past simple** to make **negative statements** about actions or situations that are now finished. 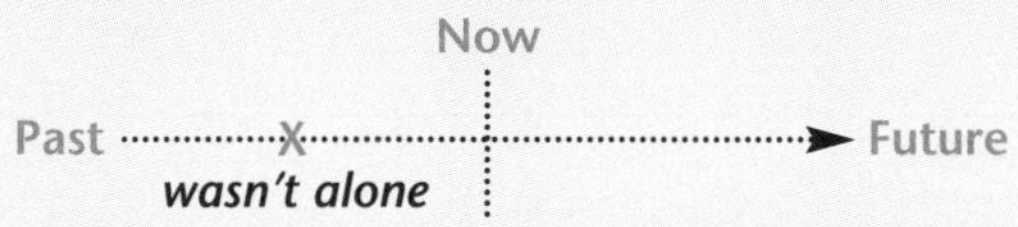 Past ····X···· Now ····► Future (*wasn't alone*)	■ She **wasn't** alone. ■ They **weren't** on an island. ■ They **didn't find** the plane. ■ He **didn't call** that night.
2. Use the **past simple** to ask **questions** about actions or situations that are now finished.	■ **Was** she alone in the plane? ■ Where **did** she **leave** from?

Check it out!

For questions about the subject, see Unit 24 on pages 102–103.

READ • *Look at some facts about Amelia Earhart.*

- She was born in the United States.
- She didn't get a degree.
- She didn't keep her first plane.
- She flew across the Atlantic Ocean.
- She received many awards.
- She married George Palmer Putnam.
- She didn't have any children.
- She wrote three books.

ANSWER • *Tick the correct box.*

	Yes	No
1. Did she get many awards?	☑	☐
2. Was she a university graduate?	☐	☐
3. Was she an American citizen?	☐	☐
4. Did she keep her first plane?	☐	☐
5. Was she an author?	☐	☐
6. Did she have a husband?	☐	☐
7. Was she a parent?	☐	☐

2

ASK & ANSWER • *Use the cues to ask questions about Amelia Earhart. Then answer the questions with the information in the box.*

~~in 1928~~ in 1937 American at Columbia University for two years New Guinea three

1. When / she / cross the Atlantic Ocean?
   When did she cross the Atlantic Ocean? ______ In 1928. ______
2. Where / she / study?
   ______ ______
3. How long / be / she / a social worker?
   ______ ______
4. Where / her last flight / leave from?
   ______ ______
5. How many books / she / write?
   ______ ______
6. What / be / her nationality?
   ______ ______
7. When / she / disappear?
   ______ ______

COMPLETE • *The magazine* Flying High (FH) *interviewed a young pilot. Complete the interview with the correct form of the verbs in brackets and with short answers.*

FH: ___Did___ you always ___want___ (1. want) to be a pilot?

SUE: ___Yes___, I ___did___ (2.). I saw a documentary about Amelia Earhart when I was six. She became my role model.

FH: ________ (3. be) your parents happy with your decision?

SUE: ________, they ________ (4.). They ________ (5. not want) me to fly.

FH: Why not? ________ they ________ (6. feel) it was too dangerous?

SUE: ________, they ________ (7.). But I was very determined, and they ________ (8. not stop) me from pursuing my dream.

FH: ________ you ever ________ (9. dream) of flying around the world?

SUE: Of course. But I ________ (10. not think) it would happen so soon.

FH: ________ (11. be) you alone on the flight?

SUE: ________, I ________ (12.). I had a co-pilot.

FH: ________ (13. be) it difficult to find a co-pilot for this flight?

SUE: ________, it ________ (14.). She's my flatmate.

EDIT • *Read this postcard. Find and correct six mistakes in the use of the past simple. The first mistake has already been corrected.*

Hi! Did you ~~received~~ receive *my last letter? I didn't knew your new address so I sent it to your old one. When you moved? Did your flatmate move with you? Right now I'm on board a plane flying to El Paso to visit Ana. Did you met her at the conference last year? I wanted to visit her in June but I no had the time. At first I was going to drive from Los Angeles but I decided to fly instead. This is only my third flight but I love flying! I didnt know flying could be so much fun! Hope to hear from you.*

—M.

To: *Sue Jacobs*
16 Beckley Avenue
Moreton
Gloucestershire
GL56 5BQ

Used to

CHECK POINT

Tick the correct answer.

The man is thinking about

❒ a habit he has now.

❒ a habit he had in the past.

CHART CHECK 1

Circle T (True) or F (False).

T F In affirmative statements, ***used to*** is used with all subjects.

AFFIRMATIVE STATEMENTS		
Subject	***Used to***	**Base Form of Verb**
I She They	**used to**	**wear** jeans.

NEGATIVE STATEMENTS		
Subject	***Didn't use to***	**Base Form of Verb**
I She They	**didn't use to**	**wear** jeans.

CHART CHECK 2

Tick the correct answer.

In questions, what form of ***used to*** is used?

❒ ***did . . . used to***

❒ ***did . . . use to***

YES/NO QUESTIONS			
Did	**Subject**	***Use to***	**Base Form**
Did	you she they	**use to**	**wear** jeans?

SHORT ANSWERS					
Affirmative			**Negative**		
Yes,	I she they	**did.**	**No,**	I she they	**didn't.**

WH- QUESTIONS				
***Wh-* Word**	***Did***	**Subject**	***Use to***	**Base Form**
What	**did**	you she they	**use to**	**wear?**

EXPRESS CHECK

Circle the correct words to complete these sentences.

- He used to / uses to wear baggy jeans.
- Did you use to / used to shop for clothes with your friends?
- What did your parents use to saying / say about your clothes?

Grammar Explanations	Examples
1. Use ***used to*** + base form of the verb to talk about **past habits** or **past situations** that no longer exist in the present. 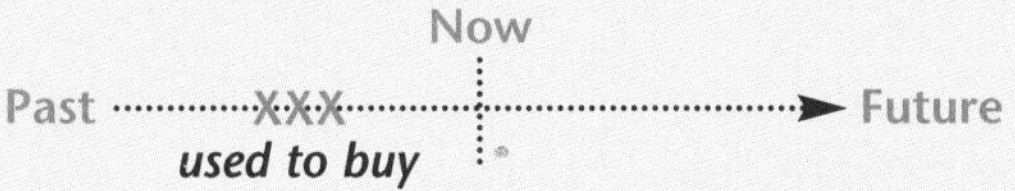 	■ Leo **used to buy** baggy jeans. *(In the past, he often bought baggy jeans. He doesn't buy baggy jeans now.)*
▶ **Be careful!** ***Used to*** always has a past meaning. There is no present form.	■ In his youth, Leo **used to be** thin. Not ~~Today Leo used to be thin.~~
2. We usually use ***used to*** in sentences that **contrast the past and the present**. We often emphasise this contrast by using time expressions such as ***now***, ***no longer*** and ***not any more*** with the present.	■ Jeans **used to come** only in blue. ***Now*** you can buy them in any colour. ■ They **used to live** in Genoa but they ***no longer*** live there. ■ She **used to wear** a size 6 but she does***n't any more***.
3. **Be careful!** Form **questions** with ***did*** + ***use to***.	■ **Did** you **use to** wear jeans? Not ~~Did you used to wear jeans?~~
Form the **negative** with ***didn't*** + ***use to***.	■ They **didn't use to** come in different colours. Not ~~They didn't used to come . . .~~
Usage Note: ***Used to*** is more common in affirmative statements than in negative statements or questions. The negative form ***used not to*** is also possible but ***didn't use to*** is more common.	■ Jeans **used not to** be so expensive.
4. **Be careful!** Do not confuse ***used to*** + base form of the verb with the following expressions:	■ I **used to wear** tight jeans. *(It was my past habit to wear tight jeans.)*
be used to *(be accustomed to)*	■ I'**m used to getting** up early. *(It's normal for me to get up early.)*
get used to *(get accustomed to)*	■ I **got used to living** in London. *(I became accustomed to living there.)*

***IDENTIFY* •** *Read this fashion article. Underline all the forms of* **used to** *that refer to a habit in the past.*

In many ways, fashion used to be much simpler. Women didn't use to wear trousers to the office and men's clothes never used to come in bright colours. People also used to dress in special ways for different situations. They didn't use blue jeans as business clothes or wear tracksuits when they travelled. Today you can go to the opera and find some women in evening gowns while others are in blue jeans. Even buying jeans used to be easier – they came only in blue denim. I'm still not used to buying green jeans and wearing them to work!

CHOOSE & COMPLETE* •** *Look at these pictures from an old magazine. Use the verbs in the box with* **used to. Write one sentence about each picture.*

~~be~~	carry	dance	dress	have	wear

1. Women's skirts ___used to be___ long and formal.
2. All men _______________ long hair.
3. Children _______________ like adults.
4. Men and women _______________ at formal balls.
5. Women _______________ many petticoats under their skirts.
6. Men _______________ walking sticks.

Rewrite the sentences so that the meaning stays the same. Use the correct form of **used to**.

1. In the past, did people worry about fashion as much as they do now?

   Did people use to worry about fashion as much as they do now?

2. When trainers were first made, they only came in two colours – black and white.

   Trainers ______

3. They didn't cost as much as they do these days.

   They ______

4. Did people wear jeans fifty years ago?

   Did ______

5. Jeans and trainers didn't cost very much thirty years ago.

   Jeans ______

6. Did women wear jeans?

   Did ______

EDIT • *Read this student's diary. Find and correct five mistakes in the use of* **used to**. *The first mistake has already been corrected.*

When I was younger, clothes didn't ~~used~~ use to be a problem. All the girls at my school used to wore the same uniform. I used to think that it took away from my freedom of choice. Now I can wear what I want but clothes cost so much! Even blue jeans, today's 'uniform', used to be cheaper. My mum uses to pay less than £30 for hers. I suppose they didn't used to sell designer jeans back then. You know, I was used to be against school uniforms, but now I'm not so sure!

UNIT 9 Past Continuous

I wasn't running for the bus, I was skiing.

CHECK POINT

Tick the correct answer.

The girl in the hospital bed is giving her version of

❑ what she usually did in the past.

❑ what she was doing at the time of her accident.

CHART CHECK 1

Circle T (True) or F (False).

T F The past continuous is made up of the past tense of ***be*** + base form of the verb.

STATEMENTS			
SUBJECT	***BE***	**(*NOT*)**	**BASE FORM OF VERB + *-ING***
I/He/She/It	**was**	**(not)**	**skiing.**
We/You*/They	**were**		

**You* is both singular and plural.

CHART CHECK 2

Tick the correct answer.

In questions, the verb ***be*** comes:

❑ after the subject

❑ before the subject

***YES/NO* QUESTIONS**		
BE	**SUBJECT**	**BASE FORM + *-ING***
Was	she	**skiing?**
Were	you	

SHORT ANSWERS					
AFFIRMATIVE			**NEGATIVE**		
Yes,	she	**was.**	**No,**	she	**wasn't.**
	we	**were.**		we	**weren't.**

***WH-* QUESTIONS**			
***WH-* WORD**	***BE***	**SUBJECT**	**BASE FORM + *-ING***
Where When Why	**was**	she	**skiing?**
	were	you	

EXPRESS CHECK

Complete this conversation with the past continuous form of the verb **stay**.

A: Where ________________ you ________________?

B: I ________________ at a ski resort in the Alps.

Grammar Explanations	Examples
1. Use the **past continuous** to describe an action that was in progress at a specific time in the past. The action began before the specific time and may or may not have continued after the specific time. 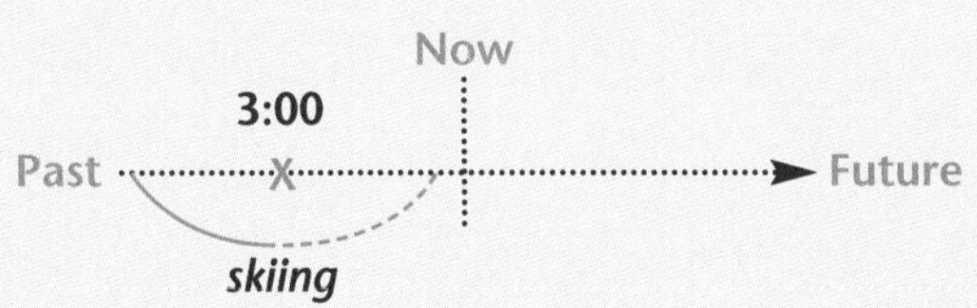	**A:** What **were** you **doing** at 3:00? **B:** We **were skiing**. **C:** I **was eating** lunch at 3:00.
▶ **Be careful!** Stative verbs are not usually used in the continuous. *(For a list of common stative verbs,* *see Appendix 2 on page 337.)*	■ I **had** a headache last night. NOT ~~I was having a headache last night.~~
2. Use the **past continuous** with ***while*** to talk about two actions in progress at the same time in the past. Use the past continuous in both clauses. Now Past ········X········ Future was skiing was reading	■ ***While*** he **was skiing**, I **was reading**. OR ■ I **was reading** ***while*** he **was skiing**.
Usage Note: In informal conversation, some people use ***when*** with the past continuous.	■ Sorry, I **wasn't listening** ***when*** you **were talking**.
3. Use the **past continuous** to focus on the duration of an action, not its completion.	■ Sheila **was reading** a book last night. *(We don't know if she finished the book.)*
Use the **past simple** to focus on the completion of an action.	■ Sheila **read** a book last night. *(She probably finished the book.)*

TRUE OR FALSE • *Read each numbered sentence. Write T (True) or F (False) for the statement that follows. Write a question mark (?) if there is not enough information.*

1. While Tanya was watching the Winter Olympics on TV, Michael was clearing the snow.

   __F__ First Michael finished clearing the snow. Then Tanya started watching TV.

2. In this photo, I was putting on my boots.

   ______ I was wearing boots in the photo.

3. At 5:00, they were drinking hot chocolate by the fire.

   ______ We don't know when they started drinking hot chocolate.

4. Last night, I was reading an article about skiing in Morocco.

   ______ I finished the article.

5. At 10:00, he drank a cup of coffee.

   ______ He finished the coffee.

6. It was snowing while she was taking the photograph.

   ______ First she took the photograph. Then it started to snow.

2

DESCRIBE • *Fritz and Karyn were at a ski café. Write about the picture. Use the past continuous.*

1. Fritz __was wearing a hat.__
   (wear / a hat)
2. Karyn __wasn't wearing a hat.__
   (wear / a hat)
3. They ______________________
   (sit / outside)
4. It ______________________
   (snow)
5. They ______________________
   (wear / sunglasses)
6. They ______________________
   (wear / their gloves)
7. The waiter ______________________
   (serve / drinks)
8. He ______________________
   (serve / lunch)
9. Karyn ______________________
   (smile)
10. She ______________________
    (use / a mobile phone)

COMPLETE • Mountain Sports Magazine (MS) *interviewed the snowboarding champion,* Rosie Happ (RH). *Complete the interview with the correct form of the verbs in brackets and with short answers.*

MS: Congratulations! You have just become a semi-finalist for the Olympic snowboarding team. ___Were___ you ___expecting___ (1. expect) to get this far in the competition?

RH: No, I ___wasn't___ (2.). During the trials, I __________ (3. recover) from a bad cold. By the last day, I still __________ (4. not perform) very well. That's what I thought, anyway.

MS: What __________ you __________ (5. think) about while you __________ (6. wait) for the announcement?

RH: Actually, I __________ (7. not think) about the competition at all. Some friends and I __________ (8. watch) a film.

MS: You're quite new to the sport. __________ you __________ (9. compete) professionally this time last year?

RH: Yes, I __________ (10.). I __________ (11. train) with Barrett Christie then and we __________ both __________ (12. take) part in local competitions.

4 **EDIT •** *Read this diary entry. Find and correct eight mistakes in the use of the past continuous. The first mistake has already been corrected.*

This evening, Sheila and I ~~was~~ were looking at some photographs from my skiing trip with Fritz's family last year. By the end of the evening, we laughing like crazy. That was my first experience on skis so the pictures were really embarrassing. In one shot, I was came down the slope on my back. In another one, my skis was falling out of the ski lift while I was riding up the slope. Fritz was taking that picture from the lift entrance. Good thing he not standing right under me! Where was I when Fritz was falling down the slope? Well, unfortunately I wasn't carry my camera. That would have been a great picture! It was amazing how fast Fritz's girlfriend, Karyn, learnt that weekend. She was doing jumps by the second day. By that time, I spent a lot of time at the ski café.

UNIT 10

Past Continuous and Past Simple

Did you see the accident?
Yes . . . The guy in the sports car **was talking** on his mobile phone when he **hit** the other car.

CHECK POINT

Number these statements in the correct time order.

_____ There was a car accident.

_____ The driver of the sports car was on the phone.

CHART CHECK

Circle T (True) or F (False).

Use ***while*** to introduce

T F a past simple action.

T F a past continuous action.

PAST CONTINUOUS AND PAST SIMPLE		
Past Continuous	***When***	**Past Simple**
He **was speeding**	when	the accident **happened**.

PAST SIMPLE AND PAST CONTINUOUS		
Past Simple	***While***	**Past Continuous**
The accident **happened**	while	you **were driving**.

PAST SIMPLE AND PAST SIMPLE		
Past Simple	***When***	**Past Simple**
The police **came**	when	the accident **happened**.

PAST CONTINUOUS AND PAST CONTINUOUS		
Past Continuous	***While***	**Past Continuous**
They **were talking**	while	they **were driving**.

EXPRESS CHECK

Circle the correct words to complete these sentences.

- When / While the car crashed, he hit his head.
- How fast was he driving / did he drive when the accident happened?

Grammar Explanations	Examples
1. Use the **past continuous** with the **past simple** when a short action interrupts a longer action in the past. Use the **past simple** for the interrupting action. 	■ I **was crossing** the street when the driver **hooted** at me. *(First, I started crossing the street. Then, the driver hooted at me.)* ■ They **were driving** too fast when they **crashed**.
Use ***when*** to introduce the past simple action OR use ***while*** to introduce the past continuous action.	■ He was speeding ***when*** the light **turned** red. ■ ***While*** he **was speeding**, the light **turned** red.
2. BE CAREFUL! Notice the difference in meaning between these two different sentences. 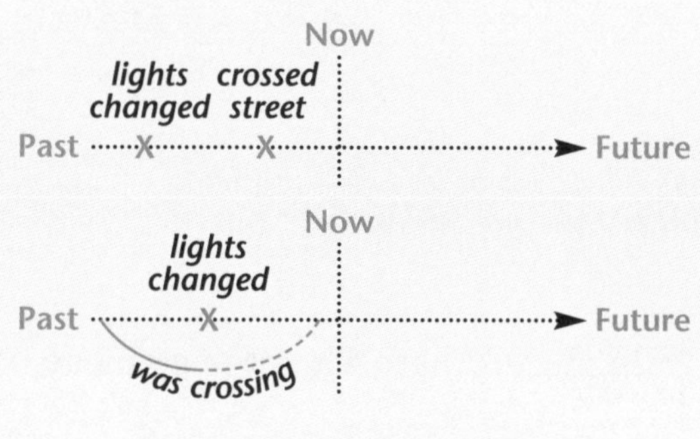	■ ***When*** the lights **changed**, I **crossed** the street. *(First the lights changed. Then I crossed the street.)* ■ ***When*** the lights **changed**, I **was crossing** the street. *(First, I started crossing the street. Then the lights changed while I was still crossing.)*
3. Use the **past continuous with *while*** to talk about two actions in progress at the same time in the past. Use the past continuous in both clauses. 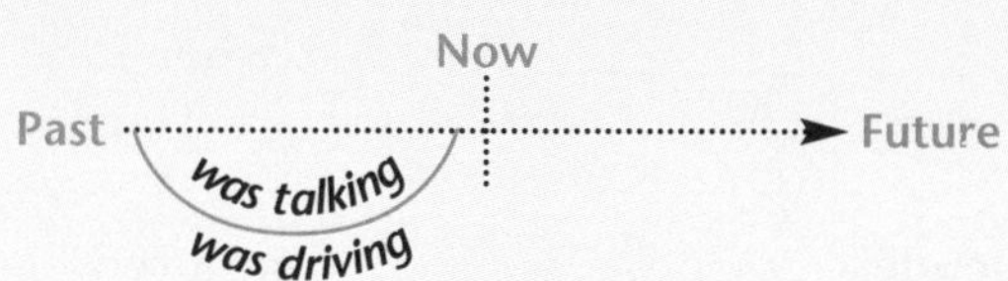	■ Joe **was talking** on the phone ***while*** he **was driving**. ■ They **weren't paying** attention ***while*** they **were crossing** the street.
4. The **time clause** (the part of the sentence beginning with ***when*** or ***while***) can come at the beginning or the end of the sentence. The meaning is the same.	■ ***When* you called,** I was leaving. ■ I was leaving ***when* you called**.
Use a **comma** after the time clause when it comes at the beginning of the sentence.	■ ***While* he was driving**, he was talking. ■ He was talking ***while* he was driving**.

TRUE OR FALSE • *Read each numbered sentence. Write T (True) or F (False) for the statement that follows.*

1. When our friends arrived, we ate lunch.

   __T__ Our friends arrived just before lunch.

2. While we were talking on the phone, I was driving to school.

   _____ We finished the conversation. Then I drove to school.

3. Jan heard about the accident while she was driving to work.

   _____ Jan knew about the accident by the time she got to work.

4. When they left the motorway, it started to rain.

   _____ It was raining while they were on the motorway.

5. When Zoe got to school, her class was taking a test.

   _____ Zoe was late for school.

2

COMPLETE • *A police officer is interviewing two witnesses of a traffic accident. Complete the interview with the correct form of the verbs in brackets and with short answers.*

OFFICER: __Were__ you __standing__ (1. stand) here when the accident __happened__ (2. happen)?

WITNESS 1: Yes, we __were__ (3.). We ________ (4. wait) at the bus stop when we first ________ (5. notice) the car.

OFFICER: ________ the car ________ (6. speed) when it ________ (7. get) to the junction?

WITNESS 1: Yes, it ________ (8.). It ________ (9. go) very fast when it ________ (10. reach) the corner.

WITNESS 2: No, it ________ (11.)! Those men ________ (12. cross) on a red light when the car ________ (13. hit) them.

OFFICER: ________ the driver ________ (14. stop) when he ________ (15. see) the men?

WITNESS 1: No, he ________ (16.). He ________ (17. talk) on his mobile phone while he ________ (18. drive). That's why he ________ (19. not stop) in time.

WITNESS 2: But the men ________ (20. not pay) attention while they ________ (21. cross).

OFFICER: ________________ it ________________ when the accident
22. (snow)

________________?
23. (happen)

WITNESS 2: Yes, it ________________. I'm sure of it. The roads were very slippery.
24.

WITNESS 1: No, it ________________. The snow ________________ when the
25. 26. (start)

ambulance ________________.
27. (arrive)

3

COMBINE • *Read each pair of sentences. Combine them into one sentence using the past simple or the past continuous form of the verbs. Use a comma where necessary.*

1. Diana attended a meeting. The blizzard started.

   When the blizzard started, Diana was attending a meeting.

2. She drove home. She listened to her car radio.

   While ________________________________

3. She pulled over to the side of the road. The visibility got very bad.

   ________________ when ________________

4. She listened to the news. She heard about the accident.

   ________________ while ________________

5. It stopped snowing. She drove to the police station.

   ________________ when ________________

6. She talked to the police. She thought about her article for the morning paper.

   While ________________________________

4

EDIT • *Read part of the first draft of Diana's article. Find and correct five mistakes in the use of past time clauses. The first mistake has already been corrected.*

Yesterday, a man was talking on his mobile phone while he was ~~drive~~ driving his car. Maybe he checking his diary while he was making his next appointment. He was certainly not concentrating on the road when the lights suddenly was turning red. The two men in the street were trying to jump out of the way when they saw him but it was too late. No one was badly hurt but that was just luck. Last year, the City Council weren't passing the 'talking and driving' law. We need that law!

SECTION ONE

Circle the letter of the correct answer to complete each sentence.

EXAMPLE:
Jennifer never ________ coffee. A (B) C D
(A) drink (C) is drinking
(B) drinks (D) was drinking

1. Roger ________ me at 9:00 last night. A B C D
(A) called (C) used to called
(B) calls (D) calling

2. Sara didn't hear the phone. She ________. A B C D
(A) sleeps (C) used to sleep
(B) slept (D) was sleeping

3. There ________ a lot of people in the park yesterday. A B C D
(A) are (C) was
(B) is (D) were

4. One day last March, I ________ a very strange letter. A B C D
(A) did get (C) used to get
(B) got (D) was getting

5. Where ________ to school? A B C D
(A) did you go (C) you go
(B) you did go (D) you went

6. Claude didn't ________ in Canada. A B C D
(A) lived (C) used to live
(B) use to live (D) used to living

7. Rick left the class early because he ________ a headache. A B C D
(A) had (C) used to have
(B) have (D) was having

8. As soon as the lights turned red, she ________ the car. A B C D
(A) did stop (C) stops
(B) stopped (D) was stopping

9. They ________ when the fire alarm rang. A B C D
(A) cook (C) was cooking
(B) cooked (D) were cooking

10. Johnny ________ the paper when I interrupted him. A B C D
(A) read (C) was reading
(B) reads (D) were reading

11. —Did you watch TV last night?
—________ I was revising for a test.
(A) Yes, I did. (C) No, I didn't.
(B) Yes, I was. (D) No, I wasn't.
A B C D

12. I remember you. You ________ to go to school here.
(A) use (C) were using
(B) used (D) were used
A B C D

SECTION TWO

Each sentence has four underlined words or phrases. The four underlined parts of the sentence are marked A, B, C and D. Circle the letter of the one underlined word or phrase that is NOT CORRECT.

EXAMPLE:
Mike usually (A) drives (B) to school but today (C) he walks (D). A B C (D)

13. Why (A) did (B) you called (C) him last week (D)? A B C D

14. They were (A) watching TV while (B) I were (C) reading (D). A B C D

15. What are (A) you doing (B) last night (C) at (D) 8:00? A B C D

16. The doctor called (A) this morning (B) while (C) you slept (D). A B C D

17. It was (A) no (B) raining (C) when the game began (D). A B C D

18. Paul was (A) drying (B) the dishes when (C) he was dropping (D) the plate. A B C D

19. When Gloria were (A) four, she used to (B) pretend (C) she had (D) a horse. A B C D

20. What do (A) you use to (B) do (C) when you felt (D) afraid? A B C D

21. As soon as (A) the alarm clock rang (B), she woke up (C) and was getting (D) out of bed. A B C D

22. Once when (A) I was (B) ten, I used to get (C) ill and went (D) to hospital. A B C D

23. While (A) I driving (B) home, I turned on (C) the car radio and heard (D) about the accident. A B C D

24. What did you do (A), (B) while (C) you were living (D) in Spain? A B C D

25. Pete and Andy were (A) driving (B) to work when (C) they were seeing (D) the accident. A B C D

Present Perfect: *Since* and *For*

Come on!
You've been a pro since 1994. Now serve the ball!
Forget it!
You haven't won a match for weeks! Go home!

CHECK POINT

Circle T (True) or F (False).

T F The man is still a professional tennis player.

CHART CHECK 1

Tick the correct answer.

The present perfect is made up of two parts:

❐ ***have*** + past simple

❐ ***have*** + past participle

The regular form of the past participle is:

❐ base form of verb + ***-d*** or ***-ed***

❐ base form of verb + ***-en***

STATEMENTS					
Subject	**Have**	**(Not)**	**Past Participle**		***Since/For***
I/We/You*/They	**have** **'ve**	**(not)** **n't**	**lived** **been**†	here	***since*** May. ***for*** a long time.
He/She/it	**has** **'s**				

* *You* is both singular and plural.
† *Been* is an irregular past participle. For a list of irregular verbs, see Appendix 1 on pages 336–337.

YES/NO QUESTIONS				
Have	**Subject**	**Past Participle**		***Since/For***
Have	they	**lived** **been**	here	***since*** May? ***for*** a long time?
Has	he			

SHORT ANSWERS					
Affirmative			**Negative**		
Yes,	they	**have.**	**No,**	they	**haven't.**
	he	**has.**		he	**hasn't.**

CHART CHECK 2

Tick the correct answer.

For is used with:

❐ a point of time

❐ a length of time

WH- QUESTIONS

WH- WORD	HAVE	SUBJECT	PAST PARTICIPLE	
How long	**have**	they	**lived**	here?
	has	he	**been**	

SHORT ANSWERS

Since January.
For a few months.

EXPRESS CHECK

Look at the past participles. Tick the correct column.

	Regular	Irregular
driven	❐	❐
competed	❐	❐
won	❐	❐
tried	❐	❐

Grammar Explanations / Examples

1. Use the **present perfect** with ***since*** or ***for*** to talk about something that began in the past and continues into the present (and may continue into the future).

Past — *1994* ✕ ······ Now ······ ► Future — ***has been***

■ Martina Hingis **has been** a professional tennis player ***since*** 1994.

■ She **has been** a professional tennis player ***for*** several years.

(She began her professional career several years ago, and she is still a professional player.)

2. Use the present perfect with ***since*** + **point in time** *(since 5:00, since Monday, since 1994)* to show when something started.

■ She **has earned** millions of dollars ***since 1994***.

3. ***Since*** can also introduce a **time clause**.

■ Martina **has loved** sports ***since she was a child***.

If the action ended in the past, use the past simple in the time clause.

■ She has won many tennis tournaments ***since*** she **moved** from Slovakia.
(She doesn't live in Slovakia now.)

If the action still continues in the present, use the present perfect in the time clause.

■ She has become extremely successful ***since*** she **has been** in Switzerland.
(She is still in Switzerland.)

4. Use the present perfect with ***for*** + **length of time** *(for ten minutes, for two weeks, for years, for a long time)* to show how long a present situation has lasted.

■ Martina's mother **has been** her coach ***for many years***.

IDENTIFY • *Read about tennis star Martina Hingis. Underline all the verbs in the present perfect. Circle all the time expressions with **since** or **for**.*

Martina Hingis picked up her first tennis racket at the age of two. Since then, she has become one of the greatest tennis players in the world. Born in Slovakia, she has lived in Switzerland for many years. She became the outdoor Swiss champion at the age of nine. Since then she has won many international competitions including Wimbledon, the US Open and the Australian Open.

For young stars like Martina, life has its difficulties. They are under constant pressure to win and they don't have time to just relax with friends. In fact, Martina hasn't been to school since 1994 and she has been in the public spotlight for years. But she seems to be handling her success well. Since she turned professional, she has played tennis all over the world and has earned millions of dollars. She sees her life as normal because tennis has been the most important thing to her since she was a little girl.

COMPLETE & CHOOSE • *Read this magazine article about a child genius. Complete it with the present perfect form of the verbs in brackets. Choose between **since** and **for**.*

Thirteen-year-old Ronnie Segal ___has loved___ (1. love) maths ___since___ (2. since / for) he was a little boy. 'I ________ (3. be) interested in numbers ________ (4. since / for) nine years, five months, three weeks, and two days,' says Ronnie. ________ (5. Since / For) the past year, Ronnie ________ (6. attend) classes at university. He ________ (7. not do) badly. ________ (8. Since / For) January, he ________ (9. take) five exams and ________ (10. not get) a mark of less than a hundred per cent on any of them. ________ (11. Since / For) Ronnie began classes, he ________ (12. meet) an average of 1.324 people a month. And his future? Young Ronnie ________ (13. not think) about it for years. He ________ (14. know) ________ (15. since / for) he was a little boy that he's going to become a famous sports announcer, get married, and have exactly 2.2 children.

ASK & ANSWER • *Complete the interview about Martina Hingis. Use the words in brackets to write questions. Then write short answers to the questions using information from Exercise 1.*

1. (How long / she / be / a tennis player?)

   Q: How long has she been a tennis player?

   A: Since she was two.

2. (How long / she / live in Switzerland?)

   Q: ______________________

   A: ______________________

3. (she / win any competitions / since the outdoor Swiss championship?)

   Q: ______________________

   A: ______________________

4. (she / go to school / since 1994?)

   Q: ______________________

   A: ______________________

5. (How much money / she / earn / since her career began?)

   Q: ______________________

   A: ______________________

6. (How long / tennis / be important to her?)

   Q: ______________________

   A: ______________________

EDIT • *Read this student's paragraph. Find and correct seven mistakes in the use of the present perfect, and* **since** *and* **for**. *The first mistake has already been corrected.*

have been

I ~~am~~ in Ms Clark's physical education class since two months. I enjoy it a lot and have only miss two classes since the beginning of the term. I especially like tennis but since September we don't play because the weather have been too cold. I also like volleyball and my team has win two matches since we have started to compete with Lincoln School. I'm looking forward to the next match.

Present Perfect: *Already, Just* and *Yet*

As you can see, the flu season **has just begun**. **Have** you **had** your flu jab **yet**? It's never too late!
FLU CHART
Well, almost never . . .

CHECK POINT

Circle T (True) or F (False).

T F The flu season will start soon.

CHART CHECK 1

Tick the correct answer.

To say that something has happened before now,

❒ use ***already*** or ***just***.

❒ use ***yet***.

To say that something has not happened before now,

❒ use ***already*** or ***just***.

❒ use ***not . . . yet***.

AFFIRMATIVE STATEMENTS: *ALREADY* AND *JUST*				
Subject	***Have***	***Already/Just***	**Past Participle**	
They	**have**	***already/just***	**developed**	a new flu vaccine.
It	**has**		**saved**	three people's lives.

NEGATIVE STATEMENTS: *YET*				
Subject	***Have not***	**Past Participle**		***Yet***
They	**haven't**	**finished**	the interview	***yet***.
It	**hasn't**	**ended**		

CHART CHECK 2

Circle T (True) or F (False).

T F ***Yet*** is used in questions.

YES/NO QUESTIONS: *YET*				
Have	**Subject**	**Past Participle**		***Yet***
Have	they	**tested**	the new vaccine	***yet***?
Has	it	**had**	approval	

SHORT ANSWERS					
AFFIRMATIVE			**NEGATIVE**		
Yes,	they	**have.**	**No,**	they	**haven't.**
	it	**has.**		it	**hasn't.**

EXPRESS CHECK

Unscramble these words to form a question. Answer the question.

you • have • yet • lunch • had

______________________________?

____

Grammar Explanations / Examples

Grammar Explanations	Examples
1. We often use the **present perfect** with ***already*** and ***just*** to talk about things that have happened before now.	**A:** Is your daughter going to get her flu jab? **B:** She**'s *already* had** it. And I**'ve *just* had** it, too.
Already means 'at some time before now'. ***Just*** means 'very recently: a moment or two ago'.	
▶ **BE CAREFUL!** Do not use the present perfect with ***already*** when you mention a specific time in the past.	DON'T SAY: ~~She's already had it last month.~~ ~~She's just had it last month.~~
Already and ***just*** usually come between ***have*** and the **past participle**.	■ Researchers **have *already* discovered** cures for many diseases. ■ I**'ve *just* recovered** from a bad cold.
Already can also come at the end of the clause.	■ They**'ve made** a lot of progress ***already***.

Grammar Explanations	Examples
2. Use the **present perfect** with ***not yet*** to talk about things that have not happened before now.	■ They **haven't discovered** a cure for the common cold ***yet***, but they hope to discover one in the future.
Notice that ***yet*** usually comes at the end of the clause.	■ The flu season **hasn't arrived *yet***.
Yet can also come between ***have not*** and the **past participle**.	■ They **haven't *yet* discovered** a cure for the common cold.

Grammar Explanations	Examples
3. We usually use ***yet* in questions** to find out if something has happened before now.	■ **Has** your son **had** his flu jab ***yet***?
USAGE NOTE: Sometimes we use ***already* in a question** to express surprise that something has happened sooner than we expected it to.	■ **Has** he ***already* had** his flu jab? The flu season hasn't begun yet.

Grammar Explanations	Examples
4. In spoken American English, people often use ***already, just*** and ***yet*** with the past simple to talk about the recent past.	■ I ***already* read** that book. ■ We ***just* got** back from Los Angeles. ■ **Did** you **do** the shopping ***yet***?

MATCH • *Match the cause with the appropriate result.*

Cause

__e__ 1. Tom has just had his flu jab, so he probably

_____ 2. Dr Meier has already finished his interview, so he

_____ 3. Dr Meier hasn't had lunch yet, so he

_____ 4. Steve hasn't had his jab yet, so he

_____ 5. Steve has just had lunch, so he

Result

a. is really hungry.

b. may get flu.

c. has left the TV studio.

d. isn't very hungry.

e. won't get flu this year.

2

COMPLETE • *Read these questions and answers from a magazine article. Complete them with the present perfect form of the verbs in brackets plus* **already** *or* **yet**. *Use short answers.*

smallpox vaccine	tetanus vaccine	flu vaccine	polio vaccine	measles vaccine	world smallpox vaccination programme	last case of smallpox	AIDS vaccine	cancer vaccine	malaria vaccine	common cold vaccine
1796	1880	1945	1954	1963	1966	1980	NOW			

Q: We plan to travel to the rain forest next year. __Have__ they __found__ (1. find) a malaria vaccine __yet__?

A: __No__, they __haven't__ (2.). Talk to your doctor about ways to prevent this disease.

Q: My doctor told me I won't need another smallpox jab. I was surprised. __________ smallpox completely __________ (3. disappear)?

A: __________, it __________ (4.).

Q: They __________ (5. develop) vaccines against flu. What about the common cold?

A: No. Because there are so many different cold viruses, they __________ (6. not be able) to develop a vaccine __________.

Q: There has been so much cancer research. __________ anyone __________ (7. make) a successful vaccine __________?

A: __________ they __________ (8.). Researchers *have* made a lot of progress in recent years, however.

DESCRIBE • *Dr Helmut Meier and his wife, Gisela, are planning a party. Look at their To Do lists and the pictures of their kitchen and dining room. Cross out the things they have already done. Then write sentences about each item on their To Do lists.*

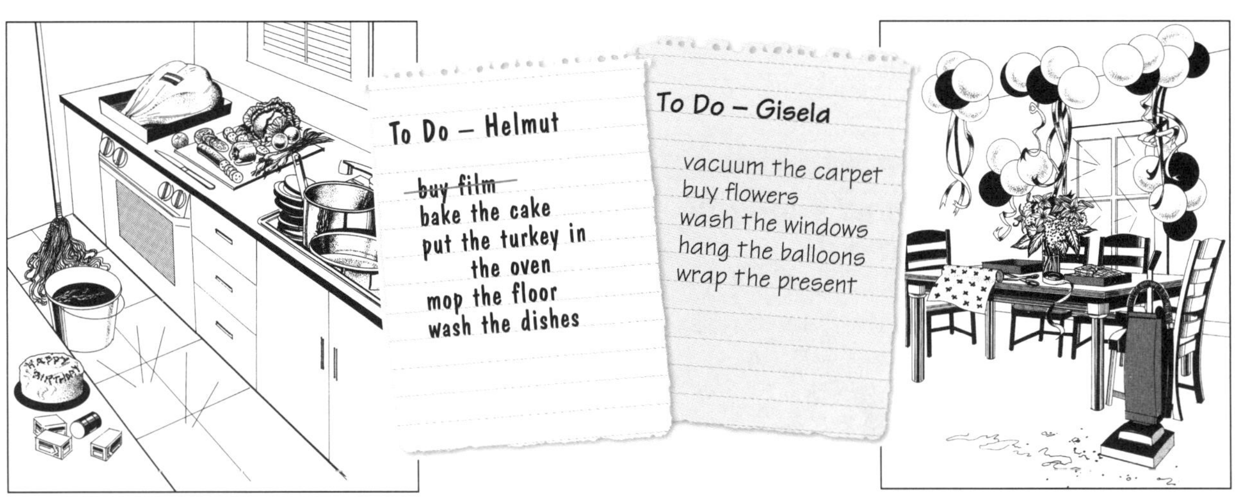

HAPPY BIRTHDAY
To Do – Helmut
~~buy film~~
bake the cake
put the turkey in the oven
mop the floor
wash the dishes
To Do – Gisela
vacuum the carpet
buy flowers
wash the windows
hang the balloons
wrap the present

1. Helmut has already bought film.
2. Gisela hasn't vacuumed the carpet yet.
3. ______
4. ______
5. ______
6. ______
7. ______
8. ______
9. ______
10. ______

EDIT • *Read this note from Gisela to Helmut. Find and correct six mistakes in the use of the present perfect with* **already** *and* **yet***. The first mistake has already been corrected.*

Helmut – I'm in a hurry. I haven't ~~went~~ been shopping already but I'll do it on the way home. Rita have just had dinner and she's already had her bath. Have you call Mr Jacobson yet? He's called already three times today. His daughter has had her flu shot yet. Is it too late? See you later.

G.

Present Perfect: Indefinite Past

CHECK POINT

Tick the correct answer.

The cast of 'Family' is talking about things of importance to them

❒ now.

❒ in the past.

CHART CHECK 1

Circle T (True) or F (False).

T F You can use the present perfect without mentioning a specific time.

STATEMENTS				
SUBJECT	**HAVE**	**(NOT)**	**PAST PARTICIPLE**	
They	**have**	**(not)**	**appeared**	on TV.
It	**has**		**been**	

For a complete presentation of present perfect forms, see Unit 11, pages 46–47.

CHART CHECK 2

Tick the correct answer.

Never comes:

❒ before the past participle

❒ at the end of the statement

STATEMENTS WITH ADVERBS				
SUBJECT	**HAVE (NOT)**	**ADVERB**	**PAST PARTICIPLE**	
They	**have**	***never***	**appeared**	on TV.
It	**has**		**been**	
They	**have (not)**		**appeared**	on TV
It	**has (not)**		**been**	

CHART CHECK 3

Circle T (True) or F (False).

T F *Ever* must be used in *yes/no* questions.

***YES/NO* QUESTIONS**			
HAVE	**SUBJECT**	**(*EVER*)**	**PAST PARTICIPLE**
Have	they	*(ever)*	**acted?**
Has	she		**won?**

SHORT ANSWERS					
AFFIRMATIVE			**NEGATIVE**		
Yes,	they	**have.**	**No,**	they	**haven't.**
	she	**has.**		she	**hasn't.**

***WH-* QUESTIONS**				
***WH-* WORD**	***HAVE***	**SUBJECT**	**PAST PARTICIPLE**	
How often	**have**	they	**acted**	on this show?
Why	**has**	it	**won**	an award?

EXPRESS CHECK

Unscramble these words to form a question. Answer the question.

you • watched • Have • 'The Simpsons' • ever

______________________________? ______________________________

Grammar Explanations	Examples
1. Use the **present perfect** to talk about things that happened at an indefinite time in the past. You can use the present perfect when you don't know when something happened or when the specific time is not important.	■ They'**ve won** several awards. ■ I'**ve interviewed** the whole cast. ■ She'**s been** on a documentary. ■ I'**ve seen** his chat show.
2. You can use ***ever*** with the **present perfect** to ask questions. It means at *any time up until now*. Use ***never*** to answer negatively.	**A:** **Have** you **won** an award? OR **Have** you ***ever*** **won** an award? **B:** No, **I've *never* won** one. OR No, ***never***.
3. BE CAREFUL! The past participles ***been*** and ***gone*** have very different meanings.	■ Tom **has *been*** to India. (He went and now he's back.) ■ Tom **has *gone*** to India. (He went to India and he's still there now.)
4. Use the ***present perfect*** with ***recently*** or ***lately*** to talk about events in the very recent past. ▶ **BE CAREFUL!** Do not use ***recently*** or ***lately*** with the present perfect and a specific past time expression.	■ I'**ve *recently* signed** a contract to write a book. ■ He **hasn't had** time ***lately***. ■ I'**ve *recently* got** back from Los Angeles. NOT ~~I've recently got back from Los Angeles last Monday~~.

TRUE OR FALSE • *Read each numbered sentence. Write T (True) or F (False) for the statement that follows.*

1. I've recently joined the programme.

   __T__ I am a new member of the cast.

2. I have never been to Scotland.

   ______ I went to Scotland a long time ago.

3. He's gone shopping.

   ______ He's shopping now.

4. Have you ever seen this film?

   ______ I want to know when you saw the film.

5. Someone asks you, 'Have you read any good books lately?'

   ______ They want to know about a book you read last year.

6. She's visited New York several times.

   ______ This is her first visit to New York.

7. She has become very popular.

   ______ She is popular now.

2

CHOOSE & COMPLETE • *Read this script from a scene from 'Family'. Complete it with the present perfect form of the verbs in the box.*

try (×2)	**have**	**eat**	**want** (×3)	**be**	**travel**

CAROL: This is a nice restaurant. ____Have____ you ever ____tried____ (1.) the steak?

JIMMY: No, but I ______________ (2.) the spaghetti. I always have it. Actually, I ______________ never ______________ (3.) meat. I think it's cruel to animals. I bet you ______________ never ______________ (4.) out with a vegetarian before, have you?

CAROL: No, I haven't actually. Tell me, ______________ you ever ______________ (5.) to live out of London? You know, out in the countryside somewhere.

JIMMY: Out of London? Are you crazy? No, seriously, I ______________ never ______________ (6) to leave London. I love it here.

CAROL: But ______________ you ever ______________ (7.) to move to another country or another city at least?

JIMMY: No, why should I? I've got everything I want here. You like London too, don't you?

CAROL: Well, yes, it's OK. But I ______________ (8.) all over the world and other places are just as nice.

JIMMY: You may be right. Anyway, ______________ you ever ______________ (9.) the new Mexican restaurant on the High Street? How about going there tomorrow?

ASK & ANSWER • *Complete the Network Online (NO) interview with Jake Stewart, the actor who plays the part of Gary. Use the words in brackets and the present perfect form of the verb.*

NO: Welcome to Live Studio, Jake. You've become very famous.

How many online interviews have you done?
1. (How many / online interviews / do?)

JAKE: None! ____________________. Very exciting!
2. (never even / be/ in a chat room)

NO: ____________________
3. (How / change / as an actor?)

JAKE: I work with a group, so ____________________
4. (become / more tolerant)

NO: As a comic actor, ____________________
5. (who / be / your role model?)

JAKE: Hard to say. ____________________
6. (Charlie Chaplin / have / great influence on me)

NO: ____________________
7. (What / be / your best moment on this show?)

JAKE: Well, you know, ____________________. That was fantastic.
8. (I / win / the award)

NO: All in all, ____________________
9. (what / find / most rewarding about the experience?)

JAKE: Free coffee! No, really, ____________________
10. (meet / some fantastic people)

EDIT • *Read this message from an online message board. Find and correct seven mistakes in the use of the present perfect. The first mistake has already been corrected.*

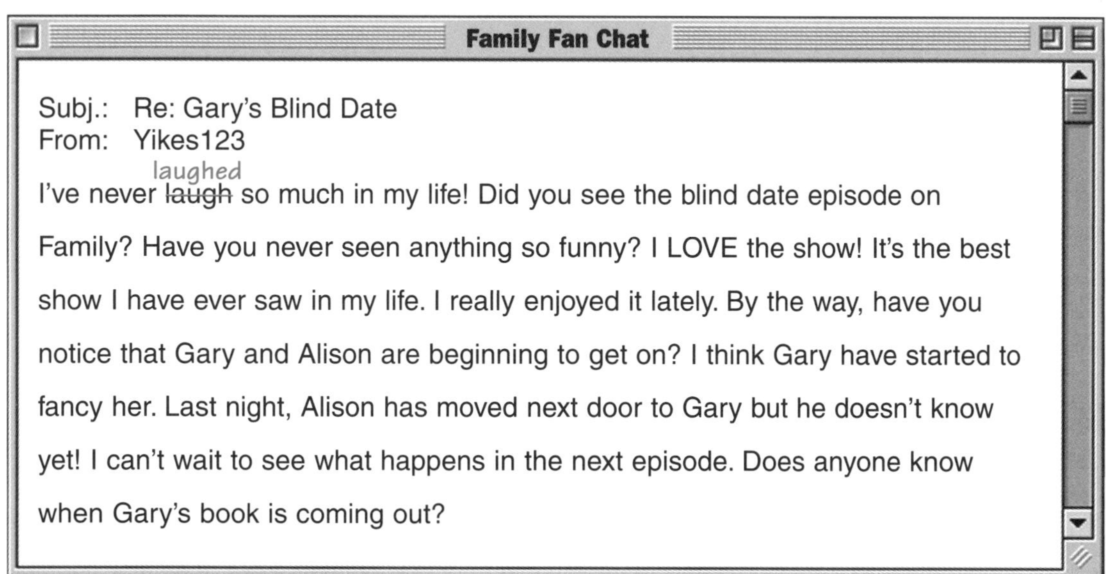

Family Fan Chat

Subj.: Re: Gary's Blind Date
From: Yikes123

I've never ~~laugh~~ laughed so much in my life! Did you see the blind date episode on Family? Have you never seen anything so funny? I LOVE the show! It's the best show I have ever saw in my life. I really enjoyed it lately. By the way, have you notice that Gary and Alison are beginning to get on? I think Gary have started to fancy her. Last night, Alison has moved next door to Gary but he doesn't know yet! I can't wait to see what happens in the next episode. Does anyone know when Gary's book is coming out?

Present Perfect and Past Simple

DEPARTURES
I can't stand this commuter marriage! I've only seen you twice this month.
Yes . . . This month has been bad . . . But last month was better. We saw each other four times!
Paris
Rome

CHECK POINT

Circle T (True) or F (False).

T F The husband and wife live in different cities.

CHART CHECK 1

Tick the correct answer.

Use ***have*** to form

❐ the past simple.

❐ the present perfect.

AFFIRMATIVE STATEMENTS	
PRESENT PERFECT	**PAST SIMPLE**
She**'s owned** the business since 2001. They**'ve met** twice this month.	She **owned** the business from '01 to '03. They **met** twice last month.

NEGATIVE STATEMENTS	
PRESENT PERFECT	**PAST SIMPLE**
She **hasn't owned** the business for long. They **haven't met** this month.	She **didn't own** the business for long. They **didn't meet** last month.

CHART CHECK 2

Tick the correct answer.

Questions in the present perfect are formed with:

❐ ***have*** + base form of verb

❐ ***have*** + past participle

YES/NO QUESTIONS	
PRESENT PERFECT	**PAST SIMPLE**
Has she **owned** it for long? **Have** they **met** this month?	**Did** she **own** it for long? **Did** they **meet** last month?

WH- QUESTIONS	
PRESENT PERFECT	**PAST SIMPLE**
How long **has** she **owned** it? How often **have** they **met** this month?	How long **did** she **own** it? How often **did** they **meet** last month?

EXPRESS CHECK

Circle the correct words to complete these sentences.

They have met / met in 1999. They have been / were married since 2000.

Grammar Explanations	Examples
1. The **present perfect** is used to talk about things that started in the past, continue up to the present and may continue into the future. 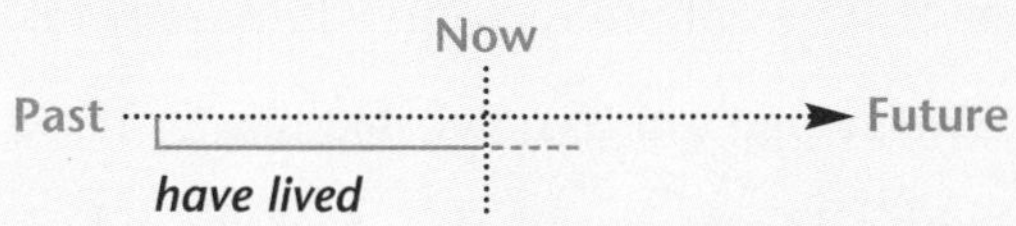	■ They**'ve decided** to live apart for a few years *(We don't know when they decided; the time is not important.)* ■ They **have lived** apart for the past three years. *(They started living apart three years ago, and they are still living apart.)* ■ They**'ve lived** apart since 1998. *(They are still living apart.)*
The **past simple** is used to talk about completed actions in the past.	■ They **lived** apart until 2000. *(They don't live apart any more.)*
2. The **present perfect** is used to talk about things that have happened in a period of time that is not finished, such as ***today***, ***this month***, ***this year***.	■ I**'ve had** three cups of coffee ***this morning***. *(It's still this morning. I might have more.)*
The **past simple** is used to talk about things that happened in a period of time that is finished, such as ***yesterday***, ***last month***, ***last year*** and ***this morning*** when it is after 12 p.m.	■ I **had** three cups of coffee ***yesterday***. *(Yesterday is finished.)* ■ I **had** three cups of coffee ***this morning***. *(It's now 2 p.m. This morning is finished.)*

IDENTIFY • *Read about Joe and Maria. Circle the verbs in the present perfect. Underline the past simple verbs.*

Many modern marriages are finding interesting solutions to difficult problems. Joe and Maria, for example, (have been) married since 1995. After their wedding, the couple <u>settled</u> down in Ipswich, where Maria opened an accounting business. Then, in 1997, Joe lost his job. By that time, Maria's new business was booming, so they didn't consider moving. Joe never found a new job in Ipswich but in 1998, he got an exciting offer on the other side of the country – in Bristol. The couple have lived apart ever since. How have they handled this 'commuter marriage' up to now? Joe notes, 'It certainly hasn't been easy. We've been geographically separated for a few years but we've grown a lot closer emotionally. For that reason, it's been worth it.'

TRUE OR FALSE • *Now write T (True) or F (False) for each statement.*

__F__ 1. Joe and Maria are divorced.

_____ 2. Maria started her own business in Oxford.

_____ 3. The couple used to live apart.

_____ 4. In 1997, they thought about moving.

_____ 5. The couple are now closer emotionally.

2

COMPLETE • *Joe is calling Maria. Complete their conversation with the correct form of the verbs in brackets and with short answers. Choose between the present perfect and the past simple.*

JOE: Hi, Maria. __Did__ you __finish__ (1. finish) that report yesterday?

MARIA: __No, I didn't__ (2.). I'm still writing it and I _____ (3. not stop) worrying about it all week.

JOE: Apart from that, how _____ the week _____ (4. be) so far?

MARIA: OK, I suppose. I'm a bit tired. I only _____ (5. sleep) for a few hours last night.

JOE: It sounds as if you _____ (6. not have) much rest this week. Listen – we _____ (7. see) each other only twice this month. I'll come tomorrow.

MARIA: OK, but I'll still have to work. Last time you came I _____ (8. not do) any work.

JOE: That's true, but it _______________ (9. not bother) us at all, remember? Listen, why don't you relax now? _______________ you _______________ (10. try) that special herbal tea yet?

MARIA: _______________ (11.). In fact, I _______________ (12. already drink) five cups so far today and it's only 3 o'clock. Yesterday I _______________ (13. drink) at least six cups.

3

ASK & ANSWER • *Lifestyle Magazine (LM) is interviewing Joe and Maria. Complete the interview using the words in brackets and information from Exercise 1. Choose between the present perfect and the past simple.*

LM: When did you get married?
1. (When / get married?)

JOE: We got married in 1995.
2.

LM: Did you live in Ipswich after that?
3. (live / in Ipswich after that?)

MARIA: Yes, we did.
4.

LM: _______________
5. (start your business / before your marriage?)

MARIA: _______________
6.

LM: _______________
7. (How long / own your own business?)

MARIA: _______________
8.

LM: _______________
9. (When / you / find your job in Bristol?)

JOE: _______________
10.

LM: _______________
11. (your commuter marriage / be very difficult?)

MARIA: _______________!
12.

EDIT • *Read this entry from Maria's diary. Find and correct six mistakes in the use of the present perfect and the past simple. The first mistake has already been corrected.*

28 December

It's 8:00 P.M. It ~~was~~ 's been *a hard week and it's not over yet! I still have to finish that report. I've started it last Monday but so far I've wrote only five pages. And it's due next week! Work was so difficult lately. I've worked late every night this week. I'm tired and I haven't got much sleep last night. I miss Joe. I've seen him last weekend but it seems like a long time ago.*

UNIT 15 Present Perfect Continuous

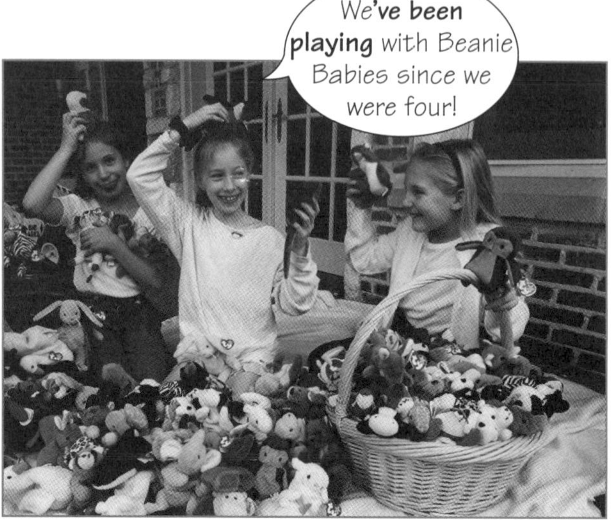

We've been playing with Beanie Babies since we were four!

Jane, Louise and Sarah **have been collecting** Beanie Babies for years.

CHECK POINT

Tick the correct sentence.

❒ The girls don't play with Beanie Babies any more.

❒ The girls are still collecting Beanie Babies.

CHART CHECK 1

Circle T (True) or F (False).

T F The present perfect continuous is always formed with the word ***been***.

STATEMENTS						
SUBJECT	***HAVE***	**(*NOT*)**	***BEEN***	**BASE FORM OF VERB + *-ING***		***SINCE/FOR***
I/We/You*/They	**have**	**(not)**	**been**	**collecting**	toys	***since*** 1992.
He/She/It	**has**	**(n't)**		**playing** with	them	***for*** a long time.

**You* is both singular and plural.

CHART CHECK 2

Check the correct answer.

In questions, which parts of the verb come after the subject?

❒ ***have been***

❒ ***been*** + base form + ***-ing***

***YES/NO* QUESTIONS**					
HAVE	**SUBJECT**	***BEEN***	**BASE FORM + *-ING***		***SINCE/FOR***
Have	you	**been**	**collecting**	toys	***since*** 1992?
Has	he		**playing** with	them	***for*** a long time?

SHORT ANSWERS					
AFFIRMATIVE			**NEGATIVE**		
Yes,	we	**have.**	**No,**	we	**haven't.**
	he	**has.**		he	**hasn't.**

WH- QUESTIONS					
WH- WORD	**HAVE**	**SUBJECT**	**BEEN**	**BASE FORM + -ING**	
How long	**have**	you	**been**	**collecting**	toys?
	has	he		**playing** with	them?

EXPRESS CHECK

Complete these conversations.

A: How long ________________ he been living here?

B: ________________ a long time.

A: I've ________________ collecting coins since last year.

B: Really? Have you been ________________ foreign coins?

Grammar Explanations

Examples

1. Use the **present perfect continuous** to talk about things that started in the past and continue up to the present. The situation is usually not finished, and it will probably continue into the future.

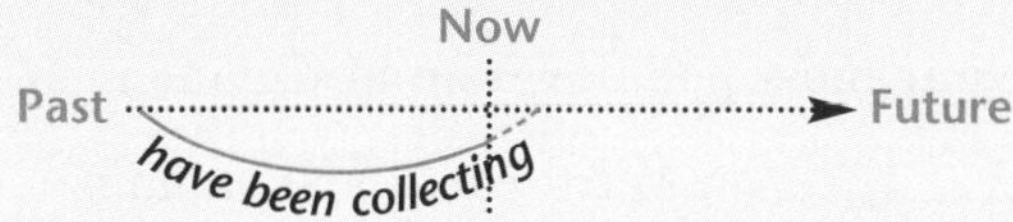

REMEMBER! Stative verbs are usually not used in the continuous.

- **I've been collecting** Beanie Babies for four years. *(I started collecting them four years ago, and I'm still collecting them.)*
- **I've owned** this doll for years. NOT ~~I've been owning this doll for years~~.

2. Use the **present perfect continuous** to describe things that have stopped very recently. The action is not happening now but you can still see the results of the action.

- The kids **have been playing** here. Their toys are all over the room.
- It's **been raining**. The streets are still wet.

Check it out!

For a list of common stative verbs, see Appendix 2 on page 337.

For the difference between the present perfect and the present perfect continuous, see Unit 16.

CHOOSE • *Read each numbered statement. Then circle the letter of the sentence (a) or (b) that best describes the information in the statement.*

1. Gina has been collecting stamps since she was at school.
   a. Gina stopped collecting stamps.
   (b.) Gina still collects stamps.
2. Edward has been writing an article about toys.
   a. The article is finished.
   b. The article isn't finished yet.
3. They've been selling a lot of Pokémon toys.
   a. People are still buying Pokémon toys.
   b. The Pokémon craze is over.
4. Daniel looked out of the window and said, 'It's been raining.'
   a. It's still raining.
   b. It stopped raining a short while ago.
5. It's been raining since 6:00.
   a. It's still raining.
   b. It stopped raining a short while ago.
6. They've been playing for hours.
   a. They've stopped playing.
   b. They're still playing.

COMPLETE • *Edward Simpson* (ES) *interviewed the manager of Toys and Us* (TAU) recently. *Complete the interview with the present perfect continuous form of the verbs in brackets. Use short answers when appropriate.*

ES: So, ___have___ you ___been selling___ (1. sell) a lot of toys this season?

TAU: ___Yes, we have___ (2.), Edward. In fact, Pokémon toys and games ________ (3. sell) very fast. They're our most popular item at the moment.

ES: In case one of our viewers ________ (4. live) on Mars, could you explain what Pokémon toys are?

TAU: Ha ha. I bet the company ________ (5. send) Pokémon to Mars, too. This product started out in Japan as a computer game. Since 1996, the characters ________ (6. appear) in collectors' cards, board games – you name it.

ES: Why ________ this craze ________ (7. attract) people all over the world?

TAU: Well, my husband ________ (8. buy) these products for our children for several years because the characters are not violent. Maybe that's why.

ES: How about Power Rangers? ________ people ________ (9. queue) up for them?

TAU: ________ (10.). People ________ (11. not ask) for Power Rangers very much lately.

DESCRIBE • *Look at the two pictures of journalist Edward Simpson. Write sentences describing what has been going on. Use the present perfect continuous form of the verbs in brackets. Choose between affirmative and negative forms.*

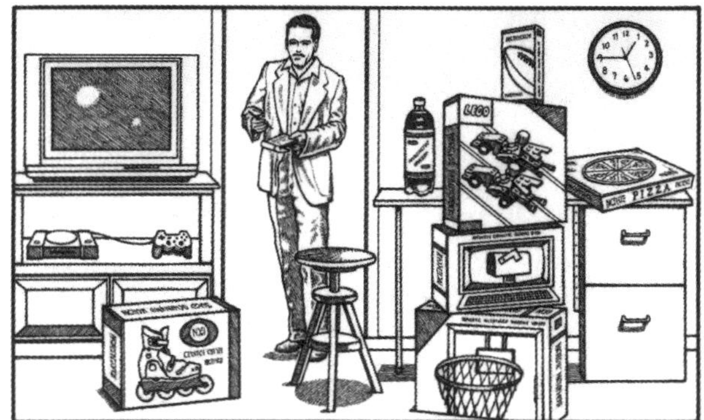

1. He's been doing research on new toys.
   (do research on new toys)
2. ______________________________
   (test the roller blades)
3. ______________________________
   (play basketball)
4. ______________________________
   (eat pizza)
5. ______________________________
   (drink Coke)
6. ______________________________
   (build a racing car)
7. ______________________________
   (play video games)
8. ______________________________
   (send emails)

EDIT • *Read the thank-you note. Find and correct six mistakes in the use of the present perfect continuous. The first mistake has already been corrected.*

Dear Aunty Sally,

Thank you very much for the Pokémon cards. My friend and I have been ~~play~~ playing with them all day. So far, I am been winning. I really love Pokémon. My mum been buying the toys for us because she thinks they're fun, too. All my friends were collecting the cards for months now. Tonya loves the computer game you sent, too. She've been asking me to play with her but I've been having too much fun with my cards.

I hope you are well. I've been thought about you a lot. I hope you can come and visit us soon.

Love,

Patrick

Present Perfect and Present Perfect Continuous

That woman has no manners. She's been following me all day. She's taken 100 rolls of film and written 42 pages of notes. But she hasn't even given me a single peanut!

CHECK POINT

Circle T (True) or F (False).

The woman has finished

T F following the elephant.

T F taking 100 rolls of film.

CHART CHECK

Circle T (True) or F (False).

T F In some sentences, you can use either the present perfect or the present perfect continuous.

PRESENT PERFECT
Elephants **have roamed** the earth for thousands of years.
I**'ve read** two books about elephants.
Dr Owen **has written** many articles.
She**'s lived** in many countries.

PRESENT PERFECT PROGRESSIVE
Elephants **have been roaming** the earth for thousands of years.
I**'ve been reading** this book since Monday.
She**'s been writing** articles since 1990.
She**'s been living** in France for a year.

EXPRESS CHECK

Complete this conversation with the correct form of the verb **eat** *and one short answer.*

A: He's been ________________ all morning!

B: What ________________ he ________________ eating?

A: Peanuts. He ________________ eaten five bags of peanuts!

B: ________________ he eaten the whole supply?

A: ________________, he ________________. There are still ten bags left.

Grammar Explanations	Examples
1. The **present perfect** often shows that something is finished. It focuses on the result of the action. 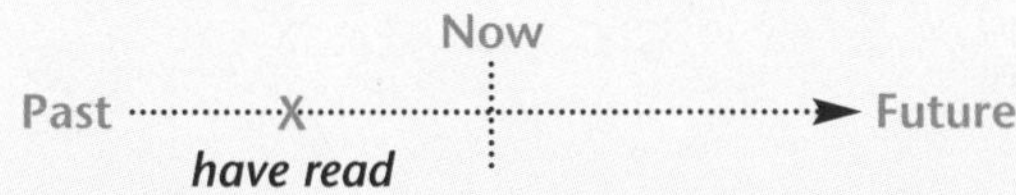	■ I**'ve read** a good book about elephants. *(I've finished reading the book and now I know a lot about elephants.)* ■ She**'s written** the article. *(She's finished writing the article.)*
The **present perfect continuous** often shows that an activity is unfinished. It focuses on the continuation of an action. 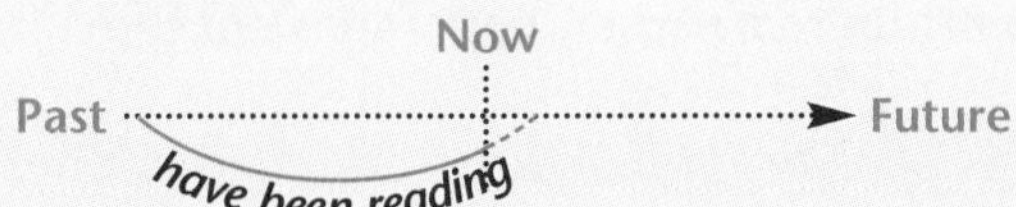	■ I**'ve been reading** a book about elephants. *(I'm still reading it.)* ■ She**'s been writing** an article. *(She's still writing it.)*
2. We often use the **present perfect** to talk about – how much someone has done. – how many times someone has done something. – how many things someone has done.	■ I**'ve read** ***a lot*** about it. ■ I**'ve been** to Africa ***twice***. ■ She**'s written** ***several*** really good articles.
We often use the **present perfect continuous** to talk about how long something has been happening.	■ I**'ve been reading** books on elephants ***for two months***.
▶ **BE CAREFUL!** We do not usually use the present perfect continuous when we mention a number of completed events.	■ I**'ve read** that book ***twice***. NOT ~~I've been reading that book twice.~~
3. Sometimes you can use either the **present perfect** OR the **present perfect continuous**. The meaning is basically the same. This is especially true when you use verbs such as ***live***, ***work***, ***study*** and ***teach*** with ***for*** or ***since***.	■ She**'s studied** elephants ***for*** two years. OR ■ She**'s been studying** elephants ***for*** two years. *(In both cases, she started studying elephants two years ago and she is still studying them.)*

TRUE OR FALSE • *Read each numbered sentence. Write T (True) or F (False) for the statement that follows.*

1. Professor Owen has been reading a book about elephants.

   __F__ She has read the whole book.

2. She's read a book about elephants.

   ______ She has read the whole book.

3. She's written a magazine article about the rain forest.

   ______ She has written the whole article.

4. She's been waiting for some supplies.

   ______ She has got the supplies now.

5. They've lived in Uganda since 1992.

   ______ They are still in Uganda.

6. They've been living in Uganda since 1992.

   ______ They still live in Uganda.

CHOOSE • *Here are some statements about Professor Owen's work. Circle the correct form of the verbs to complete these statements. In some cases, both forms are correct.*

1. Professor Owen is working on two articles for *National Wildlife Magazine*. She has written / (has been writing) these articles since Monday.
2. *National Wildlife Magazine* has published / has been publishing its annual report on the environment. It's an excellent report.
3. Five hundred and sixty African elephants have already died / have been dying this year.
4. Professor Owen has given / has been giving many talks about wildlife preservation in the last few years.
5. She has spoken / has been speaking at our school many times.
6. Professor Owen was late for a meeting. When she arrived, the chairperson said, 'At last, you're here. We have waited / have been waiting for you.'
7. Professor Owen has lived / has been living in England for the last two years.
8. She has worked / has been working with environmentalists in England and France.
9. She has set up / has been setting up a new study group to discuss the problem of endangered animals. The group has already met twice.

COMPLETE • *Read this entry from Dr Owen's field journal about an elephant she calls Grandad. Use the present perfect or the present perfect continuous form of the verbs in brackets.*

We **'ve been hearing** (1. hear) about Grandad since we arrived here in Amboseli Park. He is one of the last 'tuskers'. Two days ago, we finally saw him. His tusks are more than two metres long. I ______ never ______ (2. see) anything like them.

Grandad ______ (3. live) here for more than sixty years. He ______ (4. experience) everything and he ______ (5. survive) countless threats from human beings. Young men ______ (6. test) their courage against him and poachers ______ (7. hunt) him for his ivory. His experience and courage ______ (8. save) him so far.

For the last two days, he ______ (9. move) slowly through the tall grass. He ______ (10. eat) and ______ (11. rest). Luckily, it ______ (12. rain) a lot this year and even the biggest elephants ______ (13. find) enough food and water.

EDIT • *Read this student's report. Find and correct six mistakes in the use of the present perfect and present perfect continuous. The first mistake has already been corrected.*

Elephants and their ancestors have been ~~live~~ living on this planet for 5 million years. Scientists have found their bones in many places, from Asia to North America. Present-day elephants has also survived in different kinds of environments, including very dry areas in Niger, grasslands in East Africa and forests in West Africa.

Because of their great size and strength, elephants have always fascinating humans. Our fascination has almost caused African elephants to become extinct. Poachers (illegal hunters) have already been killing hundreds of thousands of elephants for the ivory of their tusks. After 1989, it became illegal to sell ivory. Since then, the elephant population has been grown steadily. Recently, several countries have been protecting elephants in national parks and herds have became larger and healthier.

UNIT 17 Past Perfect

By the time I was twelve, I **had** already **decided** on a career. I wanted to be paid to talk!

Chat show host Oprah Winfrey with her TV audience.

CHECK POINT

Tick the event that happened first.

❒ Oprah had her twelfth birthday.

❒ Oprah decided on a career.

CHART CHECK 1

Circle T (True) or F (False).

T F The past perfect uses ***had*** for all subjects.

STATEMENTS			
SUBJECT	**HAD (NOT)**	**PAST PARTICIPLE**	
I/He/She/We/You*/They	'd had (not) hadn't	**decided**	by then.
It		**been**	easy.

**You* is both singular and plural.

CHART CHECK 2

Tick the correct answer.

In past perfect questions, where does ***had*** go?

❒ before the subject

❒ after the subject

YES/NO **QUESTIONS**			
HAD	**SUBJECT**	**PAST PARTICIPLE**	
Had	she	**decided**	by then?
	it	**been**	easy?

SHORT ANSWERS					
AFFIRMATIVE			**NEGATIVE**		
Yes,	she	**had.**	**No,**	she	**hadn't.**
	it			it	

WH- **QUESTIONS**				
WH- **WORD**	**HAD**	**SUBJECT**	**PAST PARTICIPLE**	
Why	**had**	she	**decided**	to be a chat show host?
		it	**been**	easy?

EXPRESS CHECK

*Complete this conversation with the verb **arrive**.*

A: Had she ________________ by 9:00?

B: No, she ________________.

Grammar Explanations	Examples
1. Use the **past perfect** to show that something happened before a specific time in the past. 	■ By 1988, Oprah Winfrey **had become** famous. ■ It was 1985. She **had** already **been** in a Hollywood film.
2. The **past perfect** always shows a relationship with another past event. Use the past perfect for the earlier event. Use the past simple for the later event. ▶ **Be careful!** In these sentences with ***when***, notice the difference in meaning between the past simple and the past perfect.	■ In 1990, Oprah ***invited*** Matt on the show. He **had been** an author for two years. *(He was an author before 1990.)* ■ By the time Jill ***got*** home, 'The Oprah Winfrey Show' **had finished**. ■ ***When*** the show ended, she **left**. *(First the show ended. Then she left.)* ■ ***When*** the show ended, she **had left**. *(First she left. Then the show ended.)*
3. ***Already***, ***yet***, ***ever*** and ***never*** are often used with the **past perfect** to emphasise the event which happened first.	■ I saw *The Color Purple* last night. I **had *never* seen** it before. ■ Jason **had *already* seen** it.
4. When the time relationship between two past events is clear, you can use the **simple past for both events**. The meaning is usually clear when you use ***after***, ***before*** or ***as soon as*** to connect the events.	■ ***After*** Oprah **had appeared** in *The Color Purple*, she **got** a part in another film. OR ■ ***After*** Oprah **appeared** in *The Color Purple*, she **got** a part in another film.
5. We often use the **past perfect** with ***by*** (a certain time).	■ ***By 1966***, Oprah **had decided** on a career.

TRUE OR FALSE • *Read each numbered sentence. Write T (True) or F (False) for the statement that follows.*

1. When I got home, 'The Oprah Winfrey Show' started.

   __F__ First the Oprah show started. Then I got home.

2. When I got home, 'The Oprah Winfrey Show' had started.

   _____ First the Oprah show started. Then I got home.

3. Oprah's guest had lost 25 kilos when she interviewed him.

   _____ The guest lost the weight before the interview.

4. By the end of the show, I had fallen asleep.

   _____ I fell asleep after the show.

5. When I went to bed, I had turned off the radio.

   _____ I turned off the radio after I went to bed.

6. By midnight, I had finished the magazine article.

   _____ I finished the article before midnight.

2 **COMPLETE •** *Look at some important events in Oprah Winfrey's career. Then complete the sentences below. Use the past perfect with* **already** *or* **not yet**.

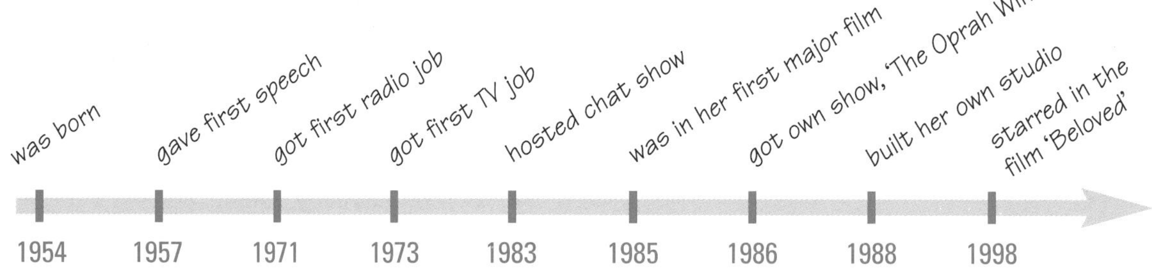

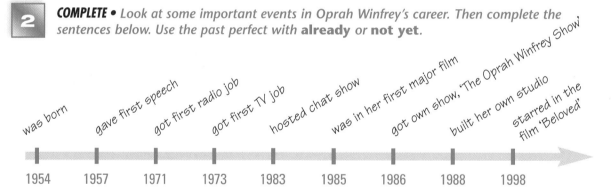

1. By 1958, Oprah ____had already given____ her first speech.
2. By 1971, she ________________ her first TV job.
3. By 1972, she ________________ her first radio job.
4. By 1973, she ________________ her first TV job.
5. By 1985, she ________________ her own TV show.
6. By 1986, she ________________ in a major film.
7. By 1987, she ________________ her own studio.
8. By 2000, she ________________ in the film 'Beloved'.

ASK & ANSWER • *Look at this typical timetable for a TV chat show host. Complete the questions about his timetable. Use the past perfect and give short answers.*

7:00 a.m.	Arrive at studio
8:00	Review day's filming
11:00	Discuss future shows with assistant producers
2:00 p.m.	Hair and make-up
2:30	Meet the day's guests
3:00	Record the show
4:30	Work out with trainer

1. It was 7:45. The host was on schedule.

   A: Had he arrived at the studio yet? **B:** Yes, he had.

2. At 7:30 the host was at his desk.

   A: ______________ the day's filming yet? **B:** ______________

3. At 10:55 he was having coffee.

   A: ______________ the day's filming by that time? **B:** ______________

4. It was 2:00. He was on his way to make up.

   A: ______________ the day's guests by then? **B:** ______________

5. At 4:00 he had a late lunch.

   A: ______________ the show yet? **B:** ______________

6. He went to bed at 10:30.

   A: ______________ with his trainer that day? **B:** ______________

EDIT • *Read this student's report. There are six mistakes in the use of the past perfect. Find and correct them. The first mistake has already been corrected.*

Oprah Winfrey is an amazing person! By the time she was twelve, she ~~has~~ had already decided on a career. Not long afterwards, she got her first radio job. Although she hadn't have any experience, she became a news reporter. When she got her own TV chat show, she has already acted in a major Hollywood film. By the late 1980s, 'Oprah Winfrey' had became a household word. Then in 1994, she decided to improve the quality of chat show themes. She also made a personal change. She had always had a weight problem but in 1995, TV viewers saw a new Winfrey. She had losed almost 40 kilos as a result of dieting and working out. She had also compete in a marathon. She has really been an inspiration to many people.

UNIT 18 Past Perfect Continuous

By the time the last runner crossed the finishing line, he **had been running** for 7 hours, 16 minutes, and 24 seconds.
RUNNER 17

CHECK POINT

Circle T (True) or F (False).

T F The race is finished.

CHART CHECK

Tick the correct answer.

What form of ***be*** does the past perfect continuous always use?

❐ ***was*** or ***were***

❐ ***is***, ***am*** or ***are***

❐ ***been***

STATEMENTS				
Subject	***Had (not)***	***Been***	**Base Form of Verb + *-ing***	
I/He/She/It/We/You*/They	**had (not)** **had(n't)**	**been**	**running** **working**	all day.

**You* is both singular and plural.

YES/NO QUESTIONS				
Had	**Subject**	***Been***	**Base Form + *-ing***	
Had	she	**been**	**running** **working**	all day?

SHORT ANSWERS	
Affirmative	**Negative**
Yes, she **had**.	No, she **hadn't**.

WH- QUESTIONS				
***Wh-* Word**	***Had***	**Subject**	***Been***	**Base Form + *-ing***
How long Why	**had**	she	**been**	**running**? **working**?

EXPRESS CHECK

Complete this conversation with the past perfect continuous form of the verb **practise**.

A: How long ____________ she ____________ when she entered the race?

B: She ____________ for more than two years.

A: ____________ she ____________ alone?

B: No, she ____________. She ____________ with a partner.

Grammar Explanations	Examples
1. Use the **past perfect continuous** to talk about an action that was in progress before a specific time in the past. The continuous emphasises the continuation of an action, not the end result.	■ It was 2:00 p.m. The runners **had been running** since 10:48 a.m. ■ I finally saw Rob at 4:00 p.m. I **had been waiting** for hours. ■ One runner fainted during the race. She **hadn't been drinking** enough water.
Now / *10:48* / *2:00* / Past / Future / *had been running*	
Remember! Stative verbs are not usually used in the continuous.	■ It was 5:00 p.m. He **had had** a headache all day. Not He ~~had been having a headache all day~~.

2. The **past perfect continuous** always shows a relationship with another past event. Use the past perfect continuous for the earlier event. Use the past simple for the later event.	■ She **had been training** for three years when she ***entered*** the race. *(First she trained. Then she entered the race.)*

3. We often use the **past perfect continuous** to draw conclusions about past events based on evidence.	■ She was out of breath. It was clear that she **had been running**. ■ The streets were wet. It **had been raining**.

4. **Be careful!** In these sentences with ***when***, notice the difference in meaning between the past continuous and the past perfect continuous.	■ ***When*** the race started, it **was raining** and the streets were wet. *(It was still raining during the race.)* ■ ***When*** the race started, it **had been raining** and the streets were wet. *(It wasn't raining during the race. It had already stopped.)*

MATCH • *Match each result with the correct cause.*

	Result		Cause
b	1. She was out of breath.	a.	He had been reading.
____	2. The ground was wet.	b.	She had been running.
____	3. Her eyes were red.	c.	They had been watching the race.
____	4. There was an open book on the sofa.	d.	She had been crying.
____	5. There was an empty box on the floor.	e.	It had been raining.
____	6. The TV was on.	f.	They had been eating pizza.

COMPLETE • *Read this story from a magazine article. Complete it with the past perfect progressive form of the verbs in brackets.*

MARATHON RUNNING

BY BERNADINE MARTIN

On 23 October, I ran the Boston Marathon with a partner, Marcia Davis. We **had been training** (1. train) together for a year. In fact, we ______________ (2. plan) to enter the race ever since we watched the Washington Marathon. The start of the race was dramatic. Up to that point, we ______________ (3. laugh and joke) but we were very serious when we lined up. I was so nervous I couldn't breathe. Marcia and I ______________ (4. train) on those same streets for a couple of weeks, so at the beginning we did well. By the time we got to Heartbreak Hill, we ______________ (5. run) for almost three hours and I really believed we could finish. Then, halfway up the hill, Marcia stopped. She just couldn't run any more. We ______________ (6. look forward) to this race for so long that I didn't want to go on alone but Marcia wanted me to finish. When I got to the finishing line, I saw Marcia. She ______________ (7. wait) for me for two hours. First we cried. Then we started talking about next year's marathon.

CHOOSE & COMPLETE • *The magazine* Runner's World (RW) *is interviewing marathon winner Paolo Esposito* (PE). *Complete the interview with the past perfect continuous form of the correct verbs from the box. Use short answers where appropriate.*

go out	expect	live	~~train~~	run

RW: You've just won the marathon. Congratulations! ___Had you been training___ (1.) for it for a long time?

PE: ___Yes, I had___ (2.). For more than five years. First in Madrid, then in Rome.

RW: You tripped during the race. How long ______________ (3.) when that happened?

PE: It was in the last hour. Luckily it didn't keep me from winning.

RW: I understand that you recently married your trainer, Emilia Leale. How long ______________ (4.) together when you decided to get married?

PE: About six months. We met in Rome and knew straightaway that we wanted to be together.

RW: ______________ (5.) in Rome for a long time when you met?

PE: ______________ (6.). In fact, I had just moved there.

RW: You looked very calm when you crossed the finishing line. ______________ (7.) to win?

PE: ______________ (8.)! I was really surprised. And very happy.

EDIT • *Read part of an entry from a runner's diary. Find and correct five mistakes in the use of the past perfect continuous. The first mistake has already been corrected.*

19 October

I've just got back from the marathon! I'm tired but very happy. When I crossed the finishing line, I ~~have~~ had *been running for four hours and twenty-five minutes. Jeremy was standing there. He had been waited for me the whole time. We were both soaking wet – I, because I had been sweating; he, because it has been raining just a little while before. I was so glad to see him. I had been look forward to this day for so long and hoping that I could finish the race in less than four and a half hours. When I got home, I called my parents. They had watching the marathon on TV and had actually seen me cross the finishing line!*

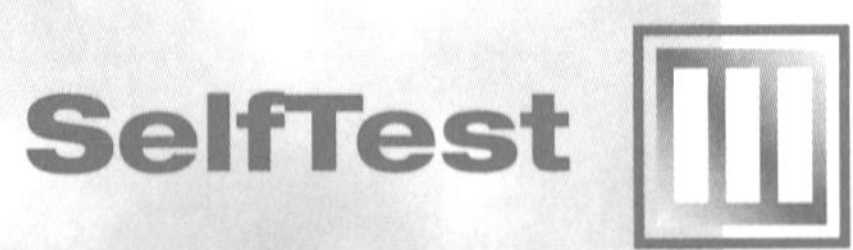

SelfTest III

SECTION ONE

Circle the letter of the correct answer to complete each sentence.

EXAMPLE:
Jennifer never ________ coffee. A (B) C D
(A) drink (C) is drinking
(B) drinks (D) was drinking

1. He ________ for the Olympics since 2002. A B C D
(A) practised (C) has been practising
(B) practises (D) was practising

2. We've known Sally ________ a long time. A B C D
(A) since (C) while
(B) by (D) for

3. We've been living in London since we ________. A B C D
(A) have graduated (C) graduated
(B) have been graduating (D) graduate

4. They haven't ________ an AIDS vaccine. A B C D
(A) yet developed (C) developed already
(B) developed yet (D) already develop

5. ________ you reserved your hotel room yet? A B C D
(A) Did (C) Do
(B) Have (D) Has

6. She hasn't ________ very often. A B C D
(A) flew (C) flown
(B) flies (D) flying

7. It ________ and the ground was still white. A B C D
(A) snows (C) would snow
(B) had been snowing (D) has snowed

8. Tina ________ last week. A B C D
(A) has arrived (C) has been arriving
(B) arrived (D) arrives

9. They ________ here for three years before they moved. A B C D
(A) live (C) had lived
(B) have lived (D) have been living

10. The show has ________ won an award. A B C D
(A) just (C) lately
(B) ever (D) yet

11. Professor Kidd ________ three books since 1999, and she's working on her fourth. A B C D
(A) has been writing (C) wrote
(B) has written (D) writes

12. We ________ to buy that car yet. A B C D
(A) haven't decided (C) have decided
(B) decided (D) are deciding

13. —Has Maria called yet?
—Yes, she ________. But she didn't leave a message. A B C D
(A) did (C) hasn't
(B) called (D) has

14. Since I ________ university, I haven't had much spare time. A B C D
(A) started (C) have started
(B) was starting (D) start

SECTION TWO

Each sentence has four underlined words or phrases. The four underlined parts of the sentence are marked A, B, C and D. Circle the letter of the one underlined word or phrase that is NOT CORRECT.

EXAMPLE:
Mike usually (A) drives (B) to school but today (C) he walks (D). A B C (D)

15. When (A) she was (B) younger, she has (C) played (D) tennis every day. A B C D

16. It's (A) already (B) 10:00, but Jane hasn't finished (C) her homework already (D). A B C D

17. I've been worrying (A) about you because you haven't (B) been seeming (C) well lately (D). A B C D

18. I've read (A) a good book recently (B), but I haven't finished (C) it yet (D). A B C D

19. Did (A) you done your homework, or have (B) you been (C) watching (D) TV? A B C D

20. Karl has (A) been (B) driving (C) since (D) ten years. A B C D

21. We've (A) been (B) here only (C) one day, but we've been taking (D) three rolls of film. A B C D

22. This hotel has been (A) already (B) in business for (C) fifty years (D). A B C D

23. How much (A) coffee did (B) you been drinking (C) last night (D)? A B C D

24. I've been studying (A) French since (B) I've (C) started (D) school. A B C D

25. Before she became (A) a film star, (B) she has (C) been (D) a stand-up comedian. A B C D

Future: *Be going to* and *Will*

CHECK POINT

Tick the main point of the cartoon.

❒ The man has forgotten his umbrella.

❒ The man is going to fall into the hole.

CHART CHECK 1

Tick the correct answer.

How many forms does ***be*** have in ***be going to***?

❒ one

❒ two

❒ three

STATEMENTS: *BE GOING TO*				
SUBJECT	***BE******	**(NOT) GOING TO**	**BASE FORM OF VERB**	
I	**am** **'m**	**(not) going to**	**leave**	soon.
He/She/It	**is** **'s**	**(not) going to**		
We/You*/They	**are** **'re**	**(n't) going to**		

*_You_ is both singular and plural.

CHART CHECK 2

Circle T (True) or F (False).

T F In questions, a form of ***be*** goes after the subject.

YES/NO QUESTIONS: *BE GOING TO*			
BE	**SUBJECT**	**GOING TO**	**BASE FORM**
Am	I	**going to**	**leave** soon?
Is	he		
Are	you		

SHORT ANSWERS					
AFFIRMATIVE			**NEGATIVE**		
Yes,	you	**are.**	**No,**	you	**aren't.**
	he	**is.**		he	**isn't.**
	I	**am.**		I	**'m not.**

WH- QUESTIONS: *BE GOING TO*				
***WH-* WORD**	***BE***	**SUBJECT**	**GOING TO**	**BASE FORM**
When Why	**am**	I	**going to**	**leave?**
	is	he		
	are	you		

CHART CHECK 3

Circle T (True) or F (False).

T F The form of ***will*** is the same for all subjects.

STATEMENTS: *WILL*			
Subject	***Will* (not)**	**Base Form**	
I/He/She/It/We/You/They	**will (not)** **(won't)**	**leave**	soon.

YES/NO QUESTIONS: *WILL*			
Will	**Subject**	**Base Form**	
Will	he	**leave**	soon?

SHORT ANSWERS	
Affirmative	**Negative**
Yes, he **will**.	**No**, he **won't**.

WH- QUESTIONS: *WILL*			
***Wh-* Word**	***Will***	**Subject**	**Base Form**
When	**will**	he	**leave**?

EXPRESS CHECK

Unscramble these words to form two sentences.

to • rain • It's • going ____.

an • get • I'll • umbrella ____.

Grammar Explanations	Examples
1. You can use ***be going to*** to talk about future plans and intentions.	■ Professor Fox **is going to attend** a conference next week. ■ I'**m going to go** with him.
You can use ***will*** to say what you think or guess will happen in the future.	■ I think it **will be** very interesting. ■ I suppose he'**ll talk** about his new invention. ■ The cars of the future **won't run** on petrol.
2. Use ***be going to*** when something in the present leads you to predict something in the future.	■ Look at those dark clouds! It'**s going to rain**. NOT ~~Look at those dark clouds! It'll rain.~~ ■ Watch out! You'**re going to fall**.
Use ***will*** to give information about the future.	■ Professor Fox's books **will be** on sale at the conference.
Use ***will*** when you decide something at the moment of speaking.	**A:** Professor Fox is speaking at noon. **B:** Oh. I think I'**ll go** to his talk.

Check it out!

There are other ways to talk about the future. See Unit 20, pages 84–85.

READ • *Look at Professor Harry Fox's email message.*

Harry's Travel Plans

Greg – Just a quick note to let you know my plans. I hear you're going to be in London next weekend. Unfortunately, I won't be there. That means I won't be able to go fishing with you on Saturday. I'm going to be in Newcastle giving a speech at the Smart Transport conference. I go every year but this is the first time I'm going to speak at it. The conference finishes on Saturday but I don't think I'm going to go back to London until Sunday night. I'm probably going to take the train instead of driving so I can get some work done. So, it doesn't look as if we'll get to see each other this time. I hope next time works out better.   Harry

ANSWER • *Tick all the things Harry Fox is going to do next weekend.*

1. ☐ be in London
2. ☑ be in Newcastle
3. ☐ go fishing
4. ☐ attend a conference
5. ☐ give a speech
6. ☐ return on Saturday
7. ☐ drive to London
8. ☐ see Greg

DESCRIBE • *Look at the pictures. They show events from a day in Professor Fox's life. Write predictions or guesses. Use the words below and a form of* **be going to** *or* **not be going to**.

answer the phone   drive   give a speech   ~~rain~~   go on a journey   watch TV

1. It's going to rain.

2. ______

3. ______

4. ______

5. ______

6. ______

COMPLETE • *After his speech, Professor Fox answered questions from the audience. Complete the questions and answers. Use the words in brackets and* **will** *or* **won't**.

WOMAN 1: My question is this, Professor Fox: ___Will___ the car of the future ___run___ (1. run) on petrol?

FOX: No, it ___won't___ (2.). It ________ probably ________ (3. use) solar energy.

WOMAN 2: ________ we still ________ (4. get) flat tyres?

FOX: No, we ________ (5.). By the year 2010, tyres ________ (6. have) a special seal so that they ________ (7. repair) themselves.

MAN 1: In what other ways ________ cars ________ (8. be) different?

FOX: Well, instead of keys, cars ________ (9. have) smart cards. These ________ (10. look) a lot like credit cards. They ________ (11. open) doors and they ________ (12. adjust) the seats, mirrors and steering wheels. They ________ even ________ (13. control) the inside temperature.

MAN 1: ________ they ________ (14. prevent) car thefts?

FOX: Yes, they ________ (15.)! Next question? That gentleman at the back.

MAN 2: How much ________ these cars ________ (16. cost)?

FOX: I don't know exactly but they certainly ________ (17. be) cheap. Nothing ever is!

EDIT • *Read this email message to Professor Fox. Find and correct nine mistakes in the use of the future with* **will** *and* **be going to**. *The first mistake has already been corrected.*

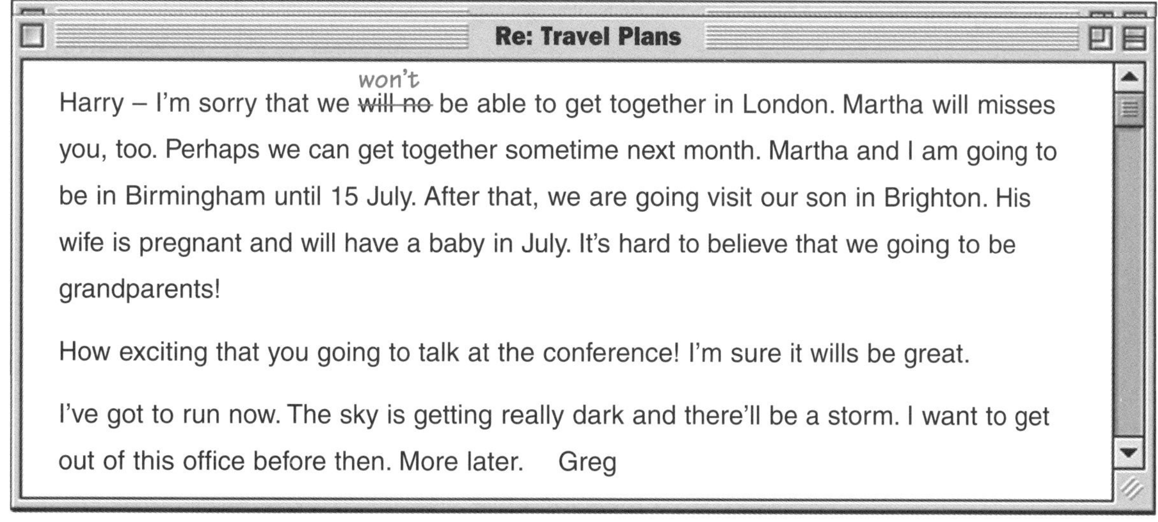

Re: Travel Plans

Harry – I'm sorry that we ~~will no~~ *won't* be able to get together in London. Martha will misses you, too. Perhaps we can get together sometime next month. Martha and I am going to be in Birmingham until 15 July. After that, we are going visit our son in Brighton. His wife is pregnant and will have a baby in July. It's hard to believe that we going to be grandparents!

How exciting that you going to talk at the conference! I'm sure it wills be great.

I've got to run now. The sky is getting really dark and there'll be a storm. I want to get out of this office before then. More later. Greg

UNIT 20 Future: Contrast

CHECK POINT

Circle T (True) or F (False).

T F The shuttle to Mars has a scheduled departure time.

T F The pilot is too late.

CHART CHECK

Circle T (True) or F (False).

T F There are several ways to talk about the future.

T F You can't use the present simple to talk about the future.

AFFIRMATIVE STATEMENTS	
We**'re going to leave**	soon.
We**'ll leave**	
We**'re leaving**	
We **leave**	

NEGATIVE STATEMENTS	
We **aren't going to leave**	until 1:00.
We **won't leave**	
We **aren't leaving**	
We **don't leave**	

YES/NO QUESTIONS	
Is she **going to leave**	soon?
Will she **leave**	
Is she **leaving**	
Does she **leave**	

SHORT ANSWERS			
AFFIRMATIVE		NEGATIVE	
Yes,	she **is.**	**No,**	she **isn't.**
	she **will.**		she **won't.**
	she **is.**		she **isn't.**
	she **does.**		she **doesn't.**

WH- QUESTIONS
When **is** she **going to leave**?
When **will** she **leave**?
When **is** she **leaving**?
When **does** she **leave**?

EXPRESS CHECK

Tick the sentences that refer to the future.

- ☐ I'm leaving in five minutes.
- ☐ What time do you normally leave the office?
- ☐ Are you going to the conference in May?
- ☐ I'm working on a report at the moment.

Grammar Explanations	Examples
1. Use ***be going to***, ***will***, the **present continuous** and the **present simple** to talk about things in the future. 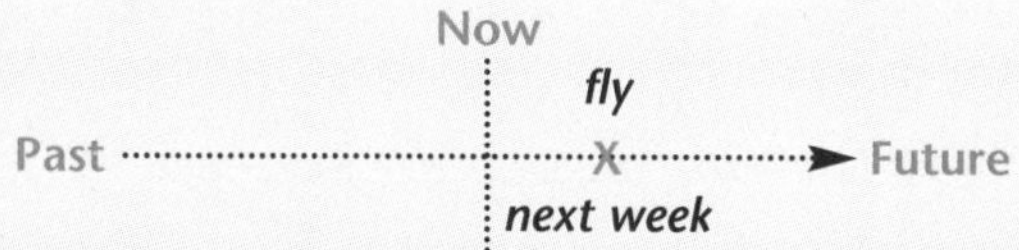	■ I'**m going to fly** to Mars next week. ■ By 2080, people **won't drive**. They'**ll fly** everywhere instead. ■ Pete's got his ticket. He'**s flying** to New York on Tuesday. ■ The plane **takes off** at 10:05 and **lands** at 16:15
2. Usage Notes: Sometimes only one form of the future is appropriate but in many cases more than one form is possible.	
a. Use ***be going to*** to make predictions when something in the present leads you to predict something in the future.	■ Look at that spaceship! It'**s going to land**. Not ~~It'll land~~.
b. Use ***will*** to say what you think or guess will happen in the future.	■ In the future, people **will spend** their holidays in space.
c. Use ***be going to*** to talk about future plans and intentions.	■ We'**re going to listen to** Dr Green's speech tomorrow.
d. Use the **present continuous** to talk about fixed arrangements that have been made for the future. You often mention the time and/or place of the arrangement.	■ Dr Green **is giving** a lecture at 10 o'clock in Lecture Room A.
e. Use ***will*** to talk about information about the future.	**A:** **Will** Dr Fisher be at the conference? **B:** No, he **won't** but Dr Green **will**. ■ Each lecture **will last** one hour.
f. Use ***will*** when you decide something at the moment of speaking and to make offers.	**A:** Dr Green is giving a talk tomorrow. **B:** Oh! Maybe I'**ll go**. **A:** Great! I'**ll get** you a ticket.
g. Use the **present simple** to talk about scheduled future events, especially timetables, programmes, etc.	■ The shuttle to Mars **leaves** at 10:00 a.m. **tomorrow**. ■ We **land** at midnight.

IDENTIFY • *Professor Ellen Green is attending a conference this week. Read her conversation with Professor David Russ. Underline all the verbs that refer to the future.*

RUSS: Ellen! It's nice to see you. Are you presenting a paper this week?

GREEN: Hi, David. Yes. In fact, my talk starts at two o'clock.

RUSS: Oh, maybe I'll come. What are you going to talk about? Robots?

GREEN: Yes. I'm dealing with personal robots for household work.

RUSS: I'd like one of those! Where's your son, by the way? Is he here with you?

GREEN: No. Tony stays in Norfolk with his grandparents in the summer. I'm going to visit him after the conference. So, what are you working on these days?

RUSS: I'm still with the Mars Association. In fact, we're holding a news conference next month about the Mars shuttle launch.

GREEN: That's exciting. Maybe I'll see you there.

RUSS: Great. The conference begins at noon on the tenth.

CHOOSE • *Circle the most appropriate words to complete these conversations.*

1. **GREEN:** Which project do you work / are you going to work on next?
   RUSS: I haven't decided for sure. Probably the Spacemobile.
2. **RUSS:** Look at those dark clouds!
   GREEN: Yes. It looks as if it's raining / it's going to rain any minute.
3. **GREEN:** I'd better get back to my hotel room before the storm.
   RUSS: OK. I'm seeing / I'll see you later.
4. **DESK:** Professor Green, your son has just called.
   GREEN: Oh, good. I'll call / I'm calling him back straightaway.
5. **GREEN:** Hi, Tony. How's it going?
   TONY: Great. I go / I'm going fishing with Grandpa tomorrow.
6. **GREEN:** Have fun, but don't forget you still have to finish your project.
   TONY: I know, Mum. I post / I'm posting it tomorrow. I've already got the envelope.
7. **TONY:** How's the conference?
   GREEN: It's great. I'm giving / I'll give a talk this afternoon.
8. **TONY:** Good luck. When are you / will you be here?
   GREEN: Tomorrow. My plane lands / will land at 7:00, so I see / I'll see you at about 8:00.

COMPLETE • *Read these conversations. Complete them with an appropriate form of the verbs in brackets. (There is more than one correct answer for some items.)*

1. **A:** Hurry up! The shuttle ___leaves___ (leave) in just a few minutes.
   B: Oh, I'm sure they ________ (wait) for us.
2. **A:** Look at those storm clouds! Do you think it ________ (rain)?
   B: I don't know. I ________ (check) the weather forecast.
3. **A:** When ________ we ________ (board) the shuttle?
   B: We ________ (fly) first class, so we should be among the first to board.
4. **A:** Wow! This suitcase is heavy.
   B: I ________ (carry) it for you. Give it to me.
5. **A:** What time ________ we ________ (land) on Mars?
   B: According to the schedule, at 9:00 a.m., but I think we ________ (be) a little late.
6. **A:** I'm hungry. I hope we ________ (get) some food soon.
   B: Me too. I ________ (have) the seafood special. I ordered it in advance.
7. **A:** Look! The flight attendant is getting ready to announce something.
   B: Great. That means we ________ (start) boarding soon.

EDIT • *Read this flight announcement on the shuttle to Mars. Find and correct seven mistakes in the use of the future. The first mistake has already been corrected. (There is often more than one way to correct a mistake).*

'Good evening, ladies and gentlemen. This ~~will be~~ is your captain speaking. We be going to leave the Earth's field of gravity in about fifteen minutes. At that time, you are able to unbuckle your seat belts and float around the cabin. Host robots take orders for dinner soon. After these storm clouds, we are having a smooth trip. The shuttle arrives on Mars tomorrow at 9:00. Tonight's temperature on the planet is a mild minus 20 degrees Celsius. By tomorrow morning the temperature is 18 degrees but it is feeling more like 28 degrees. Enjoy your flight.'

UNIT 21 Future Time Clauses

When I grow up, I'm going to be a ballet dancer.

CHECK POINT

Tick the correct answer.

❒ The child is talking about a present habit.

❒ The child is planning her future.

CHART CHECK

Circle T (True) or F (False).

T F The verb in the main clause is in the future.

T F The verb in the time clause is in the future.

STATEMENTS	
Main Clause	**Time Clause**
I'**m going to be** a ballet dancer	***when*** I **grow up**.
She'**ll join** a ballet company	***after*** she **leaves school**.

YES/NO QUESTIONS	
Main Clause	**Time Clause**
Are you **going to be** a ballet dancer	***when*** you **grow up**?
Will she **join** a ballet company	***after*** she **leaves school**?

SHORT ANSWERS			
Affirmative		**Negative**	
Yes,	I **am**.	No,	I'**m not**.
	she **will**.		she **won't**.

WH- QUESTIONS		
Main Clause		**Time Clause**
What	**are** you **going to be**	***when*** you **grow up**?
	will she **do**	***after*** she **leaves school**?

EXPRESS CHECK

Unscramble these words to form a question and an answer.

be • What • grows up • she • when • will • she

____.

she'll • scientist • a • I • think • be

____.

Grammar Explanations	Examples
1. When a sentence about future time has two clauses, the verb in the main clause is often in the **future** (*will* or *be going to*). The verb in the time clause is often in the **present**.	main clause / time clause ■ He'**ll look** for a job ***when*** he **leaves** school.
► **BE CAREFUL!** Do not use *will* or *be going to* in a future time clause.	main clause / time clause ■ I'm going to work ***after*** I **leave** school. NOT ~~after I will leave school.~~
The **time clause** can come at the beginning or the end of the sentence. The meaning is the same. Use a **comma** after the time clause when it comes at the beginning. Do not use a comma when it comes at the end.	■ ***Before she applies***, she'll visit different schools. OR ■ She'll visit different schools ***before she applies***. NOT ~~She'll visit different schools, before she applies.~~

2. Here are some **common time expressions** you can use to begin future time clauses.	
a. ***When***, ***after*** and ***as soon as*** often introduce the <u>event that happens first</u>. Now — Past ····X (leave)····X (look for a job)····► Future	■ ***When*** I leave school, I'll look for a job. ■ ***After*** I leave school, I'll look for a job. ■ ***As soon as*** I leave school, I'll look for a job. *(First I'm going to leave school. Then I'll look for a job.)*
b. ***Before***, ***until*** and ***by the time*** often introduce the <u>event that happens second</u>. Now — Past ····X (finish school)····X (get a job)····► Future	■ ***Before*** I get a job, I'll finish school. ■ ***Until*** I get a job, I'll stay at school. ■ ***By the time*** I get a job, I'll be out of school. *(First I'll finish school. Then I'll get a job.)*
c. ***While*** introduces an event that will happen <u>at the same time</u> as another event. Now — Past ········► Future (look for a job / continue to study)	■ ***While*** I look for a job, I'll continue to study. *(I will look for a job and study during the same time period.)*

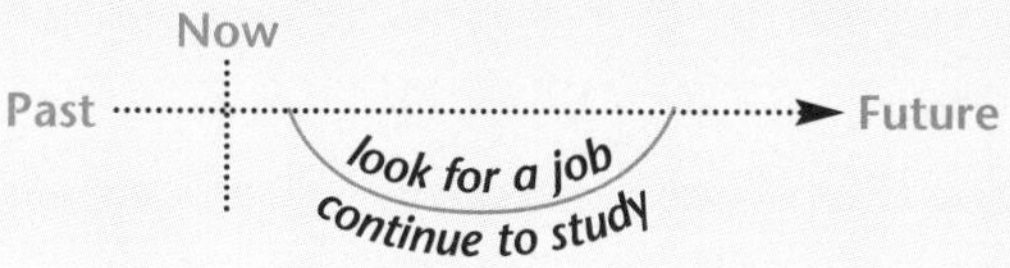

TRUE OR FALSE • *Read each numbered sentence. Write T (True) or F (False) for the statement that follows.*

1. Amber will open her own business when she finishes school.

   __F__ Amber will open her own business. Then she'll finish school.

2. Derek won't resign until he finds another job.

   _____ Derek will find another job. Then he'll resign.

3. John will retire as soon as he is sixty.

   _____ John will retire. Then he'll be sixty.

4. Marisa will call you when she gets home.

   _____ Marisa will get home. Then she'll call you.

5. While Li-jing is at school, she'll work part-time.

   _____ Li-jing will leave school. Then she'll get a part-time job.

6. By the time Carol gets her degree, she'll be twenty-one.

   _____ Carol will be twenty-one. Then she'll get her degree.

2 **COMBINE** • *Read about Sarah and Jeff. Combine the sentences.*

1. Sarah and Jeff will get married. Then Sarah will graduate from university.

   __Sarah and Jeff will get married__ before __Sarah graduates.__

2. Jeff is going to get a pay rise. Then they are going to move to a larger house.

   ______________ as soon as ______________

3. They're going to move to a larger house. Then they're going to have a baby.

   After ______________

4. They'll have their first child. Then Sarah will get a part-time job.

   ______________ after ______________

5. Their child will be two. Then Sarah will go back to work full-time.

   By the time ______________

6. Sarah will work full-time. At the same time, Jeff will go to university.

   ______________ while ______________

7. Jeff will graduate. Then he'll find another job.

   ______________ when ______________

COMPLETE • *Look at this student's worksheet. Complete it with the correct form of the verbs in brackets.*

GOAL PLANNING WORKSHEET

I. Write your major goal.

I _'ll get_ (get) a job after I ________ (graduate).

II. List three benefits of achieving your goal.

1. When I ________ (get) a job, I ________ (have) more money.
2. When I ________ (get) enough money, I ________ (buy) a car.
3. I ________ (feel) happier when I ________ (have got) a job.

III. How will you reach your goal? Write down smaller goals.

1. As soon as I ________ (get up) in the morning, I ________ (buy) the newspaper to look at the employment ads.
2. When I ________ (speak) to my friends, I ________ (ask) them if they know of any jobs.
3. I ________ (look) at the job noticeboard when I ________ (go) to the supermarket.
4. Before I ________ (go) to an interview, I ________ (improve) my computer skills.

EDIT • *Read this dancer's diary entry. Find and correct seven mistakes in the use of future time clauses. The first mistake has already been corrected. Don't forget to check for commas!*

Tomorrow is my first dance recital! By the time I ~~will~~ write my next diary entry, it will already be over! As soon as we finish the performance there are going to be a big party for us. Reporters will be there, when we enter the room. While we will celebrate, the press will interview members of the dance group. As soon as I get up on Sunday morning I'll buy the paper and read the interviews. We're going to perform this show for two weeks. As soon as it's finished, we learnt a new programme. I'm so excited. Ever since I was little, I've wanted to be a ballet dancer.

Future Continuous

I'm sorry.
I won't be here at
12:00. I'll be taking
the dog for a walk.
11:45
ROBO

CHECK POINT

Tick the correct answer.

When will Robo take the dog for a walk?

❒ before 12:00

❒ at 12:00

❒ after 12:00

CHART CHECK

Circle T (True) or F (False).

T F You form the future continuous with ***will*** plus ***be*** and the base form of the verb + *-ing*.

STATEMENTS				
Subject	**Will (not)**	**Be**	**Base Form + -ing**	
I/You/He/She/It/We/They	**will (not)** **won't**	**be**	**working** **coming**	tomorrow.

YES/NO QUESTIONS				
Will	**Subject**	**Be**	**Base Form + -ing**	
Will	I/you/he/she/it/we/they	**be**	**working** **coming**	tomorrow?

SHORT ANSWERS					
Affirmative			**Negative**		
Yes,	I/you/he/she/we/they	**will.**	No,	I/you/he/she/we/they	**won't.**

WH- QUESTIONS			
Wh- Word	**Be/Will**	**Subject**	**Be + Base Form + -ing**
Where When	**will**	she	**be working**?

EXPRESS CHECK

Unscramble these words to form two questions. Answer the questions.

working • be • Will • tomorrow • you

______________________________?

______________________________.

you • be • What • doing • will

______________________________?

______________________________.

Grammar Explanations	Examples
1. Use the **future continuous** with ***will* (*not*)** and ***won't*** to talk about things that will be in progress at a specific time in the future. 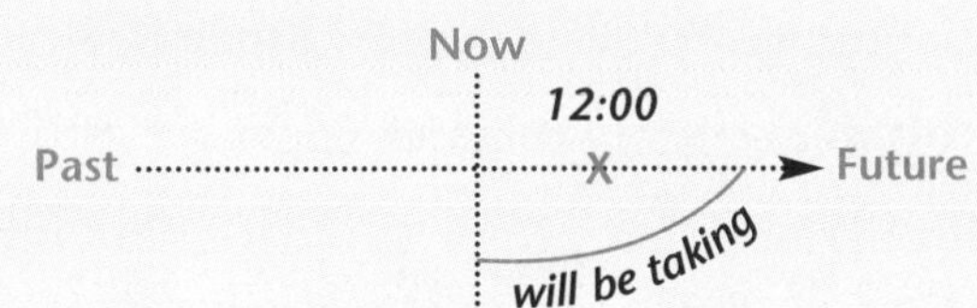	■ Robo **will be taking** the dog for a walk at noon. ■ He **won't be cleaning** the house.
2. **Usage Note:** We also use ***(not) be going to*** + ***be*** + base form + ***-ing*** but the structure with ***will*** is more common. **Remember!** Stative verbs are not usually used in the continuous form.	**A:** Robo **is going to be taking** the dog for a walk at noon. **B:** He **isn't going to be cleaning** the house. ■ **I'll know** my test results next week. Not ~~I'll be knowing my test results next week~~.
3. Remember that if the sentence has a **time clause**, use the present simple or present continuous in the time clause, not the future or future continuous.	■ I'**ll be cooking *while*** the robot **is cleaning**. Not ~~I'll be cooking while the robot will be cleaning.~~

IDENTIFY • *Read this paragraph. Underline all the future continuous forms.*

Today we find most robots working in factories around the world. But what will the robots of the future be doing? One designer predicts that in just a few years, small intelligent robots will be dealing with all the household chores. This is going to make life a lot easier. While one robot is cooking dinner, another one will be vacuuming the floor. But what about outside the home? Will robots be playing football or fighting wars? Scientists aren't sure. What is certain, however, is that robots will be playing a more and more significant role in our lives.

2

COMPLETE • *Read these conversations. Complete them with the future continuous form of the words in brackets and with short answers.*

1. **STUDENT:** ____Will____ you ____be having____ (a. Will / have) student hours today? I'd like to talk to you about my robotics paper.

   TEACHER: ____Yes, I will____ (b.). I ________ (c. will / go) to lunch at 2:00. But drop in anytime before then.

2. **MRS GEE:** When ________ you ________ (a. will / leave) the office?

   MR GEE: At 2:00. Why? Do we need something?

   MRS GEE: Would you mind picking up some milk? Robo forgot and I ________ (b. won't / get) home until late.

3. **TONY:** Dad, what time ________ you ________ (a. will / come) home today? I need some help with my science project.

   MR GEE: I ________ (b. will / take) Mia to the dentist after work but I'll be back by 4:00.

   TONY: ________ we ________ (c. Will / have) dinner before Mum comes home?

   MR GEE: ________ (d.). You know we always wait for Mum.

4. **SALESMAN:** I'm calling from Robotronics Ltd. I ________ (a. will / visit) your area soon to demonstrate our new robot.

   ROBO: I'm sorry. The Gee family ________ (b. won't / buy) a new robot for a while.

COMPLETE • *Look at Robo and Robota's schedules for tomorrow. Complete the statements.*

Robo	
8:00	make breakfast
9:00	dust bedrooms
10:00	do laundry
12:00	make lunch
1:00	give Mr Gee a massage
5:00	help Tony with homework
7:00	play chess with Tony

Robota	
8:00	pay bills
9:00	vacuum sitting room
10:00	repaint kitchen
12:00	recycle the rubbish
1:00	shop for food
5:00	cook dinner
7:00	take the dog for walk

1. While Robo __is making breakfast__, Robota __will be paying bills.__
2. Robo ______________ the bedrooms while Robota ______________
3. Robota ______________ the kitchen while Robo ______________
4. While Robo ______________ lunch, Robota ______________
5. Robo ______________ a massage while Robota ______________
6. Robota ______________ dinner while Robo ______________
7. While Robo ______________ chess, Robota ______________

EDIT • *Read this student's paragraph. Find and correct seven mistakes in the use of the future continuous. The first mistake has already been corrected.*

In the future, robots will be ~~perform~~ performing more and more tasks for humans. This will be having both positive and negative effects. On the one hand, while robots will be doing the boring and dangerous jobs, humans will be devoting more time to interesting pursuits. In this respect, robots be making life a lot easier for humans. On the other hand, the widespread use of robots will creating a lot of future unemployment. There is a risk that robots will taking on jobs that humans need in order to earn a living. And some robots could even become dangerous. I'm afraid that in the not-too-distant future, robots will be operating nuclear power stations! And before too long, robots will to be fighting in wars. Although, on second thoughts, that will be better than humans killing each other!

UNIT 23 Future Perfect and Future Perfect Continuous

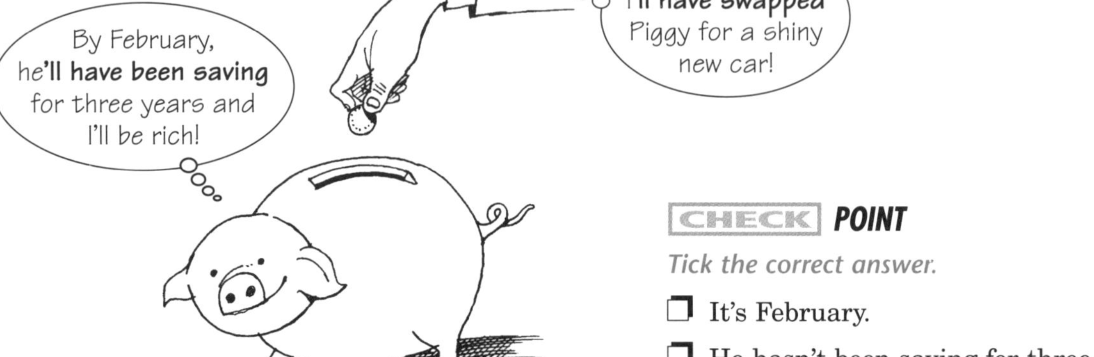

By February, he'll have been saving for three years and I'll be rich!
By February, I'll have swapped Piggy for a shiny new car!

CHECK POINT

Tick the correct answer.

❒ It's February.

❒ He hasn't been saving for three years yet.

CHART CHECK 1

Circle T (True) or F (False).

T F Both the future perfect and the future perfect continuous use ***will have been***.

FUTURE PERFECT STATEMENTS		
SUBJECT	***WILL (NOT)***	***HAVE* + PAST PARTICIPLE**
I/He/She/It/We/You*/They	**will (not)** **(won't)**	**have saved** enough money by then.

**You* is both singular and plural.

FUTURE PERFECT CONTINUOUS STATEMENTS		
SUBJECT	***WILL (NOT)***	***HAVE BEEN* + BASE FORM + *-ING***
I/He/She/It/We/You/They	**will (not)** **(won't)**	**have been saving** for three years.

CHART CHECK 2

Circle T (True) or F (False).

T F Short answer forms are the same for the future perfect and the future perfect continuous.

FUTURE PERFECT *YES/NO* QUESTIONS		
WILL	**SUBJECT**	***HAVE* + PAST PARTICIPLE**
Will	he	**have saved** enough by then?

SHORT ANSWERS	
AFFIRMATIVE	**NEGATIVE**
Yes, he **will**.	**No**, he **won't**.

FUTURE PERFECT CONTINUOUS *YES/NO* QUESTIONS		
WILL	**SUBJECT**	***HAVE BEEN* + BASE FORM + *-ING***
Will	he	**have been saving** for long?

SHORT ANSWERS	
AFFIRMATIVE	**NEGATIVE**
Yes, he **will**.	**No**, he **won't**.

EXPRESS CHECK

Complete these sentences with the verb **drive**. *Use one word for each gap.*

- By June, I'll have been ________________ my new car for a year.
- I'll have ________________ 10,000 miles by then.

Grammar Explanations / Examples

1. When we use the **future perfect**, we imagine a certain point of time in the future, and we look back at events that will be completed by that time.

■ By June, he **will have paid** his debt.
■ We **won't have saved** enough by then.

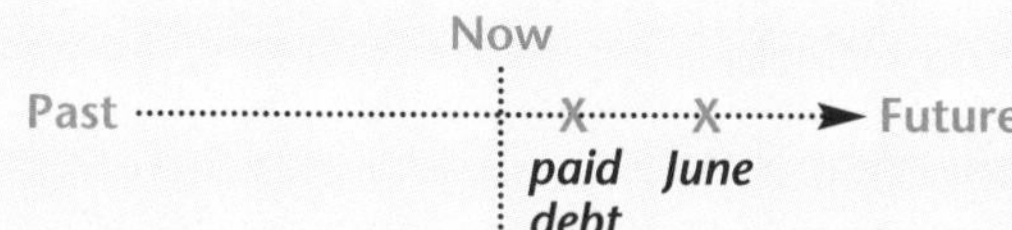

Use ***by*** **+ time expression** to identify the point in time in the future.

■ ***By June***, she'**ll have bought** a car.
■ She'**ll have looked** at a lot of cars ***by then***.

Use ***already*** to emphasise that an event will have happened by a point in time.

■ By May, he'**ll have *already* saved** £1,000.

2. When we use the **future perfect continuous**, we imagine a certain point in the future and we look back on things already in progress.

■ We moved here in 1998. By next December we **will have been living** here for several years.
■ We're moving to Paris next year. By 2009, we **will have been living** there for several years and it should feel like home.

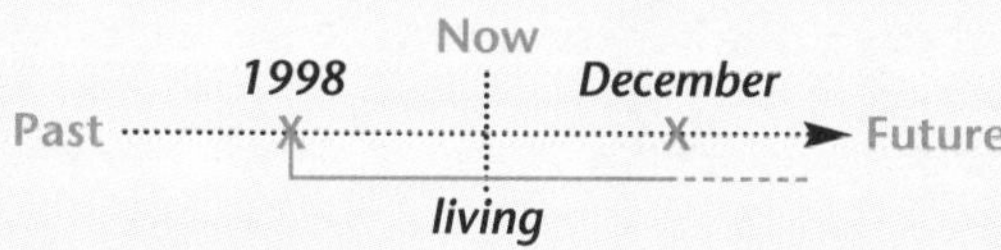

The **future perfect continuous** focuses on *how long* and often includes the length of time.

■ You'**ll have been speaking** French ***for ten years*** by then.

REMEMBER! Stative verbs are not usually used in the progressive.

■ By May, he'**ll have owned** his car for a year.
NOT ~~he'll have been owning his car . . .~~

3. Use the future perfect or the future perfect continuous **with the present simple** to show the order of events:

FIRST EVENT: future perfect (continuous)

SECOND EVENT: present simple

Now
finish dinner — *start to read* — *arrive*
Past ······X······X······X······▶ Future

■ By the time you ***arrive***, I'**ll have finished** dinner.
NOT ~~By the time you will arrive, I'll have finished dinner.~~

■ By the time you ***arrive***, I'**ll have been reading** for an hour.

TRUE OR FALSE • *Read each numbered sentence. Write T (True) or F (False) for the statement that follows.*

1. By this time tomorrow, I'll have decided which car to buy.

   __T__ I haven't decided yet which car I'm going to buy.

2. We'll have finished the shopping by the time you get home.

   _____ You will get home while we are shopping.

3. By next year, Mary will have been working at the school for five years.

   _____ Next year, Mary can celebrate her fifth anniversary at the school.

4. By ten o'clock, she won't have finished marking books.

   _____ She will finish marking books at ten o'clock.

5. We will have moved to a larger office by the year 2015.

   _____ We will move to a larger office after the year 2015.

6. By next year, we'll have been publishing the newsletter for fifteen years.

   _____ We started the newsletter less than fifteen years ago.

COMPLETE • *Look at the time line and complete the sentences about Tom and Linda's future accomplishments. Use the future perfect or the future perfect continuous form of the words in brackets. Choose between affirmative and negative.*

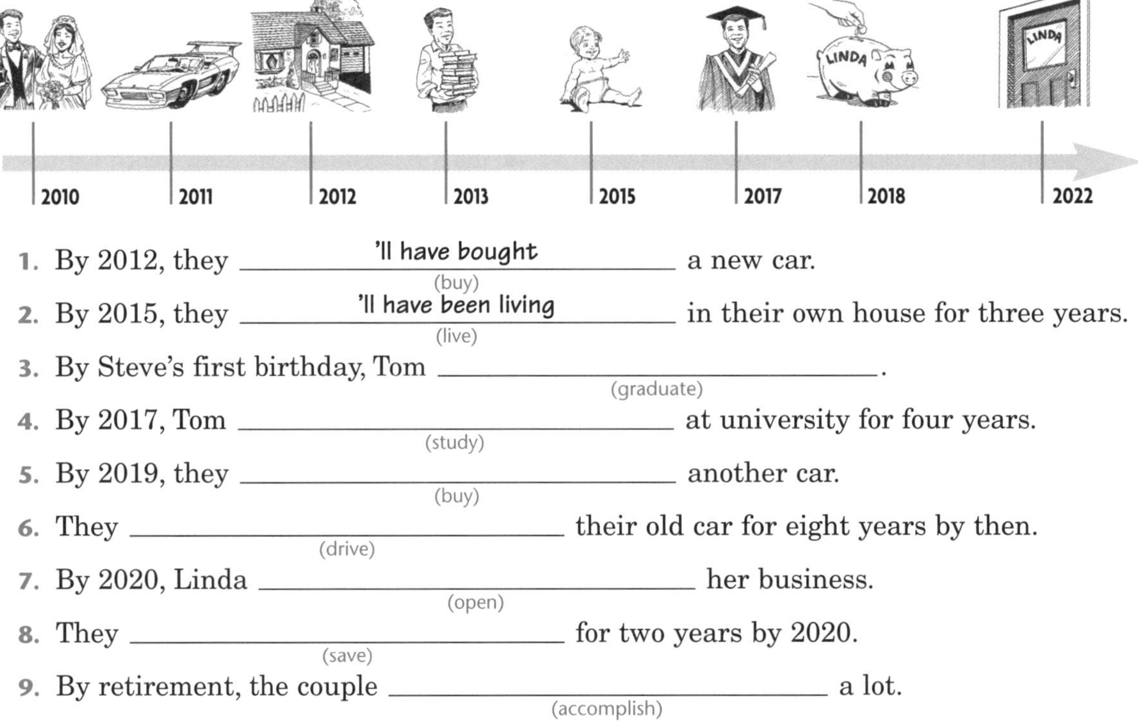

1. By 2012, they __'ll have bought__ (buy) a new car.
2. By 2015, they __'ll have been living__ (live) in their own house for three years.
3. By Steve's first birthday, Tom ______________ (graduate).
4. By 2017, Tom ______________ (study) at university for four years.
5. By 2019, they ______________ (buy) another car.
6. They ______________ (drive) their old car for eight years by then.
7. By 2020, Linda ______________ (open) her business.
8. They ______________ (save) for two years by 2020.
9. By retirement, the couple ______________ (accomplish) a lot.

COMPLETE • *Read Linda Leonard's (LL) interview with* Teenage Couples Magazine *(TC). Complete the interview with the correct form of the verbs in brackets. Use the continuous form when possible. Use* **already** *when appropriate.*

TC: You two are amazing! By the time you ___get___ (1. get) married, you ___'ll have already planned___ (2. plan) your whole life together!

LL: Well, we've been going out together since school. By the time we ______ (3. graduate) from university, we ______ (4. think) about our marriage for a long time.

TC: When Steve ______ (5. be born), Tom ______ (6. not graduate) from university. How will you manage with Tom still studying?

LL: It won't be easy but we've got a plan. Tom ______ (7. finish) most of his courses by then. He'll stay home with the baby during the day and go to evening classes.

TC: By the time you ______ (8. celebrate) your tenth wedding anniversary, you ______ (9. not start) your business. You have a lot of patience.

LL: Not really. I ______ (10. get) years of practice in my job by then. When I ______ (11. open) the doors of Linda Ltd, I ______ (12. become) a very experienced web page designer.

TC: Well, good luck to you and thanks for the interview.

EDIT • *Read this diary entry. Find and correct six mistakes in the use of the future perfect and the future perfect progressive. The first mistake has already been corrected.*

By August I'll ~~be~~ have been a secretary for ten years. And I'll earn almost the same salary for three years! That's why I've made a New Year's resolution to go back to college this year. First, I'm going to write for college magazines and start saving for tuition. By March, I'll have work out how much tuition will cost. Then I'll start applying. By summer, I had received acceptance letters. In August, I'll talk to my boss about working part-time and going to college part-time. By that time, I'll have saved already enough to pay for a term's tuition. By next New Year's Day, I'll have been study for a whole term!

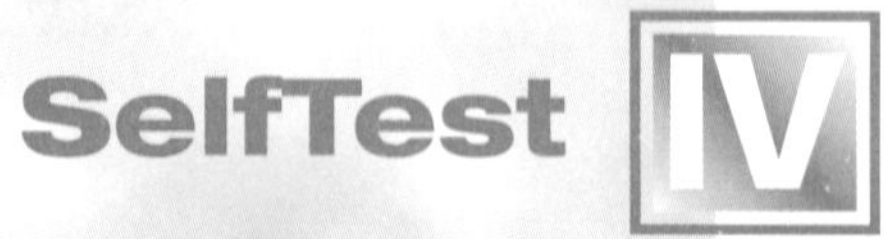

SECTION ONE

Circle the letter of the correct answer to complete each sentence.

EXAMPLE:	
Jennifer never ________ coffee.	A (B) C D
(A) drink (C) is drinking	
(B) drinks (D) was drinking	

1. It ________ tomorrow. **A B C D**
   (A) rains (C) 's going to rain
   (B) rained (D) 's raining

2. The package will ________ on Monday. **A B C D**
   (A) arrive (C) arriving
   (B) arrives (D) be going to arrive

3. Goodnight. I ________ you in the morning. **A B C D**
   (A) 'll see (C) 'm seeing
   (B) 'm going to see (D) see

4. Hurry up. The next bus ________ at 7:15. **A B C D**
   (A) leave (C) leaving
   (B) leaves (D) will have been leaving

5. Bill will be ________ to Taipei tomorrow. **A B C D**
   (A) flies (C) fly
   (B) flying (D) have flown

6. We ________ a new DVD soon. **A B C D**
   (A) have owned (C) 're owning
   (B) 'll own (D) own

7. They'll be making copies while he ________ the report. **A B C D**
   (A) finishes (C) 'll finish
   (B) 'll be finishing (D) 's been finishing

8. She'll ________ almost £1,000 by then. **A B C D**
   (A) save (C) have been saving
   (B) have saved (D) be saving

9. By next year, Roger will ________ here for ten years. **A B C D**
   (A) live (C) have been living
   (B) be living (D) be going to live

10. Will you buy an electric car when they ________ available? **A B C D**
    (A) become (C) are becoming
    (B) became (D) will become

11. She'll be married ________ June. A B C D
(A) already
(B) by
(C) since
(D) until

12. Where ________ be living? A B C D
(A) they
(B) they will
(C) will they
(D) are they

13. Look at those cars! They ________! A B C D
(A) will crash
(B) will be crashing
(C) 're going to crash
(D) will have crashed

14. How ________ for college? A B C D
(A) should pay
(B) will she pay
(C) she pays
(D) she's going to pay

SECTION TWO

Each sentence has four underlined words or phrases. The four underlined parts of the sentence are marked A, B, C and D. Circle the letter of the one underlined word or phrase that is NOT CORRECT.

EXAMPLE:
Mike usually (A) drives (B) to school but today (C) he walks (D). A B C (D)

15. Will (A) you been (B) going (C) to the supermarket tonight (D)? A B C D

16. The film starts (A) at (B) 7:30, so I think (C) I go (D). A B C D

17. We are going (A) to study (B) tonight until (C) we will finish (D) this chapter. A B C D

18. By (A) April, I'll have (B) been driven (C) my new car for (D) a year. A B C D

19. We'll travel (A) for (B) a couple of days, so you won't (C) be able to (D) call us. A B C D

20. Jan finished (A) school by (B) next summer, so we're going (C) to visit (D) her. A B C D

21. Which project will (A) he works (B) on after (C) he finishes (D) this job? A B C D

22. By (A) January, he'll (B) have yet (C) saved (D) £1,000. A B C D

23. Where you will (A) be (B) staying (C) when you go (D) to Morocco? A B C D

24. I'll (A) be studying (B) while (C) Anna will be (D) sleeping. A B C D

25. She will not (A) has (B) graduated (C) by (D) June. A B C D

Wh- Questions: Subject and Predicate

CHECK POINT

Tick the correct answers.

The lawyer wants to know

- ❐ the events on the night of 12 May.
- ❐ the witness's profession.
- ❐ the names of people who saw the witness.

CHART CHECK 1

Circle T (True) or F (False).

T F ***Wh-*** questions about the subject have the same word order as statements.

QUESTIONS ABOUT THE SUBJECT		
Wh- Word Subject	**Verb**	**Predicate**
Who	**saw**	you?

ANSWERS (STATEMENTS)		
Subject	**Verb**	**Predicate**
He	saw	me.

CHART CHECK 2

Circle T (True) or F (False).

T F ***Wh-*** questions about the predicate have the same word order as statements.

T F Questions about the predicate can include a form of the verb ***do***.

QUESTIONS ABOUT THE PREDICATE			
Wh- Word Predicate	**Auxiliary Verb**	**Subject**	**Verb**
Who(m)	**did**	you	**see**?

ANSWERS (STATEMENTS)		
Subject	**Verb**	**Predicate**
I	saw	**him**.

EXPRESS CHECK

Unscramble these words to form two questions.

night • happed • What • last ______________________________?

do • did • What • next • you ______________________________?

Grammar Explanations	Examples
1. Use ***wh-* questions** to ask for specific information. *Wh-* questions begin with question words such as ***who***, ***what***, ***where***, ***when***, ***why***, ***which***, ***whose***, ***how***, ***how many***, ***how much*** and ***how long***.	■ **Who** did you see at the café? ■ **Why** did you go there? ■ **How many** people saw you there? ■ **How long** did you stay there?
2. When you are **asking about the subject** (usually the first part of the sentence), use a *wh-* question word in place of the subject. The word order is the same as in a statement.	Someone saw you. ↓ ■ **Who** saw you?
3. When you are **asking about the predicate** (usually the last part of the sentence), the question begins with a *wh-* word, but the word order is the same as in a *yes/no* question.	You saw someone. Did you see someone? ↓ ■ **Who** did you see?
▶ **Be careful!** When you ask a *wh-* question about something in the predicate, you need either **a.** a form of the verb ***be***. OR **b.** a form of an **auxiliary** ('helping') verb such as ***do***, ***have***, ***can***, ***will***.	■ Who **is** Harry Adams? ■ Why **was** he at the café? ■ Why **does** she want to testify? Not ~~Why she wants to testify?~~
4. Usage Note: In very formal English when asking about people in the predicate, ***whom*** is sometimes used instead of ***who***.	Very Formal ■ **Whom** did you see? Informal ■ **Who** did you see?
▶ **Be careful!** If the main verb is a form of ***be***, you cannot use ***whom***.	■ **Who *is*** the next witness? Not ~~Whom is the next witness?~~

MATCH • *Each question goes with an answer. Match each question with the correct answer.*

	Question		Answer
f	1. Who did you see?	a.	His wife saw me.
____	2. Who saw you?	b.	She hit a car.
____	3. What hit her?	c.	I gave the money to Harry.
____	4. What did she hit?	d.	A car hit her.
____	5. Which man did you give the money to?	e.	Harry gave me the money.
____	6. Which man gave you the money?	f.	I saw the defendant.

2 **COMPLETE** • *Read this cross-examination. Complete it by writing the barrister's questions.*

1. **Barrister:** What time did you return home?
(What time / you / return home?)
Witness: I returned home just before midnight.

2. **Barrister:** ______________________________
(How / you / get home?)
Witness: Someone gave me a lift.

3. **Barrister:** ______________________________
(Who / give / you / a lift?)
Witness: A friend from work.

4. **Barrister:** ______________________________
(What / happen / next?)
Witness: I opened my door and saw someone on my sitting room floor.

5. **Barrister:** ______________________________
(Who / you / see?)
Witness: Deborah Collins.

6. **Barrister:** ______________________________
(Who / be / Deborah Collins?)
Witness: She's my wife's boss. I mean she *was* my wife's boss. She's dead now.

7. **Barrister:** ______________________________
(What / you / do?)
Witness: I called the police.

8. **Barrister:** ______________________________
(How many / people / call / you?)
Witness: No one called me. Why?

ASK • *Read these statements. Then ask questions about the underlined words.*

1. <u>The witness</u> recognized Harry Adams.
   Who recognized Harry Adams?
2. The witness recognized <u>Harry Adams</u>.
   Who did the witness recognize?
3. The court session begins <u>at 9:00 a.m</u>.
   ______
4. <u>Five</u> witnesses testified.
   ______
5. The jury found Adams guilty <u>because he didn't have an alibi</u>.
   ______
6. <u>Something horrible</u> happened.
   ______
7. The trial lasted <u>two weeks</u>.
   ______
8. <u>The judge</u> spoke to the jury.
   ______
9. Adams paid his barrister <u>£2,000</u>.
   ______
10. The prosecution questioned <u>the restaurant manager</u>.
    ______

EDIT • *Read this list of questions. There are six mistakes in the use of* wh- *questions. Find and correct them. The first mistake has already been corrected.*

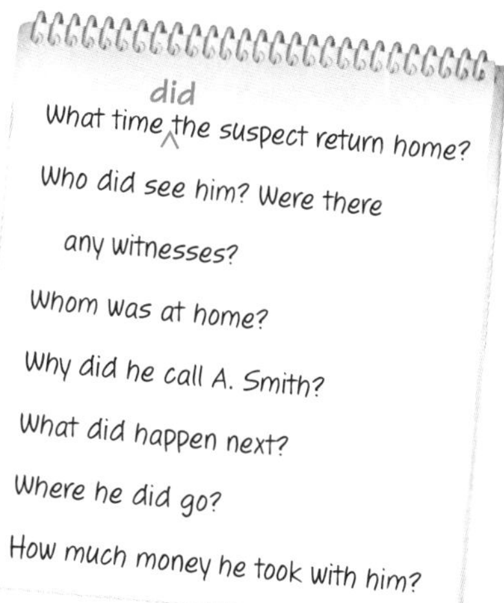

did
What time ^ the suspect return home?
Who did see him? Were there any witnesses?
Whom was at home?
Why did he call A. Smith?
What did happen next?
Where he did go?
How much money he took with him?

UNIT 25 Question Tags

CHECK POINT

Tick the correct answer.

❐ The man is asking about the weather.

❐ The man is commenting on the weather.

CHART CHECK

Circle T (True) or F (False).

T F If the statement is affirmative, the question tag is affirmative.

T F If the statement has an auxiliary, use the same auxiliary in the question tag.

T F If the statement does not have a form of ***be*** or an auxiliary, you need a form of ***do*** in the question tag.

WITH *BE* AS THE MAIN VERB

AFFIRMATIVE STATEMENT	NEGATIVE QUESTION TAG
You're from York,	**aren't you?**

NEGATIVE STATEMENT	AFFIRMATIVE QUESTION TAG
You're not from York,	**are you?**

WITH ALL AUXILIARY VERBS EXCEPT *DO*

AFFIRMATIVE STATEMENT	NEGATIVE QUESTION TAG
You're moving,	**aren't you?**
He's been here,	**hasn't he?**
They can move,	**can't they?**

NEGATIVE STATEMENT	AFFIRMATIVE QUESTION TAG
You're not moving,	**are you?**
He hasn't been here,	**has he?**
They can't move,	**can they?**

WITH *DO* AS AN AUXILIARY VERB

AFFIRMATIVE STATEMENT	NEGATIVE QUESTION TAG
You live here,	**don't you?**
They moved,	**didn't they?**

NEGATIVE STATEMENT	AFFIRMATIVE QUESTION TAG
You don't live here,	**do you?**
They didn't move,	**did they?**

EXPRESS CHECK

Unscramble these words to form a sentence with a question tag.

actor • you • an • aren't • You're ______________________, ____________?

Grammar Explanations	Examples
1. We often use question tags to: **a.** check information we believe to be true OR **b.** comment on a situation	■ Tom lives in York, **doesn't he?** *(The speaker believes that Tom lives in York and wants to check this information.)* ■ It's a nice day, **isn't it?** *(The speaker is commenting on the weather.)*
2. Question tags follow **a statement**. The statement expresses an assumption. The question tag means *Is that right?* **a.** If the verb in the statement is affirmative, the verb in the question tag is negative. **b.** If the verb in the statement is negative, the verb in the question tag is affirmative.	statement / question tag ■ You're not from York, **are you?** ■ You're Jack Davies, **aren't you?** ■ You don't drive much, **do you?** affirmative / negative ■ You **work** on Fridays, **don't** you? negative / affirmative ■ You **don't work** on Fridays, **do** you?
3. The **question tag** always uses a form of ***be*** or an auxiliary verb (***be***, ***have***, ***do*** or ***will*** or a modal such as ***can***, ***could*** or ***should***). **Usage Note:** Notice the question tag for ***I am***. ► **Be careful!** In the question tag, only use pronouns. When the subject of the statement is ***this*** or ***that***, the subject of the question tag is ***it***.	■ It's a nice day, **isn't** it? ■ You've lived here a long time, **haven't** you? ■ You come from London, **don't** you? ■ You can drive, **can't** you? ■ I'm next, **aren't** I? Not ~~I'm next, amn't I~~? ■ ***Tom*** works here, doesn't **he**? Not ~~Tom works here, doesn't Tom~~? ■ ***That's*** a good idea, isn't **it**? Not ~~That's a good idea, isn't that~~?
4. When you use a question tag to **check information** or to **comment on a situation**, your voice falls on the question tag. You expect the listener to agree or just show that he or she is listening. Question tags can also be used to **get information**. As with *yes/no* questions, your voice rises at the end, and you expect to get an answer (*Yes* or *No*).	**A:** It's getting warmer, **isn't it**? **B:** Yeah. Seems more like summer. **A:** You're not moving, **are you**? **B:** Yes. We're going back to York. OR No. We're staying here.

IDENTIFY • *Read this conversation. Underline all the question tags.*

KAY: Hi, Tom. It's a nice day, isn't it?

TOM: It certainly is. Not a cloud in the sky. How are you doing?

KAY: Fine, thanks. You don't know of any flats to rent, do you? My son is looking for one.

TOM: Is he? I thought he was staying with you.

KAY: Well, he really wants a place of his own. Do you know of anything?

TOM: As a matter of fact, I do. You know the Simpsons, don't you? Well, I've just found out that they're moving to Cheltenham next month.

KAY: Are they? What kind of flat have they got?

TOM: It's a one-bedroom flat.

KAY: It's not furnished, is it?

TOM: No. Why? He doesn't need a furnished flat, does he?

KAY: Well, he hasn't got any furniture. But I suppose he can always buy some, can't he?

TOM: Why don't you give your son my number and I'll give him some more information?

KAY: Will you? Thanks, Tom.

MATCH • *Each statement goes with a question tag. Match each statement with the correct question tag.*

	Statement		Question Tag
__i__	1. You've phoned the removers,	a.	can't we?
____	2. They're coming tomorrow,	b.	do we?
____	3. This isn't going to be cheap,	c.	is he?
____	4. You haven't finished packing,	d.	isn't it?
____	5. We don't need any more boxes,	e.	are they?
____	6. Paul is going to help us,	f.	have you?
____	7. We can put some things in storage,	g.	isn't he?
____	8. Jack isn't buying our bookcases,	h.	is it?
____	9. The removers aren't packing the books for us,	i.	haven't you?
____	10. Moving is hard,	j.	aren't they?

COMPLETE • *A radio chat show host is interviewing one of her guests, a screenplay writer. Complete the interview with appropriate question tags.*

HOST: You've lived in London for many years, ___haven't you___?
1.

GUEST: Since I was eighteen and came here to write my first screenplay.

HOST: You didn't know anyone here at first, ________________?
2.

GUEST: No. And I didn't have a penny to my name. Just some ideas and a lot of hope. It sounds crazy, ________________?
3.

HOST: But things have worked out for you, ________________?
4.

You're working on another screenplay now, ________________?
5.

GUEST: Yes. It's a comedy about some kids who become invisible.

HOST: Speaking of kids, you've got some of your own, ________________?
6.

GUEST: Two boys and a girl – all very visible!

HOST: I know what you mean. Do you ever wish they were invisible?

GUEST: Now, that's an interesting thought, ________________?
7.

4

EDIT • *Read this part of a film script. Find and correct seven mistakes in the use of question tags. The first mistake has already been corrected.*

Ben: It's been a long time, Joe, ~~haven't~~ hasn't it?

Joe: That depends on what you mean by a long time, doesn't that?

Ben: What are you doing round here, anyway? It's dangerous.

Joe: I can take care of myself. I'm still alive, amn't I?

Ben: Yes, but you're still wanted by the police, are you?

Joe: Look, I need a place to stay. You've got a place, haven't you? Just for one night.

Ben: I have to think of my wife and kids. You can find somewhere else, can you?

Joe: No. You've got to help me!

Ben: I've already helped you enough. I went to prison for you, haven't I?

Joe: Yeah, OK, Ben. You remember what happened last June, do you?

Ben: OK, OK. I can make a phone call.

Additions with *So, Too, Neither* and *Not either*

HERALD SUN

Twins Separated at Birth Are Reunited!

Mark likes hunting, fishing and Chinese food.
So does Gerald.

CHECK POINT

Tick the correct answer.

❒ The men like different things.

❒ The men like the same things.

CHART CHECK

Circle T (True) or F (False).

T F There is more than one way to make an addition.

T F Use ***so*** or ***too*** with negative statements.

T F When a statement does not have a form of ***be*** or an auxiliary verb, use a form of ***do*** in the addition.

WITH *BE* AS THE MAIN VERB

AFFIRMATIVE		NEGATIVE	
STATEMENT	**ADDITION**	**STATEMENT**	**ADDITION**
Amy **is** a twin	**and so is** Sue. and Sue **is, too.**	Amy **isn't** very tall	**and neither is** Sue. and Sue **isn't, either.**

WITH ALL AUXILIARY VERBS EXCEPT *DO*

AFFIRMATIVE		NEGATIVE	
STATEMENT	**ADDITION**	**STATEMENT**	**ADDITION**
Amy **can** swim	**and so can** Sue. and Sue **can, too.**	Amy **can't** ski	**and neither can** Sue. and Sue **can't, either.**

WITH VERBS USING *DO* AS AN AUXILIARY VERB

AFFIRMATIVE		NEGATIVE	
STATEMENT	**ADDITION**	**STATEMENT**	**ADDITION**
Amy **likes** dogs	**and so does** Sue. and Sue **does, too.**	Amy **doesn't** like cats	**and neither does** Sue. and Sue **doesn't, either.**

EXPRESS CHECK

Unscramble these words to form additions.

is • Mark • and • neither

Gerald isn't married ______________________.

does • Gerald • so • and

Mark fights fires ______________________.

Grammar Explanations	Examples
1. **Additions** are phrases or short sentences that follow a statement. Use an addition to avoid repeating the information in the statement.	■ Gerald is a firefighter **and so is Mark.** *(Gerald is a firefighter and Mark is a firefighter.)*
2. Use ***so*** or ***too*** if the addition follows an affirmative statement.	■ Gerald **is** a firefighter and ***so*** **is** Mark. OR ■ Gerald **is** a firefighter and Mark **is, *too***.
Use ***neither/nor*** or ***not either*** if the addition follows a negative statement.	■ Gerald **didn't** get married. ***Neither*** **did** Mark. OR ■ Gerald **didn't** get married. Mark **didn't, *either***.
▶ **Be careful!** Notice the word order after ***so*** and ***neither/nor***. The verb comes before the subject.	■ So **is Mark**. Not ~~So Mark is.~~ ■ Nor **did Mark**. Not ~~Nor Mark did.~~
3. **Additions** always use a form of ***be*** or an auxiliary verb (***be, have, do, will*** or a modal verb such as ***can, could, should, would***).	
a. If the statement uses a form of ***be***, use a form of ***be*** in the addition, too.	■ I'**m** a twin and so **is** my cousin.
b. If the statement uses an auxiliary verb, use the same auxiliary verb in the addition.	■ Gerald **had** resigned and so **had** Mark. ■ I **can't** drive and neither **can** my twin.
c. If the statement has a verb that uses ***do*** as an auxiliary verb, use the appropriate form of ***do*** in the addition.	■ Gerald **owns** a dog and so **does** Mark. ■ Gerald **bought** a jeep and so **did** Mark.
4. In conversation, you can use short **responses** with ***so, too, neither/nor*** and ***not either*** to agree with another speaker.	**A:** I've got a twin sister. **B:** ***So* have I.** or **I have, *too*.** **A:** I haven't got any brothers or sisters. **B:** ***Neither* have I.** or **I haven't, *either*.**
Usage Note: In informal speech, people say ***Me too*** and ***Me neither*** or ***Nor me*** to express similarity or agreement.	**A:** I'm left-handed. **B:** ***Me too***. **A:** I've never heard of these twins. **B:** ***Me neither***.

TRUE OR FALSE • *Read these short conversations between reunited twins. Write T (True) or F (False) for the statement that follows each conversation.*

1. **MARK:** I like Chinese food.
   GERALD: So do I.

   __T__ Gerald likes Chinese food.

2. **ANDREA:** I don't want to go out.
   BARBARA: Neither do I.

   _____ Barbara wants to go out.

3. **JEAN:** I'm not hungry.
   JOAN: I'm not, either.

   _____ Joan isn't hungry.

4. **AMY:** I've always felt lucky.
   KERRIE: So have I.

   _____ Kerrie has felt lucky.

5. **MIA:** I don't eat meat.
   BOB: Nor me.

   _____ Bob eats meat.

6. **JIM:** I've got a headache.
   BILL: So have I.

   _____ Both Jim and Bill have got headaches.

7. **NORA:** I can't swim.
   DINA: Nor can I.

   _____ Dina can swim.

8. **JACK:** I shouldn't work so much.
   TIM: Neither should I.

   _____ Tim wants to work less.

9. **JASON:** I'd like to leave now.
   TYLER: Me too.

   _____ Tyler wants to leave.

CHOOSE • *Circle the correct words to complete this paragraph.*

Sometimes being a twin can cause trouble. At school, I was in Mr Jacobs's history class. Neither / (So) (1.) was my brother. One day we took a test. I got questions 18 and 20 wrong. My brother did, so / too (2.). I didn't spell *hippopotamus* correctly and either / neither (3.) did he. The teacher was sure we had cheated. As a result, I got an F in the test and so did / got (4.) my brother. We tried to convince Mr Jacobs of our innocence but he didn't believe us. The headmaster didn't, either / too (5.). We finally convinced them to give us another test. This time I got questions 3 and 10 wrong. Guess what? Nor / So (6.) did my brother. Our teacher was astounded. So / Too was (7.) the headmaster. We weren't. We were just amused.

COMPLETE • *Marta and Carla are twins. They agree on everything. Complete their conversation with responses.*

MARTA: I'm so happy we finally found each other.

CARLA: So ___am I___ (1.). I always felt as if something was missing from my life.

MARTA: So ________ (2.). I always knew I had a double somewhere out there.

CARLA: I can't believe how similar we are.

MARTA: Neither ________ (3.). It's like always seeing myself in the mirror.

CARLA: Not only do we look identical but we like and dislike all the same things.

MARTA: That's true. I hate lettuce.

CARLA: I ________ (4.). And I detest liver.

MARTA: So ________ (5.). I *love* pizza, though.

CARLA: So ________ (6.). But only with tomato and cheese. I don't like pepperoni.

MARTA: Neither ________ (7.).

CARLA: This is amazing! I feel as if I've always known you.

MARTA: Me ________ (8.)!

EDIT • *Read this student's composition. There are six mistakes in the use of sentence additions. Find and correct them. The first mistake has already been corrected.*

My brother and I

My brother is just a year older than I am. We have a lot of things in common.

First of all, we look alike. I am 1.8m and so ~~he is~~ is he. I have straight black hair and dark brown eyes and so does he. We share many of the same interests, too. I love playing football and he, too. Both of us swim every day but I can't dive and either can he.

Sometimes being so similar has its problems. For example, last night I wanted the last piece of chocolate cake and so does he. Often I won't feel like doing the washing up and neither won't he. Worst of all, sometimes I'm interested in a particular girl and so he is. However, most of the time I feel our similarities are really nice. So does my brother.

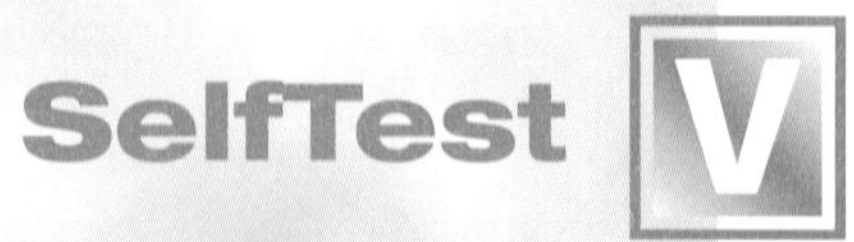

SECTION ONE

Circle the letter of the correct answer to complete each sentence.

Example:
Jennifer never ________ coffee. **A (B) C D**
(A) drink (C) is drinking
(B) drinks (D) was drinking

1. Where ________? **A B C D**
(A) does she live (C) she does live
(B) she lives (D) she lived

2. ________ has lost this wallet? **A B C D**
(A) Whom (C) Who
(B) Whose (D) Who did

3. You're Cynthia, ________ you? **A B C D**
(A) aren't (C) didn't
(B) are (D) were

4. Laura loves soap operas and ________. **A B C D**
(A) Jane does, too (C) Jane loves too
(B) so Jane does (D) so loves Jane

5. I didn't like sports and ________ my brother. **A B C D**
(A) either did (C) so did
(B) neither does (D) neither did

6. —That isn't Sam, is it? **A B C D**
—No, ________. Sam's taller.
(A) it is (C) it wasn't
(B) it doesn't (D) it isn't

7. We didn't eat here last week, ________ we? **A B C D**
(A) didn't (C) do
(B) haven't (D) did

8. —Who ________ your bike? **A B C D**
—Mike did.
(A) did give you (C) you gave
(B) did you give (D) gave you

9. —Who ________ at the party? **A B C D**
—I saw Stefan.
(A) saw you (C) you saw
(B) did you see (D) you see

10. —I hate cabbage.
—Me ________. I can't even look at it. **A B C D**
(A) too (C) neither
(B) either (D) do too

11. ________ washing up tonight? **A B C D**
(A) Whose (C) Who are
(B) Who's (D) Who does

12. Liam was born in Ireland. So ________ his brother. **A B C D**
(A) was (C) wasn't
(B) didn't (D) did

SECTION TWO

Each sentence has four underlined words or phrases. The four underlined parts of the sentence are marked A, B, C and D. Circle the letter of the one underlined word or phrase that is NOT CORRECT.

EXAMPLE:
Mike usually (A) drives (B) to school but today (C) he walks (D). **A B C (D)**

13. This (A) is a (B) good school, wasn't (C) it? (D) **A B C D**

14. We (A) went (B) to Stan's party last year, hadn't (C) we (D)? **A B C D**

15. Kevin has (A) always been (B) a great student and so (C) his brother has (D). **A B C D**

16. My sister has (A) never gone (B) skiing and neither (C) did (D) I. **A B C D**

17. Where you worked (A) last year when (B) you were (C) going (D) to school? **A B C D**

18. That (A) sign is too small to read (B), isn't (C) that (D)? **A B C D**

19. English isn't (A) an easy language to learn (B), is (C) it. (D) **A B C D**

20. My parents (A) are (B) both good cooks and (C) me,too (D). **A B C D**

21. Tom and Fred hadn't been (A) to Italy before (B) then, had (C) he (D)? **A B C D**

22. I'm (A) usually (B) right about the weather, amn't (C) I (D)? **A B C D**

23. Paul (A) likes (B) Italian food, doesn't (C) Paul (D)? **A B C D**

24. Where (A) did (B) they went (C) yesterday (D)? **A B C D**

25. Why you (A) call (B) me so late (C) last night (D)? **A B C D**

Ability: *Can, Could, Be able to*

Can you do spreadsheets?

CHECK POINT

Circle T (True) or F (False).

T F The father wants to know if his daughter has permission to do spreadsheets.

CHART CHECK 1 →

Circle T (True) or F (False).

T F The form for ***can*** and ***could*** is the same for all subjects.

STATEMENTS: *CAN/COULD*			
Subject	**Can/Could***	**Base Form of Verb**	
I/He/She/It/We/You/They	**can** **cannot** **can't**	**do**	spreadsheets now.
	could (not) **couldn't**	**use**	a computer last year.

**Can* and *could* are modals. They do not have *-s* in the third person singular.

YES/NO* QUESTIONS: *CAN/COULD			
Can/Could	**Subject**	**Base Form**	
Can	she	**do**	them?
Could	they	**use**	one?

SHORT ANSWERS			
Affirmative		**Negative**	
Yes,	she **can**.	**No,**	she **can't**.
	they **could**.		they **couldn't**.

WH-* QUESTIONS: *CAN/COULD				
***Wh-* Word**	**Can/Could**	**Subject**	**Base Form**	
How well	**can**	she	**do**	spreadsheets?
	could	they	**use**	a computer?

CHART CHECK 2 →

Tick the correct answer.

Which part of ***be able to*** changes for different subjects?

❒ ***be*** ❒ ***able to***

AFFIRMATIVE: *BE ABLE TO*				
Subject	**Be**	**Able to**	**Base Form**	
I	**am** **'m**	**able to**	**do**	graphs.
He/She/It	**is** **'s**			
We/You/They	**are** **'re**			

NEGATIVE: *BE ABLE TO*				
Subject	**Be + not**	**Able to**	**Base Form**	
I	**am not** **'m not**	**able to**	**do**	graphs.
He/She/It	**is not** **isn't** **'s not**			
We/You/They	**are** **aren't** **'re**			

CHART CHECK 3

Check the correct answer.

In questions with ***be able to***, what comes before the subject?

❒ a form of ***be***

❒ a form of ***able to***

YES/NO QUESTIONS: *BE ABLE TO*				
Be	**Subject**	***Able to***	**Base Form**	
Are	you	**able to**	**do**	spreadsheets?
Is	she			

SHORT ANSWERS			
Affirmative		**Negative**	
Yes,	I **am**.	**No,**	I'**m not**.
	she **is**.		she **isn't**.

WH- QUESTIONS: *BE ABLE TO*					
***Wh-* Word**	***Be***	**Subject**	***Able to***	**Base Form**	
How well	**are**	you	**able to**	**do**	spreadsheets?
	is	she			

EXPRESS CHECK

Complete these sentences with **can** *or* **be able to**. *Use one word for each gap.*

A: ______________ she already able ______________ use a computer?

B: Yes, she ______________, and she ______________ type and do spreadsheets, too.

Grammar Explanations	Examples
1. Use ***can*** or ***be able to*** to talk about ability in the present. **Usage Note:** In everyday speech, ***can*** is more common than ***be able to*** in the present tense.	■ She **can do** computer graphics. ■ She'**s able to do** computer graphics.
2. Use either ***could*** or ***was/were able to*** to talk about ability (but not a specific achievement) in the past.	■ Sam **could read** when he was four. ■ He **was able to use** a computer, too.
▶ **Be careful!** Use ***managed to*** or ***was/were able to*** to talk about a specific achievement or a single event in the past.	■ She **managed to** delete the virus from her computer. ■ He **was able to fix** his computer when it broke down. Not ~~He could fix his computer when it . . .~~
Use either ***could*** or ***was/were able to*** in negative sentences about past ability.	■ I **couldn't do** spreadsheets. ■ I **wasn't able to do** one problem.
3. For forms and tenses other than the present or past, use ***be able to***.	■ Jen wants **to be able to write** software. *(infinitive)* ■ By June she **will be able to complete** her computer class. *(future)*

IDENTIFY • *Read part of an article about some talented young business people. Underline the words that express ability.*

Web Businesses for Fun and Profit

An amazing number of teenagers <u>have managed to set up</u> highly successful internet businesses. Take John Davidson, for example. John could surf the net by the time he was six and by the age of eight, he could design web pages of his own. It wasn't long before he was able to persuade the bank to lend him enough money to start up his very own business. At the age of sixteen he managed to persuade his parents to allow him to leave school, and his first business, 'Webmasters', was soon up and running. Another teenager, Jim Leicester, very quickly realised he could make money doing what he enjoyed most: playing computer games. In 1999, he was able to sell five games he'd developed to a famous software company. Now Jim can earn up to £1000 a week by selling his programs. Katy Fischer, an enterprising 18-year-old from Manchester, was also able to break into the dotcom world. Although she says she can't understand why she's been so successful, her parents certainly can. 'Katy was determined to prove she could start a business when she was just fourteen,' says her father, 'and through hard work, she's managed to do just that.'

COMPLETE • *Read each description. Complete it with a name from the article.*

1. ____Jim____ sold games to a software company.
2. ________ got a bank loan.
3. ________ wanted to start a business at the age of 14.
4. ________ left school at sixteen.

2

COMPLETE • *Read these paragraphs. Complete them with* **can, could** *or* **be able to**. *Use* **can** *or* **could** *where possible. Choose between affirmative and negative.*

1. Steven is enjoying his computer class. Two weeks ago, he ____couldn't____ even use the mouse but now he ________ edit his homework. By next week, he ________ do research on the internet.
2. Eleni misses her family in Greece. She ________ visit them for years, but they've just got an email account, so now they ________ keep in touch daily.
3. I ________ work out how to set up a presentation. The software instructions don't help. I think I'll take a professional development course. In a few months maybe I ________ do that presentation.
4. Mike and I ________ get on since we started this business. He ________ work alone (he needs people) and I ________ work in a group (I have to work alone). I hope we ________ work out our problems soon.

COMPLETE • *Read this advertisement. Complete it with the appropriate form of* **can**, **could** *or* **be able to** *plus the verbs in brackets. Use* **can** *or* **could** *when possible.*

WILL B. HAPPY®

Professional Development Courses

Time Management   Presentations   Career Development   Teamwork

Think about your last presentation: ___Were___ you ___able to prepare___ it on time?
1. (prepare)

__________ you __________ your ideas?
2. (communicate)

Will B. Happy® has helped others, and he __________ YOU!
3. (help)

'Before I took Will B. Happy's course, my work was always late because

I __________ a schedule. I also had big piles of papers on my desk
4. (follow)

because I __________ what was important. Now I __________
5. (decide) 6. (manage)

my time effectively. Next month, when my workload gets heavy, I

__________ it and do the important things first.' *Scott Mathis, student*
7. (organise)

'I didn't use to __________ in front of groups. Now I can!'
8. (speak)

Mary Wells, sales manager

4

EDIT • *Read this student's diary. Find and correct seven mistakes in expressing ability. The first mistake has already been corrected.*

Today in my 'Will B. Happy' teamwork course, I learnt about work styles – 'Drivers' and 'Enthusiasts.' I'm a Driver so I can make decisions but I'm not able ^to^ listen to other people's ideas. The Enthusiast in our group can communicates well but you can't depend on her. Now I understand what was happening in my business class last year, when I couldn't got on with my team. I thought that they all talked too much and didn't able to work efficiently. I could get an A for the course but it was hard. I can do a lot more on my own but some jobs are too big for that. Our instructor says that soon the Drivers will able to listen and the Enthusiast could be more dependable.

Permission: *May, Can, Could, Do you mind if . . .?*

ENGLISH 403
FINAL EXAM
I think I've got something in my eye. **Could** I **take** the test tomorrow?

CHECK POINT

Tick the sentence that describes what's happening in the cartoon.

❒ The student wants to know if his eye will be better tomorrow.

❒ The student is asking the teacher to allow him to take the test tomorrow.

CHART CHECK 1

Tick the correct answer.

Which modal is used in questions but NOT in short answers about permission?

❒ *may*

❒ *can*

❒ *could*

QUESTIONS: *MAY/CAN/COULD*			
MAY/CAN/COULD*	**SUBJECT**	**BASE FORM OF VERB**	
May Can Could	I/we/he/she/it/they	start	now?

**May, can,* and *could* are modals. They do not have *-s* in the third person singular.

SHORT ANSWERS					
AFFIRMATIVE			**NEGATIVE**		
Yes,	you/he/she/it/they	may. can.	No,	you/he/she/it/they	may not. can't.

CHART CHECK 2

Circle T (True) or F (False).

T F After *Do you mind if . . . ?* the verb is the same for all subjects.

T F The answer *Not at all* gives permission.

QUESTIONS: *DO YOU MIND IF . . . ?*		
DO YOU MIND IF	**SUBJECT**	**VERB**
Do you mind if	I/we/they	start?
	he/she/it	starts?

SHORT ANSWERS	
AFFIRMATIVE	**NEGATIVE**
Not at all.	
No, I don't.	Yes, I do.

STATEMENTS: *MAY/CAN*		
SUBJECT	***MAY/CAN***	**BASE FORM**
I/He/She/It/We/You/They	may (not) can(not)	start.

EXPRESS CHECK

Circle the correct words to complete this conversation.

A: Do you mind if he help / helps me with my homework?

B: Not at all / Yes I do. He can help / helps you, but you should do most of the work.

Grammar Explanations	Examples
1. Use ***may***, ***could*** and ***can*** to ask for permission.	■ **May** I **call** you next Friday? ■ **Could** we **use** your car? ■ **Can** he **come** to class with me?
Usage Note: ***May*** is a little more formal than *can* and *could.*	■ **May** I **leave** the room, Professor Lee?
▶ **Be careful!** Requests for permission always refer to the present or the future. When you use ***could*** to ask for permission, it is not past.	**A:** **Could** I take the test ***tomorrow***? **B:** Certainly. The test starts at 9:00 a.m.
2. We often say ***please*** when we ask for permission. Note the possible word orders.	■ **Could** I ask a question, ***please***? OR ■ ***Please*** **could** I ask a question?
3. Use ***Do you mind if . . . ?*** to ask for permission when your action might bother someone.	**A:** **Do you mind if** I clean up tomorrow? **B:** Yes, actually, I do mind. I hate seeing a mess.
▶ **Be careful!** A negative answer to the question ***Do you mind if . . . ?*** gives permission to do something. It means *It's OK. I don't mind.*	**A:** **Do you mind if** I leave the room? **B:** ***Not at all.*** *(You may leave the room.)*
4. Use ***may*** or ***can*** in answers. Do not use ***could***.	**A:** **Could** I borrow this pencil? **B:** Yes, of course you **can**. Not ~~Yes, you could.~~
▶ **Be careful!** Do not contract ***may not***.	■ No, you **may not**. Not ~~No, you mayn't.~~
We often use **polite expressions** instead of modals to answer requests for permission.	**A:** **Could** I close the window? **B:** ***Yes, of course.*** ***Certainly.*** ***Sure.*** ***Go ahead.*** ***No, please don't.*** It's hot in here.
5. When people **refuse permission**, they often give an apology and an explanation.	**A:** Can I please have a little more time? **B:** ***I'm sorry, but the time is up.***
If the rules are very clear, someone may refuse without an apology or explanation.	**Driver:** Can I park here? **Officer:** ***No, you can't.***

MATCH • *Each request for permission goes with a response. Match each request with the correct response.*

	Request		Response
d	1. May we come in now?	a.	No, you can't. It's a bus stop.
____	2. Could I see your tickets, please?	b.	Not at all. There's plenty of time.
____	3. Please may I speak to Harry?	c.	Yes, of course they can. We've got plenty of room.
____	4. Could they come with us?	d.	Yes, you may. The test starts soon.
____	5. Can I park here?	e.	I'm sorry, he's not in.
____	6. Do you mind if I have some more tea?	f.	Certainly. Here they are.

2

COMPLETE • *Mr Smith is supervising a test. Complete his conversations with his students. Use a pronoun plus the correct form of the words in brackets and short answers.*

AHMED: Could we come (1. (Could / come)) into the test room now?

MR H: Yes, certainly (2.). Please show your registration form as you come in.

SOFIA: My brother isn't taking the test. ____________ (3. (Do you mind / stay)) in the room with me?

MR H: Yes, ____________ (4.). Only people with tickets are allowed inside.

ROSA: ____________ (5. (May / use)) a pen to write my name on the test booklet?

MR H: No, ____________ (6.). You must use a pencil. And everyone please remember, ____________ (7. (can't / start)) the test until I tell you to.

ROSA: Jamie, ____________ (8. (do you mind if / borrow)) this pencil? I only brought a pen.

JAMIE: ____________ (9.). Take it. I've brought several.

MR H: OK, ____________ (10. (may / open)) your test booklets and read the instructions now.

JEAN: I'm late because my train broke down. ____________ (11. (Can / come)) in?

MR H: No, ____________ (12.). We've already started the test.

ASK • *Lucy and Carl are going to a concert. Read each situation. Write questions to ask for permission. Use the words in brackets.*

1. Carl wants his friend Bob to come.

   Carl: I have an extra ticket. Do you mind if Bob comes?
   (Do you mind if)

2. Carl wants to use Lucy's phone to call Bob.

   Carl: Great. I'll call him right now. ______________________
   (Could)

3. Carl wants to park in front of the stadium.

   Carl: We're going to the concert, Officer. ______________________
   (May)

4. Lucy, Bob and Carl want to move up a few rows. Bob asks an usher.

   Bob: All those seats are empty. ______________________
   (Could)

5. Carl wants to record the concert. Lucy asks the usher first.

   Lucy: My friend brought a tape recorder. ______________________
   (Can)

6. Lucy hates the music. She wants to leave.

   Lucy: This music is giving me a headache. ______________________
   (Do you mind if)

4 **EDIT** • *Find the mistake in each item and fill in the space that corresponds to the letter of the incorrect word or phrase. Then correct the mistake.*

1. Can (A) he ~~comes~~ come (B) on the train with me or does (C) he need (D) a ticket? Ⓐ ● Ⓒ Ⓓ
2. I'm sorry (A), he couldn't (B). Only passengers can (C) board (D) the train. Ⓐ Ⓑ Ⓒ Ⓓ
3. Could (A) I swapped (B) seats with you (C)? I'd like to sit (D) next to my son. Ⓐ Ⓑ Ⓒ Ⓓ
4. Yes, you (A) could (B). Go ahead (C). I'm getting (D) off soon. Ⓐ Ⓑ Ⓒ Ⓓ
5. Mum, may (A) I (B) to have (C) some sweets? I'm (D) hungry. Ⓐ Ⓑ Ⓒ Ⓓ
6. No, you mayn't (A). I'm sorry (B), but (C) you've already (D) had enough sweets. Ⓐ Ⓑ Ⓒ Ⓓ
7. Do (A) you (B) mind if (C) he play (D) his computer game? Ⓐ Ⓑ Ⓒ Ⓓ
8. Yes, I do (A). He can play (B) if he wants (C). It won't (D) bother me. Ⓐ Ⓑ Ⓒ Ⓓ
9. I'm (A) still hungry. Can (B) we'll (C) get (D) a sandwich soon? Ⓐ Ⓑ Ⓒ Ⓓ
10. Not at all (A). We (B) can (C) go (D) and find the buffet car. Ⓐ Ⓑ Ⓒ Ⓓ

Requests: *Will, Can, Would, Could, Would you mind . . . ?*

'Miss Fleming, would you mind dialling 999 for me?'

CHECK POINT

Tick the correct answer.

The businessman is

❐ giving an order.

❐ asking someone to do something.

❐ asking for information.

NOTE: 999 is the emergency telephone number in the United Kingdom.

CHART CHECK 1

Circle T (True) or F (False).

T F You can use ***would*** and ***could*** in questions but NOT in short answers to requests.

QUESTIONS: *WILL/CAN/WOULD/COULD*			
WILL/CAN/ WOULD/COULD*	**SUBJECT**	**BASE FORM OF VERB**	
Will **Can** **Would** **Could**	you	**post**	this for me?

*These words are modals. They do not have *-s* in the third person singular.

SHORT ANSWERS		
AFFIRMATIVE		**NEGATIVE**
Yes, sure Of course	(I **will**). (I **can**).	I'm sorry, but I **can't**.
Certainly.		

QUESTIONS: *WOULD YOU MIND . . . ?*		
WOULD YOU MIND	**GERUND**	
Would you mind	**posting**	this for me?

CHART CHECK 2

Tick the correct answer.

Not at all means:

❐ *OK* ❐ *no*

SHORT ANSWERS	
AFFIRMATIVE	**NEGATIVE**
No, not at all. I'd be glad to.	I'm sorry, but I **can't**.

EXPRESS CHECK

Complete this conversation.

A: ______________ you mind filing these reports now?

B: ______________, ______________ at all.

A: Thanks. And ______________ you answer the phone, please?

B: Sorry, but I ______________. My hands are full.

Grammar Explanations	Examples
1. Use ***will***, ***can***, ***would*** and ***could*** to ask someone to do something.	
We often use ***will*** and ***can*** for informal requests.	**SISTER:** **Will** you **answer** the phone? **Can** you **turn down** the TV?
We use ***would*** and ***could*** to make requests more polite.	**BOSS:** **Would** you **type** this report? **Could** you **make** ten copies?
2. We also use ***please*** with ***will, can, would*** and ***could*** to make the request even more polite. Note the word order.	■ ***Please*** **could** you close the door? OR ■ **Could** you close the door, ***please***?
3. We also use ***Would you mind* + gerund** (without *please*) to make polite requests. Note that a **negative answer** means that you will do what the person requests.	**A:** **Would you mind waiting** for a few minutes? Mr Collins is still at a meeting. **B:** ***Not at all.*** *(OK. I'll do it.)*
4. People usually expect us to say ***yes*** to polite requests. When we **cannot say *yes***, we usually apologise and give a reason.	**A:** **Could** you take this to Susan Lane's office for me? **B:** ***I'm sorry, I can't.*** I'm expecting an important phone call.
▶ **BE CAREFUL!** Do not use ***would*** or ***could*** to answer polite requests.	**A:** I'm cold. **Would** you shut the window, please? **B:** ***Certainly***. NOT ~~Yes, I would~~.

IDENTIFY • *Marcia has got a new colleague. Read their conversations. Underline all the polite requests.*

1. **MARCIA:** Hi. You must be the new office assistant. I'm Marcia Jones. Let me know if you need anything.

   LORNA: Thanks, Marcia. Could you show me where the photocopier is?

   MARCIA: Certainly. It's over here.

2. **LORNA:** Marcia, would you show me how to use the fax machine?

   MARCIA: Yes, sure. Just put your fax in here and dial the number.

3. **MARCIA:** I'm going to lunch. Would you like to come?

   LORNA: Thanks, but I can't just now. I'm really busy.

   MARCIA: Do you want a sandwich from the coffee shop?

   LORNA: That would be great. Can you get me a tuna sandwich and a coffee, please?

   MARCIA: No problem. Will you answer my phone until I get back?

   LORNA: Of course.

4. **MARCIA:** Lorna, would you mind making some tea?

   LORNA: I'm sorry, but I can't do it now. I've got to finish this letter by 2:00.

2

CHOOSE • *Lorna's flatmate, Jane, is having problems today. Tick the appropriate response to each of Jane's requests.*

1. Lorna, please would you drive me into town today? My car won't start.

   a. ______ Yes, I would. b. __✓__ I'd be glad to.

2. Would you mind lending me five pounds? I'm getting paid tomorrow.

   a. ______ Not at all. b. ______ Yes.

3. Lorna, can you take these books back to the library for me? I'm running late.

   a. ______ I'm late, too. Sorry. b. ______ No, I can't.

4. Could you lock the door on your way out? My hands are full.

   a. ______ Yes, I could. b. ______ Of course.

5. Can you turn the radio down? I need to study this morning.

   a. ______ Certainly. b. ______ Not at all.

6. Will you pick up some milk on the way home this afternoon?

   a. ______ No, I won't. b. ______ Sorry. I'll be at work until 8:00.

CHOOSE & COMPLETE • *Use the appropriate imperative from the box to complete these requests. Use* **please** *when possible, and make any necessary changes.*

Buy some cereal.	**Call back later.**	**~~Close the window.~~**
File these reports.	**Shut the door.**	**Turn on the lights.**

1. Can ___you close the window, please?___ It's freezing in here.
2. Could ______________________ I've finished reading them.
3. Would you mind ______________________ It's too dark in here.
4. Will ______________________ We don't have any left.
5. Could ______________________ Ms Blake is on another call just now.
6. Would ______________________ There's too much noise in the hall!

EDIT • *Read these requests from Marcia's boss and Marcia's answers (in bold type). Find and correct six mistakes in making and responding to requests. The first mistake has already been corrected.*

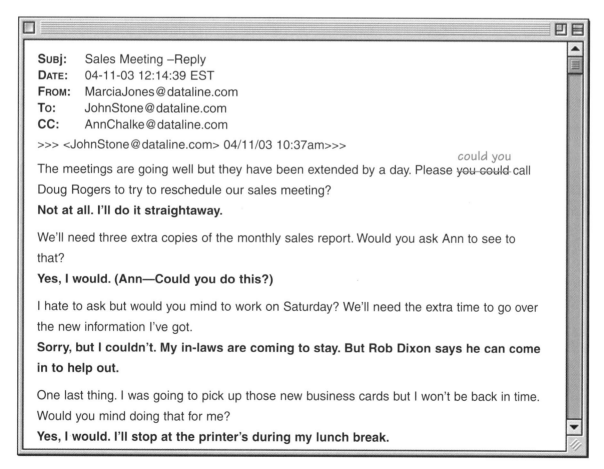

Subj: Sales Meeting –Reply
Date: 04-11-03 12:14:39 EST
From: MarciaJones@dataline.com
To: JohnStone@dataline.com
CC: AnnChalke@dataline.com

>>> <JohnStone@dataline.com> 04/11/03 10:37am>>>

The meetings are going well but they have been extended by a day. Please ~~you could~~ *could you* call Doug Rogers to try to reschedule our sales meeting?

Not at all. I'll do it straightaway.

We'll need three extra copies of the monthly sales report. Would you ask Ann to see to that?

Yes, I would. (Ann—Could you do this?)

I hate to ask but would you mind to work on Saturday? We'll need the extra time to go over the new information I've got.

Sorry, but I couldn't. My in-laws are coming to stay. But Rob Dixon says he can come in to help out.

One last thing. I was going to pick up those new business cards but I won't be back in time. Would you mind doing that for me?

Yes, I would. I'll stop at the printer's during my lunch break.

Advice: *Should, Ought to, Had better*

EMPLOYMENT AGEN
I really don't mind starting at the bottom and working my way to the top.
Maybe you **ought to consider** a job as a lift operator.

CHECK POINT

Check the correct answer.

❒ The interviewer is suggesting a type of job for the applicant.

❒ The interviewer is telling the applicant how to be successful.

CHART CHECK 1

Circle T (True) or F (False).

T F The same form of the verb follows ***should***, ***ought to*** and ***had better***.

STATEMENTS: *SHOULD/OUGHT TO/HAD BETTER*			
Subject	***Should/Ought to/ Had better****	**Base Form of Verb**	
I/He/She/We/You/They	**should (not)** **ought to** **had better (not)**	**look**	for a new job.

**Should* and *ought to* are modals. *Had better* is similar to a modal. These forms do not have *-s* in the third person singular.

NOTE: For contractions of *should not* and *had better*, see Appendix 24 on page 346.

CHART CHECK 2

Tick the correct answer.

In questions about advice, we usually use:

❒ ***should***

❒ ***ought to***

❒ ***had better***

YES/NO QUESTIONS: *SHOULD*		
Should	**Subject**	**Base Form**
Should	I he	**look?**

SHORT ANSWERS					
Affirmative			**Negative**		
Yes,	you he	**should.**	**No,**	you he	**shouldn't.**

WH- QUESTIONS: *SHOULD*				
***Wh-* Word**	***Should***	**Subject**	**Base Form**	
Where	**should**	I he	**look**	for a new job?

EXPRESS CHECK

Complete this conversation.

A: They're looking for a cashier at McDonald's. ________________ I apply for the job?

B: ________________, you ________________. You can get more money working at the bookshop.

Grammar Explanations	Examples
1. Use ***should*** and ***ought to*** to say that something is advisable. **Usage Note:** ***Should*** is more common than ***ought to***.	■ Mark **should get** a new job. ■ He **shouldn't leave** school yet. ■ He **ought to read** the job ads. Not common ~~He ought not to quit.~~
2. Use ***had better*** for urgent advice – when you believe that something bad will happen if the person does not follow the advice. **Usage Note:** We usually use the contraction for *had better*. The negative of *had better* is ***had better not***. ► **Be careful!** *Had better* always refers to the present or the future, never to the past (even though it uses the word *had*).	■ You**'d better leave** now ***or you'll be late***. ■ You**'d better** apply for more than one job. Not ~~You had better apply . . .~~ ■ You**'d better not** be late. Not ~~You'd not better be late.~~ ■ We**'d better take** the bus ***now***. ■ You**'d better call** them back ***tomorrow***.
3. Use ***should*** for questions. We do not usually use *ought to* or *had better* for questions.	■ **Should** I **apply** for that job? ■ When **should** I **apply**?
4. It is usually considered impolite to give **advice to people of equal or higher status** (such as friends or bosses) unless they ask for it. When we give unasked-for advice, we often soften it with ***maybe***, ***perhaps*** or ***I think***.	**Friend:** **Should** I **shake** hands with the interviewer? **You:** Yes, you **should**. **Boss:** Where **should** I **take** our client to lunch? **You:** I think you **should go** to Luigi's. ■ Myra, ***maybe*** you **ought to apply** for this job.

READ • *Look at these job search tips.*

- You should tell all your friends that you are looking for a job.
- You'd better not leave your present job before you find a new one.
- You shouldn't tell your boss that you are looking for a new job.
- You ought to apply for several jobs at once.
- You shouldn't immediately ask an interviewer about job benefits.
- You should always give the interviewer accurate salary information.

ANSWER • *Tick the things that are OK to do, according to the tips.*

1. ☑ tell your friends about your job search
2. ☐ tell your boss about your job search
3. ☐ ask about job benefits straight away
4. ☐ leave your job during your search
5. ☐ apply for several jobs at once
6. ☐ tell the interviewer your real salary

CHOOSE • *Read this advice for job seekers. Complete it with the correct words.*

Reader's Weekly Volume II, Issue 23

ADVICE FOR JOB SEEKERS

Want or need a new job? When's the best time to start looking? Right now! You ___'d better not___ (1. ought to / 'd better not) delay, or you'll start to feel 'stuck in a rut'.

These tips will help:

☛ A lot of people wait until after the holidays to look for a job. That means there's less competition for you at this time of year. You ______________ (2. shouldn't / should) wait!

☛ Too busy at work to go to interviews? Early morning interviews have fewer interruptions. You ______________ (3. should / 'd better not) ask for interviews before nine o'clock.

☛ If you are laid off, you ______________ (4. 'd better / shouldn't) take a lower-paid job just to get work. If your new salary is low, your employer won't appreciate your skills. If possible, you ______________ (5. 'd better not / should) ask for a salary that matches your skills.

☛ However, money isn't everything! You ______________ (6. ought to / 'd better not) take a position with a company you dislike, or you won't do a good job there.

☛ Don't talk about salary too soon. You ______________ (7. 'd better / shouldn't) wait – learn about the job and talk about your skills first.

COMPLETE • *Ken Lang's boss has invited him to dinner at his home. Complete Ken's conversation with his friend, Scott. Use* **should, ought to** *or* **had better** *and the words in brackets. Choose between affirmative and negative.*

KEN: How should I dress? In a suit?
1. (How / dress?)

SCOTT: You don't have to wear a suit. ________________________________,
2. (look / neat)

but you can wear casual clothes.

KEN: ________________________________
3. (What time / arrive?)

SCOTT: It's really important to be on time. Your boss and his wife are expecting you at 7:00, so ________________________________. It's OK to be a little
4. (arrive after 7:15)

late but don't make them wait too long for you!

KEN: ________________________________
5. (take a gift?)

SCOTT: Yes, but get something small. ________________________________.
6. (buy an expensive gift)

It would embarrass them.

KEN: ________________________________
7. (What / buy?)

SCOTT: I think ________________________________.
8. (get some flowers)

EDIT • *Read this letter. Find and correct six mistakes in expressing advice. The first mistake has already been corrected.*

Dear Tom,

We are so happy to hear about your new job. Congratulations! Just remember – you shouldn't ~~to~~ work too hard. The most important thing just now is your studies. Maybe you better work only two days a week instead of three. Also, we think you'd better ask your boss for time off during the exams. That way you'll have plenty of time to study. You would better give this a lot of careful thought, OK? Please take good care of yourself. You'd not better start skipping meals and you definitely shouldn't worked at night. At your age, you shall always get plenty of sleep. Do you need anything from home? Should we send any of your books? Let us know.

With love,

Mum and Dad

Suggestions: *Could, Why don't?, Why not?, Let's, Shall we?, How about?*

Let's Travel!

Going to Germany?

Why not stay at a youth hostel?

How about a magnificent one like Altena Castle? Altena is also fun and cheap. So, **why don't** you **make** our castle your home?

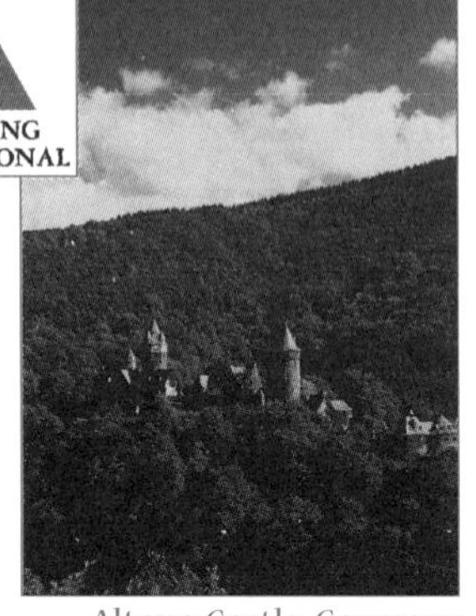

Altena Castle, Germany

CHECK POINT

Circle T (True) or F (False).

T F The questions in the advert are asking for information about youth hostels.

CHART CHECK 1

Tick the correct answer.

The verb after ***could***, ***why don't***, ***why not***, ***shall we*** or ***let's***

❐ changes for different subjects.

❐ does not change for different subjects.

COULD				
(Maybe)	**Subject**	***Could******	**Base Form**	
(Maybe)	I/he/she/we/you/they	**could**	**stay**	in a castle.

**Could* is a modal. It does not have *-s* in the third person singular.

WHY DON'T?				
Why	***Don't***	**Subject**	**Base Form**	
Why	**don't**	I/we/you/they	**stay**	in a castle?
	doesn't	he/she		

WHY NOT?		
Why not	**Base Form**	
Why not	**stay**	there?

LET'S		
Let's (Not)	**Base Form**	
Let's (not)	**stay**	there.

CHART CHECK 2

Circle T (True) or F (False).

T F Suggestions with ***How about?*** have only one form.

HOW ABOUT?		
How about	**Gerund/Noun**	
How about	**staying**	in a castle?
	a castle?	

SHALL WE?		
Shall we	**Base form**	
Shall we	**stay**	at Altena?

EXPRESS CHECK

Add the correct punctuation.

Let's take the train____ Maybe we could take the train____

Why not take the train____ How about the train____

Grammar Explanations	Examples
1. Use ***Let's***, ***(Maybe)*** . . . ***could***, ***Why don't/ doesn't***, ***Why not***, ***Shall we*** and ***How about*** to make suggestions.	**A:** **Let's go** somewhere this summer. **B:** **Maybe** we **could go** to Germany. **A:** **Why don't** we **ask** Luke to go with us? **B:** Good idea. **Why doesn't** Tom **call** him tonight? **A:** **Why not call** him right now? **B:** **How about staying** at a youth hostel? **A:** **How about** Altena Castle? **B:** **Shall we go** by train?
► **Be careful!** When someone uses ***Why not*** and ***Why don't/doesn't*** to make a suggestion, these expressions are not information questions. The speaker does not expect to receive information from the listener.	SUGGESTION **A:** **Why don't** you **visit** Jill in Hong Kong? **B:** That's a good idea. INFORMATION QUESTION **A:** **Why don't** you **eat** meat? **B:** Because I'm a vegetarian.
2. ***Let's*** and ***Shall we*** always include the speaker. They mean: *Here's a suggestion for you and me.*	■ **Let's go** to Hong Kong. *(I suggest that we go to Hong Kong.)* ■ **Shall we visit** Jill?
3. Note the **different forms** to use with these expressions.	BASE FORM OF THE VERB ■ **Let's *take*** the train. ■ **Maybe** we **could *take*** the train. ■ **Why don't** we ***take*** the train? ■ **Why not *take*** the train? GERUND OR NOUN ■ **How about *taking*** the train? ■ **How about *the train***?
4. Notice the **punctuation** at the end of each kind of suggestion.	STATEMENTS ■ **Let's** stay at a hostel**.** ■ **Maybe** we **could** stay at a hostel**.** QUESTIONS ■ **Why don't** we stay at a hostel**?** ■ **Why not** stay at a hostel**?** ■ **Shall we** stay at a hostel**?** ■ **How about** staying at a hostel**?** ■ **How about** a hostel**?**

IDENTIFY • *Emily and Megan are visiting Hong Kong. Read their conversation. Underline all the suggestions.*

EMILY: Why don't we go to the races? I hear they're really exciting.

MEGAN: I'd like to but I need to go shopping.

EMILY: Then let's go to the Temple Street Market tonight. We might even see some Chinese opera in the street while we're there.

MEGAN: That sounds like fun. If we do that, why not go to the races this afternoon?

EMILY: OK, but let's get something to eat first in one of those floating restaurants.

MEGAN: I don't think we'll have time. Maybe we could do that tomorrow. Shall we get *dim sum* at the Kau Kee Restaurant next door? Then we could take the Star Ferry to Hong Kong Island and the racecourse.

EMILY: Sounds good. For tomorrow, why not take one of those small boats – *kaido* – to Lantau Island? When we come back, we could have dinner at the Jumbo Palace.

MEGAN: Let's do that. It's a bit expensive but at least it floats!

COMPLETE • *Read these conversations. Complete them with the appropriate expression in brackets.*

1. **A:** I feel like having seafood for dinner but we went to Tai Pak for seafood last night.
   B: ______Why not______ go again? The food's great and so is the view. (Why not / Let's not)
2. **A:** I'm really tired. ____________________ have a rest before we go out? (Let's / Shall we)
   B: That's a good idea. I'm tired, too.
3. **A:** I want to explore downtown Hong Kong.
   B: ____________________ take a minibus? We'll see a lot more that way. (Let's not / Why don't we)
4. **A:** A group of foreign students has just checked in at the hostel.
   B: ____________________ ask them to join us for dinner. (How about / Maybe we could)
5. **A:** I still need to buy some souvenirs before we leave.
   B: ____________________ go shopping after dinner. (Let's / Shall we)
6. **A:** I don't want to go home tomorrow. I'm having a really good time here.
   B: So am I. ____________________ leave tomorrow. (Let's not / Why not)

CHOOSE & COMPLETE • *Read these conversations. Complete the suggestions with phrases from the box. Add pronouns and change the verbs as necessary. Punctuate correctly.*

take a trip together	try that new seafood place	~~buy tickets~~
go to the beach	buy another one	

1. **A:** There's an Oasis concert at the Hong Kong Convention Centre next weekend.
   B: We're near there now. Maybe we could buy tickets.
2. **A:** It's going to be hot tomorrow.
   B: I know. How about ______
3. **A:** These jackets are in the sale. Maybe we could buy one for Brian's birthday.
   B: We got him a jacket last year. Let's not ______
4. **A:** I don't know what to do next summer. I'm sick of doing nothing.
   B: Me too. Shall we ______
5. **A:** I'm hungry.
   B: Let's ______

EDIT • *Read these notes. Find and correct seven mistakes in the use of suggestions. The first one has already been corrected. Don't forget to check the punctuation.*

3:00

Emily

I'm going shopping. I'll be back at 5:00. Let's ~~eating~~ eat at 7:00. OK?

Megan

4:00

Megan

7:00 for dinner is fine.

Shall we going to see a film afterwards.

See you later.

E.

5:00

Emily

I'm going to be too tired for a film. Maybe we could just hanging around the hostel after dinner. Let's talk about it later. I'm going to have a nap.

M.

6:00

M–

Let's not eat at the same restaurant tonight? Why don't we trying a new place? How about Broadway Seafood. I'll meet you downstairs at 7:00.

E.

Preferences: *Prefer, Would prefer, Would rather*

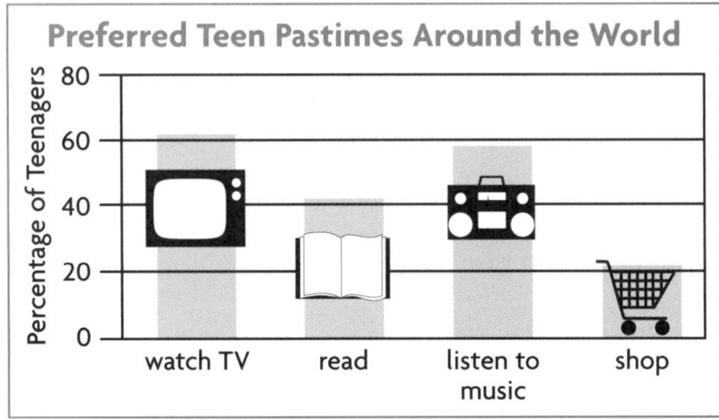

Teenagers around the world **prefer watching** TV to all other leisure-time activities.

CHECK POINT

Tick the main point of the bar graph.

❒ Teenagers like watching TV, reading books and listening to music.

❒ Teenagers like watching TV more than they like doing other things.

CHART CHECK 1

Tick the correct answer.

Which word(s) can you use with all subjects?

❒ ***prefer***

❒ ***would prefer* (*'d prefer*)**

STATEMENTS: *PREFER/WOULD PREFER*		
SUBJECT	**(WOULD) PREFER**	**NOUN/GERUND/INFINITIVE**
I/We/You*/They	**prefer**	**newspapers** (to magazines). **reading** newspapers (to reading books). **(not) to read** newspapers.
He/She	**prefers**	
I/He/She/We/You/They	**would prefer** **'d prefer**	**newspapers** (to magazines) **(not) to read** newspapers.

**You* is both singular and plural.

CHART CHECK 2

Tick the correct answer.

Which two forms of the verb can follow ***prefer***?

❒ the base form or the gerund

❒ the gerund or the infinitive

YES/NO QUESTIONS: *PREFER/WOULD PREFER*			
DO/WOULD	**SUBJECT**	**PREFER**	**NOUN/GERUND/INFINITIVE**
Do	you/they	**prefer**	**newspapers**? **reading** newspapers? **to read** newspapers?
Does	he/she		
Would	you/they/he/she		**newspapers**? **to read** newspapers?

SHORT ANSWERS					
AFFIRMATIVE			**NEGATIVE**		
Yes,	I/we/they	**do.**	**No,**	I/we/they	**don't.**
	he/she	**does.**		he/she	**doesn't.**
	I/we/they/he/she	**would.**		I/we/they/he/she	**wouldn't.**

STATEMENTS: *WOULD RATHER*		
Subject	***Would rather***	**Base Form of Verb**
I/He/She/We/You/They	**would rather** **'d rather**	**read** newspapers (than read magazines). **(not) read** newspapers.

YES/NO QUESTIONS: *WOULD RATHER*			
Would	**Subject**	***Rather***	**Base Form**
Would	she	**rather**	**read**?

SHORT ANSWERS	
Affirmative	**Negative**
Yes, she **would**.	**No**, she **wouldn't**. She**'d rather not**.

EXPRESS CHECK

Circle the correct words to complete this sentence.

I'd rather read / to read than / to shop, but Jo prefers shop / shopping.

Grammar Explanations	Examples
1. Use ***prefer***, ***would prefer*** and ***would rather*** to talk about things that you like more than other things.	■ We usually **prefer** ***Italian food*** to French. ■ I'**d prefer** ***to have*** Chinese food tonight. ■ I'**d rather** ***cook*** at home than at Jane's place.
Usage Note: We often use ***prefer*** for a general preference and ***would prefer*** or ***would rather*** for a preference in a particular situation.	■ Which **do** you **prefer** – chicken or prawn? ■ **Would** you **prefer** chicken or prawn curry tonight?
2. ***Prefer*** may be followed by a noun, a gerund or an infinitive.	■ I usually **prefer** ***vegetables*** (noun) to ***meat***. ■ **Does** Bill **prefer** ***staying*** (gerund) in or ***going*** out? ■ I **prefer** ***to read*** (infinitive) whenever I have any free time.
Would prefer may be followed by a noun or an infinitive.	■ I think Sam **would prefer** ***the book*** (noun) to the CD. ■ We'**d** both **prefer** ***to go out*** (infinitive) tonight.
Would rather can be followed by only the base form of the verb.	■ I'**d rather** ***stay*** (base form) at home tonight.
Usage Note: We often use ***I'd rather not***, by itself, to refuse an offer, suggestion or invitation.	**A:** Would you like some dessert? **B:** **I'd rather not**. I've had enough to eat.
▶ **Be careful!** The negative of *I'd rather* is *I'd rather not.*	■ **I'd rather not** have dessert. Not ~~I wouldn't rather have dessert.~~
3. For **comparisons**, we can use ***to*** after *prefer* + noun or gerund.	■ Jack **prefers** comedies (noun) ***to*** action films (noun). ■ I'**d prefer** walking (gerund) ***to*** swimming (gerund).
We can also use ***than*** after *would prefer* + infinitive.	■ I'**d prefer** to stay (infinitive) at home tonight ***than*** go to a restaurant.
We can use ***than*** after *would rather* + base form of the verb.	■ I'**d rather** watch (base form) football ***than*** play (base form) it.

TRUE OR FALSE • *Jim ranked some activities from 1 to 8 according to his preferences (1 = his favourite). Look at his list. Then read each numbered sentence and write T (True) or F (False).*

Preferred Activities	
3	listen to music
5	go swimming
4	go cycling
1	watch TV
8	cooking
6	play the guitar
7	go hiking
2	read

T 1. He prefers listening to music to playing the guitar.

_____ 2. He'd rather go hiking than go swimming.

_____ 3. He prefers swimming to cycling.

_____ 4. He'd rather not watch TV.

_____ 5. He prefers cooking to reading.

_____ 6. He prefers watching TV to reading.

_____ 7. He'd probably prefer a concert to a walk in the countryside.

CHOOSE & COMPLETE • *Jim and Anna are discussing their evening plans. Complete their conversation. Use* **would rather (not)** *with one of the verbs in the box or by itself in short answers.*

have	cook	see	~~stay~~	go

ANNA: Would you like to go to the cinema tonight?

JIM: I'd rather stay (1.) at home and watch TV.

ANNA: Sounds good. Maybe we could make some dinner later.

JIM: ______________ (2.) tonight. I'm too tired.

ANNA: OK. ______________ you ______________ (3.) to a restaurant instead?

JIM: Let's order some pizza.

ANNA: How about a pepperoni pizza?

JIM: ______________ (4.). Pepperoni gives me indigestion.

______________ (5.) mushrooms than pepperoni if that's OK.

ANNA: No problem. Do you want to watch the Stephen King thriller at 8:00?

JIM: ______________ (6.). I don't like his films.

ANNA: Well . . . there's a comedy on at 8:00 and a documentary at 8:30.

JIM: ______________ (7.) the comedy. I need a laugh.

COMPLETE • *Read these conversations. Complete them with* **prefer, would prefer** *or* **would rather**. *Use* **prefer** *to state general preferences. Complete the comparisons with* **to** *or* **than**.

1. **A:** We're going to Rome again next week. ___Would___ you ___prefer___ to take the train or ___to___ fly this time?

   B: You know me. I always __________ the plane __________ the train.

2. **A:** I __________ have the aisle seat __________ the window seat.

   B: That's fine with me. I __________ the window seat. That way I can look out.

3. **A:** Where would you like to stay? In a hotel or a *pensione*?

   B: Oh, I __________ to stay in a *pensione* this time. It's more personal.

4. **A:** I __________ eating in small *trattorias* __________ eating in big restaurants.

   B: Me too. They're less expensive and the food is always delicious.

5. **A:** Speaking of food, you make the best spaghetti in the world.

   B: Thanks, but I __________ order it in a restaurant __________ make it at home!

6. **A:** When in Rome, __________ you __________ drinking tea or coffee?

   B: I definitely __________ coffee __________ tea. You know what they say, 'When in Rome, do as the Romans do!'

EDIT • *Read Anna's report. Find and correct six mistakes in the use of* **prefer** *and* **would rather**. *The first mistake has already been corrected.*

For my research, I interviewed fifty men and women. There was no difference in men's and women's TV preferences. I found that everyone prefers watching TV ~~than~~ to going to the cinema. Men and women both enjoy news programmes and documentaries. However, men would rather watching adventure programmes and science fiction, while women prefer soap operas. Men also like to watch all kinds of sport but women would rather see game shows to sports. Reading preferences differ, too. Men prefer to reading newspapers, while women would rather read magazines and books. When men read books, they prefer read non-fiction and adventure stories. Women are preferring novels.

SelfTest VI

SECTION ONE

Circle the letter of the correct answer to complete each sentence.

EXAMPLE:
Jennifer never ________ coffee. A (B) C D
(A) drink (C) is drinking
(B) drinks (D) was drinking

1. —Would you shut the door, please? A B C D
—________
(A) Certainly. (C) Yes, I could.
(B) No, I can't. (D) Yes, I would.

2. Why ________ a movie tonight? A B C D
(A) about seeing (C) not seeing
(B) don't we see (D) we don't see

3. Sonia can't speak German yet but after a few lessons she ________ speak a little. A B C D
(A) can (C) is able to
(B) could (D) will be able to

4. In 1998, Tara Lipinski ________ win the gold medal in figure skating at the Winter Olympics. A B C D
(A) can (C) will be able to
(B) could (D) was able to

5. I ________ make new friends since I moved here. A B C D
(A) can't (C) haven't been able to
(B) couldn't (D) 'm not able to

6. She ________ better not arrive late. A B C D
(A) did (C) 'd
(B) has (D) would

7. —Do you mind if I borrow a chair? A B C D
—________ Do you need only one?
(A) I'm sorry. (C) Yes, I do.
(B) Not at all. (D) Yes, I would.

8. Would you mind ________ me tomorrow? A B C D
(A) call (C) to call
(B) calling (D) if you call

9. I'd rather ________ the film. I hear it's very good. A B C D
(A) watch (C) watching
(B) to watch (D) not watch

10. You ________ miss the deadline or you'll have to pay a fine. A B C D
(A) better not
(B) 'd better
(C) 'd better not
(D) had no better

11. ________ take the train instead of the bus? It's faster. A B C D
(A) How about
(B) Let's
(C) Why don't
(D) Why not

12. Could my sister ________ to class with me tomorrow? A B C D
(A) come
(B) comes
(C) coming
(D) to come

13. I ________ have dessert. I'm trying to lose some weight. A B C D
(A) 'd rather
(B) 'd rather not
(C) 'd prefer
(D) 'd prefer not

14. Jamie prefers working at home ________ working in an office. A B C D
(A) more
(B) than
(C) that
(D) to

SECTION TWO

Each sentence has four underlined words or phrases. The four underlined parts of the sentence are marked A, B, C and D. Circle the letter of the one underlined word or phrase that is NOT CORRECT.

EXAMPLE:
Mike usually (A) drives (B) to school but today (C) he walks (D). A B C (D)

15. When (A) I was ten, I could (B) swim but I wasn't (C) able dive (D). A B C D

16. Why don't (A) we have (B) dinner and then go (C) and see *Possible Dreams*. (D) A B C D

17. You drove (A) for seven hours today so maybe (B) you'd not better (C) drive (D) tonight. A B C D

18. Will (A) you mind bringing (B) your camera to the party tomorrow (C) ? (D) A B C D

19. Dad, may (A) Jim borrows (B) the car tomorrow or does (C) Mum need (D) it? A B C D

20. I can't (A) help (B) you so maybe (C) you should to ask (D) Mary. A B C D

21. Should (A) I bring (B) flowers to Lisa's or should (C) I giving (D) her chocolates? A B C D

22. Maybe (A) you ought (B) than (C) just bring (D) flowers. A B C D

23. Sarah celebrated (A) last year (B) because she could (C) win (D) the race. A B C D

24. It's (A) really late so let's (B) we (C) go (D) out to dinner tonight. A B C D

25. Why would (A) you rather (B) stay (C) at home to (D) go out tonight? A B C D

Necessity: *Have (got) to* and *Must*

Tick the correct answer.

Using a seat belt is:

❐ a requirement

❐ a choice

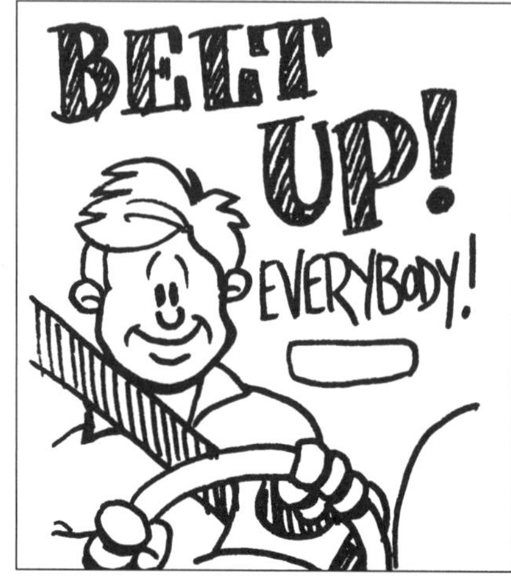

You **must fasten** your seat belt. It's the law.

CHART CHECK 1

Circle T (True) or F (False).

T F We use ***have got to*** in affirmative and negative statements.

AFFIRMATIVE STATEMENTS: *HAVE (GOT) TO*		
Subject	***Have to/ Have got to***	**Base Form of Verb**
I/We/You/They	**have (got) to**	**go.**
He/She/It	**has (got) to**	

CONTRACTIONS
Have got to = **'ve got to**
Has got to = **'s got to**

NEGATIVE STATEMENTS: *HAVE TO*			
Subject	***Do not***	***Have to***	**Base Form**
I/We/You/They	**don't**	**have to**	**go.**
He/She/It	**doesn't**		

CHART CHECK 2

Tick the correct answer.

In questions with ***have to***, what comes before the subject?

❐ a form of ***do***

❐ a form of ***have to***

YES/NO QUESTIONS: *HAVE TO*			
Do	**Subject**	***Have to***	**Base Form**
Do	we	**have to**	**go?**
Does	he		

SHORT ANSWERS					
Affirmative			**Negative**		
Yes,	you	**do.**	**No,**	you	**don't.**
	he	**does.**		he	**doesn't.**

STATEMENTS: *MUST*		
Subject	***Must* (not)***	**Base Form**
I/He/She/It/We/You/They	**must (not)**	**go.**

CONTRACTION
must not = **mustn't**

**Must* is a modal. It does not take *-s* in the third person singular.

EXPRESS CHECK

Complete this conversation. Use one word for each blank.

A: Why ______________ she ______________ ______________ wear her seat belt?

B: It's the law. Everyone ______________ wear a seat belt.

Grammar Explanations	Examples
1. Use ***have to***, ***have got to*** and ***must*** to express necessity.	
a. ***Have to*** is the most common expression in everyday use.	■ Everyone **has to pass** a driving test before getting a driving licence.
b. ***Have got to*** often expresses strong feelings in speaking and informal writing.	■ He'**s got to drive** more slowly. I'm afraid he's going to have an accident.
c. ***Must*** is used in writing (forms, signs, notices).	■ You **must stop** completely at a stop sign.
Must is used in spoken English, when	
• the speaker is in a position of power.	■ Jamie, you **must clean** your room today. *(mother talking to her young child)*
• there is urgent necessity.	■ You really **must talk** to your boss about a pay rise. *(friend talking to a friend)*
▶ **BE CAREFUL!** ***Don't have to*** and ***must not*** have very different meanings. *(See Unit 34.)*	■ You **don't have to park** here. *(It isn't necessary to park here.)* ■ You **must not park** here. *(You can't park here. It's not allowed.)*

2. Use the correct form of ***have to*** for all tenses and forms.	■ After his accident, Gary **had to take** time off work. *(past simple)* ■ Sheila **has had to wear** glasses since she was five years old. *(present perfect)* ■ I'**ll have to drive** tomorrow. *(future)*
Use ***have got to*** and ***must*** only for the present or the future.	■ I'**ve got to wear** glasses all the time. ■ Everyone **must take** an eye test tomorrow.

3. Use ***have to*** for most questions. (We rarely use ***have got to*** or ***must*** for questions.)	■ **Does** Paul **have to drive**? ■ When **will** he **have to leave**?

IDENTIFY • Ben Leonard is moving from London to California. Read his telephone conversation with the Department of Motor Vehicles (DMV). *Underline the words that talk about necessity.*

DMV: Department of Motor Vehicles. May I help you?

BEN: I'm moving to the States soon. Will I have to get an American licence when I move?

DMV: Yes, you will. Residents must have an American licence.

BEN: When will I have to get my licence?

DMV: You have to replace your old licence ten days after you become a resident. So come in and apply for your licence when you get here.

BEN: Do I have to take any tests to exchange my British licence for an American one?

DMV: Since you already have a British licence, you won't have to take the full driving test. You will only have to take the written test.

BEN: How about an eye test?

DMV: Oh, everyone has got to take an eye test.

BEN: OK. Thanks a lot. You've been very helpful.

COMPLETE • Read this conversation. Complete it with the correct form of **have to** *or* **have got to** *and the verbs in brackets. Use* **have got to** *and give short answers whenever possible.*

BEN: When ___do___ you ___have to use___ the car?
1. (use)

ANN: I ____________ Jim's football gear pretty soon. Why?
2. (pick up)

____________ you still ____________ the oil?
3. (change)

BEN: No, ____________. I did it early this morning. Oh, and I bought some film.
4.

ANN: Oh, you ____________ that. I bought three rolls yesterday.
5. (not do)

BEN: We ____________ lots of pictures on the trip.
6. (take)

____________ Jim still ____________?
7. (pack)

ANN: No, ____________. He's done his packing and gone to Sara's to say goodbye. Why?
8.

BEN: He ____________ me clean out the car. It's full of his stuff.
9. (help)

ANN: I'll call him again. It's difficult for him to leave his friends.

I ____________ him to come home twice already.
10. (call)

CHOOSE & COMPLETE • *Look at these signs. Use the verbs from the box to complete the sentences about things you* **must** *do and* **must not** *do.*

turn drive ride walk

1. You ______must turn______ left.
2. You ____________________ right.
3. You ____________________ over 40 mph.
4. You ____________________ over 55 mph.
5. Cyclists ____________________ on the left.
6. Pedestrians ____________________ on the left.

EDIT • *Read Jim's letter to Sara. Find and correct seven mistakes in expressing necessity. The first mistake has already been corrected.*

Dear Sara,

How are you doing? We've been here about six weeks. It's strange living in the United States.

There's no public transport, so you've ~~get~~ got to drive everywhere. I had to signs up for driving lessons so I can get my licence by the summer. It's the law here that everyone musts wear a seat belt. I used to hate wearing a seat belt but with the traffic here, I have changed my mind. There are a lot of motorways and you've got know how to change lanes with a lot of fast traffic. Even my mum have had to get used to it. Dad works from home, so he hasn't has to do a lot of driving.

Have you beaten those computer games yet? I'm having a lot of trouble with 'Doom'. You got to write to me and tell me how to get past the fifth level!

Jim

Choice: *Don't have to* No Choice: *Must not* and *Can't*

CHECK POINT

Check the correct answer.

The driver can choose to

❒ park on the zebra crossing. ❒ stop to ask for directions.

CHART CHECK 1

Tick the correct answer.

Which part of ***do not have to*** changes for different subjects?

❒ ***do*** ❒ ***have***

DON'T HAVE TO				
SUBJECT	***DO NOT***	***HAVE TO***	**BASE FORM OF VERB**	
I/We/You/They	**don't**	**have to**	**stop**	here.
He/She/It	**doesn't**		**park**	

CHART CHECK 2

Circle T (True) or F (False).

T F The form of ***must not*** and ***can't*** changes for different subjects.

MUST NOT			
SUBJECT	***MUST* NOT***	**BASE FORM**	
I/He/She/It/We/You/They	**must not**	**stop**	here.

CAN'T			
SUBJECT	***CAN'T****	**BASE FORM**	
I/He/She/It/We/You/They	**can't**	**stop**	here.

*These words are modals. They do not take *-s* in the third person singular.

EXPRESS CHECK

Unscramble these words to form two sentences.

stop • He • have • here • to • doesn't

____

must • fast • You • not • drive • too

____

Grammar Explanations	Examples
1. ***Have to*** and ***must*** have similar meanings. They both express the idea that something is necessary or required.	■ You **have to stop** at the stop sign. ■ You **must stop** at the stop sign.
Don't/Doesn't have to and ***must not*** have very different meanings.	
a. ***Don't/Doesn't have to*** expresses that something is not necessary. It means that there is another possibility. There is a **choice**.	■ You **don't have to drive**. I can do it. ■ He **doesn't have to turn** here. He can turn at the next junction.
b. ***Must not*** expresses **prohibition**. It means that something is not allowed or is against the law. There is **no choice**.	■ You **must not use** the car without my permission. ■ You **must not drive** without a licence. It's against the law.
2. ***Must not*** is used to express prohibition in writing, including official forms, signs and notices.	■ You **must not use** your hooter unnecessarily.
Usage Note: In spoken English, we do not usually use *must not* when talking to or about another adult. We use ***can't*** instead.	■ We **can't park** here. There are double yellow lines.
Sometimes people use ***must not*** to tell a child that there is no choice in a situation.	■ Jane, you **mustn't take off** your seat belt while the car is moving.
3. You can use ***not have to*** for all tenses and forms.	■ You **don't have to drive**. *(present simple)* ■ She **won't have to renew** her driving licence next year. *(future)* ■ We **haven't had to pay** a lot of parking fines this year. *(present perfect)* ■ They **didn't have to take** a written test last year. Now it's compulsory. *(past simple)*
Must not refers only to the present or the future, not the past.	■ Drivers **must not park** on double yellow lines. ■ I **must not forget** to fill up with petrol tomorrow.
To refer to the past, use ***had/didn't have to***.	■ I **didn't have to** take a driving test when I moved here ten years ago.
To refer to the future, use ***will/won't have to***.	■ You**'ll have to** renew your driving licence next year.

IDENTIFY • *Read this article. Underline the words that show that there is a choice about doing something. Circle the words that show that there is no choice.*

A New Alternative to Car Ownership

New drivers are usually excited about their new freedom: 'My mum doesn't have to drive me everywhere any more! I don't have to ask my friends for lifts to school!' When you haven't got your own car yet, any price seems worth paying. But once you buy a car, you can't forget your car payments and insurance premiums or you won't be a driver for very long. You can't leave petrol and servicing out of the budget, either. Car sharing offers an alternative to these problems, however. Members of car-sharing groups have a car when they need one for either short trips or holidays but they don't have the high expenses of ownership. They pay very little to use a shared car and they don't have to worry about servicing the car or paying the insurance. Fees for short trips are only about £5.00 an hour plus 50p per mile. Groups do not have strict requirements, either. Members must not have bad driving records or poor credit and they must not return the cars in bad condition or they will pay extra.

2 **COMPLETE** • *Read this conversation. Complete it with* **can't** *or the correct form of* **not have to** *and the verb in brackets.*

JIM: Austin ___doesn't have to sit___ (1. sit) in a child seat. Who do I have to? It's not fair.

ANN: Jim, you really ________________ (2. yell) like that in the car. Your father needs to concentrate on driving. Ben, turn left for the restaurant.

BEN: I ________________ (3. turn) left. It's a one-way street. I'll go round the block.

ANN: There's the restaurant. Uh-oh. You ________________ (4. park) here. It's a bus stop.

BEN: Maybe I'll park in that car park. That way we ________________ (5. worry) about our stuff while we're eating. Remind me to buy some petrol after lunch.

ANN: We ________________ (6. get) petrol, do we? The tank is still half full.

BEN: I know. But we ________________ (7. buy) petrol for a long time. I'm not sure the gauge is working.

AUSTIN: You ________________ (8. bring) your bicycle into the restaurant, Jim! It's too big.

JIM: Mum said it was OK. Anyway, I ________________ (9. listen) to you.

READ & COMPLETE • *Look at this sign at the hotel swimming pool. Complete each sentence with* **must not** *or* **don't have to** *and the correct form of the verb in brackets.*

Swimming Pool Rules and Regulations

Pool Hours 10:00 a.m.–10:00 p.m.

Children under 12 years NOT ALLOWED in pool without an adult.

Towels available at front desk.

NO
- ball playing
- radios
- diving
- glass bottles
- alcoholic beverages

1. Children under 12 years old ___must not swim___ (swim) without an adult.
2. You ______________ (bring) your own towel.
3. You ______________ (play) ball in or around the pool.
4. You ______________ (dive) into the pool.
5. Teenagers ______________ (be) with an adult.
6. You ______________ (leave) the pool at 8:00 p.m.

EDIT • *Read Austin's postcard to his friend. Find and correct five mistakes in expressing necessity. The first mistake has already been corrected.*

Holiday Hotel

Hi, Janet!

We got to the hotel late this evening because we got lost. But we were lucky – they kept our room so we ~~must not~~ didn't have to find another hotel. Jimmy is really happy because he don't have to go to bed until after 10:00, when the swimming pool closes. We mustn't leave until 11:00 tomorrow (checkout time) so we can stay up later. Plymouth is only four hours away so we won't had to drive the whole day tomorrow. It's going to be exciting. My parents say we absolutely must not to go to the beach by ourselves because there are sharks there. I'd love to see a shark (from a safe distance). I'll send a postcard of one.

Austin

To:

Janet Edwards

55 Amherst Lane

Harlow

Essex CM20 2EJ

Expectations: *Be supposed to*

Oh no! I **was supposed to prepare** a speech!
He'd better hurry up with these pictures. It**'s supposed to rain**.
best man
bride's parents
brides-maid
bride
groom
groom's parents

CHECK POINT

Tick the correct answers.

The best man is thinking about

❒ something he has forgotten to do.

❒ the usual way something is done at a wedding.

CHART CHECK

Circle T (True) or F (False).

T F You can use ***be supposed to*** in the present simple and past simple.

STATEMENTS				
Subject	**Be**	**Supposed to**	**Base Form of Verb**	
I	**am** / **was**	**(not) supposed to**	**stand** / **be**	here.
He/She/It	**is** / **was**			
We/You*/They	**are** / **were**			

*You is both singular and plural.

SHORT FORMS				
Subject	**Be**	**Supposed to**	**Base Form of Verb**	
I	**'m (not)** / **wasn't**	supposed to	stand / be	here.
He/She/It	**'s (not)** / **wasn't**			
We/You*/They	**'re (not)** / **weren't**			

YES/NO QUESTIONS				
Be	**Subject**	**Supposed to**	**Base Form**	
Am / **Was**	I	**supposed to**	**stand**	here?
Is / **Was**	he			
Are / **Were**	you			

SHORT ANSWERS					
AFFIRMATIVE			**NEGATIVE**		
Yes,	you	are. were.	No,	you	aren't. weren't.
	he	is. was.		he	isn't. wasn't.
	I	am. was.		I	'm not. wasn't.

EXPRESS CHECK

Complete these sentences.

A: What ______________ we supposed to wear yesterday?

B: Our suits. It ______________ supposed to be a dress rehearsal.

A: Oops.

Grammar Explanations	Examples
1. Use ***be supposed to*** to talk about different kinds of expectation:	
a. rules and **usual ways** of doing things	■ The groom **is supposed to arrive** at the ceremony early. It's a custom.
b. predictions	■ It**'s not supposed to rain** tomorrow. I heard the weather forecast on the radio.
c. hearsay (what everyone says)	■ The beach **is supposed to be** beautiful in August. Everyone says so.
d. plans or **arrangements**	■ The ceremony **isn't supposed to begin** 'till noon.
2. Use ***be supposed to*** only in the **present simple** or in the **past simple**.	■ The bride **is supposed to wear** white. ■ The ceremony **was supposed to begin** at 12:00. ■ It **wasn't supposed to rain.**
Use the **present simple** to refer to both the **present** and the **future**.	■ I**'m supposed to be** at the wedding rehearsal ***tomorrow***. NOT ~~I will be supposed to be there tomorrow.~~
USAGE NOTE: The **past simple** often suggests that something did not happen.	■ Carl **was supposed to bring** flowers ***but*** he forgot.

IDENTIFY • *Read this article and underline the phrases that express expectations.*

It Wasn't Supposed to Be a Big Wedding

19 July The Stricklands wanted a quiet wedding – that's why they went to the Isle of Skye, an island off the coast of Scotland. The island is quite small so the Stricklands packed their bikes for the ferry trip. The weather was supposed to be lovely and they had asked the Registrar to marry them on a hill overlooking the ocean.

'When we got there, we found a crowd of cyclists admiring the view,' laughed Beth.

When Bill kissed his bride, the cyclists burst into loud applause and rang their bicycle bells. 'We weren't supposed to have fifty wedding guests but we love cycling and we're not sorry,' Bill said.

While packing the next day, Beth left her wedding bouquet at the hotel. Minutes before the ferry was supposed to leave, Bill jumped on his bike, got the flowers and made it back to the ferry on time. 'Cyclists are supposed to stay fast and fit,' he said.

TRUE OR FALSE • *Read the article again. Write T (True) or F (False) for each sentence.*

__F__ 1. The Stricklands planned a big wedding.

_____ 2. The weather forecaster predicted rain.

_____ 3. The Stricklands invited fifty wedding guests.

_____ 4. There was a scheduled time for the ferry to leave.

_____ 5. People generally think that cyclists should be fit.

2 **COMPLETE** • *Read these conversations. Complete them with a form of* **be supposed to** *and the verb in brackets. Give short answers. Choose affirmative or negative.*

1. **A:** Nessie, Gary called while you were out.

   B: ____Am____ I ____supposed to call____ him back?
   a. (call)

   A: ____No, you aren't____. He'll call you this afternoon.
   b.

2. **A:** The bridal shop rang, too. They've delivered your wedding dress to your office.

   ________ they ________________ that?
   a. (do)

   B: ________________! That's why I stayed at home today. They
   b.

   ________________ it here.
   c. (deliver)

3. **A:** Come on, hurry up! The rehearsal ________________ in a few minutes.
   a. (start)

   B: We're the bridesmaids. Where ________ we ________________?
   b. (stand)

4. **A:** Gary! You ______________ here!
a. (be)

B: Why not?

A: You ______________ Nessie until she gets to the church. It's bad luck.
b. (see)

5. **A:** Sophie, could I borrow your handkerchief, please? I ______________ something old, something new, something borrowed and something blue. I haven't got anything borrowed.
a. (wear)

B: It ______________ today. Maybe I should lend you my umbrella instead.
b. (rain)

6. **A:** I hear Gary and Nessie are going to Egypt for their honeymoon.

B: Oh, that ______________ a really beautiful place.
a. (be)

EDIT • *Read Sophie's letter to a friend. Find and correct six mistakes in the use of* **be supposed to**. *The first mistake has already been corrected.*

Dear Katy,

I'm so sorry – I know I ~~am~~ was *supposed to let you know about my plans to visit. I've been awfully busy. My friend Nessie is getting married soon and she's asked me to be her chief bridesmaid. She and Gary want a big wedding. They're supposed to have about two hundred guests. I've got a lot of responsibilities. I will be supposed to give Nessie a hen party before the wedding (that's a party where everyone brings presents for the bride). I am also suppose to help her choose the bridesmaids' dresses. The best man's name is Jim. He's going to help Gary get ready. I haven't met him yet but he's supposes to be very nice.*

I'd better say goodbye now. I supposed to be at the rehearsal five minutes ago.

Love,
Sophie

P.S. About my visit—I'm supposing to get some time off in July. Would that be convenient?

Future Possibility: *May, Might, Could*

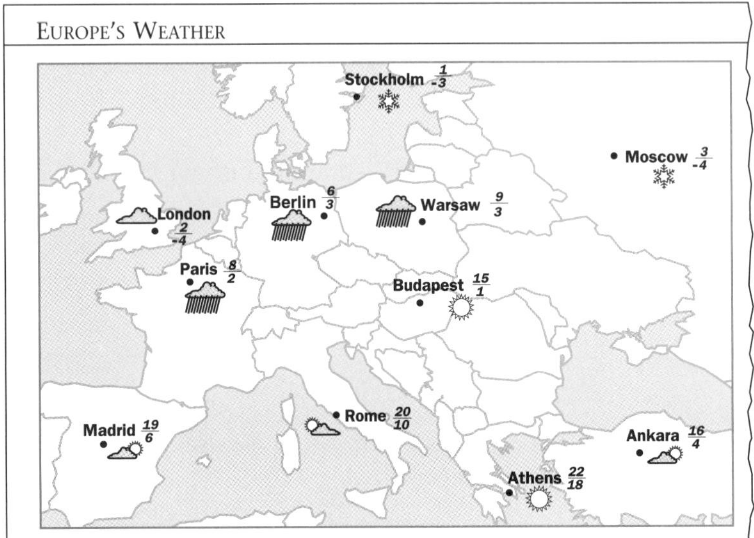

Temperatures in London **may drop** as much as eleven degrees by tomorrow morning. We **might** even **see** some snow flurries later on in the day. Winds **could reach** 60 kph.

CHECK POINT

Circle T (True) or F (False).

T F It's definitely going to snow in London tomorrow.

CHART CHECK 1

Circle T (True) or F (False).

T F ***May***, ***might*** and ***could*** have only one form for all subjects.

STATEMENTS			
SUBJECT	***MAY/MIGHT/COULD****	**BASE FORM OF VERB**	
I/He/She/It/We/You/They	**may (not)** **might (not)** **could**	**get**	cold.

*These words are modals. They do not take *-s* in the third person singular.

CHART CHECK 2

Tick the correct answer.

When do you use ***may***, ***might*** or ***could*** for future possibility?

❒ in questions

❒ in answers

***YES/NO* QUESTIONS**
Are you going to fly to Paris? Are you taking the train?

SHORT ANSWERS	
I/We	**may (not).** **might (not).** **could.**

***WH-* QUESTIONS**
When are you **going** to Paris?
How long will you **be** there?

ANSWERS			
I/We	**may** **might** **could**	**go**	tomorrow.
		be	there a week.

EXPRESS CHECK

Complete this conversation with **might** *or* **might not**.

A: Are you going home after this lecture?

B: I ______________. It's possible. Why?

A: I ______________ call you about the assignment. I don't understand it.

B: Maybe you should call Jean instead. I ______________ understand it either.

Grammar Explanations	Examples
1. Use ***may***, ***might*** and ***could*** to talk about future possibility.	■ It **may be** windy later. ■ It **might get** cold. ■ It **could rain** tomorrow.
▶ **BE CAREFUL!** Notice the difference between ***may be*** and ***maybe***. Both express possibility.	
May be is a modal + verb. It is always two words.	■ He **may be** late today.
Maybe is not a modal. It is an adverb. It is always one word and it comes at the beginning of the sentence.	■ **Maybe** he'll take the train. NOT ~~He'll maybe take the train.~~

Grammar Explanations	Examples
2. Use ***may not*** and ***might not*** to express the possibility that something will not happen.	■ There are a lot of clouds but it **might not rain**.
▶ **BE CAREFUL!** We don't usually contract ***might not*** and we never contract ***may not***.	■ You **may not** need a coat. NOT ~~You mayn't need a coat.~~

Grammar Explanations	Examples
3. **Questions about possibility** are not usually formed with *may, might* or *could.* Instead, they are formed with the future (*will, be going to,* the present continuous) or phrases such as *Do you think . . . ?* or *Is it possible that . . . ?* It's the **answers to these questions** that often have ***may***, ***might*** or ***could***.	**A:** When ***will*** it ***start*** snowing? **B:** It **might start** around lunchtime. **A:** ***Are*** you ***going to drive*** to work? **B:** I **might take** the bus instead. **A:** When ***are*** you ***leaving***? **B:** I **may leave** in about an hour or so.
In short answers to *yes/no* questions, use ***may***, ***might*** or ***could*** alone.	**A:** Will your office close early for Christmas? **B:** It **might**.
USAGE NOTE: If a form of ***be*** is the main verb, it is common to include ***be*** in the short answer.	**A:** ***Is*** our train going to be late? **B:** It **might *be***.

IDENTIFY • *Alice is a university student who works part time; Bill is her boyfriend. Read their conversation. Underline the words that express future possibility or impossibility.*

Alice: I've just heard that it may snow today. Are you going to drive to work?

Bill: No. I'll take the 7:30 train instead.

Alice: I'll take the train with you. I've got some work to do in the library.

Bill: Great. Why don't you miss your afternoon class and have lunch with me, too?

Alice: Oh, I couldn't do that. But let's meet at the station at 6:00 and go home together, OK?

Bill: I might have to work until 8:00 tonight. I'll call you and let you know.

ANSWER • *What will Alice and Bill do together? Tick the appropriate box for each activity.*

	Certain	Possible	Impossible
1. Take the train at 7:30 a.m.	❒	❒	❒
2. Have lunch.	❒	❒	❒
3. Meet at the station at 6:00 p.m.	❒	❒	❒

2

COMPLETE • *Alice is graduating from university with a degree in Early Childhood Education. Complete this paragraph from her diary. Choose the appropriate words in brackets.*

I ___'m going to___ (1. might not / 'm going to) graduate in June but I still haven't got any plans. Some day-care centres employ students before they graduate so I ________ (2. could / couldn't) apply for a job now. Or I ________ (3. might / might not) apply to do a master's degree. I'm just not sure though – these past two years have been hard and I ________ (4. may / may not) be ready to study for two more.

At least I am sure about my career: I ________ (5. 'm going to / might) work with children. That's certain. I've made an appointment to discuss my plans with my tutor, Mrs Humphrey, tomorrow. I ________ (6. maybe / may) talk it over with her. She ________ (7. won't / might) have an idea about what to do.

DESCRIBE • *Look at Alice's timetable for Monday. She's put a question mark (?) next to each item she isn't sure about. Write sentences about Alice's plans for Monday. Use* **may** *or* **might** *for things that are possible and* **be going to** *for things that are certain.*

MONDAY

call Bill at 9:00	go to work at 1:00
buy some stationery ?	go shopping after work ?
go to meeting with Mrs Humphrey at 11:00	take 7:00 train ?
have coffee with Sue after lectures ?	pick up pizza

1. Alice is going to call Bill at 9:00.
2. She may buy some stationery.
3. ______________________________
4. ______________________________
5. ______________________________
6. ______________________________
7. ______________________________
8. ______________________________

EDIT • *Read this student's report about El Niño. Find and correct eight mistakes in expressing future possibility. The first mistake has already been corrected.*

Every few years, the ocean near Peru becomes warmer. Called El Niño, this variation in temperature ~~maybe~~ may cause weather changes all over the world. The west coasts of North and South America might to have heavy rains. On the other side of the Pacific, New Guinea might becomes very dry. Northern areas could have warmer, wetter winters and southern areas could become much colder. These weather changes affect plants and animals. Some fish mayn't survive in warmer waters. Droughts could causing crops to die and food may get very expensive. El Niño may happen every two years or it could not come for seven years. Will El Niños get worse in the future? They could be. Pollution holds heat in the air and it will increase the effects of El Niño but no one is sure yet.

Deduction: *May, Might, Could, Must, Have (got) to, Can't*

Gina Lemont
Hmm. You must be Gina Lemont.
Right again! This man has got to be a genius!

CHECK POINT

Tick the correct answer.

The famous detective, Sherlock Holmes, is

❒ guessing.

❒ talking about an obligation.

CHART CHECK 1

Circle T (True) or F (False).

T F The third person singular modal does not end in *-s*.

STATEMENTS			
Subject	**Modal**	**Base Form of Verb**	
I/He/She/It/We/You/They	may (not) might (not) could (not) must can't	be	right.
		work	there.

AFFIRMATIVE STATEMENTS: *HAVE (GOT) TO*			
Subject	***Have (got) to***	**Base Form**	
I/We/You/They	have (got) to	be	right.
He/She/It	has (got) to	work	there.

CHART CHECK 2

Circle T (True) or F (False).

T F All modals of deduction are used in questions.

YES/NO QUESTIONS			
Could	**Subject**	**Base Form**	
Could	he	work	there?

NOTE: For contractions with *could not* and *cannot*, see Appendix 24 on page 346.

SHORT ANSWERS	
Subject	**Modal/ *Have (got) to***
He	must. may (not). might (not). could(n't). can't. has (got) to.

EXPRESS CHECK

Circle the correct words to complete this conversation.

A: I heard a sound coming from the basement. What could / must it be?

B: I'm not sure. It can / can't be the dog. The dog's upstairs. It can / might be the cat.

Grammar Explanations	Examples
1. We often make **deductions** or 'best guesses', based on information we have about a present situation. The modal that we choose depends on how certain we are about our deduction.	100% certain AFFIRMATIVE: **must**, **have (got) to**, **may**, **might, could** NEGATIVE: **can't, couldn't**, **may not**, **might not** 0% certain
2. When you are almost 100 per cent certain that something is **possible**, use ***must***, ***have to*** or ***have got to***. **USAGE NOTE:** We use ***have got to*** in informal speech and writing and we usually contract it. When you are less certain, use ***may***, ***might*** or ***could***.	Holmes is a brilliant detective. DEDUCTION ■ He **must solve** a lot of crimes. ■ He**'s got to be** a genius! Watson knows a lot about medicine. DEDUCTION ■ He **might be** a doctor.
3. When you are almost 100 per cent certain that something is **impossible**, use ***can't*** or ***couldn't***. Use ***may not*** or ***might not*** when you are less certain. ► **BE CAREFUL!** *Have to* and *have got to* are not used to make negative deductions.	■ He **can't be** a doctor! He's only sixteen! ■ He **may not know** about the plan. His boss doesn't tell him everything. ■ It **can't be** true! NOT ~~It doesn't have to be true~~!
4. Use ***could*** in **questions**. **USAGE NOTE:** We rarely use ***might*** and we never use ***may*** in questions about possibility.	■ Someone's coming. Who **could** it be? ■ **Could** she have gone home? RARE: **Might** he be at home? NOT ~~May he be at home~~?
5. In **short answers**, use a modal alone or with a form of ***do***. Use ***be*** in short answers to questions that include a form of ***be***.	**A:** *Could* Ann know Marie? **B:** She **must do**. They're neighbours. **A:** *Is* Ron still with National Bank? **B:** I'm not sure. He **might not *be***.

MATCH* • *Each fact goes with a deduction. Match each fact with the correct deduction.

	Fact		Deduction
f	1. Her last name is Lemont. She	a.	can't be at home.
______	2. He's only thirteen. He	b.	must be married.
______	3. Her eyes are red. She	c.	has to be older than twenty.
______	4. She's wearing a wedding ring. She	d.	can't be married.
______	5. His initials are M.B. He	e.	might be tired.
______	6. The house is completely dark. They	f.	may be French.
______	7. She's got grey hair. She	g.	could be Marc Brunner.

CHOOSE* • *Look at the picture and circle the correct words to complete this conversation.

WATSON: Look! What's going on over there?

HOLMES: I don't know. It (could) / couldn't (1.) be some kind of delivery.

WATSON: At this hour? It can't / must (2.) be almost midnight! Nothing's open now.

HOLMES: Hmm. 27 Carlisle Street. That can't / 's got to (3.) be the bank.

WATSON: It *is* the bank.

HOLMES: Can you see what that man is taking out of the carriage?

WATSON: It looks like a box. What do you suppose is in it?

HOLMES: I don't know but it seems heavy. It could / might not (4.) contain gold.

WATSON: Look at that man in front of the bank. Could / Must (5.) he be the bank manager?

HOLMES: He might / might be (6.).

WATSON: But why are they making a delivery at this time? It can / can't (7.) be normal.

HOLMES: The manager might not / must (8.) want people to know about it. He couldn't / may (9.) be worried about robbers.

COMPLETE • *Read Sherlock Holmes's conversation with a murder suspect. Complete it with the words in brackets and a modal that shows the degree of certainty. (There may be more than one correct answer.)*

HOLMES: You must be Gina Lemont.
1. Almost certain (You / be / Gina Lemont)

LEMONT: ____________________. Who wants to know?
2. Possible (I / be)

HOLMES: Sherlock Holmes. I can hear something in the next room.

LEMONT: ____________________. I'm alone.
3. Possible (It / be / the cat)

HOLMES: Alone? ____________________. There are two plates on the table. ____________________ that you are mistaken?
4. Almost certain (You / eat a lot)
5. Possible (it / be)

LEMONT: No, ____________________. I was expecting someone but he didn't turn up.
6. Impossible (it / be)

HOLMES: Does your cat smoke? I can smell pipe tobacco.

LEMONT: ____________________
7. Almost certain (It / come / from your own pipe)
____
8. Impossible (There / be / any other explanation)

HOLMES: Oh, ____________________. May we have a look at this 'cat'?
9. Possible (there / be)

EDIT • *Read this student's summary of a mystery novel. Find and correct six mistakes in expressing deductions. The first mistake has already been corrected.*

The main character, Molly Smith, is a university professor. She is trying to find her dead grandparents' first home in Scotland. It may ~~being~~ be in a nearby town. The villagers there seem scared. They could be have a secret or they must just hate strangers. Molly has some old letters that might lead her to the place. They are in Gaelic but one of her students mights translate them for her. They got to be important because the author mentions them at the beginning of the novel. The letter must contain family secrets. Who is the bad guy? It couldn't be the student because he wants to help. It might to be the newspaper editor in the town.

Expressing Regret about the Past

I could have become a doctor.

My parents might have encouraged me more.

I ought to have applied to college.

I shouldn't have missed that opportunity.

I could have been rich and famous.

CHECK POINT

Tick the correct answer.

The man

❐ is planning his future.

❐ regrets things in his past.

CHART CHECK 1

Circle T (True) or F (False).

T F You can add ***not*** to all modals that express past regret.

STATEMENTS			
Subject	**Modal**	***Have***	**Past Participle**
I/He/She/We/You/They	should (not) (shouldn't) ought (not) to (oughtn't to) could might	have	applied.

CHART CHECK 2

Circle T (True) or F (False).

T F In questions and short answers, we usually only use ***should have***.

YES/NO QUESTIONS			
Should	**Subject**	***Have***	**Past Participle**
Should	he	have	applied?

SHORT ANSWERS	
Affirmative	**Negative**
Yes, he should have.	No, he shouldn't have.

WH- QUESTIONS				
***Wh-* Word**	***Should***	**Subject**	***Have***	**Past Participle**
When	should	he	have	applied?

CHART CHECK 3

Tick the correct answer.

Which words are NOT usually contracted?

❐ ***should have***

❐ ***could have***

❐ ***ought to have***

CONTRACTIONS		
should have	=	**should've**
could have	=	**could've**
might have	=	**might've**
should not have	=	**shouldn't have**

EXPRESS CHECK

Complete this conversation.

A: Should I ______________ called you yesterday?

B: Yes, you ______________. I waited all day for your call.

Grammar Explanations	Examples
1. Use ***should have***, ***ought to have***, ***could have*** and ***might have*** to talk about things that were advisable in the past but didn't happen. These modals often express regret or blame.	■ I **should've applied** to go to university. *(I didn't apply and I'm sorry.)* ■ I **ought to have taken** that job. *(I didn't take the job. That was a mistake.)* ■ She **could've gone** to a better university. *(She didn't go to a good university. Now she regrets her choice.)* ■ You **might've told** me. *(You didn't tell me. That was wrong.)*
2. ***Should not have*** and ***ought not to have*** are the only forms used in negative statements. ***Should not have*** is more common. ***Should have*** is the most common form used in questions.	■ He **shouldn't have missed** the exam. ■ He **ought not to have missed** the exam. ■ **Should he have phoned** the lecturer?

TRUE OR FALSE* • *Read each numbered sentence. Write T (True) or F (False) for the statement that follows.

1. I shouldn't have called him.
   ___T___ I called him.
2. I should have told them what I thought.
   ______ I didn't tell them. Now I'm sorry.
3. He might have warned us about it.
   ______ He knew but he didn't tell us.
4. Felicia could have been a doctor.
   ______ Felicia is a doctor.
5. I ought to have practised more.
   ______ I didn't practise enough.
6. They shouldn't have lent him their car.
   ______ They lent him their car.

COMPLETE* • *Read this extract from a magazine article. Complete it with the correct form of the words in brackets and a short answer. Choose between affirmative and negative.

Regrets . . .

It's not unusual to feel regret about things in the past that you think you ___should have done___ **1.** (should / do) and did not do – or the opposite, about things you did do and feel you ______________ **2.** (should / do). In fact, we learn by thinking about past mistakes. For example, a student who fails a test learns that he or she ______________ **3.** (should / study) more and can improve on the next test. Often, however, people spend too much time thinking about what they ______________ **4.** (could / do) differently. Many regrets are simply not based in fact. A mother regrets missing a football game in which her son's leg was injured. 'I ______________ **5.** (ought to / go),' she keeps telling herself. 'I ______________ **6.** (should / stay) home. I ______________ **7.** (could / prevent) the injury. The coach ______________ at least ______________ **8.** (might / call) me as soon as it happened.' Did she *really* have the power to prevent her son's injury? ______________ the coach ______________ **9.** (Should / contact) her *before* looking at the injury? No, of course, he ______________ **10.** There is an Italian proverb that says, 'When the ship has sunk, everyone knows how they ______________ **11.** (could / save) it.' It's easy to be wise about the past; the real challenge is to solve the problems you face at the moment.

REWRITE • *Read Lisa's regrets. Rewrite them using the modals in brackets and choose between affirmative and negative.*

1. I didn't go to university. Now I'm unhappy with my job.
   (should) I should have gone to university.
2. I feel sick. I ate all the chocolate.
   (should) ______________________________
3. Christina didn't come round. She didn't even call.
   (might) ______________________________
4. I didn't have enough money to buy the shirt. Why didn't Ed offer to lend me some?
   (could) ______________________________
5. I jogged five miles yesterday and now I'm exhausted.
   (should) ______________________________
6. The supermarket charged me for the plastic bags. They used to be free.
   (should) ______________________________
7. I didn't invite Cynthia to the party. Now she's angry with me.
   (ought to) ______________________________
8. Yesterday was my birthday and my brother didn't send me a card. I'm hurt.
   (might) ______________________________

EDIT • *Read this diary entry. Find and correct six mistakes in the use of modals. The first mistake has already been corrected.*

15 December

About a week ago, Jennifer was late for work again and Doug, our boss, told me he wanted to get rid of her. I was really upset. Of course, Jennifer shouldn't ~~had~~ have been late so often but he might has talked to her about the problem before he decided to let her go. Then he told me to make her job difficult for her so that she would resign. I just pretended I hadn't heard him. What a mistake! I ought have confronted him right away. Or I could at least have warned Jennifer. Anyway, Jennifer is still here but now I'm worried about my own job. Should I told Doug's boss? I wonder. Maybe I should handle things differently last week. The company should never has employed this man.

Deduction in the Past

EASTER ISLAND: **Could** visitors from another planet **have built** these giant statues?

CHECK POINT

Check the correct answer.

The question under the photograph asks

❒ if it was possible that something happened.

❒ if people had permission to do something.

CHART CHECK 1

Circle T (True) or F (False).

T F The form of the modal does not change for different subjects.

STATEMENTS				
SUBJECT	**MODAL/ HAD TO**	**HAVE**	**PAST PARTICIPLE**	
I/He/She/We/You/They	may (not) might (not) can't could (not) must had to	have	seen	the statues.

CHART CHECK 2

Tick the correct answer.

Which modal can be used in both questions and short answers for deductions about the past?

❒ *can*

❒ *could*

❒ *might*

YES/NO QUESTIONS: *COULD*			
COULD	**SUBJECT**	**HAVE**	**PAST PARTICIPLE**
Could	he	have	seen aliens?

SHORT ANSWERS		
SUBJECT	**MODAL/ HAD TO**	**HAVE**
He	may (not) might (not) can't could (not) must had to	have.

EXPRESS CHECK

Circle the correct words to complete these sentences.

Could they carved / have carved the statues? They might / might have.

Grammar Explanations	Examples
1. We often **make deductions** or 'best guesses', about past situations based on the facts that we have. The modal that we choose depends on how certain we are about our deductions.	100% certain ↑ AFFIRMATIVE: **must have**, **had to have**, **may have**, **might have**, **could have** NEGATIVE: **can't have**, **couldn't have**, **may not have**, **might not have** ↓ 0% certain
2. When you are almost 100 per cent certain that something was **possible**, use ***must have*** or ***had to have***. When you are less certain, use ***may have***, ***might have*** or ***could have***.	The statues are very big. DEDUCTION ■ They **must have been** hard to move. The islanders were able to carve the stone. DEDUCTION ■ The stone **may have been** quite soft.
3. When you are almost 100 per cent certain that something was **impossible**, use ***can't have*** or ***couldn't have***. Use ***may not have*** or ***might not have*** when you are less certain. ► **BE CAREFUL!** We do not usually use ***had to have*** for negative deductions.	■ The islanders **couldn't have moved** the statues! They were too heavy. ■ The islanders **might not have moved** the statues over land. They could have taken them by boat.
4. Use ***could have*** in **questions about possibility** or use questions without modals.	■ **Could** the islanders **have moved** the statues? OR ■ Do you think they moved the statues?
5. Use ***been*** in **short answers** to questions that include a form of ***be***. Use only the **modal +** ***have*** in short answers to questions with other verbs.	**A:** **Could** von Däniken **have** ***been*** wrong? OR ***Was*** he wrong? **B:** He certainly **could have** ***been***. **A:** Did the islanders ***work*** on their own? **B:** They **could have**.

MATCH • *Each fact goes with a deduction. Match each fact with the correct deduction about author Erich von Däniken.*

Fact

__e__ 1. The original title of *Chariots of the Gods?* was *Erinnerungen an die Zukunft*.

_____ 2. Von Däniken visited every place he described in his book.

_____ 3. In 1973, he wrote *In Search of Ancient Gods*.

_____ 4. He didn't have a degree in archaeology.

_____ 5. Von Däniken's books sold millions of copies.

_____ 6. As soon as von Däniken published his books, scientists attacked him.

Deduction

a. He must have travelled a lot.

b. They can't have believed his theories.

c. He could have learnt about the subject on his own.

d. He must have made a lot of money.

e. He must have written it in German.

f. He might have written other books, too.

2

ANSWER • *Some archaeology students are asking questions in class. Use the modals in brackets to write short answers.*

1. **A:** Do you think the people on Easter Island built the giant statues themselves?

   B: __They could have__ (could). They had the knowledge and the tools.

2. **A:** Were many people impressed by von Däniken's theories?

   B: ______________________ (must). His books were read all over the world.

3. **A:** Von Däniken says that many ancient artifacts show pictures of astronauts. Could these pictures have illustrated anything closer to Earth?

   B: ______________________ (may). It's possible that the pictures show people dressed in local costumes.

4. **A:** Was von Däniken upset by all the criticism he received?

   B: ______________________ (might not). After all, it helped to sell his books.

5. **A:** Do you think von Däniken helped increase general interest in archaeology?

   B: ______________________ (must). Just look at the size of this class!

COMPLETE • *Read part of a review of Erich von Däniken's book* Chariots of the Gods? *Complete it with the verbs in brackets.*

Who could have made (1. could / make) the Easter Island statues? According to Erich von Däniken, our ancestors ______ (2. could not / build) these structures on their own because their cultures were too primitive. According to him, they ______ (3. had to / get) help from aliens. When he wrote his popular book, von Däniken ______ (4. can't / know) about the Easter Island experiments that proved that the ancient islanders ______ (5 could / carve) and ______ (6 transport) these statues without any help from alien visitors. Not only that, the island's population ______ (7. might / be) much larger than von Däniken believes. One scientist speculates that as many as 20,000 people ______ (8. may / live) on Easter Island – enough people to have done the job. Visitors from another planet? A more logical answer is to think that our ancestors ______ (9. must / have) great skill, intelligence and strength to create these wonderful things.

EDIT • *Read part of a student's essay. Find and correct six mistakes in the use of modals for deductions about the past. The first mistake has already been corrected.*

In 1927, Toribio Mexta Xesspe of Peru must ~~be~~ have been very surprised to see lines in the shapes of huge animals on the ground below his aeroplane. Created by the ancient Nazca culture, these forms are too big to recognise from the ground. However, from about 200m in the air, the giant forms take shape. Without aeroplanes, how could an ancient culture had made them? What purpose could they have had? Author Erich von Däniken believes that the drawings might have mark a landing strip for the spacecraft of astronauts from another planet. Archaeologists, however, now believe that the ancient Nazcan civilisation might develop flight. They could built hot-air balloons and design the pictures from the air.

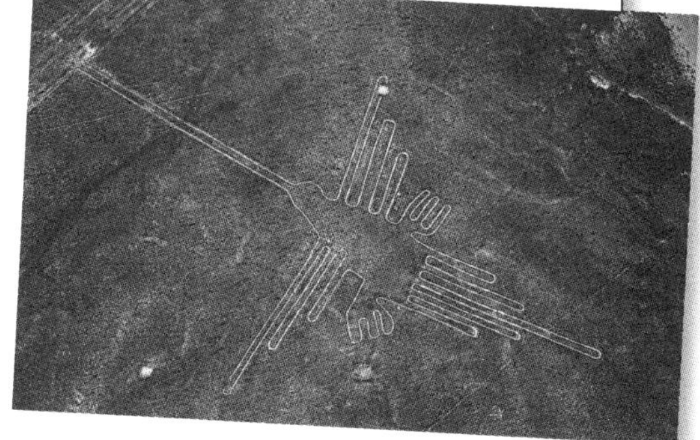

SECTION ONE

Circle the letter of the correct answer to complete each sentence.

EXAMPLE:
Jennifer never ________ coffee. **A (B) C D**
(A) drink (C) is drinking
(B) drinks (D) was drinking

1. —Wasn't that Malcolm in class? **A B C D**
—It ________. Malcolm left last week.
(A) couldn't (C) couldn't have been
(B) could have been (D) couldn't have

2. Frank watches all the United games. He ________ to be one of their biggest fans. **A B C D**
(A) must (C) couldn't
(B) has got (D) should have

3. Children under five years old ________ swim without an adult. **A B C D**
(A) don't have to (C) have to
(B) must not (D) are supposed to

4. Where ________ we supposed to go for the test tomorrow? **A B C D**
(A) do (C) will
(B) are (D) should

5. Bring your umbrella. It ________ later. **A B C D**
(A) might rain (C) couldn't rain
(B) rains (D) might have rained

6. —Will your plane be late this afternoon? **A B C D**
—It ________. The airport was closed this morning.
(A) couldn't be (C) maybe
(B) may be (D) will

7. You ________ told Mark. You knew it was a secret. **A B C D**
(A) should have (C) couldn't have
(B) might have (D) shouldn't have

8. They built this temple 3,000 years ago. This must ________ a great civilization. **A B C D**
(A) has been (C) was
(B) have been (D) not have been

9. John ________ to call Myra yesterday but he forgot. **A B C D**
(A) supposed (C) supposes
(B) is supposed (D) was supposed

10. 'Could Amy have been at home yesterday?' 'She ________. I really don't know.' **A B C D**
(A) could have been (C) had to have been
(B) might be (D) couldn't have

11. Chris ________ to clean up his room. It's a mess. **A B C D**
(A) have got (C) must
(B) has got (D) got

12. I failed the test. I ________ studied harder. **A B C D**
(A) should have (C) should
(B) must have (D) may

13. Lisa was in Oxford recently. She might ________ me to say hello! **A B C D**
(A) call (C) have called
(B) has called (D) be calling

SECTION TWO

Each sentence has four underlined words or phrases. The four underlined parts of the sentence are marked A, B, C and D. Circle the letter of the one underlined word or phrase that is NOT CORRECT.

EXAMPLE:
Mike usually (A) drives (B) to school but today (C) he walks (D). **A B C (D)**

14. Tom didn't (A) wave (B) to me so he must have known (C) I was (D) here. **A B C D**

15. We'd better (A) hurry (B) or the train might (C) leaves (D) without us. **A B C D**

16. His English is (A) excellent so he had to (B) has (C) studied (D) hard. **A B C D**

17. We ought to have (A) look (B) at more cars before (C) we bought (D) ours. **A B C D**

18. You got (A) get (B) dressed because (C) Sasha may be (D) here soon. **A B C D**

19. You have to (A) fasten your seat belt now or you couldn't (C) drive (D). It's the law. **A B C D**

20. You don't have to (A) drive (B) faster than (C) 40 kph or you might (D) get a ticket. **A B C D**

21. Hardy and Co must (A) has (B) gone (C) out of business recently (D). **A B C D**

22. It must (A) rain (B) tonight so I'd better (C) stay (D) home. **A B C D**

23. Jason will be (A) supposed (B) to be there tomorrow (C) but he can't (D) attend. **A B C D**

24. It must (A) be (B) almost 11:00 so we really has to (C) leave (D) now. **A B C D**

25. You should had (A) seen (B) that film with us because it may not (C) be (D) here long. **A B C D**

Adjectives and Adverbs

CHECK POINT

Tick the correct answer.

The owner thinks the flat is:

❒ perfect

❒ warm and cosy

CHART CHECK

Circle T (True) or F (False).

T F Adverbs often come before nouns.

T F Adjectives often come after action verbs.

T F Adverbs often end in *-ly*.

ADJECTIVES
They are **quiet** tenants.
There's a **fast** lift.
The flat sounds **nice**.
It's absolutely **perfect**.
The flat felt **warm**.

ADVERBS
They work **quietly**.
It moves **very fast**.
She described it **nicely**.
It's **absolutely** perfect.
The owner greeted the tenants **warmly**.

EXPRESS CHECK

Complete these sentences with the correct form of **slow**.

A: There's a ________________ lift. It moves very ________________.

B: It's not ________________. It just seems ________________.

Grammar Explanations	Examples
1. Use **adjectives** to describe nouns or pronouns (for people, places and things).	■ The **houses** (noun) are ***beautiful*** (adjective). **They** (pron.) are ***new*** (adjective).
Adjectives usually come immediately before the noun they describe.	■ This is a ***small*** (adjective) **flat** (noun).
Adjectives can also come after stative verbs such as *be, look, sound* or *seem.*	■ This flat **seems** (verb) ***small*** (adjective).
2. Use **adverbs** to describe verbs, adjectives and other adverbs.	■ They **furnished** (verb) it ***nicely*** (adverb).
Adverbs that describe adjectives and other adverbs usually come immediately before the word they describe.	■ It's an ***extremely*** (adverb) **nice** (adjective) house. ■ They found it ***very*** (adverb) **quickly** (adverb).
3. Use **adverbs of manner** to describe action verbs. These adverbs often answer *How?* questions. They come after the verb they describe.	■ It'**ll sell** ***quickly***. (Quickly *describes how fast it will sell.*)
▶ **Be careful!** Do not put an adverb of manner between the verb and its direct object.	■ She'**ll rent** (verb) this flat (direct object) ***quickly***. Not ~~She'll rent quickly this flat~~.
4. **Adverbs of manner** are often formed by adding *-ly* to adjectives.	■ We need a **quick** (adjective) decision. ■ You should decide **quickly** (adverb).
▶ **Be careful!** Some adjectives also end in *-ly*, for example, *silly, friendly, lovely* and *lonely.*	■ It's a **lovely** (adjective) flat.
5. Some **common adverbs of manner** do not end in *-ly.*	
a. The adverb form of *good* is ***well***.	■ She's a **good** (adjective) writer. She writes **well** (adverb).
b. Some adverbs have the same form as their related adjectives, for example, ***early***, ***fast***, ***wrong***, ***late*** and ***hard***.	Adjective: Bob was **late**. / She's a **hard** worker. Adverb: Bob came **late**. / She works **hard**.
▶ **Be careful!** ***Lately*** is not the adverb form of *late. Lately* means 'recently'. ***Hardly*** is not the adverb form of *hard. Hardly* means 'almost not'.	■ She hasn't met any new people ***lately***. ■ There's ***hardly*** enough time to prepare for her classes. Her part-time job takes up most of her time.

Check it out!

For a discussion of adverbs of frequency, see Unit 2, page 7.

IDENTIFY • *Read this notice about a flat for rent. Underline the adjectives and circle the adverbs. Then draw an arrow from the adjective or adverb to the word it is describing.*

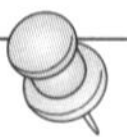

FOR RENT

Students! Are you looking for a special place to live? Come to 140 Grant Street, Flat 4B. This flat is absolutely perfect for two serious students who are looking for a quiet neighbourhood, just 15 minutes from campus. This lovely flat is in a new building.

It is a short walk to the bus stop. The bus goes directly into town. At night the bus hardly makes any stops at all. You can walk safely through the wonderful parks on your way home. The rent is very affordable.

Call us on 020 551 6116.

Don't delay! This flat will go fast.

2

COMPLETE • *Many people went to see the flat described in the advert above. Complete their comments about the flat with the correct form of the words in brackets.*

1. I'm very interested. I think the flat is ___extremely nice___. (extreme / nice)
2. I was expecting much bigger rooms. I was ______________. (terrible / disappointed)
3. I thought the flat would be hard to find but it was ______________. (surprising / easy)
4. I was happy to hear that the park is ______________. (extreme / safe)
5. It's a great place and the price is reasonable. It will go ______________. (incredible / fast)
6. The owner seems nice but she talks ______________. (awful / slow)
7. The advert said it was quiet but I heard the neighbours ______________. (very / clear)
8. I heard them, too. I thought their voices were ______________. (unusual / loud)
9. All in all, it's an ______________ place. (exceptional / pleasant)

3 **CHOOSE** • *Complete Maggie's letter with the correct word in brackets.*

Dear Mum and Dad,

Life in London is very **exciting** (1. exciting / excitingly). Paul and I weren't sure we'd like such a ________ (2. large / largely) city but it's so interesting! Yesterday we saw a street musician. He played the violin so ________ (3. beautiful / beautifully) we couldn't believe he wasn't in a big concert hall. You'd be surprised to see us. We walk ________ (4. happy / happily) down the ________ (5. busy / busily) streets and the noise doesn't bother us at all! I'm sending a photo of our flat. It looks ________ (6. nice / nicely), doesn't it? It's so ________ (7. quiet / quietly) we can ________ (8. hard / hardly) believe it's in London. Our next-door neighbour is very ________ (9. nice / nicely). At first she seemed ________ (10. shy / shyly) but now we're ________ (11. good / well) friends.

We hope you're both well. Please give our love to everyone and write soon.

Love,

Maggie

4 **EDIT** • *Read this student's diary entry. Find and correct seven mistakes in the use of adjectives and adverbs. The first mistake has already been corrected.*

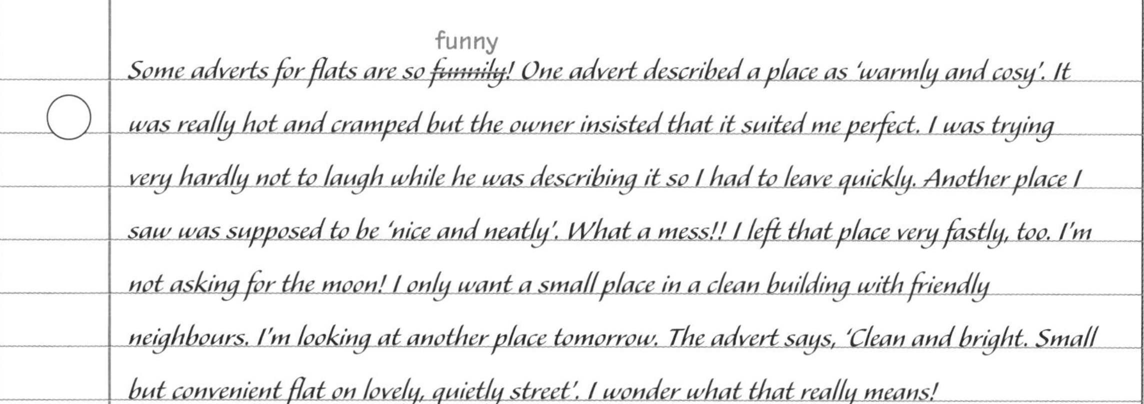

Some adverts for flats are so ~~funnily~~ funny! One advert described a place as 'warmly and cosy'. It was really hot and cramped but the owner insisted that it suited me perfect. I was trying very hardly not to laugh while he was describing it so I had to leave quickly. Another place I saw was supposed to be 'nice and neatly'. What a mess!! I left that place very fastly, too. I'm not asking for the moon! I only want a small place in a clean building with friendly neighbours. I'm looking at another place tomorrow. The advert says, 'Clean and bright. Small but convenient flat on lovely, quietly street'. I wonder what that really means!

Participles used as Adjectives

NEW FRIENDS
New to the Area
Screen Name: newgal@XYZ.com
Age & Sex: 20 year old Female
Location: Cambridge
Looking for: Friends
Tired of doing things alone? Me too! 20-year-old university student, new to the area, is interested in meeting interesting people for friendship and fun.
Send me email!
Send me an online greeting!
Send this to a friend!
print/save

CHECK POINT

Circle T (True) or F (False).

T F The writer of the advert says that she is an interesting person.

CHART CHECK

Circle T (True) or F (False).

T F There are two types of participles used as adjectives.

PARTICIPLES USED AS ADJECTIVES

-ing Adjectives	*-ed* Adjectives
He is **boring**. They had a **boring** date.	She is **bored**. They had a **bored** look on their faces.
She is **amusing**. They had an **amusing** date.	He is **amused**. They had an **amused** look on their faces.
The film was **frightening**. They saw a **frightening** film.	They were **frightened**. They had a **frightened** look on their faces.
The job is **tiring**. She's got a **tiring** job.	She's **tired**. She's got a **tired** look on her face.
The weekend was **relaxing**. He had a **relaxing** weekend.	He felt **relaxed**. He had a **relaxed** manner.

EXPRESS CHECK

Complete the chart.

-ING ADJECTIVES	-ED ADJECTIVES
exciting	
	interested
frightening	
	amused
tiring	

Grammar Explanations	Examples
1. Participles used as adjectives are adjectives that end with *-ing* or *-ed*. They usually describe feelings or reactions. The two forms have different meanings.	**A:** The last *Star Wars* film was **amazing**! **B:** I know. I was **amazed** by the special effects.
2. Participles used as adjectives that end in *-ing* describe someone or something that **causes** a feeling or reaction.	■ That actor is always **amusing**. *(He causes amusement.)* ■ These directions are **confusing**. *(They cause confusion.)*
3. Participles used as adjectives that end in *-ed* describe someone who **experiences** a feeling or reaction.	■ We were **amused** by that actor. *(We felt amusement.)* ■ I'm really **confused** by these directions. *(I feel confusion.)*
4. To the right are some common pairs of **participles used as adjectives.**	**annoying** — **annoyed** **boring** — **bored** **depressing** — **depressed** **embarrassing** — **embarrassed** **exciting** — **excited** **frightening** — **frightened** **relaxing** — **relaxed** **shocking** — **shocked** **surprising** — **surprised**

Check it out!

For a list of common participles used as adjectives, see Appendix 11 on page 339.

IDENTIFY • *Read this article. Underline all the* **-ed** *participles used as adjectives. Circle all the* **-ing** *participial adjectives.*

14 • SECTION 4 • LIFESTYLES

Not Personal Enough?

In some countries, people who are interested in meeting others turn for help to personal ads in newspapers and magazines, and online. A surprising number of busy people view these ads as a practical way of increasing their social circle. 'I've tried hard to meet people on my own,' said one satisfied customer. 'I was new to the town and wanted to make friends fast. The personals provided me with a quick way of meeting many interesting people in a short period of time.' Others are not so impressed. 'I think it's kind of depressing when people need to resort to placing ads to make friends,' observed one man. 'A friend of mine tried the ads several times and was really disappointed with the results. It's just not personal enough.'

CHOOSE • *Read this conversation between Martin and Louise about their friend Alice. Circle the correct words to complete the conversation.*

MARTIN: What's the matter with Alice?

LOUISE: Who knows? She's always annoyed / annoying about something. (1.)

MARTIN: I know. I try to understand her but this time I'm really puzzled / puzzling. (2.)

LOUISE: Really? What's so puzzled / puzzling this time? (3.)

MARTIN: I thought she was happy. She met an interested / interesting guy last week. (4.)

LOUISE: That's nice. Was she interested / interesting in him? (5.)

MARTIN: I thought she was. She said they saw a fascinated / fascinating film together. (6.)

LOUISE: Well, maybe she was fascinated / fascinating by the film but disappointed / disappointing with the guy. (7.) (8.)

MARTIN: I don't know. It's hard to tell with Alice. Her moods are always very surprised / surprising. (9.)

LOUISE: I'm not surprised / surprising at all. That's just the way she is. (10.)

COMPLETE • *Read this conversation between Alice and her date, Jake. Complete it with the correct form of the words in brackets. Choose between* **-ed** *and* **-ing** *participles used as adjectives.*

ALICE: That was a very ___interesting___ (**1.** interest) film. What did you think?

JAKE: To be honest, I found it rather ______________ (**2.** bore). I'm not that ______________ (**3.** interest) in science fiction.

ALICE: Really? I find it ______________ (**4.** fascinate). What kind of films *do* you enjoy?

JAKE: Mostly comedies. Have you seen *Home Again*?

ALICE: Yes, but I wasn't ______________ (**5.** amuse) at all. In fact, I thought it was ______________ (**6.** horrify). The story line was ______________ (**7.** confuse) and I couldn't find any humour in the characters' problems. When I left the cinema, I felt kind of ______________ (**8.** depress).

JAKE: I'm ______________ (**9.** amaze) that you felt that way! I thought it was very ______________ (**10.** amuse).

ALICE: Well, I guess it's a matter of taste.

JAKE: Speaking of taste, would you like to get a bite to eat?

ALICE: Thanks, but it's late and I'm ______________ (**11.** exhaust).

EDIT • *Read Alice's diary entry. Find and correct six mistakes in the use of participles used as adjectives. The first mistake has already been corrected.*

Just got home. I'm ~~disappointing~~ disappointed with the evening. At first I thought Jake was an interested guy but tonight I felt somewhat bored with his company. We saw a very entertained film but Jake didn't like it. In fact, it seems like we have completely different tastes in things. After the film, I tried to make conversation but all I really wanted was to go home. So, I told him I was exhausting and didn't want to get home late. If he asks me out again – I'm not interesting. Trying to meet people can be very frustrated.

Adjectives and Adverbs: *As . . . as . . .*

She cycles **as fast as** he does. She controls her bike just **as well**.
But her shoulders aren't **as wide** and her arms aren't **as long as** his.
Why should she ride a bike designed for him?
TRAX – made to fit *you.*

CHECK POINT

Tick the things the boy and girl have in common.

- ❒ cycling speed
- ❒ width of shoulders
- ❒ control of bike
- ❒ length of arms

CHART CHECK

Tick the correct answers.

Which words are always used in comparisons with *as . . . as*?

- ❒ ***not***
- ❒ ***a verb***
- ❒ an adjective or an adverb

ADJECTIVES					
	Verb* (*not*)	***As***	**Adjective**	***As***	
The girl			**fast**		the boy.
She	is		**good**		he is.
Her bike	isn't	**as**	**big**	**as**	his.
The girl's bike			**heavy**		the boy's.

*Stative verbs like *be, look, seem*

ADVERBS					
	Verb* (*not*)	***As***	**Adverb**	***As***	
The girl			**fast**		the boy.
She	cycles		**well**		he does.
Her bike	doesn't cycle	**as**	**smoothly**	**as**	his.
The girl's bike			**consistently**		the boy's.

*Action verbs

EXPRESS CHECK

Complete these sentences with as … as and the words in brackets.

A: My old bike wasn't ____________________ (expensive) my new one. Of course, it didn't perform ____________________ (well) the new one.

B: And it didn't look ____________________ (good) the new one, either.

Grammar Explanations	Examples
1. You can use ***as*** **+ adjective +** ***as*** to compare two people, places or things.	■ Trax bikes are **as expensive as** Gordos. *(The Trax bike costs a lot of money. The Gordo bike costs the same amount of money.)* ■ The Trax bike is**n't as light as** the Gordo, though. *(The two bikes are not the same weight.)*
Use ***as*** **+ adjective +** ***as*** to compare two people, places or things that are equal in some way. Use ***just*** to emphasise the equality.	■ This helmet is **as good as** yours. ■ It's ***just*** **as expensive as** yours, too.
Use ***not as*** **+ adjective +** ***as*** to talk about two people, places or things that are different in some way.	■ The new adverts are **not as effective as** the old ones. ■ They are**n't as funny as** the old ones, either.
2. You can also use ***as*** **+ adverb +** ***as*** to compare two actions.	■ He rides **as fast as** she does. *(They ride equally fast.)* ■ He does**n't** ride **as safely as** she does, though. *(They don't ride the same way. She rides more safely than he does.)*
Use ***as*** **+ adverb +** ***as*** to talk about two actions that are the same or equal. Use ***just*** to emphasise the equality.	■ Kleen brightens **as thoroughly as** Brite. ■ It removes stains ***just*** **as effectively as** Brite.
Use ***not as*** **+ adverb +** ***as*** to talk about two actions that are not the same or equal.	■ Kleen does**n't** clean **as well as** Brite.
3. You do not always have to mention both parts of a comparison. Sometimes the meaning is clear from the context.	■ Trax and Gordo are both great bikes but Trax is**n't as light** (as Gordo). ■ Jake and Christopher both ride fast but Christopher does**n't ride as skilfully** (as Jake).

IDENTIFY • *Read this article on washing powders. Underline all the comparisons with adjectives. Circle the comparisons with adverbs.*

PRODUCT REVIEWS ✦ WASHING POWDERS

So you were riding the trails this weekend and you hit the dirt. Now your clothes look as bad as your bike. Never mind. They'll look as good as new next weekend. We checked out three major brands of powder and we can tell you which ones clean best and which ones don't remove trail stains (as effectively as) others.

Overall, Brite and Kleen aren't as expensive as Trend but they didn't perform as well, either. However, they were almost as good in particular categories. Trend removed both mud and grass stains effectively. Brite removed mud just as effectively as Trend but it didn't remove grass stains as well. Kleen was effective on grass stains but not on mud. Brite cleaned clothes as thoroughly as Kleen but again, Brite and Kleen weren't as good as Trend in this category. On the other hand, Brite came out on top in brightening. Colours washed in Kleen and Trend just didn't look as bright as the ones washed in Brite.

2 **COMPLETE** • *Read these conversations. Complete them with* **(not) as . . . as . . .** *and the correct form of the words in brackets.*

1. **THOMAS:** ___Does___ your new bike ___handle as comfortably as___ (a. handle / comfortable) the old one?

   DIANA: It's great. The handlebars ________ (b. not be / wide) and the brakes ________ (c. not be / hard) to reach. This bike was made for a small person like me.

2. **CHARLIE:** We need a name for this product. It should show that this washing powder ________ (a. clean / effective) the others but ________ (b. not be / unfriendly) to the environment.

   EVA: I like 'GreenKleen'. It ________ (c. sound / exciting) other product names and it ________ the message ________ (d. express / clear) theirs, too.

3. **SAM:** The last group I cycled with ________ (a. be / noisy) a herd of elephants. I prefer to cycle alone but I know it's dangerous.

   JACK: Come cycling with me next weekend. I ________ (b. pedal / quiet) a mouse, I promise.

COMPARE & COMPLETE • *Read the chart comparing several models of bicycle. Complete the sentences with* **(not)** ***as . . . as*** *and the correct form of the words in brackets. Choose between affirmative and negative.*

PRODUCT RATINGS ✦ BICYCLES — KEY: BETTER ● → ◒ → ○ WORSE

MODEL	PRICE	COMFORT	BRAKING SPEED, DRY GROUND	BRAKING SPEED, WET GROUND	GEAR CHANGING EASE	ON-ROAD HANDLING	OFF-ROAD HANDLING
Trax	£999	◒	●	◒	●	◒	●
Huff	£550	●	◒	●	◒	●	◒
Gordo	£225	◒	○	○	◒	◒	○

1. The Gordo _doesn't stop as quickly as_ the Trax and the Huff. (stop / quick)
2. On wet ground, the Huff ______________ the Trax. (stop / slow)
3. The Gordo ______________ the Trax and the Huff. (be / expensive)
4. The Trax ______________ the Huff. (feel / comfortable)
5. The Trax ______________, either. (be / cheap)
6. Even the Gordo ______________ the Trax. (ride / comfortable)
7. On the road, the Gordo ______________ the Trax. (handle / good)
8. Off the road, the Gordo and the Huff ______________ the Trax. (handle / good)
9. The Gordo's gears ______________ the Huff's but (be / easy to change)

______________ the Trax's.
10. (be / easy to change)

EDIT • *Read these forum postings. Find and correct six mistakes in the use of comparisons. The first mistake has already been corrected.*

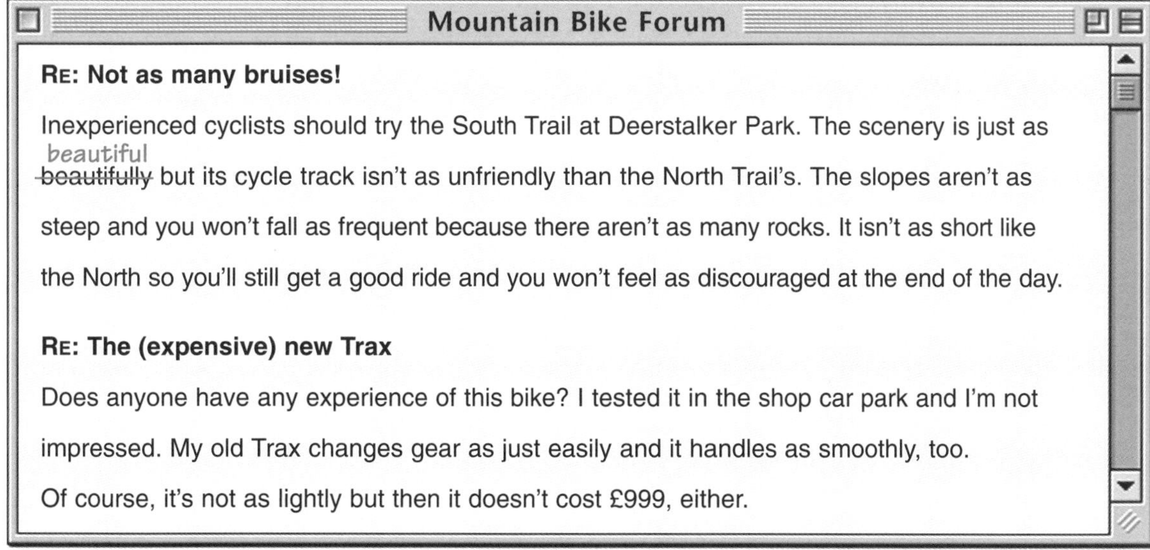

Mountain Bike Forum

RE: Not as many bruises!

Inexperienced cyclists should try the South Trail at Deerstalker Park. The scenery is just as ~~beautifully~~ beautiful but its cycle track isn't as unfriendly than the North Trail's. The slopes aren't as steep and you won't fall as frequent because there aren't as many rocks. It isn't as short like the North so you'll still get a good ride and you won't feel as discouraged at the end of the day.

RE: The (expensive) new Trax

Does anyone have any experience of this bike? I tested it in the shop car park and I'm not impressed. My old Trax changes gear as just easily and it handles as smoothly, too. Of course, it's not as lightly but then it doesn't cost £999, either.

Adjectives: Comparatives

CHECK POINT

Check the correct answer.

The new restaurant will be

❒ different from the old restaurant.

❒ the same as the old restaurant.

CHART CHECK

Circle T (True) or F (False).

T F The comparative adjective form always ends in *-er*.

T F You can use the same comparative adjective twice in a statement to show a change in a situation.

COMPARATIVES

	Comparative		Than	
The new restaurant is	brighter better		than	the old one.
	more less	comfortable beautiful		

REPEATED COMPARATIVES

	Comparative	And	Comparative	
The food is getting	better	and	better.	
	worse		worse.	
	more		more	delicious.
	less		less	interesting.

DOUBLE COMPARATIVES

The	Comparative		The	Comparative	
The	more crowded	the restaurant,	the	slower	the service.

EXPRESS CHECK

Complete this sentence.

Mo's is bigger and ________________ popular ________________ Val's.

Grammar Explanations	Examples
1. Use the **comparative** form of adjectives to focus on a difference between people, places and things.	■ The new menu is **bigger than** the old menu. ■ The new waiters are **more experienced than** the old waiters.

Grammar Explanations	Adjective	Comparative
2. There is more than one way to **form the comparative of adjectives**.		
a. For one-syllable adjectives and two-syllable adjectives ending in *-y*, use **adjective** + ***-er***.	bright friendly	**brighter** **friendlier**
▶ **Be careful!** There are often spelling changes when you add ***-er***.	nice big pretty	**nicer** **bigger** **prettier**
▶ **Be careful!** Some adjectives have irregular comparative forms.	good bad	**better** **worse**
b. For most other adjectives of two or more syllables, use ***more/less*** + **adjective**.	comfortable	**more comfortable** **less comfortable**
c. For some adjectives, use either ***-er*** or ***more/less***.	■ The River Inn is **quieter** than Joe's. ■ The River Inn is **more quiet** than Joe's.	

Grammar Explanations	Examples
3. Use the comparative **with *than*** when you mention the things you are comparing.	■ The apple pie is **better *than*** the cake.
Use the comparative **without *than*** when it is clear which things you are comparing.	■ The new desserts are **better**. *(The new desserts are better than the old desserts.)*
4. Repeat the same comparative to talk about change – an increase or a decrease: **comparative adjective** + ***and*** + **comparative adjective** OR ***more/less*** + ***and*** + ***more/less*** + **adjective**	■ It's getting **harder and harder** to find an inexpensive restaurant. ■ The prices of mobile phones are going **lower and lower**. ■ It's getting **more and more difficult**. *(The difficulty is increasing.)* ■ Cars are becoming **less and less** expensive.
5. Use a double comparative to show cause and effect: ***the*** + **comparative adjective** + ***the*** + **comparative adjective**	■ **The shorter** the queue, **the faster** the service. *(When the queue is shorter, the service is faster.)* ■ **The more expensive** the restaurant, **the bigger** the bill.

Check it out!

For spelling rules for the comparative form of adjectives, see Appendix 22 on page 344.
For a list of irregular comparative adjectives, see Appendix 10 on page 339.
For a list of some adjectives that form the comparative in two ways, see Appendix 12 on page 339.

TRUE OR FALSE • *Look at these two restaurant ads. Then read the statements below and decide if they are True (T) or False (F).*

Luigi's
Italian Restaurant

Family-style eating since 1990
Open Tuesday – Sunday, 12:00–9:00
EARLY-BIRD SPECIAL
(full dinner for £10.95 if ordered before 6:00)
No reservations necessary
No credit cards
87 High Street

Antonio's
Ristorante Italiano
Established in 1990
Relaxed dining in a romantic atmosphere
open seven days a week – dinner only
reservations suggested
all credit cards accepted
12 Broad Street
one free drink with this ad

__F__ 1. Luigi's is older than Antonio's.

_____ 2. Antonio's is more romantic than Luigi's.

_____ 3. Luigi's is probably less crowded.

_____ 4. Antonio's seems cheaper than Luigi's.

_____ 5. On Tuesdays, Luigi's has shorter business hours.

COMPARE & COMPLETE • *Look at part of Luigi's menu. Then complete the comparisons. Use the comparative form of the words in brackets.*

♥ **Spaghetti Primavera** *(with lightly sautéed vegetables)* £6.95
🌶 **Spaghetti Arrabbiata** *(with hot chilli peppers and tomatoes)* £7.50
Fettuccini Alfredo *(with butter and cream)*....................................£8.95
Linguine Aglio e Olio *(with garlic and oil)*..................................£5.60

♥ low fat, low salt 🌶 hot and spicy

1. The spaghetti primavera is __cheaper than__ (cheap) the spaghetti arrabbiata.
2. The linguine aglio e olio is __________ (expensive) the fettuccini Alfredo.
3. The spaghetti arrabbiata is __________ (hot) and __________ (spicy) the linguine aglio e olio.
4. The fettuccini Alfredo is __________ (fattening) the spaghetti primavera.
5. The spaghetti primavera is __________ (healthy) the fettuccini Alfredo.

COMPLETE • *Read these comments about a restaurant. Complete them with the comparative form of the words in brackets to show cause and effect or a change.*

1. **A:** I can't believe the size of this menu. It's going to take me forever to choose.

   B: The longer (long) the menu, the more difficult (difficult) the choice.

2. **A:** They say the food here is getting ________ and ________ (good).

   B: And ________ (good) the food, ________ (expensive) it is.

3. **A:** The service seems a little slow tonight.

   B: Yes, ________ (popular) the restaurant, ________ (slow) the service.

4. **A:** The cigarette smoke here is getting ________ and ________ (bad).

   B: ________ (smoky) the room, ________ (bad) my cough gets.

5. **A:** It's pretty loud in here.

   B: ________ (crowded) the restaurant, ________ (noisy) it is.

6. **A:** They certainly give you a lot of food. I can't eat any more.

   B: ________ (big) the portions, ________ (hard) it is to finish.

7. **A:** Their desserts keep getting ________ and ________ (delicious).

   B: And I keep getting ________ and ________ (heavy)!

EDIT • *Read this restaurant review. Find and correct eight mistakes in the use of the comparative of adjectives. The first mistake has already been corrected.*

Dining Out

BY BRUCE NEWHART

Pete's Place has just reopened under new management. The dining room looks bigger, ~~more bright~~ brighter and prettier as the old one. Although the food isn't better, it *is* just as good. The menu is more varied and less expensiver. Try one of their pasta dishes. You won't find a more fresher tomato sauce in town. And leave room for dessert. They just keep getting good and better.

The waiters are friendly but not able to handle large numbers of people – the crowded the restaurant, the slower the service. At dinnertime, the queues outside this popular restaurant are getting longer and more long. Try lunchtime for a quieter and relaxeder meal.

Adjectives: Superlatives

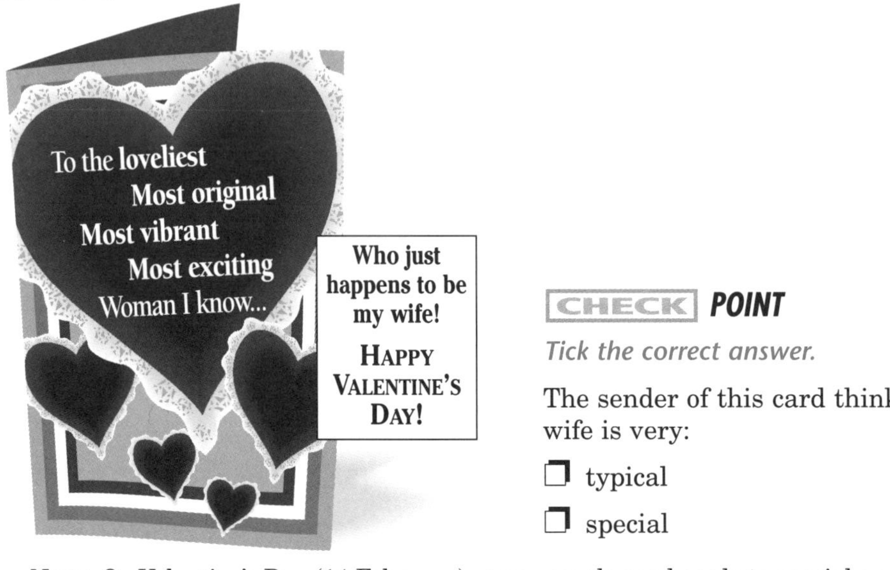

To the loveliest
Most original
Most vibrant
Most exciting
Woman I know...
Who just happens to be my wife!
HAPPY VALENTINE'S DAY!

CHECK POINT

Tick the correct answer.

The sender of this card thinks his wife is very:

❒ typical

❒ special

NOTE: On Valentine's Day (14 February), many people send cards to special people in their lives to tell them how much they love them.

CHART CHECK

Tick the correct answers.

Which word always goes before the superlative form of the adjective?

❒ ***a*** or ***an***

❒ ***the*** ❒ ***most***

Which letters do you add to the end of a short adjective to form the superlative?

❒ ***-er*** ❒ ***-est***

Which words do you add before a long adjective to form the superlative?

❒ ***more*** or ***less***

❒ ***most*** or ***least***

SUPERLATIVES		
	SUPERLATIVE ADJECTIVE FORM	
You are	**the sweetest** **the funniest** **the best** **the most wonderful** **the least selfish**	person in the world.
That's	**the nicest** **the loveliest** **the worst** **the most amusing** **the least original**	card I've ever received.

Complete the chart.

Adjective	Superlative
nice	
beautiful	
warm	
happy	

Grammar Explanations / Examples

Grammar Explanations	Examples
1. Use the **superlative** form of adjectives to single out people, places and things from other people, places and things.	■ You are **the best** parents in the world. ■ You are **the most wonderful** friend I've ever had.

Grammar Explanations	Adjective	Superlative
2. There is more than one way to **form the superlative of adjectives.**		
a. For one-syllable adjectives, or two-syllable adjectives ending in *-y*, use ***the*** + **adjective** + ***-est***.	bright friendly	**the brightest** **the friendliest**
▶ **Be careful!** There are often spelling changes when you add *-est*.	nice big pretty	**the nicest** **the biggest** **the prettiest**
▶ **Be careful!** Some adjectives have irregular superlative forms.	good bad	**the best** **the worst**
b. For most other adjectives of two or more syllables, use ***the most/the least*** + **adjective**.	comfortable	**the most comfortable** **the least comfortable**
c. For some adjectives use either ***the . . . -est*** or ***the most/the least***.	■ The third hotel was **the quietest**. ■ The third hotel was **the most quiet**.	

Grammar Explanations	Examples
3. The superlative is often used **with expressions beginning with *in* or *of***, such as *in the world* and *of all*.	■ You're **the best** mother ***in the world***. ■ He's **the cleverest** one ***of us all***.
4. The superlative is sometimes **followed by a clause**. Often the clause uses the present perfect with ***ever***.	■ That's **the nicest** card ***I've ever received***. ■ You have **the loveliest** smile ***I've ever seen***.

Check it out!

For spelling rules for the superlative form of adjectives, see Appendix 22 on page 344.
For a list of irregular superlative adjectives, see Appendix 10 on page 339.
For a list of some adjectives that form the superlative in two ways, see Appendix 12 on page 339.

IDENTIFY • *Read this Mother's Day card written by a young child. Underline all the superlative adjectives.*

MUM
You are the best mother
in the whole wide world.
You are the cleverest, the brightest and
the funniest of all mums I've ever known.
You are the nicest mum I've ever had.
You are the most wonderful and definitely
the least impatient.
No mum in the whole wide world is
better than you.
You are the greatest mother of all.
I love you very very much!
Happy Mother's Day!
Love,
Holly

CHOOSE & COMPLETE • *Read these sentences from Valentine's Day cards. Complete them with the superlative form of the adjectives in brackets and the expressions in the box.*

of all	in the school	of my life	in our family	~~in the world~~	of the year

1. You are so good to me. I am the luckiest (lucky) person in the world.
2. The day we were married was ________ (happy) day ________.
3. You are a terrific teacher. You are ________ (good) teacher ________.
4. You make me feel warm even in ________ (cold) months ________.
5. You are ________ (nice) cousin ________.
6. Grandma, you are ________ (wise) person ________. Maybe that's why I love you the most.

DESCRIBE • *Look at these items. Write sentences about them. Use the superlative form of the words in brackets.*

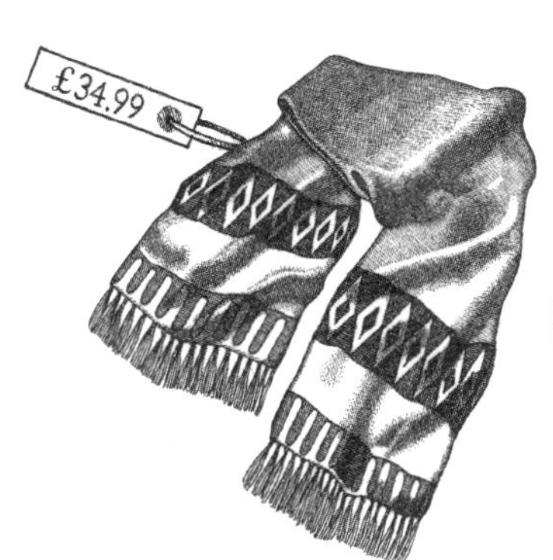

1. The book is the least expensive gift. (expensive)
2. The painting ______ (unusual)
3. The painting ______ (practical)
4. The book ______ (small)
5. The painting ______ (big)
6. The scarf ______ (expensive)
7. The toy ______ (funny)

EDIT • *Read this paragraph from a student's essay. Find and correct five mistakes in the use of superlative adjectives. The first mistake has already been corrected.*

Ramadan is the ~~seriousest~~ most serious time in Muslim culture. During Ramadan, we do not eat from dawn to sunset. This is difficult for everyone but teenagers have the hardest time. Immediately after Ramadan is the Eid al-Fitr. This holiday lasts three days and it's the most happiest time of the year. On the morning of Eid, my family gets up early and goes to the mosque. After we've greeted our neighbours by saying 'Eid Mubarek' (Happy Eid), we go home. We eat the big breakfast you have ever seen. Our parents give us presents, usually new clothes and money. One year, Eid came round the time I graduated from university. That year, I got the most beautiful clothes and the fatter envelope of money of all the children in my family. Eid Mela is part of Eid al-Fitr. On that day, we all go to a big park. Last year at Eid Mela, I had the better time of my life. I met my old friends and we all ate junk food and showed off our new clothes.

UNIT 45

Adverbs: Comparatives and Superlatives

Watch Jordan. **The more** he plays, **the better** he gets.
Come on, Steve, try **harder**, man!

CHECK POINT

Circle T (True) or F (False).

T F Jordan improves every time he plays.

CHART CHECK

Tick the correct answer.

What do you add to long adverbs to form the comparative?

❐ ***more*** or ***less***

❐ ***-er*** or ***-est***

Which word do you always add to form the superlative?

❐ ***most***

❐ ***the***

COMPARATIVES				
	COMPARATIVE ADVERB FORM		***THAN***	
Jordan played	**harder** **better**		**than**	Steve.
	more **less**	**aggressively** **consistently**		

SUPERLATIVES			
	SUPERLATIVE ADVERB FORM		
He threw	**the fastest** **the best**		of anyone in the game.
	the most **the least**	**accurately** **frequently**	

EXPRESS CHECK

Circle the correct words to complete these sentences.

Sims threw faster <u>than / of</u> Jones. He played <u>better / the best</u> of all.

Grammar Explanations	Examples
1. Use the **comparative form of adverbs** to focus on differences between actions.	■ The Bulls played **better than** the Lakers. ■ Jordan played **more skilfully than** O'Neal.
Use the comparative **without *than*** when it is clear which things you are comparing.	■ He played **less aggressively**, though.

2. Use the **superlative form of adverbs** to single out something about an action.	■ Steve tried **the hardest**.
We often use the superlative **with expressions beginning with *of***, such as *of any player*.	■ He scored **the most frequently *of any player*** on the team.

3. There is more than one way to **form the comparative and superlative of adverbs.**

	Adverb	Comparative	Superlative
a. For one-syllable adverbs, use **adverb + *-er*** or ***the* + adverb + *-est***.	fast hard	**faster** **harder**	**the fastest** **the hardest**
► **Be careful!** Some adverbs have irregular comparative and superlative forms.	well badly	**better** **worse**	**the best** **the worst**
b. For most adverbs of two or more syllables, use ***more/less* + adverb** or ***the most/the least* + adverb.**	skilfully	**more/less skilfully**	**the most/the least skilfully**
c. Some adverbs use either ***more/less*** or ***-er*** and ***the most/the least*** or ***the . . . -est***.	quickly	**more quickly** **quicker**	**the most quickly** **the quickest**

4. Repeat the same comparative to talk about change – an increase or a decrease: **comparative adverb** + ***and*** + **comparative adverb**	■ Steve is playing **better and better** as the season continues. *(His performance keeps improving.)*
OR ***more/less*** + ***and*** + ***more/less*** + **adverb**	■ He is shooting **more and more accurately**. *(His shooting keeps getting more accurate.)*

5. Use a double comparative to show cause and effect: ***the*** + **comparative adverb** + ***the*** + **comparative adverb**	■ **The harder** he played, **the better** he performed. *(When he played harder, his performance improved.)* ■ **The more** you practise, **the better** you become.

Check it out!

For a list of irregular comparisons of adverbs, see Appendix 10 on page 339.

IDENTIFY • *Read this feature story from the sports section of the newspaper. Underline all the comparative forms once. Underline all the superlative forms twice.*

Section 3 **Sports**

Norwich Beat Stowe!

In the first football game of the season, Norwich beat Stowe, 6 goals to 3. The Stowe team played a truly fantastic game but its defence is still weak. Norwich defended the ball much more aggressively than the Stowe team did. Of course, Joe Jackson helped win the game for Norwich. Norwich's star player was back on the field today, to the delight of his many fans. He was badly hurt at the end of last season but he has recovered quickly. Although he didn't play as well as people expected, he still handled the ball like the old Joe. He certainly handled it the most skilfully of anyone on the team. He controlled the ball the best, kicked the ball the furthest and ran the fastest of any of the players on either team. He played hard and helped the Norwich team look good. In fact, the harder he played, the better Norwich performed. Watch Joe this season.

And watch Stowe, too. They've got a new coach and they're training more seriously this year. I think we'll see them play better and better as the season progresses.

2

COMPLETE • *Read this conversation between friends. Complete it with the comparative or superlative forms of the words in brackets. Add* **the** *and* **than** *where necessary.*

BILLY: Did you hear about that new speed-reading course? It helps you read ___faster___ (1. fast) and __________ (2. well).

MICHAEL: I don't believe it! The __________ (3. fast) you read, the __________ (4. little) you understand.

BILLY: The advert says that after the course, you'll read ten times __________ (5. rapidly) and understand five times more. And the best thing is that you won't have to work any __________ (6. hard).

MICHAEL: I'd like to see that. When I was at school, I read __________ (7. slowly) of any student in my class but I also remembered details __________ (8. clearly) and __________ (9. long) of any of my classmates.

BILLY: Maybe you could read even __________ (10. quickly) that and still remember details. That way, you'd have more time to go to the gym.

MICHAEL: Did you read the course description properly?

BILLY: I read it __________ (11. thoroughly) I read most things.

CHOOSE & COMPLETE • *Look at the chart. Then complete the sentences with the comparative or superlative form of the words in the box. You will use some words more than once.*

far good fast bad slow high

ATHLETE	LONG JUMP	POLE VAULTING	5-MILE RUN
CLARKE	4.3 m	2.2 m	24 minutes
SMITH	4.2 m	2.1 m	28 minutes
ROGERS	4.6 m	2.3 m	30 minutes
DAVIES	4.7 m	2.5 m	22 minutes

1. Clarke jumped ______ further than ______ Smith.
2. Davies vaulted ______ the highest ______ of all.
3. Rogers ran ______________________.

4. Smith ran ______________________ Davies.
5. Davies jumped ______________________.
6. Clarke ran ______________________ Smith.
7. Davies vaulted ______________________ Smith.
8. All in all, Davies did ______________________.
9. All in all, Smith did ______________________.

EDIT • *Read this student's report about a basketball game. Find and correct seven mistakes in the use of adverbs. The first mistake has already been corrected.*

Last night, I watched the Lakers and the Bulls. Both teams played more aggressively ^than I've ever seen them. In fact, they played the better of any game I've watched this season. In the first half, Michael Jordan sprained his left ankle and Shaquille O'Neal was out of the game because of fouls. But they still didn't start the second half any slower that the first. With Jordan out, Kukoc scored the most frequenter of any player. He's been playing more and more better as the season goes on. In fact, more he plays, the better he gets. The Bulls won by 97 to 88. The Lakers seemed to get tired at the end. They played little and less consistently as the game went on.

SECTION ONE

Circle the letter of the correct answer to complete each sentence.

EXAMPLE:
Jennifer never ________ coffee. A (B) C D
(A) drink (C) is drinking
(B) drinks (D) was drinking

1. I've got ________ job in the world. A B C D
(A) a good (C) the best
(B) best (D) the better

2. This apple pie smells ________! A B C D
(A) wonderful (C) more wonderfully
(B) wonderfully (D) the most wonderfully

3. Our team didn't play ________ I expected. I was disappointed. A B C D
(A) as well as (C) as badly as
(B) well (D) better

4. I passed my driving test. It seemed much ________ this time. A B C D
(A) easy (C) easiest
(B) easier (D) easily

5. The faster Daniel walks, ________. A B C D
(A) more tired (C) the more tired he gets
(B) he gets tired (D) he gets more tired

6. Could you talk ________? I'm trying to work. A B C D
(A) more quietly (C) more quiet
(B) quieter than (D) quiet

7. Lisa is staying at home. Her cold is a lot ________ today. A B C D
(A) bad (C) worst
(B) worse (D) the worst

8. Sorry we're late. Your house is much ________ than we thought. A B C D
(A) far (C) further
(B) the furthest (D) the further

9. The film was so ________ that we couldn't sleep last night. A B C D
(A) excitingly (C) excite
(B) excited (D) exciting

10. Chris is working very ________ these days. A B C D
(A) hardly (C) harder
(B) hard (D) hardest

11. Write the report first. It's more important ________ your other work. A B C D
(A) than (C) from
(B) as (D) then

12. The lunch menu is very short. It's ________ than the dinner menu. A B C D
(A) varied (C) less varied
(B) more varied (D) the least varied

13. Thank you! That's ________ I've ever received. A B C D
(A) the nicer gift (C) nicest gift
(B) a nice gift (D) the nicest gift

14. It's getting more ________ to find a cheap flat. A B C D
(A) hardly (C) the most difficult
(B) and more difficult (D) and very difficult

SECTION TWO

Each sentence has four underlined words or phrases. The four underlined parts of the sentence are marked A, B, C and D. Circle the letter of the one underlined word or phrase that is NOT CORRECT.

EXAMPLE:
Mike usually (A) drives (B) to school but today (C) he walks (D). A B C (D)

15. The harder (A) Sylvia tries (B), less (C) she succeeds (D). A B C D

16. This has been the (A) best (B) day than (C) my whole (D) life! A B C D

17. We're always (A) amazing (B) by (C) John's incredible (D) travel stories. A B C D

18. We took a lot of (A) photos because she was such (B) a sweetly (C) little (D) baby. A B C D

19. Our new (A) car is hard (B) to drive than (C) our old (D) one. A B C D

20. Patrick doesn't run quickly (A) as (B) Lee but (C) he can run further (D). A B C D

21. You did much (A) more (B) better (C) in the last test than (D) in this one. A B C D

22. What's the (A) more (B) popular (C) of all the new (D) TV shows? A B C D

23. The (A) more (B) I practise the piano, the most (C) skilled (D) I get. A B C D

24. The rubbish in the street is (A) more (B) disgusted (C) than (D) the potholes. A B C D

25. Today seems as (A) hotter (B) as (C) yesterday but the humidity is lower (D). A B C D

Gerunds: Subject and Object

I'm all
out of breath again.
I really need to
give up jogging!

CHECK POINT

Tick the correct answer.

What does the woman want to give up?

❒ cigarettes

❒ exercise

CHART CHECK

Tick the correct answer.

What does the gerund end with?

❒ *-ed*

❒ *-ing*

What goes before the gerund to make it negative?

❒ *not*

❒ *don't* or *doesn't*

GERUND AS SUBJECT

GERUND (SUBJECT)	VERB	OBJECT
Smoking	harms	your health.
Not smoking	makes	you healthier.

GERUND AS OBJECT

SUBJECT	VERB	GERUND (OBJECT)
You	should give up	**smoking**.
My doctor	suggests	**not smoking**.

EXPRESS CHECK

Complete this conversation with the correct form of the verb **drink**. *Use the affirmative or negative.*

A: ________________ too much coffee isn't good for you.

B: I know. I gave up ________________ coffee last year.

A: My doctor suggested ________________ fizzy drinks, either.

Grammar Explanations	Examples
1. A **gerund** (base form of verb + ***-ing***) is a verb that functions like a noun.	■ **Drinking** too much coffee is bad for your health.
A gerund can be the **subject** of a sentence.	■ **Smoking** is also unhealthy.
▶ **Be careful!** There are often spelling changes when you add ***-ing*** to the base form of the verb.	smoke **smoking** jog **jogging**
Notice that a gerund is always singular and is followed by the third person singular form of the verb.	■ **Eating** sweets ***is*** bad for your teeth. ■ **Inhaling** smoke ***gives*** me bronchitis.
▶ **Be careful!** Don't confuse a gerund with the continuous form of the verb.	gerund ■ **Drinking** coffee isn't healthy. continuous form ■ He **is drinking** coffee at the moment.
2. A **gerund** can also be the **object** of certain verbs.	■ I **enjoy** ***exercising***. ■ I've **considered** ***joining*** a gym.
To the right is a short list of verbs that can be followed by a gerund.	**admit** **miss** **avoid** **practise** **consider** **stop** **deny** **resent** **enjoy** **suggest** **finish** **(dis)like**
3. There are many common expressions with ***go*** **+ gerund**. These expressions usually describe activities, such as *shopping, fishing, skiing, swimming* and *camping*.	■ We often **go** ***swimming*** in the lake. ■ Yesterday I **went** ***shopping*** for a new pair of running shoes.

Check it out!

For more complete lists of common verbs that can be followed by the gerund, see Appendix 3 on page 337 and Appendix 6 on page 338.

IDENTIFY • *Read part of an article from a magazine. Underline the words ending in* **-ing** *that are gerunds.*

YOUR HEALTH

SWIMMING is great exercise. It's healthy, fun and relaxing. Because swimming is a 'low-impact' sport, most people enjoy participating in this activity without fear of injury to their bones or muscles. Jogging, which is a 'high-impact' activity, can at times be harmful. I know this from personal experience. Last year while I was jogging, I injured my right knee. I don't go jogging any more. After a painful month of recovery, I stopped running and switched to water sports. I'm now considering joining a swimming team and competing in races.

CHOOSE & COMPLETE • *Read these statements about health issues. Complete them with the gerund form of the verbs in the box. Choose between affirmative and negative.*

increase	eat	do	walk	drink	~~smoke~~	swim	run	go

1. ___Smoking___ is bad for your heart and lungs.
2. ________________ too much fat and sugar is also unhealthy.
3. ________________ enough water is bad for your general health.
4. Doctors suggest ________________ the amount of fruit and vegetables in your diet.
5. Avoid ________________ too many high-impact sports such as jogging and jumping.
6. Instead, consider ________________ in a pool every day. It's an excellent low-impact activity.
7. Many health experts think that ________________ is better than ________________ because there is less stress on your body when your feet come into contact with the ground.
8. Some people are afraid of the doctor but ________________ for regular checkups is a mistake.

SUMMARISE • *Read each numbered statement. Complete the following summary using the appropriate verb from the box and the gerund form of the verb in brackets.*

admit	can't stand	avoid	consider	deny	~~enjoy~~	go	stop

1. **Tom:** Ann jogs but I don't really like that kind of exercise.
   Summary: Tom doesn't <u>enjoy jogging</u> . (jog)
2. **Martina:** Oh, no thanks. I don't smoke any more.
   Summary: Martina ______________________ . (smoke)
3. **Carl:** I'm going to that new swimming pool. Would you like to come with me?
   Summary: Carl is going to ______________________ . (swim)
4. **Jim:** I can smell smoke, too. But don't look at me! I didn't have a cigarette!
   Summary: Jim ______________________ . (smoke)
5. **Izzy:** I know I should exercise but I don't want to. I guess you're right. I *am* lazy.
   Summary: Izzy ______________________ lazy. (be)
6. **Phil:** No, thanks. The cake looks great but I'm trying to stay away from sweet things.
   Summary: Phil ______________________ sweet things. (eat)
7. **Vicky:** I'm not sure but I *may* go on holiday.
   Summary: Vicky ______________________ a holiday. (take)
8. **Myles:** Traffic jams are what I hate most about commuting.
   Summary: Myles ______________________ in traffic jams. (be)

4 ***EDIT*** • *Read Jim's notes. Find and correct nine mistakes in the use of the gerund. The first mistake has already been corrected.*

SMOKING

WAYS I CAN GIVE UP ~~SMOKE~~ CIGARETTES

Choose an exact date to give up smoke.

Stop smoking completely. (Cut down is harder than stopping all at once.)

Avoid to be around other smokers (at least at the beginning).

Start exercising daily. To exercise can reduce stress.

No drinking coffee may help, too.

Imagine been a non-smoker. Positive mental images can help.

Consider to join a support group.

Don't delay to ask for help. Call Dr Burns right away!

Keep trying and don't give up!

Gerunds after Prepositions

GET INVOLVED!

Interested **in improving** life on campus?

Tired **of hearing** complaints and not **finding** solutions?

Join the Student Council!

Next Meeting: Mon. 25 March, 8:00 p.m., Main Auditorium

We look forward **to seeing** you there.

You CAN make a difference!

CHECK POINT

Circle T (True) or F (False).

The Student Council is looking for students who

T **F** want to make new friends.

T **F** want to improve life on campus.

T **F** like to complain.

CHART CHECK

Tick the correct answers.

What part of speech is the word ***to*** in ***look forward to***?

❐ part of the infinitive

❐ a preposition

What form of the verb follows a preposition?

❐ the base form

❐ the gerund

❐ the infinitive

GERUNDS AFTER PREPOSITIONS

	Preposition	Gerund	
Do you have ideas	**for**	**improving**	life on campus?
We're good	**at**	**planning**	ahead.
You can help	**by**	**taking**	notes.
She believes	**in**	**compromising**.	
Are you tired	**of**	**hearing**	complaints?
Let's work	**instead of**	**complaining**.	
They insist	**on**	**coming**	to the meeting.
I look forward	**to**	**having to**	study next summer.
She's interested	**in**	**working with**	other students.

EXPRESS CHECK

Complete this conversation with the correct form of the verb **join***.*

A: Are you happy about ________________ the Student Council?

B: Yes, I am. I'd been looking forward to ________________ a group for a while.

Grammar Explanations	Examples
1. A **preposition** is a word such as ***about***, ***against***, ***at***, ***by***, ***for***, ***in***, ***instead of***, ***of***, ***on***, ***to***, ***with*** and ***without***. A preposition can be followed by a noun or a pronoun.	■ The council insists **on** ***elections***. (noun) ■ The council insists **on** ***them***. (pronoun)
Because a **gerund** (base form of verb + ***-ing***) acts as a noun, it can follow a preposition, too.	■ The council insists **on** ***voting***. (gerund)
2. Many **common expressions** are made up of a verb or an adjective followed by a preposition.	VERB + PREPOSITION: advise **against**, believe **in**, count **on** ADJECTIVE + PREPOSITION: afraid **of**, bored **with**, excited **about**
These expressions can be followed by a gerund.	■ She's **counting on** ***going*** to university. ■ He **is bored with** ***working*** in a shop.
3. BE CAREFUL! **a.** In the **expressions** on the right, ***to*** is a preposition, not part of an infinitive form. For this reason it can be followed by the gerund.	VERB + PREPOSITION: look forward **to**, object **to**, resort **to** ADJECTIVE + PREPOSITION: accustomed **to**, opposed **to**, used **to** ■ I'**m looking forward to** ***seeing*** you. NOT ~~I'm looking forward to see you~~. ■ She'**s used to** coming top in her class. NOT ~~She's used to come top in her class~~.
b. Do not confuse ***used to*** + **base form** of verb (for habits in the past) with ***be/get used to*** + **gerund** (meaning 'be/get accustomed to').	■ I **used to take** the train. *(It was my habit to take the train but I no longer take the train.)* ■ I'**m used to** ***taking*** the train. *(I'm accustomed to taking the train.)* ■ I'**m getting used to** ***taking*** the train. *(I'm becoming accustomed to taking the train.)*

Check it out!

For a list of common verb plus preposition combinations, see Appendix 7 on page 338.
For a list of common adjective plus preposition combinations, see Appendix 8 on page 338.

IDENTIFY • *The Student Council wrote a letter to the Dean of the university. Read it and underline all the preposition + gerund combinations.*

We, the members of the Student Council, would like to share with you the thoughts and concerns of the general student body. As you probably know, many students are complaining about life on campus. We are interested in meeting with you to discuss our ideas for dealing with these complaints.

We know that you are tired of hearing students complain and that you are not used to working with the Student Council. However, if you really believe in giving new ideas a try, we hope you will think about speaking to our representatives. We look forward to hearing from you soon.

CHOOSE & COMPLETE • *Read these comments from the university newspaper. Complete the students' statements with the appropriate preposition from the box (you will use one of them several times) and the gerund form of the verb in brackets.*

at on in to about for

1. I don't have any plans for the holidays but I'm not concerned about getting (get) bored. I can always go for a walk or something. *Jim Clark*
2. What are my plans for the holidays? I'm very interested ________ (listen) to jazz. I'm going to go to the Spring Jazz Festival. *Lisa Smith*
3. My friends and I are driving to Scotland. I'm excited ________ (go) but I'm nervous ________ (drive) at night. *Emily Latham*
4. I'm really looking forward ________ (stay) at home and just ________ (relax). *Don Peters*
5. I'm driving to Wales. It's famous ________ (have) great scenery. *Ed Davies*
6. I love languages but I'm not good ________ (learn) them so I'm studying for my Japanese class over the break. *Claire Kaplan*
7. My friends and I are going camping but my little brother insists ________ (come) with us. A lot of fun that'll be! *Oscar Stephens*
8. My girlfriend is keen ________ (read) and ________ (go) to the cinema so I guess I'll read a lot and see a lot of films. *Tim Riley*

COMBINE • *Read these pairs of sentences about student life. Combine them with the prepositions in brackets.*

1. You can't walk on campus late at night. You have to worry about your safety.
   You can't walk on campus late at night without worrying about your safety.
   (without)
2. We can make changes. We can tell the Dean about our concerns.
   ____
   (by)
3. The Dean can help. He can listen to our concerns.
   ____
   (by)
4. In some cases, students just complain. They don't make suggestions for improvements.
   ____
   (instead of)
5. Students get annoyed with some lecturers. Some lecturers come late to class.
   ____
   (for)
6. You can improve your work. Study regularly.
   ____
   (by)

EDIT • *Read this student's letter. Find and correct seven mistakes in the use of gerunds after prepositions. The first mistake has already been corrected.*

Dear Brian,

I have been attending Bedford College for a year. I'm very happy about ~~study~~ studying here. At first, it was quite hard getting used to speak English all the time but now I feel very comfortable about communicate in my second language.

I've just joined an international student group and I'm excited with meeting new people. The summer break is coming and a few of us are planning on do some travelling together. Before to join this group, I used to spend holidays alone.

Please write. I look forward to hear from you!

K.

UNIT 48 Infinitives after Certain Verbs

Lifestyles Section 4

ASK ANNIE

Dear Annie,

A month ago I met this great woman, Megan, and I **asked her to marry** me straight-away. She says things are 'moving too fast' and she **wants me to think** about my proposal a bit longer. I've told her I **can't afford to wait** forever. Am I right? *Impatient*

CHECK POINT

Tick the correct answer.

❒ Megan wants more time to consider the marriage proposal.

❒ Megan thinks 'Impatient' should consider his proposal more.

CHART CHECK

Circle T (True) or F (False).

T F The infinitive = base form + *to*.

T F The negative infinitive = *not* + infinitive.

T F All verbs need an object before the infinitive.

STATEMENTS: WITHOUT AN OBJECT

Subject	Verb	(Not)	Infinitive	
They	**decided** **agreed**	(not)	**to call** **to ask**	Annie.

STATEMENTS: WITH AN OBJECT

Subject	Verb	Object	(Not)	Infinitive	
They	**urged** **advised**	John him	(not)	**to call** **to ask**	her.

STATEMENTS: WITH OR WITHOUT AN OBJECT

Subject	Verb	(Object)	Infinitive	
They	**wanted** **needed**	(John) (him)	**to call** **to ask**	her.

EXPRESS CHECK

Unscramble these words to form a sentence.

to • want • Annie • write • to • I ______________________

Grammar Explanations	Examples
1. Certain **verbs** can be followed by an **infinitive** (***to*** + base form of the verb).	■ I **want** ***to get*** married. ■ I **asked** Annie ***to help*** me.
2. Some of these verbs are **immediately** followed **by an infinitive**.	■ He **decided** ***to write*** to Annie. ■ He **hoped** ***to get*** a quick reply.
The verbs on the right can be followed by an infinitive.	**agree** **plan** **begin** **refuse** **fail** **seem**
3. Some verbs need an **object** (noun or pronoun) **before the infinitive**.	■ I **invited** ***Mary*** (object) **to celebrate** with us. ■ I **reminded** ***her*** (object) **to come**.
The verbs on the right need an object before the infinitive.	**advise** **tell** **encourage** **urge** **order** **warn**
4. Some verbs can be followed by either: • **an infinitive** OR • **an object + infinitive**	■ He **wants** ***to leave***. He's tired. OR ■ He **wants** ***you to leave***. You're tired.
The verbs on the right can be followed either by an infinitive or by an object + infinitive.	**ask** **need** **expect** **want** **help** **would like**
5. Form a **negative infinitive** by placing ***not*** before the infinitive.	■ Lee remembered **not *to call*** after 5:00. *(Lee didn't call after 5:00.)* ■ Anna told me **not *to go*** to class. *(Anna: 'Don't go. The teacher is sick.')*
▶ **BE CAREFUL!** A sentence with a negative infinitive can have a very different meaning from a sentence with a negative main verb.	■ Jim told me **not *to give up***. *(Jim: 'Don't give up.')* ■ Jim **didn't tell** me to give up. *(Jim didn't say I should give up.)*

Check it out!

For a list of common verbs followed directly by the infinitive, see Appendix 4 on page 338.

For a list of verbs followed by objects and the infinitive, see Appendix 5 on page 338.

For a list of verbs that can be followed either directly by an infinitive or by an object + infinitive, see Appendix 5 on page 338.

IDENTIFY • *Read Annie's response to 'Impatient'. Underline all the verb + infinitive and verb + object + infinitive combinations.*

Lifestyles 17

Dear Impatient,

Slow down! You appear to be in too much of a hurry. You've only known this person for a month and yet you've asked her to marry you! What's the big rush? *Why* can't you afford to wait? Are you afraid that if she gets to know you better, she may decide not to tie the knot? I agree with your girlfriend. You need to consider things more carefully. You can't expect her (or yourself) to make such an important decision so quickly. If you don't want to regret a hasty decision, I advise you both to get to know each other better before you hurry to the altar.

Annie

COMPLETE • *Read this article. Complete it with the correct form of the verbs in brackets. Use the present simple or the imperative form of the first verb.*

Planning for Love

Most people make careful plans when they ___decide to have___ **1.** (decide / have) a holiday. Yet when they ________ **2.** (attempt / find) a mate, they depend on luck.

Edward Driscoll, PhD, ________ **3.** (warn / single people / not / leave) love to chance.

He ________ **4.** (urge / them / use) his four-step plan when they search for a partner.

Remember: When you ________ **5.** (fail / plan), you ________ **6.** (plan / fail).

STEP ONE: **Make a list.** What kind of person do you ________ **7.** (wish / meet)? Someone intelligent? Someone who loves sports? List everything.

STEP TWO: **Make another list.** What kind of person are you? ________ **8.** (Ask / two friends / read) your list and comment on it. The two lists should match.

STEP THREE: **Increase your chances.** ________ **9.** (Choose / participate) in activities you like.

STEP FOUR: **Ask for introductions.** Dr Driscoll ________ **10.** (advise / people / not / feel) embarrassed to ask. Everyone ________ **11.** (want / be) a matchmaker!

SUMMARISE • *Read each numbered statement. Complete the summary using the appropriate verb from the box followed by an infinitive or an object + infinitive.*

agree	remind	would like	~~urge~~	invite	need	forget	encourage

1. **ANNIE:** I really think you should take things more slowly, Mark.
   SUMMARY: Annie urged Mark to take things more slowly.
2. **KAREN:** Tom, could you call me at 10:00?
   SUMMARY: Karen ______
3. **CHRIS:** Emily, please remember to buy petrol today.
   SUMMARY: Chris ______
4. **JOHN:** We're going out for coffee, Mel. Would you like to join us?
   SUMMARY: John ______
5. **JASON:** OK, OK, Dad. I'll be home by 10:30 if that's what you want.
   SUMMARY: Jason ______
6. **JEFF:** Oh, no! It's 4:15. I didn't go to the two o'clock staff meeting!
   SUMMARY: Jeff ______
7. **MUM:** Come on, Lisa, don't be scared. Just try again.
   SUMMARY: Lisa's mother ______
8. **TERRY:** I'm using the car tonight. I'm taking Sue to the cinema.
   SUMMARY: Terry ______

EDIT • *Read this entry from a diary. Find and correct seven mistakes in the use of infinitives after certain verbs. The first mistake has already been corrected.*

Annie advised me ~~joining~~ to join a club or take a class and I finally did it! I decided become a member of the Outdoor Adventure Club and I went to my first meeting last night. I'm really excited about it. The club is planning a hiking trip next weekend. I definitely want to go rafting in the spring. At first I didn't want signing up but the leader was so nice. He urged me to not miss this trip so I put my name on the list. After the meeting, a group of people asked me to go out with them. We went to a coffee shop and talked for hours. Well, I hoped make some friends when I joined this club but I didn't expect everyone being so friendly. I'm glad Annie persuaded me no to give up.

Infinitives after Certain Adjectives and Nouns

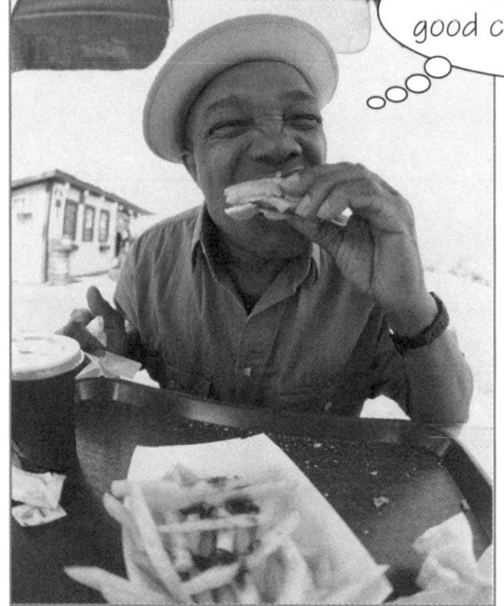

It's **hard to find** good chips these days.

CHECK POINT

Check the correct answer.

❒ Finding good chips is difficult.

❒ The man hardly eats anything but chips.

CHART CHECK

Tick the correct answers.

The infinitive is formed with:

❒ ***to*** + base form of verb

❒ ***to*** + base form of verb + ***-ing***

The infinitive follows:

❒ certain nouns and adjectives

❒ certain prepositions

INFINITIVES AFTER CERTAIN ADJECTIVES

	Adjective	Infinitive	
It's	**hard**	**to find**	nutritious fast food.
We're	**eager**	**to hear**	about the new restaurant.
He seemed	**surprised**	**to find out**	about the amount of fat in a burger.

INFINITIVES AFTER CERTAIN NOUNS

	Noun	Infinitive	
It's	**time**	**to go.**	
That's a high	**price**	**to pay.**	
Does he have	**permission**	**to stay**	out late?

EXPRESS CHECK

Unscramble these words to form two sentences.

convenient • It's • eat • fast • food • to ______________________.

pay • a • price • low • That's • to ______________________.

Grammar Explanations	Examples
1. Certain **adjectives** can be followed by an **infinitive** (*to* + base form of the verb).	adjective infinitive ■ They were **eager** ***to try*** the new burger.
Many of these adjectives describe a feeling about the action in the infinitive.	■ She was **glad** ***to hear*** that it was low in calories.
Adjectives that express praise or blame are often followed by an infinitive.	■ I was **wrong** ***to leave***. ■ They were **brave** ***to tell*** him.
Adjectives that show the order of actions are often followed by an infinitive.	■ We were **last** ***to order***. ■ When the bill came, she was the **first** ***to leave*** the restaurant.
2. We often use ***It's*** + **adjective** + **infinitive**.	adjective infinitive ■ **It's great** ***to see*** you again.
When the action in the infinitive is done by a person, we often use ***of*** or ***for*** + **noun/pronoun**.	■ It was **silly** ***of Tom*** **to leave**. ■ It's **hard** ***for us*** **to get** there on time.
It's + **adjective** + **infinitive** is often used to make general observations.	■ **It's convenient** ***to eat*** fast food. ■ **It's difficult** for students ***to work*** full time.
3. Certain **nouns** can be followed by an **infinitive**.	noun infinitive ■ It's **time** ***to take*** a break. ■ I have the **right** ***to eat*** what I want. ■ They made a **decision** ***to lose*** weight. ■ It's a high **price** ***to pay***. ■ He's got **permission** ***to stay*** out late.
The **noun** + **infinitive** combination often expresses advisability or necessity.	■ Robin is the **person** ***to ask*** about that. *(You should ask Robin about that.)* ■ I have a **test** ***to study*** for. *(I must study for my test.)*

Check it out!

For a list of common adjectives that can be followed by the infinitive, see Appendix 9 on page 338.

IDENTIFY • *Read this questionnaire. Underline all the adjective + infinitive and noun + infinitive combinations. Write* **A** *over the adjectives and* **N** *over the nouns.*

FAST-FOOD QUESTIONNAIRE

Please take a few minutes to complete this questionnaire about fast-food restaurants. (N over "minutes"; "minutes to complete" underlined)

Tick (✓) all the answers that apply to you.

1. How often are you likely to eat at a fast-food restaurant? (A over "likely"; "likely to eat" underlined)
   - ☐ 1–3 times a week
   - ☐ 4–6 times a week
   - ☐ more than 6 times a week
   - ☐ never
2. In your opinion, fast food is:
   - ☐ good to eat
   - ☐ a way to save time
   - ☐ fun to order occasionally
   - ☐ unhealthy to have every day
3. Which statement best describes your feelings about the cost of fast food?
   - ☐ It's a high price to pay for convenience.
   - ☐ You get a lot for not very much money.
4. Is it a good idea to include healthy choices in fast-food menus?
   - ☐ Yes
   - ☐ No

2 ***COMPLETE*** • *Read these excerpts from letters to the editor of a university newspaper. Complete them with the correct form of the words in brackets.*

Last year, I stopped eating in the cafeteria because the food was so bad and it was such a terrible ___place to have___ (1. place / have) a meal. Yesterday, I went back for the first time. I was ______________ (2. delighted / find) *Burgers Unlimited* there. Fast foods are the ______________ (3. way / go)! They're ______________ (4. fun / eat) and the cheerful atmosphere has made the cafeteria a ______________ (5. pleasure / eat) in. I'll be eating lunch there every day from now on. Jeff

It was a ______________ (6. mistake / bring) fast-food chains to the campus. It's ______________ (7. outrageous / see) the exact same restaurants everywhere you go. The food they serve isn't ______________ (8. good / eat). It contains much too much sugar, salt and fat. For students, it's ______________ (9. essential / have) a healthy meal every day and it's ______________ (10. difficult / go) off campus to eat. We just don't have the time. Alice

CHOOSE & COMPLETE • *Read these conversations between colleagues. Complete them with the words in brackets and the infinitive form of a verb from the box.*

get	cry	hear	keep	work	find	decide	wake up	show	~~take~~

CHRIS: Hey, Dawn. I've got to talk to you. Have you got ___time to take___ (1. time) a break?

DAWN: Of course, Chris. What's wrong? You look like you're __________ (2. ready).

CHRIS: Mr Kay's just asked me if I'd be __________ (3. willing) from 4:00 p.m. to midnight.

DAWN: But lectures start early tomorrow! It's __________ (4. hard) early after working late.

CHRIS: When I told him that, he said, 'I'm __________ (5. suprised) that, Chris. I thought you were __________ (6. eager) a promotion to shift manager.'

DAWN: It's __________ (7. important) your work up, too. Did he give you __________ (8. time)?

CHRIS: He just said, 'OK. I'll ask Steve. We'll give *him* the __________ (9. chance) his loyalty to the company.'

DAWN: Fast-food jobs are __________ (10. easy). Don't worry! Just concentrate on university.

EDIT • *Read Mr Kay's journal. Find and correct seven mistakes in the use of infinitives. The first mistake has already been corrected.*

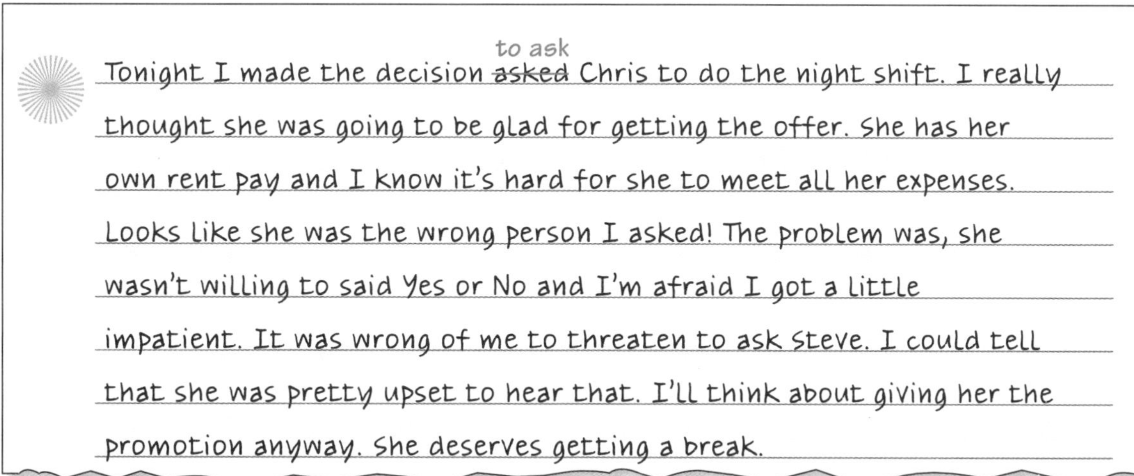

Tonight I made the decision ~~asked~~ to ask Chris to do the night shift. I really thought she was going to be glad for getting the offer. She has her own rent pay and I know it's hard for she to meet all her expenses. Looks like she was the wrong person I asked! The problem was, she wasn't willing to said Yes or No and I'm afraid I got a little impatient. It was wrong of me to threaten to ask Steve. I could tell that she was pretty upset to hear that. I'll think about giving her the promotion anyway. She deserves getting a break.

UNIT 50 Infinitives with *Too* and *Enough*

'Son, your mother and I think that you are now old enough to get your own drink of water.'

CHECK POINT

Circle T (True) or F (False).

T F The man's parents want the man to get them a drink of water.

T F The man wants his parents to get him a drink of water.

CHART CHECK →

Tick the correct answer.

Which word comes before the adjective or adverb?

❒ ***too***

❒ ***enough***

INFINITIVES WITH *TOO*

	Too	Adjective/ Adverb	(*For* + Noun/ Object Pronoun)	Infinitive	
We're (not)	too	**young**	(for people)	**to trust**	us.
The teacher talked		**quickly**	(for me)	**to take**	notes.
It's (not)		**hard**	(for us)	**to decide**.	

INFINITIVES WITH *ENOUGH*

	Adjective/ Adverb	*Enough*	(*For* + Noun/ Object Pronoun)	Infinitive	
They're (not)	**old**	enough	(for people)	**to trust**	them.
She hasn't come	**often**		(for me)	**to recognise**	her.
It's (not)	**easy**		(for us)	**to decide**.	

EXPRESS CHECK

Unscramble these words to form two sentences.

vote • She's • to • young • too ____________________

to • enough • old • We're • work ____________________

Grammar Explanations	Examples
1. Use ***too*** + **adjective/adverb** + **infinitive** to give a reason.	■ I'm **too young *to drive***. *(I'm not seventeen yet so I can't drive.)* ■ She is**n't too young *to drive***. *(She's over seventeen so she can drive.)* ■ She arrived **too late *to take*** the test. *(She arrived twenty minutes after the test started so she couldn't take the test.)* ■ She did**n't** arrive **too late *to take*** the test. *(She arrived only two minutes after the test started so she could still take the test.)*
2. You can also use **adjective/adverb** + ***enough*** + **infinitive** to give a reason.	■ I'm **old enough *to go*** into the army. *(I'm over eighteen so I can go into the army.)* ■ He is**n't old enough *to go*** into the army. *(He isn't eighteen yet so he can't go into the army.)* ■ I ran **fast enough *to get*** into the final. *(I ran very fast so I managed to get into the final.)* ■ She did**n't** run **fast enough *to get*** into the final. *(She didn't run very fast so she didn't manage to get into the final.)*
3. Notice that you don't need to use the infinitive when the meaning is clear from the context.	■ I'm seventeen years old and I can't vote yet. I'm **too young**. I'm not **old enough**.
▶ **Be careful!** Note the position of ***too*** and ***enough***.	
Too comes before the adjective or adverb.	■ She's ***too* old**.
Enough comes after the adjective or adverb.	■ I'm not **old *enough***. Not ~~I'm not enough old.~~
4. Sometimes we use ***for*** + **noun** or ***for*** + **object pronoun** before the infinitive.	■ We are too young **for our parents *to allow*** us to go out alone. *(Our parents won't allow us to go out alone.)* ■ We are too young **for them *to allow*** us go out alone. *(They won't let us go out alone.)*

CHOOSE • *People have different opinions about things. Read each numbered statement of opinion. Then circle the letter of the sentence* (a) *or* (b) *that best summarises that opinion.*

1. Teenagers are responsible enough to stay out past 10:00 p.m.
   (a.) Teenagers should have permission to stay out past 10:00 p.m.
   b. Teenagers shouldn't have permission to stay out past 10:00 p.m.
2. Teenagers are too immature to vote.
   a. Teenagers should be able to vote.
   b. Teenagers shouldn't be able to vote.
3. Teenagers are responsible enough to use the internet without censorship.
   a. Teenagers can use the internet without censorship.
   b. Teenagers can't use the internet without censorship.
4. Adults are too afraid of change to listen to children's ideas.
   a. Adults listen to children's ideas.
   b. Adults don't listen to children's ideas.
5. At the age of seventy, people are not too old to work.
   a. At the age of seventy, people can work.
   b. At the age of seventy, people can't work.
6. Sixteen-year-olds are not experienced enough to drive.
   a. Sixteen-year-olds can drive.
   b. Sixteen-year-olds can't drive.

UNSCRAMBLE • *Gina wants to drive to Milton Keynes for a concert but her mother thinks she's too young. Make sentences with the words in brackets. Then write* **G (Gina)** *or* **M (Mother)** *to show whose opinion each sentence represents.*

1. You're too young to be out so late. M
   (too / You're / young / to / out / be / so / late)
2. ______________________________
   (get / It's / to / by ten / us / too / home / far / for)
3. ______________________________
   (take care of / mature / myself / I'm / to / enough)
4. ______________________________
   (dangerous / too / night / It's / to / drive / at)
5. ______________________________
   (too / give / worry / I / much / to / permission / you)
6. ______________________________
   (that / experienced / drive / aren't / far / enough / to / You)

COMPLETE • *Some teenagers are leaving a concert. Complete the sentences. Use the words in brackets with the infinitive and* **too** *or* **enough**.

1. I couldn't hear that last song. The guitar was too loud for me to hear the words. (loud / me / hear)
2. Let's get tickets for the concert at Hampton. They're _______________. (cheap / us / afford)
3. I hope the concert hall is _______________ all the fans! (large / hold)
4. I hope my mother lets me go. This concert is going to be _______________. (good / me / miss)
5. Let's get a pizza at Luigi's. The large ones are _______________. (big / share)
6. It's 9:30 already. It's _______________ for pizza. (late / stop)
7. I hate this! I think we're _______________ out past 10:00! (old / stay)
8. Tom didn't get out of work _______________ tonight. (early / come)
9. Zak, I'm playing basketball tomorrow. Are you still _______________ me? (slow / beat)
10. Let's find out. But I want to walk. Your car isn't _______________. (safe / drive)

EDIT • *Read this student's diary entry. Find and correct eight mistakes in the use of infinitives with* **too** *or* **enough**. *The first mistake has already been corrected.*

The Phish concert was brilliant! Now I'm too excited ~~for sleeping~~ to sleep. That Mike Gordon really can sing. My voice isn't enough good to sing in the shower! After the concert, we were really hungry but it was to late to go for pizza. I HATE going home so early! It's too weird understand. My friend Stan works and has to pay taxes but the law says he's too young for staying out past 10:00! That's crazy enough to make me want to scream. That reminds me. I sure hope my mother changes her mind soon enough for I to buy a ticket to the Hampton concert. They sell out very quickly. Why doesn't she think I'm mature to drive fifty miles? I'll have to do it sometime! Well, I'd better try to get some sleep or I'll be too tired too get up in the morning.

UNIT 51 Infinitives of Purpose

DATALATOR 534 F

Personal Digital Assistant **£99**

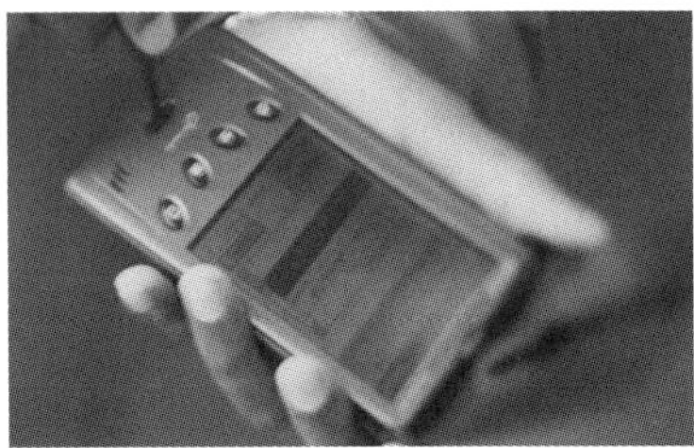

Use me
- ✔ **to look up** words
- ✔ **to check** meaning and pronunciation
- ✔ **to store** names and phone numbers
- ✔ **to add** and **subtract**
- ✔ **to write down** ideas
- ✔ **to surf** the net!

CHECK POINT

Tick all the correct answers.

What can you use the Personal Digital Assistant (PDA) as?

❐ an address book ❐ a telephone ❐ a dictionary ❐ a note pad ❐ a radio

CHART CHECK

Circle T (True) or F (False).

T F There are two ways to form the affirmative infinitive of purpose.

T F There are two ways to form the negative infinitive of purpose.

AFFIRMATIVE	NEGATIVE
I put his number in my PDA **(in order) to save** it.	I put his number in my PDA **in order not to lose** it.
I made a note **(in order) to remember** our meeting.	I made a note **in order not to forget** our meeting.
I left at 9:00 **(in order) to arrive** early.	I left at 9:00 **in order not to arrive** late.
I ran **(in order) to catch** the bus.	I ran **in order not to miss** the bus.

EXPRESS CHECK

Unscramble these words to form two sentences.

store • addresses • use • I • a • PDA • to

____

in order • I • not • set • oversleep • my • alarm clock • to

____

Grammar Explanations	Examples
1. Use an **infinitive** (***to*** + **base form** of the verb) to explain the purpose of an action. It often answers the question ***Why?***	**A:** ***Why*** did you go to Lacy's? **B:** I went there **to buy** one of those PDAs I saw in an advert.
Usage Note: In spoken English, you can answer the question ***Why?*** with an incomplete sentence beginning with ***To***.	**A:** ***Why*** did you go to Lacy's? **B:** **To buy** a PDA.
2. You can also use the longer form ***in order to*** + **base form** of the verb to explain a purpose.	■ I bought a PDA **in order to store** names and phone numbers.
Usage Note: ***To*** + **base form** of the verb is more common in informal speech and writing.	■ I bought a PDA **to store** names and phone numbers.
3. Use ***in order not to*** + **base form** of the verb to express a negative purpose.	■ I use my PDA **in order not to make** mistakes in pronunciation. *(I don't want to make mistakes.)*
4. You can also use **noun/pronoun** + **infinitive** to express the purpose of an object.	■ I need a **PDA to help** me remember my appointments. ■ I need **it to help** me remember my appointments.

IDENTIFY • *Read this conversation. Underline all the infinitives that express a purpose.*

JUDITH: It's 5:00. Aren't you going home?

LEE: No. I'm staying late to finish this report. What about you? Are you going straight home?

JUDITH: No. I'm going to stop at the bank to get some cash. Then I'm going to Lacy's to take advantage of the sale they're having.

LEE: Oh, what are you going to get?

JUDITH: One of those new PDAs they're advertising. I've been looking for something to help me with my work.

LEE: What's wrong with a normal organiser?

JUDITH: Nothing. But sometimes I need to surf the net.

LEE: What else are you going to use it for?

JUDITH: Oh, to store important names and phone numbers and to do my accounts.

LEE: What did we do before they invented all these electronic gadgets?

JUDITH: We made a lot of mistakes!

ANSWER • *Look at Judith's list of things to do. Then write a phrase to answer each question.*

To Do
- Check tyres
- Make dental appointment
- Buy batteries
- Withdraw £100
- Invite Rick and Tina to dinner
- Buy milk and eggs

1. Why did she ring the surgery? *To make a dental appointment.*
2. Why did she go to the bank? ____________________
3. Why did she ring her friends? ____________________
4. Why did she go to the supermarket? ____________________
5. Why did she go to the electrical shop? ____________________
6. Why did she go to the petrol station? ____________________

MATCH • *Find the correct purpose for each action.*

	Action	Purpose
g	1. He enrolled on the course because he	a. didn't want to get any phone calls.
b	2. She caught a bus because she	b. didn't want to be late.
______	3. She went to the shop because she	c. wanted to store information.
______	4. We disconnected our phone because we	d. wanted to listen to the news.
______	5. He turned on the radio because he	e. didn't want to worry me.
______	6. He didn't tell me he was ill because he	f. needed to buy some pasta.
______	7. She bought a PDA because she	g. wanted to learn a new language.

REWRITE • *Combine the sentence parts above. Use the infinitive of purpose.*

1. He enrolled on the course to learn a new language.
2. She took a bus in order not to be late.
3. ______________________________
4. ______________________________
5. ______________________________
6. ______________________________
7. ______________________________

EDIT • *Read this student's diary entry. Find and correct six mistakes in the use of the infinitive of purpose. The first mistake has already been corrected.*

I went to the dentist ~~for getting~~ to get my teeth cleaned today. While I was waiting, I used my PDA to study for the test. Then I used it to helps me pronounce 'dental floss' for my appointment. After the dentist, I checked my calendar and saw 'Rick and Tina, dinner, 7:30'. I should use it in order to not forget appointments! Luckily, my recipes are already on the PDA so I used them for making a quick shopping list. When I got home, there was a note on my door – 'Call PLB'. I checked the PDA dictionary to find 'PLB'. The 'plumber' wanted to come in order fix the taps! Rick, Tina and I played with the PDA all evening. You can programme it for to play computer games, too. I don't know how I lived without it!

UNIT 52 Gerunds and Infinitives

I'm so embarrassed. I didn't **remember meeting** Bob.
How could you forget?
Hi! I'm Bob.

CHECK POINT

Circle T (True) or F (False).

T F The woman had an appointment with Bob but she forgot to go.

T F The woman forgot that she had met Bob once before.

CHART CHECK

Circle T (True) or F (False).

T F Some verbs can be followed by either the gerund or the infinitive.

T F The infinitive sometimes follows a preposition.

T F A gerund can be the subject of a sentence.

GERUNDS	INFINITIVES
Joan **enjoys going** to parties.	Joan **wants to go** to parties.
She **loves meeting** new people.	She **loves to meet** new people.
She **stopped buying** ice cream.	She **stopped to buy** ice cream.
She's worried **about forgetting** people's names.	
Meeting new people is fun.	**It's** fun **to meet** new people.

EXPRESS CHECK

Complete these sentences with the correct form of the verbs **go** *or* **talk**.

- Phil wants ________________ to the party.
- ________________ to parties is exciting.
- Phil enjoys ________________ about a lot of different things.
- It's fun ________________ to new people.

Grammar Explanations	Examples
1. Some **verbs** are **followed by a gerund**.	■ Joan **enjoys** ***meeting*** people. ■ She **misses** ***going*** to parties.
2. Some **verbs** are **followed by an infinitive**.	■ Joan **wants** ***to meet*** people. ■ She'**d like** ***to go*** to parties.
3. Some **verbs** can be followed by either **a gerund** or **an infinitive**.	■ Joan **loves** ***meeting*** new people. OR ■ Joan **loves** ***to meet*** new people.
4. **Be careful!** A few verbs can be followed by either a gerund or an infinitive but the **meanings are very different**.	■ Joan **stopped eating** ice cream. *(She doesn't eat ice cream anymore.)* ■ Joan **stopped to eat** ice cream. *(She stopped another activity in order to eat some ice cream.)* ■ Richard **remembered posting** the invitation. *(First, he posted the invitation. Then, he remembered that he had done it.)* ■ Richard **remembered to post** the invitation. *(First, he remembered. Then, he posted the invitation.)* ■ Joan never **forgot meeting** Richard. *(Joan met Richard. It was an important meeting that she still remembers.)* ■ Joan **forgot to meet** Richard. *(Joan had plans to meet Richard but she didn't meet him because she forgot about the plans.)*
5. A **gerund** is the only verb form that **can follow a preposition**.	preposition ■ Joan's worried **about** ***forgetting*** names.
6. To make **general statements**, you can use: • **gerund as subject** OR • ***It's*** + **adjective/noun** + **infinitive**	■ **Meeting** new people is fun. OR ■ **It's** fun **to meet** new people

Check it out!

For a list of common verbs followed by the gerund, see Appendix 3 on page 337.
For a list of common verbs followed by the infinitive, see Appendix 4 on page 338.
For a list of verbs that can be followed by the gerund or the infinitive, see Appendix 6 on page 338.

TRUE OR FALSE • *Read each numbered sentence. Write T (True) or F (False) for the statement that follows.*

1. Joan remembered meeting Mr Jackson.

   __T__ Joan has already met Mr Jackson.

2. Richard stopped smoking.

   ______ Richard doesn't smoke any more.

3. She didn't remember to buy a cake for the party.

   ______ She bought a cake.

4. She stopped eating desserts.

   ______ She used to eat desserts.

5. Richard forgot to invite his boss to the party.

   ______ Richard invited his boss.

6. Richard never forgot seeing Jane for the first time.

   ______ Richard forgot about Jane.

7. Richard thinks giving a party is fun.

   ______ Richard thinks it's fun to give a party.

8. Joan likes going to parties.

   ______ Joan likes to go to parties.

CHOOSE • *Circle the correct words to complete these ideas from a book about memory.*

1. Get into the habit of (repeating) / to repeat things aloud.
2. Never rely on someone else's memory. Learn trusting / to trust your own.
3. It's easy forgetting / to forget what you don't want remembering / to remember.
4. Study immediately before going / to go to sleep. You'll remember a lot more.
5. Our memories are filled with things we never meant remembering / to remember.
6. Make it a habit to look back at your car every time you get out and you'll never forget turning off / to turn off your headlights.
7. Playing / To play games is a fun way of improving / to improve your memory skills.

SUMMARISE • *Read each numbered statement or conversation. Complete the summary statement using a gerund or an infinitive.*

1. **ROGER:** Hi, Richard. I brought the drinks. Where do you want me to put them?
   SUMMARY: Roger remembered to bring the drinks.
2. **JOAN:** You're Natalie! We met last year at Richard's party! How have you been?
   SUMMARY: Joan remembers ______________________________
3. **ROGER:** Don't look at *me*! I didn't spill juice on the sofa!
   SUMMARY: Roger denied ______________________________
4. **NATALIE:** I'm so glad Richard plays jazz at his parties. I listen to it a lot at home, too.
   SUMMARY: Natalie enjoys ______________________________
5. **LEO:** Would you like to go dancing some time?
   JOAN: Sure. I'd like that very much.
   SUMMARY: Leo suggested ______________________________
   Joan agreed ______________________________
6. **NATALIE:** Joan, can we give you a lift home?
   JOAN: Thanks, but I think I'll stay a little longer.
   SUMMARY: Natalie offered ______________________________
   Joan decided ______________________________

EDIT • *Read Joan's diary entry about Richard's party. Find and correct seven mistakes in the use of the gerund and infinitive. The first mistake has already been corrected.*

What a great party! I usually avoid ~~to go~~ going to parties because it's such a problem for me to remember people's names. I'm so glad I read that book about improve your memory. The author suggested to do exercises and they really helped. I stopped to worry about what people would think of me and I tried to pay attention to what people were saying. As a result, I had a great time! I'm even planning going dancing with this guy Leo next week.

I have an English test tomorrow so I should stop writing now and start studying. The book even had some good tips about study for an exam. I hope I remember using some of them tonight!

Make, Let, Help and *Get*

Oh no! She's not going to let us leave when the bell rings!

She'll make me do my essay again.

Alice Roberts with two of her students.

CHECK POINT

Circle T (True) or F (False).

T F The teacher in the picture has very strict rules.

CHART CHECK

Circle T (True) or F (False).

T F ***Make*** and ***let*** are always followed by the base form of the verb.

T F ***Get*** can be followed by either the base form of the verb or the infinitive.

T F ***Help*** can be followed by either the base form of the verb or the infinitive.

MAKE, LET, HELP					
SUBJECT	***MAKE/LET/HELP***		**OBJECT**	**BASE FORM OF VERB**	
The teachers	**(don't)**	**make** **let** **help**	us students	**do**	homework.

GET, HELP					
SUBJECT	***GET/HELP***		**OBJECT**	**INFINITIVE**	
The teachers	**(don't)**	**get** **help**	us students	**to do**	homework.

EXPRESS CHECK

Complete these sentences with the correct form of the verbs **correct** *or* **stay**.

A: Did the teacher get the students ________________ their essays?

B: Yes. He got them ________________ their essays in groups.

A: Do you think he'll make them ________________ late again today?

B: I don't think so. But he'll let them ________________ late if they need help.

Grammar Explanations	Examples
1. Use ***make*** and ***let*** followed by **object + base form** of the verb to talk about things that someone can require or permit another person to do.	■ The teacher **makes *his students* do** homework every night. *(He requires them to do homework.)* ■ He **lets *them choose*** their own essay topics. *(He allows them to choose their own essay topics.)*
You can also use ***make*** to mean 'cause to'.	■ This will **make *you become*** a better student. *(This will cause you to become a better student.)*

2. ***Help*** can be followed by either: • **object + base form** of the verb OR • **object + infinitive**. The meaning is the same. **USAGE NOTE:** ***Help*** + base form of the verb is more common.	■ She **helped *me understand*** the homework. OR ■ She **helped *me to understand*** the homework.

3. ***Get*** has a similar meaning to *make* but it is followed by **object + infinitive**, not the base form of the verb.	■ The teacher **got *us to help*** the weaker students. NOT ~~The teacher got us help the weaker students~~. *(The teacher persuaded us to help the weaker students.)* ■ She always **gets *me to do*** my best. *(She always motivates me and I do my best in her lessons.)*

TRUE OR FALSE • *Read each numbered sentence. Write T (True) or F (False) for the statement that follows.*

1. My teacher made me rewrite the report.

   __T__ I wrote the report again.

2. Ms Trager let us use our dictionaries during the test.

   ______ We had to use our dictionaries.

3. Mr Goldberg got us to translate a short story.

   ______ We translated a short story.

4. Paul helped Annie do her homework.

   ______ Paul did Annie's homework for her.

5. Ms Bates got the director to arrange a class trip.

   ______ The director arranged a class trip.

6. Professor Washington let us choose our own topic for our essay.

   ______ We didn't choose our own topic.

CHOOSE • *Circle the correct words to complete this article about Bill Roberts.*

Miracle Teacher

The day Bill Roberts arrived to start his first teaching job at Sunnyfields, he was amazed to see that the other teachers made / (let) (1.) students hand in their homework late and miss classes altogether. Even in sports lessons, no one made / let (2.) students take part: they could just sit on the grass and chat if they wanted to. But Bill believed in teaching too much to help / let (3.) his own students waste their education. So from the start, he decided to help / make (4.) them to achieve their best. Every morning, he got / let (5.) them to do five minutes of aerobics exercises, then he made / let (6.) them sing the school song, whether they wanted to or not! By the time each lesson began, he had got / made (7.) his students to pay attention to every word he said. Bill knew his methods were unconventional but he couldn't make / let (8.) his students miss out on an education. He believed in them too much to help / let (9.) that happen. He intended to get / help (10.) them see the value of learning, and that's exactly what he achieved. As an ex-student of Bill's once said, 'He made / let (11.) me realise that I could do anything if I really tried.'

SUMMARISE • *Read each numbered statement. Complete the summary with the correct form of the verbs in brackets. Choose between affirmative and negative forms.*

1. **Ms Allen:** Peter, you can rewrite this essay but only if you want to.

   Summary: She didn't make Peter rewrite his essay. (make / rewrite)

2. **Ms Allen:** I know you prefer working alone, Anna, but you really need to work in a group today.

   Summary: She ______ in a group. (make / work)

3. **Ms Allen:** Listen, everyone! No dictionaries during the test, please. You should be able to guess the meaning from the context.

   Summary: She ______ dictionaries. (let / use)

4. **Ms Allen:** Freddy, could you do me a favour and clean the board before you leave?

   Summary: She ______ the board. (got / clean)

5. **Ms Allen:** Simon, show your teeth and say é –, école. Yes! That's it!

   Summary: She ______ a French *é*. (get / pronounce)

6. **Ms Allen:** Julie, please use French in class!

   Summary: She ______ in English. (let / speak)

7. **Ms Allen:** Janet, you can take the test in the classroom. Just move your desk to a corner.

   Summary: She ______ the room. (make / leave)

4 ***EDIT*** • *Read this student's diary entry. Find and correct seven mistakes in the use of* **make**, **let**, **help** *and* **get**. *The first mistake has already been corrected.*

When I was a teenager, my parents never let me ~~to play~~ play until I had finished all my homework. They even made me helping my brothers with their homework before I could have any fun. On the one hand, they certainly got me learn a lot. On the other hand, they made me became too serious. I wish they had let me to have a little more fun. When I become a parent, I want to get my child learns about responsibility but also I would want to let he or she have fun. As Ben Franklin said, 'All work and no play makes Jack a dull boy'. I want to avoid that mistake.

SelfTest IX

SECTION ONE

Circle the letter of the correct answer to complete each sentence.

EXAMPLE:
Jennifer never ________ coffee. A (B) C D
(A) drink (C) is drinking
(B) drinks (D) was drinking

1. Maria's going to stop ________ dinner so she may be late. A B C D
(A) eating (C) to eat
(B) for eating (D) eat

2. My glasses are in my bag but I don't remember ________ them there. A B C D
(A) putting (C) I put
(B) to put (D) put

3. I asked him ________ but he went anyway. A B C D
(A) not to go (C) not going
(B) to not go (D) he doesn't go

4. ________ in a foreign country is sometimes difficult. A B C D
(A) I live (C) Live
(B) Living (D) Lives

5. He's not used to ________ up so early. A B C D
(A) wake (C) wakes
(B) waken (D) waking

6. We're eighteen so we're ________ vote. A B C D
(A) too old to (C) old enough to
(B) young enough to (D) old enough for

7. I don't think Tom enjoyed ________ me study for the test. A B C D
(A) helping (C) helped
(B) to help (D) helps

8. I bought this new software ________ Chinese. A B C D
(A) for learning (C) to learn
(B) learning (D) learned

9. We got a new card holder ________ lose our credit cards. A B C D
(A) in order not to (C) not to
(B) not (D) for not

10. It isn't difficult ________ this textbook. A B C D
(A) understand (C) for understanding
(B) in order to understand (D) to understand

11. Are you ready? It's time ________.　　A B C D
(A) for going　　(C) going
(B) to go　　(D) go

12. I resented ________ that. He could have been more polite.　　A B C D
(A) he said　　(C) his saying
(B) he saying　　(D) him to say

13. I talked to the students about working harder but I couldn't ________ them to study.　　A B C D
(A) make　　(C) got
(B) get　　(D) let

14. My mother ________ do my homework before I go out.　　A B C D
(A) makes me　　(C) gets me
(B) helps me　　(D) lets me

SECTION TWO

Each sentence has four underlined words or phrases. The four underlined parts of the sentence are marked A, B, C and D. Circle the letter of the one underlined word or phrase that is NOT CORRECT.

EXAMPLE:
Mike usually [A] drives [B] to school but today [C] he walks [D].　　A B C (D)

15. I decided [A] changing [B] jobs because my boss makes [C] me work [D] overtime.　　A B C D

16. Most students appreciate [A] their head teacher [B] try [C] to improve [D] school conditions.　　A B C D

17. I succeeded in [A] to find [B] a job so my parents didn't make [C] me go [D] to university.　　A B C D

18. Get [A] more exercise appears [B] to be [C] the best way to lose [D] weight.　　A B C D

19. In order [A] to not [B] forget [C] things, I put [D] a string around my finger.　　A B C D

20. Harry is [A] only fourteen but he seems [B] enough old [C] to stay [D] out until ten.　　A B C D

21. I know you're too busy [A] to stay [B] but I look forward [C] to see [D] you again.　　A B C D

22. I forgot buying [A] petrol but I got [B] to a petrol station before [C] I ran out [D].　　A B C D

23. Getting [A] enough sleep is [B] important in order [C] not fall [D] asleep in class.　　A B C D

24. Let's stop [A] to watch [B] so much TV and read [C] or go out [D] instead.　　A B C D

25. I'm trying [A] to persuade [B] my sister to drive [C] but I can't get her do [D] it.　　A B C D

Phrasal Verbs: Inseparable

CHECK POINT

Tick the correct answer.

Where does the woman suggest eating?

- ❒ at home
- ❒ in a restaurant
- ❒ in a park

CHART CHECK

Tick the correct answer.

Where does the particle go?

- ❒ before the direct object
- ❒ after the direct object

INSEPARABLE PHRASAL VERBS

SUBJECT	VERB	PARTICLE	DIRECT OBJECT
They	**came**	**back**.	
	gave	**up**.	
	ate	**out**.	
	ran	**into**	his teacher.
	stuck	**to**	their decision.

EXPRESS CHECK

Unscramble these words to form two sentences.

into • We • Bob • ran

____

out • was • He • eating

____

Grammar Explanations	Examples
1. A **phrasal verb** (also called a multi-word verb) consists of a **verb + particle**.	verb + particle ■ We often **eat out**.
2. Particles look the same as prepositions. However, particles are part of the verb phrase and they often change the meaning of the verb.	verb + preposition ■ She **ran into** another runner because she wasn't paying attention. *(She collided with another runner.)* verb + particle ■ I **ran into** John at the supermarket. *(I met John by accident.)*
3. The verb and particle are usually common words but their separate meanings may not help you guess the **meaning of the phrasal verb**. **USAGE NOTE:** Phrasal verbs are very common in everyday speech.	■ Please **go on**. I didn't mean to interrupt. *(Please continue.)* ■ We **got back** after dark. *(We returned after dark.)* ■ They **called off** the meeting. *(They cancelled the meeting.)*
4. Most phrasal verbs are **transitive**. (They take direct objects). Some transitive phrasal verbs are **inseparable**. This means that both noun and pronoun objects always go after the particle. You cannot separate the verb from its particle.	direct object ■ You should **go after *your goals***. direct object ■ She **ran into *her friend*** at the library. NOT ~~She ran her friend into at the library~~. direct object ■ She **ran into *her***. NOT ~~She ran her into~~.
5. Some phrasal verbs are used in combination with certain prepositions. These combinations are usually **inseparable**.	■ She **came up *with*** a brilliant idea. ■ I **dropped out *of*** school and got a job.

Check it out!

For a list of some common inseparable phrasal verbs, see Appendix 17 on pages 341–342.
To learn about separable phrasal verbs, see Unit 55, pages 236–237.

IDENTIFY • *Read this article. Circle all the phrasal verbs.*

The Art of Feng Shui

Ho Da-ming's new restaurant was failing. His customers rarely (came back). Why? Mr Ho contacted a feng shui consultant to find out. Feng shui (meaning 'wind and water') is the ancient Chinese art of placing things in your surroundings. According to this art, the arrangement of furniture, doors and windows affects our health, wealth and happiness. Mr Ho was concerned about his business but he didn't give up. Following the consultant's advice, he remodelled and redecorated his restaurant. His actions paid off. Soon business picked up and Mr Ho became rich. 'It was the best decision I ever made,' he says happily. And he isn't alone in his enthusiasm. Feng shui has caught on with modern architects and homeowners everywhere.

MATCH • *Write each phrasal verb from the article next to its meaning.*

	Phrasal Verb	Meaning		Phrasal Verb	Meaning
1.	________	has become popular	4.	________	learn information
2.	came back	returned	5.	________	stop trying
3.	________	were worthwhile	6.	________	improved

CHOOSE • *Complete this student's diary entry by circling the correct particles.*

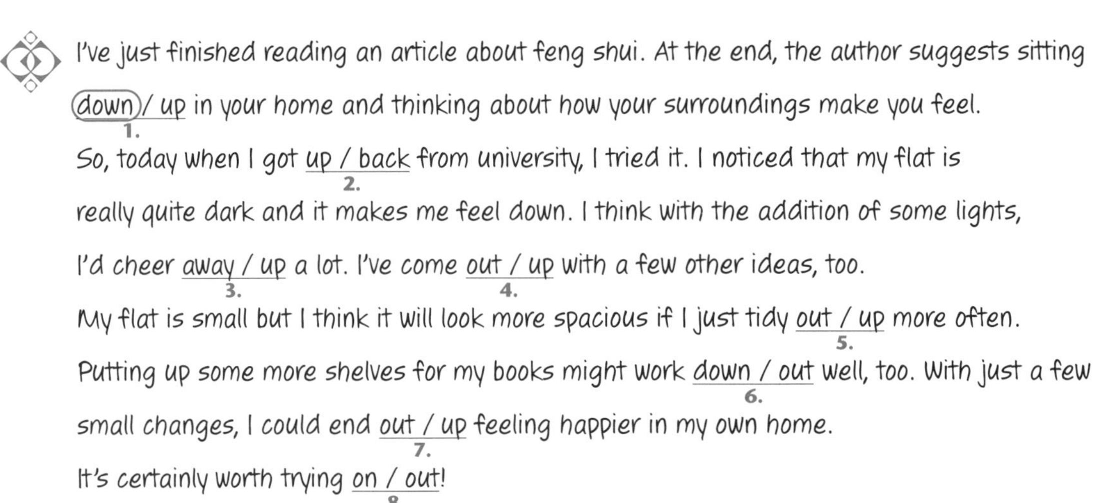

I've just finished reading an article about feng shui. At the end, the author suggests sitting (down) / up (1.) in your home and thinking about how your surroundings make you feel.

So, today when I got up / back (2.) from university, I tried it. I noticed that my flat is really quite dark and it makes me feel down. I think with the addition of some lights, I'd cheer away / up (3.) a lot. I've come out / up (4.) with a few other ideas, too.

My flat is small but I think it will look more spacious if I just tidy out / up (5.) more often. Putting up some more shelves for my books might work down / out (6.) well, too. With just a few small changes, I could end out / up (7.) feeling happier in my own home.

It's certainly worth trying on / out (8.)!

CHOOSE & COMPLETE • *Read this article about the architect I. M. Pei. Complete it using the correct form of the phrasal verbs in the box.*

come up with   give up   go back   go up   ~~grow up~~   carry on   pay off   turn out

Born in 1917, Ieoh Ming Pei (better known as I. M. Pei) ___grew up___ (1.) in Canton, China. When he was seventeen, he went to the United States to learn about building. As it ______________ (2.), Pei became one of the most famous architects of the twentieth century.

Pei is famous for his strong geometric forms. One of his most controversial projects was his glass pyramid at the Louvre in Paris. The old museum had a lot of problems but no one wanted to destroy it. Pei had to ______________ (3.) a solution. Many Parisians were shocked with his proposal for a 71-foot-high glass pyramid. It ______________ (4.) anyway, blending with the environment. Today many people say that it is a good example of the principles of feng shui.

Pei ______________ (5.) despite criticism. He strongly believed that 'you have to identify the important things and press for them and not ______________ (6.)'. His determination ______________ (7.). He continued to build structures that reflected the environment. Pei received many prizes for his work. He used some of the prize money to start a scholarship fund for Chinese students to study architecture in the United States and then to ______________ (8.) to China to work as architects.

EDIT • *Read Bob's note to his flat mate. Find and correct eight mistakes in the use of inseparable phrasal verbs. The first mistake has already been corrected.*

> Sorry the flat is such a mess. I got ~~down~~ up late this morning and didn't have time to tidy out. I'm going to the gym now to work off for an hour. I should get across before you and I'll clean up then. How about eating tonight out? Afterwards, we can get together with some of the guys and maybe see a film. Or maybe we'll come over with a better idea.   Bob
>
> P.S. I ran Tom into at the library. He'll drop off to see you later.

Phrasal Verbs: Separable

Glove sticks to burr.
Burr sticks to fur.
Why? **Work** this **out**!
Uh-oh. I can see another weird invention coming. George **is dreaming** it **up** right now!
Burr

CHECK POINT

Tick the correct answer.

The dog thinks that

❒ George is dreaming.

❒ George is getting an idea for an invention.

SEPARABLE PHRASAL VERBS

CHART CHECK

Tick the correct answer.

❒ Direct objects that are nouns can go before or after the particle.

❒ Direct objects that are pronouns always go after the particle.

NOT SEPARATED			
Subject	**Verb**	**Particle**	**Direct Object**
He	**dreamt**	**up**	the idea.
	worked	**out**	the details.

SEPARATED			
Subject	**Verb**	**Direct Object**	**Particle**
He	**dreamt**	the idea it	**up**.
	worked	the details them	**out**.

EXPRESS CHECK

Complete these sentences with the correct form of the words in brackets.

Who ______________________? Did *you* ______________________?
(dream up / that idea) (dream up / it)

Grammar Explanations	Examples
1. A **phrasal verb** consists of a **verb + particle**.	verb + particle ■ She **set up** an experiment.
Particles look the same as prepositions but they are part of the verb phrase. They often change the meaning of the verb.	verb + preposition ■ He **looked up** at the sky. *(He looked in the direction of the sky.)* verb + particle ■ He **looked up** the information on the internet. *(He found the information on the internet.)*
The separate meanings of the verb and particle may be very different from the **meaning of the phrasal verb**.	■ They **turned down** my application. *(They rejected my application.)*
2. Most phrasal verbs are transitive (they take direct objects). Most transitive phrasal verbs are **separable**. This means the **direct object** can go:	
a. after the particle (verb and particle are not separated)	verb + particle + direct object ■ I just **dreamt up *a new idea***.
OR	OR
b. between the verb and the particle (verb and particle are separated)	verb + direct object + particle ■ I just **dreamt *a new idea* up**.
Notice that when the direct object is **in a long phrase**, it comes after the particle.	direct object ■ She **dreamt up *an unusually complicated new device***. NOT ~~She dreamt an unusually complicated new device up.~~
► **BE CAREFUL!** When the direct object is a pronoun, it **must** go between the verb and the particle.	■ She **dreamt *it* up**. NOT ~~She dreamt up it.~~
3. With a small group of phrasal verbs, the verb and particle **must be separated**.	
keep *something* ***on***	■ **Keep *your hat* on**. NOT ~~Keep on your hat.~~
talk *someone* ***into***	■ She **talked *her boss* into** (giving her) a pay rise. NOT ~~She talked into her boss a pay rise.~~

Check it out!

For a list of common separable phrasal verbs, see Appendix 17 on pages 341–342.
For a list of common phrasal verbs that must be separated, see Appendix 17 on pages 341–342.
For information about inseparable phrasal verbs, see Unit 54, pages 232–233.

IDENTIFY • *Read this article. Underline the phrasal verbs. Circle the direct objects.*

Eureka!

Did you know that two university dropouts thought up the idea of the first personal computer? What's more, they put it together in a garage. Inventions don't have to come out of fancy laboratories. Average people in classrooms, kitchens and home workshops often dream up new and useful ideas.

The ability to think of something new seems like magic to many people but in fact anyone can develop the qualities of an inventor. First, inventors follow their curiosity. The Swiss inventor George de Mestral wanted to find out the reason it was so hard to remove burrs from his dog's coat. His answer led to the idea for Velcro®, now used to fasten everything from trainers to space suits. Second, inventors use imagination to put things together in new ways. Walter Morrison watched two men throwing a pan to each other and thought up the Frisbee®, one of the most popular toys in the world. Perhaps most important, successful inventors don't give up. They continuously look up information about their ideas and try new designs out until they succeed.

CHOOSE & COMPLETE • *Read about one of history's greatest inventors. Complete the information with the correct form of the appropriate phrasal verbs from the box.*

fill up keep away bring about ~~try out~~ set up carry out pay back pick up

As a child, Thomas Alva Edison (1847–1931) ___tried out___ (1.) almost everything he heard about – he even tried to hatch goose eggs by sitting on them! Before he was twelve, he __________ (2.) his first laboratory using money he had earnt himself. He had hundreds of bottles and he __________ them __________ (3.) with chemicals for his experiments. He labelled the bottles 'poison' to __________ his family __________ (4.). When he was fifteen, Edison __________ (5.) a new skill. He had saved a child's life and the grateful father, a telegraph operator, __________ Edison __________ (6.) by teaching him telegraphy. After that, Edison was able to work at night and __________ (7.) his experiments during the day.

In 1869, Edison made a piece of equipment for a company that supplied prices to gold brokers. This ________________ (8.) his first useful invention – the stock ticker – for which he received $40,000. He was then able to spend all his time working on his new inventions. During his lifetime, Edison was issued with 1,093 patents!

3

COMPLETE • *Read these conversations that take place in a school laboratory. Complete them with phrasal verbs and pronouns.*

1. **A:** Please **put on** your lab coats.
   B: Do we really have to ___put them on___? It's hot in here.
2. **A:** I can't **figure out** this problem.
   B: I know what you mean. I can't ________________ either.
3. **A:** Remember to **fill in** these forms.
   B: Can we ________________ at home or do we have to do it now?
4. **A:** Are you going to **hand out** the next assignment today?
   B: I ________________ a few minutes ago. Weren't you here?
5. **A:** I can't get this to work. We'd better **point** the problem **out** to the teacher.
   B: OK, I'll ________________ to her.
6. **A:** Are we supposed to **hand in** our lab reports today?
   B: No. Please ________________ next week.

EDIT • *Read an inventor's notes. Find and correct seven mistakes in the use of phrasal verbs. The first mistake has already been corrected.*

3 May I dreamt ~~over~~ up a really good idea – a jar of paint with an applicator like the kind used for shoe polish. It can be used to touch on spots on a wall when people don't want to paint a whole room. I know a manufacturer. I'll call up him and order several types so I can try them in.

3 July I filled down an application for a patent and posted it yesterday. I'll be able to set a strong and convincing demonstration of the product up soon.

30 August I demonstrated the product at an exhibition for decorators. I wanted to point out that it's very clean to use so I put white gloves for the demonstration. It went very well.

SECTION ONE

Circle the letter of the correct answer to complete each sentence.

EXAMPLE:

Jennifer never ________ coffee. A (B) C D

(A) drink (C) is drinking
(B) drinks (D) was drinking

1. Come in. Please sit ________. A B C D
   (A) down (C) it down
   (B) down it (D) up

2. Your mother called. She wants you to call her ________ tonight. A B C D
   (A) in (C) back
   (B) off (D) over

3. Could you turn ________ the music so we can sleep? A B C D
   (A) down (C) over
   (B) away (D) up

4. Please put ________ your lab coats before you leave the laboratory. A B C D
   (A) off (C) up
   (B) away (D) in

5. Mark works so hard that he's sure to ________. A B C D
   (A) give up (C) turn over
   (B) work off (D) get ahead

6. Kevin is going to ________ from holiday tomorrow. A B C D
   (A) call back (C) get back
   (B) give back (D) get along

7. A lamp will ________ this corner nicely. A B C D
   (A) turn on (C) put up
   (B) blow up (D) light up

8. Instead of arguing about the problem, let's ________. A B C D
   (A) look it over (C) take it away
   (B) charge it up (D) talk it over

9. That's very original. How did you dream ________ that idea? A B C D
   (A) about (C) of
   (B) down (D) up

10. That kettle is hot. Don't pick ________! A B C D
    (A) it up (C) up
    (B) up it (D) it

11. —It's cold outside. You need your jacket.
—OK. I'll put ________. **A B C D**
(A) it on
(B) it over
(C) on it
(D) over it

12. She ran ________ on the way home. **A B C D**
(A) him into
(B) into
(C) into Jason
(D) Jason into

13. Slow down. I can't keep up ________ you! **A B C D**
(A) of
(B) with
(C) after
(D) to

SECTION TWO

Each sentence has four underlined words or phrases. The four underlined parts of the sentence are marked A, B, C and D. Circle the letter of the one underlined word or phrase that is NOT CORRECT.

> **EXAMPLE:**
> Mike usually (A) drives (B) to school but today (C) he walks (D). **A B C (D)**

14. Could we talk over it (A) before you turn (B) the whole idea (C) down (D)? **A B C D**

15. I know I let (A) Andy (B) down (C) when I forgot to pick his suit out (D) from the dry cleaner's. **A B C D**

16. I ran into (A) him (B) while I was getting (C) the bus off (D). **A B C D**

17. As soon as I hand (A) in (B) my report (C), I'm going to take all these books on (D) to the library. **A B C D**

18. We'd better (A) get the bus on (B) now or we (C)'re going to miss it (D). **A B C D**

19. Instead of calling (A) off (B) the meeting, maybe we can just put it (C) over (D) until next week. **A B C D**

20. If you don't use out (A) the milk by Monday, please throw (B) it (C) away (D). **A B C D**

21. Jim had to cheer (A) up her (B) after the company turned down (C) her application (D). **A B C D**

22. Do you want to get up (A) by yourself or would you like (B) me (C) to wake up you (D)? **A B C D**

23. Tom asked (A) me to pick (B) some stamps for him (C) at the post office up (D). **A B C D**

24. Did you find (A) out (B) how Jane talked (C) into Meg (D) working on Saturday? **A B C D**

25. We got (A) over (B) well after we found (C) out (D) we were both from Dublin. **A B C D**

Nouns

ACROSS THE ATLANTIC ON A REED BOAT

Barbados—17 **May** 1970. Norwegian **explorer Thor Heyerdahl**, along with an international **crew**, has crossed the **Atlantic Ocean** on **Ra II**. The **reed boat**, modelled on those of the ancient **Egyptians**, made the **journey** in 57 **days**.

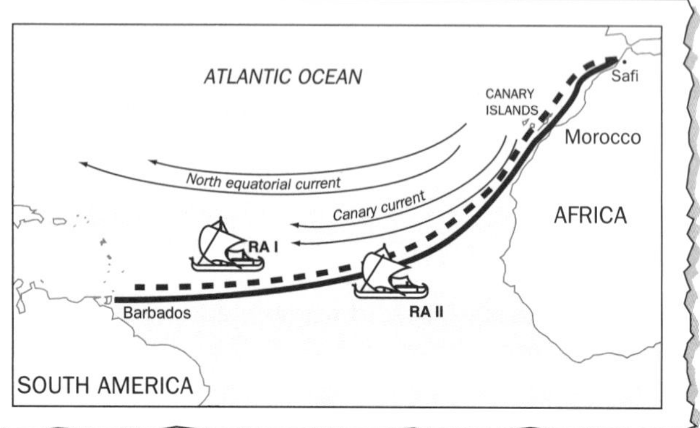

CHECK POINT

Tick the correct answer.

The name of Heyerdahl's boat was: ❐ Ra II ❐ Reed Boat

CHART CHECK 1

Circle T (True) or F (False).

T F Common nouns are written with capital letters.

PROPER NOUNS
Heyerdahl sailed **Ra II** across the **Atlantic**.

COMMON NOUNS
The **explorer** sailed his **boat** across the **ocean**.

CHART CHECK 2

Circle T (True) or F (False).

T F Countable nouns can be plural.

T F Uncountable nouns can be plural.

COUNTABLE NOUNS			
Article/ Number	**Noun**	**Verb**	
A One	**sailor**	is	brave.
(The) Two	**sailors**	are	

UNCOUNTABLE NOUNS		
Noun	**Verb**	
Fire	is	dangerous.
Sailing		

EXPRESS CHECK

Circle the correct words to complete these sentences.

The boats was / were made of reed. The voyage was / were hard.

Grammar Explanations	Examples
1. **Proper nouns** are the names of particular people, places and things. On the right are some categories and examples of proper nouns.	**People** Heyerdahl, Egyptians **Places** Africa, Morocco, the United States **Months** September, October **Days** Monday, Tuesday **Holidays** Easter, Passover, Ramadan **Languages** Arabic, Spanish
Capitalise the first letter of most proper nouns. We do not usually use an article (*a/an* or *the*) with proper nouns.	
Note that ***the*** is used with some nouns of places.	■ Heyerdal sailed across ***the* Atlantic**.

2. **Common nouns** refer to people, places and things but not by their individual names. For example, *explorer* is a common noun but *Heyerdahl* is a proper noun.	**People** explorer, sailor, builder, doctor **Places** continent, country, city, mountain **Things** pots, eggs, fish, honey, table

3. Common nouns are either countable or uncountable. **Countable nouns** are things that you can count separately. They can be singular or plural. For example, you can say *a ship* or *three ships*. You can use *a/an* or *the* before countable nouns.	■ **a** sailor, **the** sailor, **two** sailors ■ **an** island, **the** island, **three** islands ■ **a** ship, **the** ship, **four** ships
Form the **plural** of most nouns by adding *-s* or *-es* to the noun. There are sometimes spelling changes when you form the plural.	ship ship**s** potato potato**es** watch watch**es** country countr**ies**
▶ **Be careful!** Some nouns are irregular. They do not form the plural by adding *-s* or *-es*.	foot **feet** man **men** child **children** mouse **mice**

4. **Uncountable nouns** are things that you cannot count separately. For example, in English you can say *gold* but you cannot say *a gold* or *two golds*. Uncountable nouns usually have no plural forms. We usually do not use *a/an* with uncountable nouns. On the right are some categories and examples of uncountable nouns.	**Abstract words** courage, education, time **Activities** exploring, sailing, farming **Fields of study** geography, history, medicine **Food** corn, chocolate, fish, meat **Gases** air, oxygen, steam **Liquids** water, milk, coffee, petrol **Materials** cotton, plastic, silk, leather **Natural forces** cold, electricity, weather, wind **Particles** dust, sand, sugar, salt, rice
Some common uncountable nouns do not fit into these categories. You need to memorise nouns such as the ones on the right.	advice, furniture, jewellery, money clothing, rubbish, luggage, news equipment, homework, post, work food, information
▶ **Be careful!** Uncountable nouns take singular verbs and pronouns.	■ ***Reed* is** a good material for boats. ■ ***It* floats** in the heaviest storm.

Check it out!

For a list of some common irregular plural nouns, see Appendix 18 on page 343.

IDENTIFY • *Read this article about Thor Heyerdahl. Circle all the proper nouns. Underline once all the common countable nouns. Underline twice the common uncountable nouns.*

Who Really Discovered America?

Was (Columbus) really the first <u>explorer</u> to discover the Americas? Thor Heyerdahl didn't think so. He believed that ancient people were able to build boats that could cross oceans. To test his ideas, he decided to build a copy of the reed boats that were pictured in ancient paintings and sail across the Atlantic from North Africa to Barbados. Heyerdahl's team also copied ancient Middle Eastern pots and filled them with <u>food</u> for their journey – dried fish, honey, oil, eggs, nuts and fresh fruit. Ra, the expedition's boat, carried an international group including a Norwegian, an Egyptian, an Italian, a Mexican and a Chadian.

The first trip failed but everyone survived and wanted to try again. Departing on 17 May 1970, under the flag of the United Nations, Ra II crossed the Atlantic in 57 days. The expedition proved that ancient civilisations had the skill to reach the Americas long before Columbus.

2 ***COMPLETE*** • *Megan and Jason McKay are planning a hiking trip. Complete their conversation with the correct form of the words in brackets.*

JASON: There __'s__ (1. be) still a lot of __work__ (2. work) to do this evening. We have to plan the food for the trip.

MEGAN: You're right. ________ (3. Food) certainly ________ (4. be) important. I've been reading this book about camping. There ________ (5. be) some good ________ (6. idea) in it.

JASON: Oh? What does it say?

MEGAN: We should bring a lot of ________ (7. bean) and ________ (8. rice).

JASON: ________ (9. Potato) ________ (10. be) good on camping ________ (11. trip), too.

MEGAN: No, fresh ________ (12. vegetable) ________ (13. be) too heavy to carry. Maybe we can get some when we go through a town.

JASON: ______ (14. Be) the ______ (15. equipment) ready? We should go through the list.

MEGAN: I've done that. We need ______ (16. battery) for the radio.

JASON: Why do we need a radio? I thought we were running away from civilisation.

MEGAN: But the ______ (17. news) never ______ (18. stop). I still want to know what's happening.

JASON: That's OK with me. By the way, have we got enough warm ______ (19. clothing)? It gets chilly in the mountains.

MEGAN: That's true. And the ______ (20. cold) really ______ (21. bother) me at night.

JASON: But we've got warm sleeping ______ (22. bag).

***EDIT** • Tina Jameson sailed around the world alone on a small boat. Read her diary entries. There are fifteen mistakes in the use of nouns and subject–verb agreement. Find and correct them. The first two mistakes have already been corrected.*

27 October I've been on the ~~canary~~ Canary Islands for three days now. I'll start back home when the ~~weathers are~~ weather is better. I was so surprised when I picked up my posts today. My family sent me some birthday presents. My Birthday is the 31st. I won't open the presents until then.

29 october I think the weather is getting worse. I heard thunders today but there wasn't any rain. I stayed in bed with my cat, Typhoon. Every time it thundered, typhoon and I snuggled up closer under the covers. I started reading a Novel, 'Brave New World'.

30 October I left the Canary Islands today – just like columbus. There's a strong wind and plenty of sunshine now. I travelled 500 Kilometres.

31 October I'm 21 today! To celebrate, I drank some coffees for breakfast and I opened my presents. I got some perfume and pretty silver jewelleries.

1 November The electricities are very low. I'd better not use much until I get near plymouth. I'll need the radio then. It rained today so I collected waters for cooking.

Quantifiers

I'm glad I bought a lot of batteries.
Are there any candles?
I hope we've got enough chocolate.

CHECK POINT

Tick the correct answer.

The child wants to know if they've got

❒ chocolate.

❒ a good supply of chocolate.

CHART CHECK

Circle T (True) or F (False).

T F ***A lot of*** is used with both countable and uncountable nouns.

T F ***Several*** is used with uncountable nouns.

T F ***A few*** is used with countable nouns.

T F ***Any*** is used in negative sentences.

QUANTIFIERS AND COUNTABLE NOUNS		
	QUANTIFIER	**NOUN**
I've got	*some* *enough* *a lot of*	**batteries.** **biscuits.**
I've got	*a few* *several*	
I haven't got	*any* *enough* *a lot of* *many*	

QUANTIFIERS AND UNCOUNTABLE NOUNS		
	QUANTIFIER	**NOUN**
I 've got	*some* *enough* *a lot of*	**coffee.** **water.**
I 've got	*a little* *a great deal of*	
I haven't got	*any* *enough* *a lot of* *much*	

EXPRESS CHECK

Complete this conversation with **much** *or* **many**.

A: We didn't buy ________________ batteries.

B: Well, we didn't have ________________ time before the storm.

Grammar Explanations	Examples
1. **Quantifiers** are expressions of quantity such as *a lot of* and *many*. They are used before a noun.	■ We used ***a lot of* water** last summer. ■ There aren't ***many* sweets** left in the bag.
Quantifiers can also be used alone, when it is clear what they refer to. Note that in ***a lot of***, *of* is dropped.	**A:** How many **eggs** do we have? **B:** Not ***a lot***, just ***a few***.
2. Use ***some***, ***enough***, ***a lot of*** and ***any*** with both countable and uncountable nouns.	■ We've got ***some* batteries** (countable) and ***some* petrol** (uncountable). ■ We've got ***enough* water** (uncountable) and **eggs** (countable) for a week. ■ We've got ***a lot of* beans** (countable) and **rice** (uncountable) left.
Use ***any*** in questions and in negative sentences.	**A:** Have we got ***any* milk** (uncountable) or **teabags** (countable)? **B:** No, and we haven't got ***any* coffee** or **paper plates**, either.
Use ***some*** when you make an offer.	■ Would you like ***some* coffee**?
3. Use ***a few***, ***several*** and ***many*** with plural countable nouns in affirmative sentences.	■ ***A few* people** got ill. ■ ***Several* children** went to hospital. ■ ***Many* people** agreed.
Use ***a little***, ***a great deal of*** and ***much*** with uncountable nouns in affirmative sentences.	■ They had ***a little* trouble** with the radio. ■ They threw away ***a great deal of* food**. ■ ***Much* planning** went into the rescue.
Usage Note: In affirmative sentences, ***many*** is more formal than *a lot of*; ***much*** is very formal.	More Formal: ***Many* rescue workers** arrived. Less Formal: ***A lot of* rescue workers** arrived. Very Formal: He showed ***much* courage**. Less Formal: He showed ***a lot of* courage**.
▶ **Be careful!** Don't confuse ***a few*** and ***a little*** with *few* and *little*. ***Few*** and ***little*** usually mean 'not enough'.	■ They received ***a little* news** last night. *(not a lot but probably enough)* ■ They received ***little* news** last night. *(probably not enough news)*
4. Use ***many*** with countable nouns and ***much*** with uncountable nouns in questions and negative sentences.	**A:** **How *many* people** did you see? **B:** We **didn't** see ***many***.
Usage Note: In questions and negative sentences, ***many*** and ***much*** are used in both formal and informal English.	**A:** **How *much* food** did they carry? **B:** **Not *much***.

IDENTIFY • *Read this article about preparing for natural disasters. Underline the quantifiers + countable nouns. Circle the quantifiers + uncountable nouns.*

Be Prepared

Are you ready? Many people don't realise that some natural disasters such as earthquakes can strike with little warning. It may take several days for assistance to reach you. Prepare your disaster kit in advance! Here are a few tips.

Water may be unsafe to drink. Store enough water for several days. Each person needs five litres per day for cooking and washing.

You will also need food for several days. It's a good idea to store a lot of of tinned meat, fruit, vegetables and milk. However, also include several kinds of high-energy food, such as peanut butter and raisins. And don't forget some 'comfort food' like biscuits and chocolate!

If you haven't got any electricity, you might not have any heat, either. Keep some blankets, sleeping bags and extra clothes for everyone.

Prepare a first aid kit with some pain killers, several sizes of plaster and an antiseptic.

The cash machines might not be working. Have you got any cash? You shouldn't keep much money in the house but you should have a lot of small notes and a few larger notes, too.

CHOOSE • *Circle the correct words to complete this radio interview between* This Morning (TM) *and food psychologist Angie Webber* (AW).

TM: Dr Webber, in a crisis, a lot of / much (1.) people crave chocolate. Does comfort food have any / many (2.) real benefit?

AW: Yes. Several / A little (3.) types of food help give emotional balance. Chocolate gives an emotional lift because it contains a great deal of / many (4.) sugar, for example.

TM: What about mashed potatoes? When I'm down, I cook a lot of / much (5.) potatoes.

AW: They remind you of childhood, when you felt safe. Much / Many (6.) traditional foods comfort us in this way.

TM: I have a few / a little (7.) friends who eat comfort food to celebrate. Why?

AW: We have much / many (8.) changes in our lives today and a few / few (9.) ways to calm down. Comfort food tells us, 'Don't worry. Some / A little (10.) things are still the same.'

TM: We only have a few / a little (11.) time left. Tell us – what is *your* favourite comfort food?

AW: Strawberry ice cream. I always feel better after I've eaten a few / few (12.) spoonfuls.

COMPLETE • *Read these conversations. Complete them with the correct words.*

1. **much, many, a few, a little**

A: Hi, Barbara. Did you and Jim lose ____many____ (a.) trees in the storm?

B: Just one. And the house is OK. We only lost ____________ (b.) windows. How about you?

A: We didn't have ____________ (c.) problems either. We didn't have ____________ (d.) time to shop before the storm but, thanks to the disaster kit, we had ____________ (e.) candles and ____________ (f.) food on hand.

2. **little, a little, a few, few**

A: It's interesting to see what we used up from the disaster kit. I noticed we've only got ____________ (a.) hot chocolate left.

B: That's because ____________ (b.) things taste better in a crisis. I bet there are more than ____________ (c.) tins of spinach, though.

A: Six tins. I suppose there's ____________ (d.) reason to buy more of that.

B: We learnt ____________ (e.) things about comfort foods during the storm, didn't we?

4 **EDIT** • *Read this child's diary entry. Find and correct seven mistakes in the use of quantifiers. The first mistake has already been corrected.*

We had a big storm last week and we lost the electricity for ^a few days. Once I got over being scared, it was fun – a bit like camping. We've got an electric heater so we didn't have some heat. We slept in our sleeping bags around the fireplace. We used up many wood! Mum baked some bread in a pan in the fireplace. She had to try several times but it was really good when it worked. We ate it with little butter. The first night, we had much problems working out what to do. It got dark early and we only had a little candles – and no TV! Jane is five and she was really frightened until we made hot chocolate over the fire. Finally, everybody took turns telling stories. I found out that Dad knows a lot good stories.

Articles: Indefinite and Definite

An evil magician from **a** universe beyond ours is trying to conquer **the** Earth.

The magician is Zado. He has four helpers—and only YOU can destroy him!

SPACE DEFENDER

A NEW GAME FROM PLAYZAP

CHECK POINT

Tick the correct answer.

According to the advert for the video game:

❐ There is only one universe beyond ours.

❐ There is only one Earth.

CHART CHECK

Circle T (True) or F (False).

T F ***A/An*** can be used with uncountable nouns.

T F ***The*** can be used with singular and plural nouns.

T F Use ***the*** when you mention a noun for the second time.

INDEFINITE

SINGULAR COUNTABLE NOUNS		
	A/An	**Noun**
Let's rent	**a**	**video game**.
It's	**an**	**adventure**.

PLURAL COUNTABLE NOUNS/ UNCOUNTABLE NOUNS		
	(Some)	**Noun**
Let's play	**(some)**	**video games**.
I won		**gold**.

DEFINITE

SINGULAR COUNTABLE NOUNS			
	The	**Noun**	
Let's rent	**the**	**game**	by Playzap.
It's		**adventure**	of Zado.

PLURAL COUNTABLE NOUNS/ UNCOUNTABLE NOUNS			
	The	**Noun**	
Let's play	**the**	**games**	we rented.
It's		**gold**	Zado lost.

EXPRESS CHECK

Circle the correct articles to complete these sentences.

Playzap has <u>a / the</u> new video game. <u>A / The</u> game is called *Space Defender*.

Grammar Explanations	Examples
The article you use before a noun depends on the kind of noun it is (countable or uncountable) and on how you are using the noun.	
1. Use **the indefinite article *a / an*** with singular countable nouns when you mention a person, place or thing for the first time or when you are not referring to a particular person, place or thing.	■ Let's buy ***a* video game**. *(Any video game. Not a particular game.)* ■ I'm reading about ***a* magician**. *(This is the first time I've mentioned the magician.)*
Also use ***a / an*** for singular countable nouns when you are classifying a person, place or thing.	■ I'm ***a* pilot**. ■ Rome is ***a* city**. ■ A Dalmatian is ***a* type of dog**.
Use ***a*** before consonant sounds. Use ***an*** before vowel sounds.	■ ***a*** **m**agician, ***a*** **d**og, ***a*** **ch**air ■ ***an*** **au**thor, ***an*** **u**mbrella, ***an*** **o**range
► **Be careful!** It is the sound, not the letter, that determines whether you use ***a*** or ***an***.	■ ***a*** **u**niverse ■ ***a*** **h**ostile army ■ ***an*** h**o**nest man
2. Use **no article** or ***some*** with plural countable nouns, and with uncountable nouns when you mention a person, place or thing for the first time or when you are not referring to a particular person, place or thing.	■ There are (**some**) books on the shelf. *(It isn't important which books they are.)* ■ I need to buy (**some**) sugar. *(I haven't mentioned this before.)*
3. Use the **definite article *the*** with singular and plural nouns and countable and uncountable nouns when you mention a person, place or thing for the second time, or when you are referring to a particular person, place or thing that your listener knows about.	■ ***The* magician** I told you about is on TV tonight. *(This is the second time I've mentioned him.)* ■ Your glasses are in ***the* kitchen**. *(You know which kitchen I'm talking about.)*
4. Use ***the*** when the person, place or thing is unique – there is only one.	■ ***The* moon** is 250,000 miles away. *(There's only one moon.)* ■ Jack's in ***the* garden**. *(We've only got one garden.)*
5. Use ***the*** when a phrase or adjective such as *first, best, right, wrong* or *only* identifies which person, place or thing you are talking about.	■ *Donkey Kong* was ***the first* video game** that had a story. ■ *Moonraker* is ***the last* Bond film** I saw. ■ The beach is ***the only* place** to be on a hot summer's day.

CHOOSE & DESCRIBE • *Read these conversations. Circle the letter of the statement that best describes each conversation.*

1. **LIZ:** I'm bored. Let's rent a video game.
   FRED: OK.
   a. Fred knows which game Liz is going to rent.
   (b.) Fred and Liz aren't talking about a particular game.

2. **LIZ:** Mum, where's the new video game?
   MUM: Sorry, I haven't seen it.
   a. Mum knows that Liz has rented a new game.
   b. Mum doesn't know that Liz has rented a new game.

3. **FRED:** I'll bet it's in the kitchen. You always leave your things there.
   LIZ: I'll go and look.
   a. There are several kitchens in Fred and Liz's house.
   b. There is only one kitchen in Fred and Liz's house.

4. **FRED:** Was I right?
   LIZ: You weren't even close. It was on a chair in the hall.
   a. There is only one chair in the hall.
   b. There are several chairs in the hall.

5. **FRED:** Wow! Look at that! The graphics are brilliant.
   LIZ: So is the music.
   a. All video games have good graphics and music.
   b. The game Liz has rented has good graphics and music.

6. **LIZ:** That was fun. But why don't we rent a sports game next time?
   FRED: Good idea. I love sports games.
   a. Fred is talking about sports games in general.
   b. Fred is talking about a particular sports game.

CHOOSE & COMPLETE • *Circle the correct articles to complete this paragraph.*

Board games are popular all over a / (the) (1.) world. Mah Jong is an / the (2.) example of a / an (3.) very old one. I had an / a (4.) uncle who had an / the (5.) old set from Singapore. He kept a / the (6.) set in the / a (7.) beautiful box in a / the (8.) living room. He used to open the / a (9.) box and tell me about the / a (10.) pieces. They were made of bamboo and each one had a / the (11.) Chinese character on it. To me, they were the / a (12.) most fascinating things in a / the (13.) world.

COMPLETE • *Read each conversation. Complete it with the appropriate article (**a**, **an**, or **the**).*

1. **A:** ____A____ car has just pulled up. Are you expecting someone?

   B: No, I'm not. I wonder who it is.

2. **A:** Can we use ________ car?

   B: OK, but bring it back by 11:00 o'clock.

3. **A:** Let's turn off ________ game system before we leave.

   B: We don't have to. We can just leave it on pause.

4. **A:** Have you got ________ game system?

   B: Yes, I have. I've just bought a Sega Genesis.

5. **A:** Can you see the video shop? I was sure it was on the High Street.

   B: I think it's on ________ side street but I'm not sure which one.

6. **A:** There it is.

   B: Good. You can park opposite ________ shop.

7. **A:** Excuse me, have you got any new games?

   B: ________ newest games are over there.

8. **A:** We'd better go. We've been here for ________ hour.

   B: That was ________ shortest hour I've ever spent.

9. **A:** Excuse me. I'd like to rent this game.

   B: Just take it to ________ cash desk.

EDIT • *Read this magazine article about video games. Find and correct nine mistakes in the use of articles. The first mistake has already been corrected.*

Once there was a plumber called Mario. ~~Plumber~~ The plumber had beautiful girlfriend. One day, a ape fell in love with the girlfriend and kidnapped her. The plumber chased ape to rescue his girlfriend.

This simple tale became *Donkey Kong,* a first video game with a story. It was invented by Sigeru Matsimoto, a artist with Nintendo, Inc. Matsimoto loved the video games but he wanted to make them more interesting. He liked fairy tales so he invented story similar to a famous fairy tale. Story was an immediate success and Nintendo followed it with *The Mario Brothers.* The rest is video game history.

Ø (No Article) and *The*

Roller coaster **rides** are like **life**. You just have to relax and enjoy yourself.
Thunderball

So how are you enjoying **the ride**?

CHECK POINT

Tick the correct answer.

Who is talking about roller coaster rides in general?

❒ the little girl ❒ the little boy

CHART CHECK

Tick the correct answer.

You can use **Ø** (no article) for a noun that is:

❒ indefinite

❒ definite

You can use **Ø** for a countable noun that is:

❒ singular

❒ plural

NO ARTICLE (INDEFINITE)	*THE* (DEFINITE)
Ø + UNCOUNTABLE NOUN	***THE* + UNCOUNTABLE NOUN**
Do you like **candy floss**?	**The candy floss** in this park is great.
Ø + PLURAL COUNTABLE NOUN	***THE* + PLURAL COUNTABLE NOUN**
Rides can be very exciting.	**The rides** in this park are exciting.
	***THE* + SINGULAR COUNTABLE NOUN**
	The ride near the entrance is exciting.

EXPRESS CHECK

Circle **the** *or* **Ø** *(no article) to complete these sentences.*

A: Did you enjoy Ø / the roller coaster ride?

B: Yes, I love Ø / the roller coaster rides.

A: And did you try Ø / the candy floss?

B: No. I don't like Ø / the candy floss. It's always too sweet.

Grammar Explanations	Examples
1. We often use **Ø (no article)** before uncountable nouns and plural countable nouns that are **indefinite** (not specific). Use **Ø** when you:	
a. have **no specific** person, place or thing in mind.	**A:** What do you want to do tonight? **B:** Let's stay at home. We can listen to **music** or watch **videos**.
b. **classify** (say what something or someone is).	**A:** What's that? **B:** It's **candy floss**. **A:** And what are those? **B:** They're **tickets** for the roller coaster. I bought them while you were on the phone.
c. make **general statements**.	■ **Candy floss** is very sweet. *(candy floss in general)* ■ **Roller coasters** are popular. *(roller coasters in general)*
2. Use ***the*** with uncountable nouns and countable nouns (singular and plural) that are **definite** – when you are talking about a **specific or unique** person, place or thing that you and your listener know about.	**A:** Can I taste ***the* candy floss**? **B:** Of course. Have as much as you like. **A:** Where are ***the* tickets** for ***the* roller coaster**? **B:** I put them in my pocket. **A:** This is ***the* best roller coaster** in ***the* world**.
3. **Be careful!** Singular countable nouns cannot stand alone. You must always use either an article, a pronoun, *one* or a word such as *this, that, each* or *every* before a singular countable noun.	■ This is ***a*** delicious **meal**. Not ~~This is delicious meal~~. ■ It's hard to eat just ***one* biscuit**, isn't it? ■ Give me ***that* biscuit**! You've had enough. ■ It's ***my* biscuit**.

IDENTIFY • *Read this announcement for a new theme park. Underline all the common nouns that have no articles. Circle all the nouns with* **the**.

Grand Opening!

Do you enjoy theme parks? Tomorrow, Blare Gardens will open to the public for the first time. The park features a wide variety of rides and games that will appeal to both adults and children. And, of course, a theme park would not be complete without candy floss and hot dogs. The food at Blare Gardens promises to be very good. Come early, bring the whole family and be sure to stay for the firework display that takes place just after the sun sets. So check it out! You won't be disappointed.

CHOOSE • *Circle the correct words to complete this magazine article.*

Thrills and Spills

Why do people around the / Ø (1.) world flock to the / Ø (2.) theme parks? The / Ø (3.) places like Disney World and Alton Towers offer the / Ø (4.) fun, relaxation and escape from the / Ø (5.) problems and boredom of everyday life. They offer the / Ø (6.) adults and children alike a chance to take the / Ø (7.) risks without the / Ø (8.) consequences. Thanks to advances in the / Ø (9.) technology, the / Ø (10.) accidents in the / Ø (11.) theme parks are now rare. You can go on the / Ø (12.) rides that look scary but are actually safe. You can scream and laugh as the / Ø (13.) roller coaster races down toward the / Ø (14.) ground and loops up to the / Ø (15.) sky again, leaving your cares and troubles behind.

Even though the / Ø (16.) roller coasters are the / Ø (17.) most popular of all the / Ø (18.) rides, they are not for everyone. But don't worry. Today's theme parks offer a lot more than the / Ø (19.) thrills and spills. There are train rides through a replica of the / Ø (20.) rain forest. And there are the / Ø (21.) games with the / Ø (22.) prizes, too. The / Ø (23.) hot dogs, ice cream and candy floss complete the / Ø (24.) picture of this perfect getaway for the / Ø (25.) whole family.

COMPLETE • *Read this conversation about a theme park. Complete the sentences with* **the** *where necessary. Use* **Ø** *if you don't need an article.*

A: I'm going to Blare Gardens next weekend. You work there. What's it like?

B: That depends. Do you like ___Ø___ (1.) scary rides? If you do, then you're going to love __________ (2.) rides at Blare Gardens.

A: What's __________ (3.) most exciting ride there?

B: The Python. I've seen people actually shaking with fear before they got on it.

A: Sounds like __________ (4.) fun. By the way, what's __________ (5.) food like? I hate __________ (6.) hot dogs.

B: Then you might have a little problem. They sell __________ (7.) hot dogs and __________ (8.) pizza and that's about all. But do you like __________ (9.) music?

A: I love it. I listen to __________ (10.) music all the time. Why?

B: __________ (11.) music at Blare Gardens is great. They have __________ (12.) best pop groups in __________ (13.) whole country.

A: What exactly do you do there? Maybe we'll see you.

B: I dress up like a cartoon character and guide people around __________ (14.) park.

4 **EDIT** • *Read this postcard from Blare Gardens. Find and correct eight mistakes in the use of* **the** *and* **Ø** *(no article). The first mistake has already been corrected.*

Blare Gardens Amusement Park

Hi! Blare Gardens is excellent! This is ^the best holiday we've ever been on! I love the rides here. I've been on the roller coasters before but nothing is like the one they've got here! And food is great, too. I usually don't eat the hot dogs but hot dogs here are great. So is pizza. Do you like the theme parks? If so, you've got to get your family to come. The only problem is crowds here. People have to queue to get into everything – even the toilets!

See you soon.

Nicky

24p

To: *Richard Turner*
27 Park Street
OXFORD
OX2 6PP

Reflexive Pronouns and Reciprocal Pronouns

'I will not talk to myself, I will not talk to myself.'

CHECK POINT

Circle T (True) or F (False).

T F The man is talking to another person.

CHART CHECK

Circle T (True) or F (False).

T F Singular reflexive pronouns end in ***-selves***.

T F Reciprocal pronouns always refer to more than one person.

REFLEXIVE PRONOUNS		
SUBJECT PRONOUN		**REFLEXIVE PRONOUN**
I	looked at	**myself**.
You		**yourself**.
He		**himself**.
She		**herself**.
It		**itself**.
We		**ourselves**.
You		**yourselves**.
They		**themselves**.

RECIPROCAL PRONOUNS		
SUBJECT PRONOUN		**RECIPROCAL PRONOUN**
We You They	looked at	**each other**. **one another**.

EXPRESS CHECK

Circle the correct words to complete this conversation.

A: Is someone in there with you or are you talking to yourself / themselves?

B: No one's here. I'm just talking to one another / myself.

Grammar Explanations	Examples
1. Use a **reflexive pronoun** when the subject and object of a sentence refer to the same people or things.	subject = object ■ **Sara** looked at ***herself*** in the mirror. *(Sara looked at her own face.)*
In **imperative sentences** use: – ***yourself*** when the subject is singular	■ 'Don't push ***yourself*** so hard, **Tom**,' Sara said.
– ***yourselves*** when the subject is plural	■ 'Don't push ***yourselves*** so hard, **guys**,' Sara said.
2. Use a **reflexive pronoun** to emphasise a noun. In this case, the reflexive pronoun usually follows the noun directly.	■ Tom was upset when he lost his job. The **job *itself*** wasn't important to him but he needed the money.
3. ***By*** **+ a reflexive pronoun** means *alone* or *without any help*.	■ Sara lives **by herself**. *(Sara lives alone.)* ■ We painted the house **by ourselves**. *(No one helped us.)*
Be **+ a reflexive pronoun** means *behave in the usual way*.	■ Just **be yourself** at your interview. *(Behave the way you usually behave.)* ■ He **wasn't himself** after he lost his job. *(He seemed different.)*
4. Use a **reciprocal pronoun** when the subject and the object of a sentence refer to the same people and these people have a two-way relationship. Use ***each other*** when the subject is two people. Use either ***one another*** or ***each other*** when the subject is more than two people.	subject = object ■ **Tom and Sara** met ***each other*** at work. *(Tom met Sara and Sara met Tom.)* subject = object ■ **We all** told ***one another*** about our jobs. OR subject = object ■ **We all** told ***each other*** about our jobs. *(Each person swapped information with every other person.)*
► **BE CAREFUL!** Reciprocal pronouns and plural reflexive pronouns have different meanings.	■ Fred and Jane talked to ***each other***. *(Fred talked to Jane and Jane talked to Fred.)* ■ Fred and Jane talked to ***themselves***. *(Fred talked to himself and Jane talked to herself.)*
5. **Reciprocal pronouns** have possessive forms: ***each other's***, ***one another's***.	■ Tom and Sara took ***each other's*** numbers. *(Tom took Sara's number. Sara took Tom's number.)*

Check it out!

For a list of verbs and expressions commonly used reflexively, see Appendix 16 on page 340.

IDENTIFY • *Read this article about self-talk. Underline the reflexive pronouns once and the reciprocal pronouns twice. Draw an arrow to the word that each pronoun refers to.*

SELF-TALK

Self-talk is the way we explain a problem to ourselves. It can affect the way we feel and the way we behave. Tom and Sara, for example, both lost their jobs when their company laid off a lot of people. Sara kept herself fit and spent time with friends. Tom gained ten pounds and spent all his time by himself. They were both unemployed so the situation itself can't explain why they acted so differently from each other. The main difference was the way Tom and Sara explained the problem to themselves. Sara believed that she herself could change her situation. Tom saw himself as helpless. Later, everyone got their jobs back. When they all talked to one another back at the office, Tom grumbled, 'They must have been desperate.' Sara replied, 'They finally realised they need us!'

2

CHOOSE • *Tom and Sara's company held an office party. Choose the correct reflexive or reciprocal pronouns to complete the conversations.*

1. **A:** Do you mind if we pour ___ourselves___ (myself / ourselves) a drink?
   B: Of course not. And there's food, too. Please help ______ (yourselves / themselves).
2. **A:** That's the new head of Marketing. She's standing by ______ (herself / himself).
   B: Let's go and introduce ______ (himself / ourselves).
3. **A:** I'm nervous about my date with Niki. I cut ______ (myself / herself) twice shaving.
   B: You'll be fine. Just relax and be ______ (yourselves / yourself).
4. **A:** My boss and I always give ______ (ourselves / each other) the same presents. Every year I give him a book and he gives me a scarf.
   B: Funny. I always thought you bought ______ (yourself / himself) a lot of scarves.
5. **A:** The new software is so easy, it just seems to run by ______ (itself / myself).
   B: Really? In our department, we're still teaching ______ (themselves / ourselves) how to use it.
6. **A:** Did you and Andrew go to Japan by ______ (yourself / yourselves) or with a tour group?
   B: With a group. We've all kept in touch with ______ (one another / ourselves) since the trip.

COMPLETE • *George Prudeau is a French teacher. Complete his talk to a group of new teachers. Use reflexive and reciprocal pronouns.*

I teach French but the subject ___itself___ (1.) isn't that important. I think my experience applies to all subjects. Your first year may be hard so teach ______ (2.) to think positively and keep things simple. Remember that a good teacher helps students learn by ______ (3.). Recently, John, one of my students, was having trouble teaching ______ (4.) how to bake French bread. I encouraged him to keep trying and in the end he succeeded. As far as discipline goes, I have a few rules. I tell my students, 'Keep ______ (5.) busy. Discuss the lessons but don't interfere with ______ (6.) 's work.' Keep teaching materials simple, too. I pride ______ (7.) on being able to teach anywhere, even on a street corner. Finally, the salary for teachers is not great but you have a lot of freedom. I run my class by ______ (8.) – just the way I want to. You will all have to decide for ______ (9.) if it's worth it. I can't afford to travel much but I satisfy ______ (10.) with trips to Calais!

EDIT • *Read this woman's diary. Find and correct eight mistakes in the use of reflexive and reciprocal pronouns. The first mistake has already been corrected.*

I forgot to call Sam on his birthday. I reminded ~~me~~ myself all day and I still forgot! I felt terrible. My sister, Anna, said, 'Don't be so hard on yourselves,' but I didn't believe her. She prides her on remembering everything. Then I read an article on self-talk. It said that people can change the way they explain problems to theirselves. I realised that the way I talk to me is insulting – like the way our maths teacher used to talk to us. I thought, Sam and I treat each other well. He forgave myself for my mistake straightaway and I forgave him for forgetting our dinner date two weeks ago. Sam and I could forgive themselves so I suppose I can forgive me.

SelfTest XI

SECTION ONE

Circle the letter of the correct answer to complete each sentence. Choose Ø when no article is needed.

EXAMPLE:

Jennifer never ________ coffee. A (B) C D

(A) drink (C) is drinking
(B) drinks (D) was drinking

1. I introduced ________ to Bill as soon as I saw him. A B C D
   (A) himself (C) myself
   (B) me (D) each other

2. The job ________ isn't a problem. It's my boss. A B C D
   (A) myself (C) himself
   (B) itself (D) it

3. The students write cards to ________ during the holidays. A B C D
   (A) themselves (C) each other's
   (B) ourselves (D) one another

4. What a beautiful bracelet! Is it made of ________ gold? A B C D
   (A) the (C) Ø
   (B) some (D) a

5. I bought ________ bottled water before the trip. A B C D
   (A) a lot of (C) twelve
   (B) a few (D) many

6. How ________ eggs do you need for the cake? A B C D
   (A) many (C) Ø
   (B) much (D) more

7. She was lonely because she had ________ friends at first. A B C D
   (A) little (C) few
   (B) a little (D) a few

8. That's ________ best film I've ever seen. A B C D
   (A) a (C) the
   (B) an (D) Ø

9. Sue's in ________ Germany on holiday. A B C D
   (A) a (C) Ø
   (B) an (D) the

10. Frank's ________ astronaut. There are six of them on this mission. A B C D
    (A) Ø (C) an
    (B) a (D) the

11. – I've just rented ________ video.
– Great! Which one?
(A) the
(B) some
(C) a
(D) any

A B C D

12. We haven't got ________ fruit left. Could you buy some apples?
(A) much
(B) some
(C) little
(D) many

A B C D

SECTION TWO

Each sentence has four underlined words or phrases. The four underlined parts of the sentence are marked A, B, C and D. Circle the letter of the one underlined word or phrase that is NOT CORRECT.

EXAMPLE:
Mike usually [A] drives [B] to school but today [C] he walks [D]. A B C (D)

13. There are [A] a lot of [B] food [C] in the fridge so help yourself [D]. A B C D

14. Do your [A] families come [B] for christmas [C] or do you celebrate by yourselves [D]? A B C D

15. The news [A] are starting [B] so let's watch TV [C] in the [D] living room. A B C D

16. Lee wants to open his [A] business in may [B] and start [C] working for himself [D]. A B C D

17. I myself [A] don't eat chilli but it's the most [B] popular spice [C] in a [D] world. A B C D

18. A money [A] isn't [B] everything – the job itself [C] has to [D] be interesting. A B C D

19. Mathematics [A] isn't [B] Jeff's best [C] subject but he succeeds with the [D] hard work. A B C D

20. How [A] many times [B] do we [C] have before the [D] film starts? A B C D

21. Smith [A] was an [B] unpopular MP so he had a few [C] friends in politics [D]. A B C D

22. We [A] have only a few [B] milk left so could you pick some [C] up for us [D]? A B C D

23. We [A] didn't know one another [B] names before Maria [C] introduced us [D]. A B C D

24. Ben [A] has to save a few [B] money so that he can go to school [C] in the [D] autumn. A B C D

25. I met an accountant [A] and a lawyer [B] at your party [C] and an accountant [D] said he'd help me. A B C D

UNIT 61 The Passive: Overview

The World Keeps
Informed With
Reader's Digest
Reader's Digest

Reader's Digest **was founded** in 1922.
Today it **is read** by people in every country in the world.
Shouldn't you be one of them? Subscribe today.

CHECK POINT

Tick the information you can get from the advert.

- ❒ the name of the founder
- ❒ the number of years the magazine has existed
- ❒ the price of the magazine

CHART CHECK

Circle T (True) or F (False).

T F The object of an active sentence becomes the subject of the passive sentence.

T F Passive statements always have a form of the verb ***be***.

T F Passive statements always have an object.

ACTIVE	PASSIVE
OBJECT	SUBJECT
Millions of people **buy *it***.	***It* is bought** by millions of people.
OBJECT	SUBJECT
Someone **published *it*** in 1922.	***It* was published** in 1922.

PASSIVE STATEMENTS

SUBJECT	*BE* (*NOT*)	PAST PARTICIPLE	(*BY* + OBJECT)	
It	**is not/isn't**	**bought**	by millions of people.	
It	**was not/wasn't**	**published**		in 1922.

***YES/NO* QUESTIONS**

BE	SUBJECT	PAST PARTICIPLE	
Is / **Was**	it	**sold**	in China?

SHORT ANSWERS

AFFIRMATIVE		NEGATIVE	
Yes, it	**is.**	No, it	**isn't.**
	was.		**wasn't.**

***WH-* QUESTIONS**

WH- WORD	*BE*	SUBJECT	PAST PARTICIPLE
Where	**is**	it	**sold**?

EXPRESS CHECK

Complete this sentence with the passive form of the verb **print**.

How many copies of *Reader's Digest* ________________ last year?

Grammar Notes	Examples
1. Active and **passive sentences** usually have the same meaning but the focus is different.	ACTIVE ■ Millions of people **read** the magazine. *(The focus is on the people.)* PASSIVE ■ The magazine **is read** by millions of people. *(The focus is on the magazine.)*
2. Form the **passive** with the **correct** form of ***be*** + **past participle**.	■ It **is written** in nineteen languages. ■ It **was published** in 1922. ■ These copies have just **been printed**.
3. Use the **passive** when:	
a. the agent (the person or thing doing the action) is unknown or not important.	■ The magazine **was founded** in 1922. *(I don't know who founded it.)*
b. the identity of the agent is clear from the context.	■ The magazine **is sold** in newsagents. *(We can assume that the people who work in the newsagent's sell it. We don't need to mention them.)*
c. you want to avoid mentioning the agent.	■ Some mistakes **were made** in that article. *(I know who made the mistakes but I don't want to blame the person who made them.)*
4. Use the **passive with *by*** if you mention the agent. Mention the **agent** when:	■ The article **was written *by a psychologist***.
a. you introduce necessary new information about the agent.	■ John Dent is a famous sports writer. He **has** just **been hired *by Sports Weekly*** to write a monthly column. *(The name of John's employer is necessary new information.)*
b. you want to give credit to someone who created something.	■ The article **was written *by John Dent***.
c. the agent is surprising or interesting.	■ Our windows **are washed *by a robot***.
► **BE CAREFUL!** In most cases, you do not need to mention an agent in passive sentences. Do not include an agent unnecessarily.	■ The magazine **is published** once a week. NOT ~~The magazine is published by the publisher once a week.~~

CHOOSE • *Read these sentences and decide if they are* **Active (A)** *or* **Passive (P).**

__P__ 1. *Reader's Digest* was founded in 1922.

______ 2. Millions of people read it.

______ 3. A large-type edition is also printed.

______ 4. They also record it.

______ 5. *Reader's Digest* is published once a month.

______ 6. It has been translated into many languages.

______ 7. Many readers subscribe to the magazine.

______ 8. It is sold in newsagents throughout the country.

______ 9. I read an interesting article in it.

______ 10. The article was written by a famous scientist.

READ & COMPLETE • *Look at the chart. Then complete the sentences. Use the verb* **speak** *in the active or the passive form.*

Language	Number of Speakers (in Millions)
Arabic	246
Cantonese (China)	71
English	508
Ho (Bihar and Orissa States, India)	1
Japanese	126
Spanish	417
Swahili (Kenya, Tanzania, Uganda, Democratic Republic of Congo)	49
Tagalog (Philippines)	57

1. Japanese __is spoken by 126 million people__.
2. One million people __speak Ho__.
3. ______________________ by 57 million people.
4. Spanish ______________________.
5. ______________________ Cantonese.
6. ______________________ 246 million people.
7. More than 500 million people ______________________.
8. ______________________ in Uganda.

COMPLETE • *Use the passive form of the verbs in the first set of brackets to complete this report. Include the agent (from the second set of brackets) only if absolutely necessary.*

Modern Reader Newsletter

TENTH ANNIVERSARY ISSUE

DID YOU KNOW . . . ?

- *Modern Reader* was founded by A. J. Thompson ten years ago.
  1. (found) (A. J. Thompson)
- At first it was printed only in English.
  2. (print) ~~(the printer)~~
- Today it ______________ in three foreign-language editions.
  3. (publish) (the publisher)
- It ______________ in more than ten countries.
  4. (read) (readers)
- Since 2000, twenty new employees ______________.
  5. (hire) (our international offices)
- Back at home, ten new computers ______________ last month.
  6. (purchase) (the company)
- They ______________ to write our award-winning articles.
  7. (use) (our writers)
- *Modern Reader* ______________ all over the world.
  8. (advertise) (advertisers)
- Our editorial staff ______________ last month.
  9. (interview) (*Live at Ten TV*)
- The interview ______________.
  10. (see) (millions of viewers)

4 **EDIT** • *Read an editor's notes for a story for* Modern Reader. *Find and correct eight mistakes in the use of the passive. The first mistake has already been corrected.*

Two-thirds of Bolivia's five million people ~~locate~~ are located in the cool western highlands known as the Altiplano. For centuries, the grain quinoa has been grew in the mountains. Llamas bred for fur, meat and transportation. And tin, Bolivia's richest natural resource, is mining by miners in the high Andes.

The Oriente, another name for the eastern lowlands, is mostly tropical. Rice is the major food crop and cows are raised for milk. Oil is also find there.

Although Spanish is the official language, Native American languages are still spoken by people. Traditional textiles are woven by hand and music played on reed pipes whose tone resembles the sound of the wind blowing over high plains in the Andes.

UNIT 62 The Passive with Modals

Bill, something should be done about Ed. He snores so loudly he's going to knock us out of orbit!
zZzZzZ
I know, Carla. He can be heard back on Earth!

CHECK POINT

Tick the correct answer.

According to Carla,

❒ Ed needs to do something about his snoring.

❒ somebody should do something about Ed's snoring.

CHART CHECK 1

Circle T (True) or F (False).

T F Passives with modals always use *be*.

T F You cannot use modals with the passive to talk about the future.

STATEMENTS				
SUBJECT	**MODAL***	***BE***	**PAST PARTICIPLE**	
The crew	**will not/won't** **should not/shouldn't** **must not/mustn't**	**be**	**replaced**	next month.

SUBJECT	***HAVE* (*GOT*) *TO*/ *BE GOING TO***	***BE***	**PAST PARTICIPLE**	
The crew	**have (got) to** **don't have to** **are (not) going to**	**be**	**replaced**	next month.

*Modals have only one form. They do not have *-s* in the third person singular.

CHART CHECK 2

Tick the correct answer.

What comes before the subject in questions?

❒ *be*

❒ a modal or an auxiliary verb

YES/NO QUESTIONS			
MODAL	**SUBJECT**	***BE***	**PAST PARTICIPLE**
Will	they	**be**	**replaced?**
Should			

SHORT ANSWERS			
AFFIRMATIVE		**NEGATIVE**	
Yes, they	**will.**	**No,** they	**won't.**
	should.		**shouldn't.**

YES/NO QUESTIONS				
Auxiliary Verb	**Subject**	***Have to/ Going to***	***Be***	**Past Participle**
Do	they	**have to**	**be**	**replaced?**
Are		**going to**		

SHORT ANSWERS			
Affirmative		**Negative**	
Yes, they	**do.**	**No,** they	**don't.**
	are.		**aren't.**

EXPRESS CHECK

Complete this conversation with the passive form of **will prepare**.

A: ______________ food ______________ on board?

B: No, it ______________. It ______________ on Earth.

Grammar Explanations	Examples
1. To form the passive with a modal, use **modal + *be* + past participle.**	■ The Space Shuttle ***will* be launched** soon. ■ The launch ***won't* be postponed**. ■ The crew ***must* be given** time off. ■ Decisions ***shouldn't* be made** too quickly.
2. Use ***will*** or ***be going to*** with the passive to talk about the **future**.	■ It ***will* be launched** very soon. OR ■ It***'s going to* be launched** very soon.
3. Use ***can*** with the passive to express **present ability**. Use ***could*** with the passive to express **past ability**.	■ The blastoff ***can* be seen** for miles. ■ It ***can't* be done**. ■ It ***could* be seen** very clearly last year. ■ The reports ***couldn't* be filed** in time.
4. Use ***could***, ***may*** and ***might*** with the passive to express **future possibility.**	■ It ***could* be launched** very soon. ■ French scientists ***may* be invited** to participate. ■ Plants ***might* be grown** on board.
5. Use ***should***, ***ought to***, ***had better***, ***have (got) to*** and ***must*** with the passive to express: **a. advisability** **b. necessity**	 ■ The crew ***should* be prepared** to work hard. ■ Crew members ***had better* be given** a day off. ■ Privacy ***ought to* be respected**. ■ Reports ***have to* be filed**. ■ Everyone ***must* be consulted**.

IDENTIFY • *Read this article about the International Space Station,* Unity*. Underline all the passives with modals.*

Living in Outer Space

Space Station *Unity* will be completed within the next decade and international teams of astronauts will then be sharing close quarters for long periods of time. What can be done to improve living conditions in space? Here's what former astronauts suggest:

- FOOD It doesn't taste as good in zero gravity. Food should be made spicier to overcome those effects. International tastes must also be considered.
- CLOTHING Layered clothing could help astronauts stay comfortable. The top layer could be removed or added as temperatures vary.
- SLEEPING Because of weightlessness, sleep is often interrupted in space. Comfortable restraints must be provided to give a sense of stability.
- EMOTIONAL NEEDS People need rest time in space just as they do on Earth. Time ought to be provided for relaxation and privacy.

2

COMPLETE • Comet Magazine (CM) *is interviewing aerospace engineer Dr Bernard Kay* (BK). *Complete the interview with the passive form of the verbs in brackets.*

CM: Dr Kay, I'd like to ask how meals ___will be handled___ in the Space Station.
1. (will / handle)
________________ food ________________ on board or
2. (Be going to / prepare)
________________ from tubes?
3. (squeeze)

BK: Neither. Gourmet meals ________________ on Earth and then they
4. (will / prepackage)
________________ on board.
5. (can / warm up)

CM: The Space Station will have an international crew. How ________________ food ________________ to suit everyone's taste?
6. (should / choose)

BK: An international menu ________________. Food ________________
7. (have to / offer) **8.** (could / select)
from food preference forms that the crew members complete.

CM: ________________ dishes ________________ on board?
9. (Will / use)

BK: Probably. But utensils ________________ to the plates so they won't fly
10. (had better / attach)
around! Meals ________________ as pleasant as possible.
11. (ought to / make)

CHOOSE & COMPLETE • *Some scientists have just completed a simulation of life on the Station. Complete their conversations with the modals in brackets and the correct verbs from the box.*

design	improve	keep	remove	~~solve~~

BRUCE: These simulations showed that there are still some problems. I hope they ___can be solved___ (1. (can)) before the real thing. For example, the temperature __________ (2. (should)) at 68°F but I was uncomfortably warm most of the time.

JOHN: The material for our clothing __________ (3. (ought to)). Maybe clothing __________ (4. (could)) in layers. A layer __________ (5. (can)) if it's too warm.

do	deliver	give	store

DAVID: I didn't like the food very much. We __________ (6. (ought to)) more fresh food.

STEPHEN: Well, fresh fruits and vegetables __________ (7. (be going to)) by the shuttle regularly.

DAVID: What __________ (8. (will)) with the rubbish? Litter is already a problem.

STEPHEN: I'm sure it __________ (9. (will)) on board and carried to Earth by the shuttle.

EDIT • *Read an astronaut's diary notes. Find and correct seven mistakes in the use of the passive with modals. The first mistake has already been corrected.*

I used the sleeping restraints last night and slept a lot better. They ought to ~~make~~ be made more comfortable, though. I felt trapped. I've just looked in the mirror. My face is puffy and my eyes are red. I'd better be got on the exercise bike right away. I can be misunderstanding when I look like this. Last night, Max thought I was angry with him for turning on 'Star Trek'. Actually, I love that programme. I might be given early lunch shift today. I hope they have more chilli. It's nice and spicy and the sauce can actually been tasted, even at zero gravity. Some of it had better be fly in on the shuttle pretty soon or there might be some unhappy astronauts! Speaking of unhappy, last night, Katy called and told me she was planning to leave school. I think she could be talk out of it but I'm afraid I'll get angry and shout if we discuss it. I might overheard by others. We need some privacy here!

The Causative

Bye, Emily,
see you
next week.

One week later . . .
Hi, Emily! . . .
Hmm . . . Something's
different. Have you
had your hair cut?

CHECK POINT

Tick the correct answer.

The man wants to know if his girlfriend

❒ cut her own hair.

❒ went to a hairdresser's.

CHART CHECK

Circle T (True) or F (False).

T F The causative always has a form of the verb ***be***.

T F You can form the causative with ***have*** or ***get***.

T F The causative always needs an agent.

STATEMENTS

SUBJECT	HAVE/GET	OBJECT	PAST PARTICIPLE	(BY + AGENT)
She	**has**	***her hair***	**cut**	by Colin.
He	**has had**	***his beard***	**trimmed.**	
I	**got**	***my car***	**repaired.**	
She	**is going to get**	***her lawn***	**cut.**	

***YES/NO* QUESTIONS**

AUXILIARY VERB	SUBJECT	HAVE/GET	OBJECT	PAST PARTICIPLE	(BY + AGENT)
Does	she	**have**	***her hair***	**cut**	by Colin?
Has	he	**had**	***his beard***	**trimmed?**	
Did	you	**get**	***your car***	**repaired?**	
Is	she	**going to get**	***her lawn***	**cut?**	

EXPRESS CHECK

Complete this conversation with the correct form of the verb **do**.

A: Where do you have your hair ________________?

B: I don't have it ________________. I ________________ it myself.

Grammar Explanations	Examples
1. Use the **causative** to talk about services that you arrange for someone to do for you.	■ I used to colour my own hair but now I **have *it* coloured** at the hairdresser's. ■ I **get *my groceries* delivered** by Derek.
► **BE CAREFUL!** Do not confuse the past simple causative *(had something done)* with the past perfect in active sentences *(had done something).*	SIMPLE PAST CAUSATIVE ■ I **had *it* done** last week. *(Someone did it for me.)* PAST PERFECT ■ I **had done *it*** before. *(I did it myself.)*
2. Form the **causative** with the appropriate form of ***have*** or ***get*** + **object** + **past participle**. The causative can be used in all tenses and with modals.	■ I always **have *my hair* cut** by Colin. ■ I **haven't had *it* done** since June. ■ Last year I **got *my jacket* cleaned** once. ■ Next week I**'m going to have *my windows* cleaned**. ■ I**'m getting *them* done** by *Spotless*. ■ I **had *them* cleaned** a long time ago. ■ You **should get *the car* serviced**. ■ You **ought to have *it* done** soon.
3. Use ***by*** when it is necessary to mention the person doing the service (the agent). Do not mention the agent unnecessarily.	■ Lynne has her hair done ***by Colin***. ■ Where does Lynne **get her hair done**? NOT ~~Where does Lynne get her hair done by a hairdresser~~?

Check it out!

For more information about when to use an agent, see Unit 61, page 265.

TRUE OR FALSE • *Read each person's statement. Write T (True) or F (False) for the sentence that follows.*

1. **Jack:** I'm going to get my hair cut tomorrow after work.
   F Jack cuts his own hair.
2. **Debra:** I'm colouring my hair this afternoon.
   ______ Debra colours her own hair.
3. **Amy:** I didn't pack any nail polish because I had done my nails before the trip.
   ______ Amy did her own nails.
4. **Jack:** I'm thinking of getting the floors polished before the party.
   ______ Jack might hire someone to polish the floors.
5. **Marie:** I had my flat painted two months ago.
   ______ Marie painted her own flat.
6. **Tony:** I'll wash the car this weekend.
   ______ Tony is going to wash the car himself.

FIND OUT & REPORT • *It's 15 February. Look at the Davies's calendar and write sentences about things they* **had done** *and things they* **are going to have done**.

FEBRUARY						
SUNDAY	MONDAY	TUESDAY	WEDNESDAY	THURSDAY	FRIDAY	SATURDAY
1	2	3	4	5	6	Debra – hairdresser 7
8	9	10	11	Jack – barber 12	carpets 13	Amy – dog groomer 14
Today's date 15	windows 16	17	18	19	food and drinks 20	party! 21
22	23	24	Amy – ears pierced 25	26	27	family photos 28

1. They / have / photos / take They are going to have photos taken.
2. Debra / get / her hair / perm Debra got her hair permed.
3. Amy / have / the dog / groom ______
4. They / get / the windows / clean ______
5. They / have / the carpets / shampoo ______
6. Amy / have / her ears / pierce ______
7. Jack / get / his hair / cut ______
8. They / have / food and drinks / deliver ______

CHOOSE & COMPLETE* • *Debra and Jack are going to have a party. Complete the conversations with the passive causative of the appropriate verbs in the box.

dry clean	colour	cut	paint	~~shorten~~	clean

1. **DEBRA:** Your new dress is a bit long. Why don't you get it shortened?
   AMY: OK. They do alterations at the cleaners. I'll take it in tomorrow.
2. **DEBRA:** My blue dress has a small stain on it. I have to ______________.
   AMY: I can drop it off at the cleaners with my dress.
3. **JACK:** The house is ready, except for the windows. They look pretty dirty.
   DEBRA: Don't worry. We ______________ tomorrow.
4. **DEBRA:** Your hair is getting really long. I thought you were going to cut it.
   AMY: I decided not to do it myself this time. I ______________ by Colin.
5. **DEBRA:** My hair's getting a lot of grey in it. Should I ______________?
   JACK: It looks fine to me but it's up to you.
6. **GUEST:** The house looks beautiful. ______________ you ______________?
   JACK: No, actually we did it ourselves last summer.

EDIT* • *Read Amy's diary entry. Find and correct seven mistakes in the use of the passive causative. The first mistake has already been corrected.

21 February

The party was last night. It went really well! The house looked great. Mum and Dad had the floors polished and all the windows ~~clean~~ cleaned professionally so everything sparkled. And of course we had the whole house painted ourselves last summer. (I'll never forget *that*. It took us two weeks!) I wore my new black dress that I have shortened by Jill and I got cut my hair by Colin. He did a great job. There were a lot of guests at the party. We had almost fifty people invited and they almost all turned up! The food was great too. Mum made most of the main dishes herself but she had the rest of the food prepare by a caterer. Mum and Dad hired a professional photographer so at the end of the party we all took our photos. Dad's getting them back next week. I can't wait to see them!

SECTION ONE

Circle the letter of the correct answer to complete each sentence.

EXAMPLE:
Jennifer never _______ coffee. A (B) C D
(A) drink (C) is drinking
(B) drinks (D) was drinking

1. This book _______ written in 2002. A B C D
(A) is (C) was
(B) has (D) were

2. Coffee is _______ in Colombia. A B C D
(A) grow (C) been growing
(B) grew (D) grown

3. Millions of people _______ the film. A B C D
(A) saw (C) will be seen
(B) were seen (D) must be seen

4. The meeting won't _______. A B C D
(A) cancel (C) been cancelled
(B) be cancelled (D) cancelled

5. Sally doesn't cut her own hair. She _______ at the hairdresser's. A B C D
(A) cuts it (C) has it cut
(B) has cut it (D) gets it

6. That book was written _______ Maya Angelou. A B C D
(A) at (C) from
(B) by (D) of

7. The report _______ soon. A B C D
(A) publishes (C) will be published
(B) is published (D) will publish

8. —When will the work be completed? A B C D
—It _______ be by June, but I'm not really sure.
(A) has (C) will
(B) might (D) won't

9. How often _______ your car serviced since you bought it? A B C D
(A) do you get (C) had you got
(B) did you get (D) have you got

10. I need to get my photo _______ for my website. A B C D
(A) take (C) taking
(B) taken (D) took

SECTION TWO

Each sentence has four underlined words or phrases. The four underlined parts of the sentence are marked A, B, C and D. Circle the letter of the one underlined word or phrase that is NOT CORRECT.

EXAMPLE:
Mike usually (A) drives (B) to school but today (C) he walks (D). A B C (D)

11. Tomorrow I'm getting (A) my car serviced (B) from (C) the mechanic that Jake uses (D). A B C D

12. The reports were (A) arrived (B) late so I had (C) them sent (D) to you this morning. A B C D

13. Some mistakes were (A) made (B) in the brochure but they might corrected (C) before you get (D) back. A B C D

14. You'll see (A) a copy before they're (B) printed (C) by the printer (D). A B C D

15. A funny thing was (A) happened when your office (B) was (C) painted (D) yesterday. A B C D

16. Will (A) your stay be (B) extended (C) or will you be returned (D) next week? A B C D

17. I used to do (A) my own taxes but now I have (B) done them (C) by (D) an accountant. A B C D

18. Before a final decision is reached (A), the various possibilities should (B) probably discussed (C) by (D) the whole team. A B C D

19. The house painted (A) more than three years ago but I'm not going to (B) have (C) it done (D) again for a while. A B C D

20. We didn't (A) know (B) about the problem so it shouldn't (C) be handled (D) in time. A B C D

21. A lot of crops can't (A) be grew (B) in the mountains because it (C) gets (D) too cold. A B C D

22. That bit of pottery was (A) found (B) by (C) an archaeologist while she was worked (D) in this area. A B C D

23. Does (A) the lightbulb have to replaced (B) or is it (C) still working (D)? A B C D

24. Have (A) you had (B) your teeth clean (C) yet by (D) the new hygienist? A B C D

25. The last payment shouldn't make (A) until all the work has been (B) completed (C) and carefully checked (D). A B C D

UNIT 64 Zero Conditionals

Sorry, Sir.
If you don't fit,
you can't board.

CHECK POINT

Circle T (True) or F (False).

T F The man may not be able to board the plane.

CHART CHECK

Circle T (True) or F (False).

T F The verbs in both clauses are in the present.

T F The *if* clause always comes first.

T F There is always a comma between the two clauses.

STATEMENTS

If Clause		Result Clause
If	it **snows**,	the airport **closes**.
	it's foggy,	planes **can't leave**.

STATEMENTS

Result Clause	*If* Clause	
The airport **closes**	*if*	it **snows**.
Planes **can't leave**		it's foggy.

***YES/NO* QUESTIONS**

Result Clause	*If* Clause	
Does the airport **close**	*if*	it **snows**?
Can planes **leave**		it's foggy?

SHORT ANSWERS

Affirmative		Negative	
Yes,	it **does**.	No,	it **doesn't**.
	they **can**.		they **can't**.

***WH-* QUESTIONS**

Result Clause	*If* Clause
Why **does** air **get** lighter	*if* it **expands**?

EXPRESS CHECK

Match the if *clauses with the result clauses.*

_____ 1. If you hate aeroplane food, — a. they often get jet lag.

_____ 2. You might not be able to board — b. you can order a special meal.

_____ 3. If people travel a long distance, — c. if you don't check in at the gate.

Grammar Explanations	Examples
1. Use **zero conditionals** to talk about general truths and scientific facts. The *if* clause talks about the condition and the result clause talks about what happens if the condition occurs. Use the **present simple** in both clauses.	*if clause* / result clause ■ ***If*** it'**s** noon in Lima, it'**s** 6:00 p.m. in Rome. *if clause* / result clause ■ ***If*** air **expands**, it **becomes** lighter. Note: *If* means *when* in these contexts.
2. You can also use **zero conditionals** to talk about habits and recurring events (things that happen again and again). Use the present simple or present continuous in the *if* clause. Use the present simple in the result clause.	*if clause* / result clause ■ ***If*** Bill **flies**, he **orders** a special meal. *if clause* / result clause ■ ***If*** I'**m travelling** a long way, I always **fly**.
3. You can also use **modals** in the result clause.	■ If you practise your Chinese every day, you ***can* improve** quickly. ■ You ***might* learn** more if you listen to Chinese CDs.
4. Use the **imperative** in the result clause to give instructions, commands and invitations that depend on a certain condition.	■ If you want the seat to recline, **press** the button. ■ If the seat belt light is on, **don't leave** your seat. ■ If you come to Tokyo, **stay** with us.
5. You can **begin conditional sentences** with the *if* clause or the result clause. The meaning is the same. Use a **comma** between the two clauses only when the *if* clause comes first.	■ **If the light goes on**, fasten your seat belt. OR ■ Fasten your seat belt **if the light goes on**.

IDENTIFY • *Read this article. In each zero conditional sentence, underline the result clause once. Underline the clause that expresses the condition twice.*

Passengers' Rights

If you run into problems on your journey, remember your rights as a passenger. Often the airline company is required to compensate you for delays or damages. For example, the airline provides meals and hotel rooms if a flight is unduly delayed. However, the airline owes you a lot more if it caused the delay by overbooking. This can occur especially during holidays if airlines sell more tickets than there are seats. If all the passengers actually turn up, then the flight is overbooked. Airlines usually award upgrades or additional free travel to passengers who volunteer to take a later flight. However, if no one volunteers, your flight may be delayed. In that case, the airline must repay you 100 per cent of the cost of your ticket for a delay of up to four hours on an international flight. If the delay is more than four hours, you receive 200 per cent of the cost of your ticket.

SUMMARISE • *Read these conversations about Hong Kong. Summarise the advice with zero conditional sentences.*

1. **A:** I hate hot weather.
   B: The best time to go to Hong Kong is November or December.
   If you hate hot weather, the best time to go to Hong Kong is November or December.

2. **A:** I'm travelling with my children.
   B: Take them to Lai Chi Kok Amusement Park in Kowloon.
   ____

3. **A:** We need a moderately priced hotel.
   B: I suggest the Harbour View International House.
   ____

4. **A:** We like seafood.
   B: There are wonderful seafood restaurants on Lamma Island.
   ____

5. **A:** I'm fascinated by Chinese opera.
   B: You might like the street opera in the Shanghai Street Night Market.
   ____

6. **A:** I'd like to get a good view of Hong Kong.
   B: You should take the funicular to the Peak.
   ____

COMBINE • *Complete this interview between* Careers Magazine (CM) *and flight attendant Mary Soames* (MS). *Combine the sentences in brackets to make a zero conditional sentence. Use the same order. Make necessary changes in capitalisation and punctuation.*

CM: How long are you usually away?

MS: If I go to the Bahamas, I have a two-day stopover.
1. (I go to the Bahamas. I have a two-day stopover.)

CM: What do you do for two days?

MS: ______________________________
2. (I spend a lot of time at the pool. I stay at a hotel.)

____
3. (I stay with friends. I spend time with them.)

CM: Sounds nice.

MS: ______________________________
4. (It's not so nice. I get a 'Dracula' flight.)

That's when you fly somewhere at midnight, spend four hours, and then fly back.

CM: Sounds like a tough job. Is it worth it?

MS: ______________________________
5. (It's very rewarding. You don't mind hard work.)

CM: Who walks the dog and waters the plants when you're away?

MS: ______________________________
6. (You have three flatmates. You don't have trouble finding dogwalkers.)

CM: What's the best thing about this job?

MS: Free trips. ______________________________
7. (A flight has an empty seat. I travel free!)

EDIT • *Read Mary's diary entry. Find and correct seven mistakes in the use of zero conditionals. The first mistake has already been corrected. Don't forget to check punctuation!*

What a great weekend! If Lou and Tony aren't the best hosts in the world, I ~~won't~~ don't know who is. I've invited them to London but if you live in the Bahamas, you rarely want to leave. Tomorrow at midnight, I am doing a round trip from London to Singapore. There's always a price to pay. If I get a free weekend, I always get a 'Dracula' flight afterwards. Oh, well. If I won't fall asleep, I can usually get a lot of reading done. Pat and Ken both flew to London yesterday. I hope someone can walk Frisky for me. Usually, if I'll be working, one of them is off. If Frisky is alone for a long time, he barked a lot. That disturbs the neighbours. Maybe I should just leave the TV on for him. He's always very calm, if the TV is on. Or maybe I'd better call Pat and ask her about her timetable. If it was 6:00 p.m. here in Singapore, it's 11:00 a.m. in London.

First Conditionals

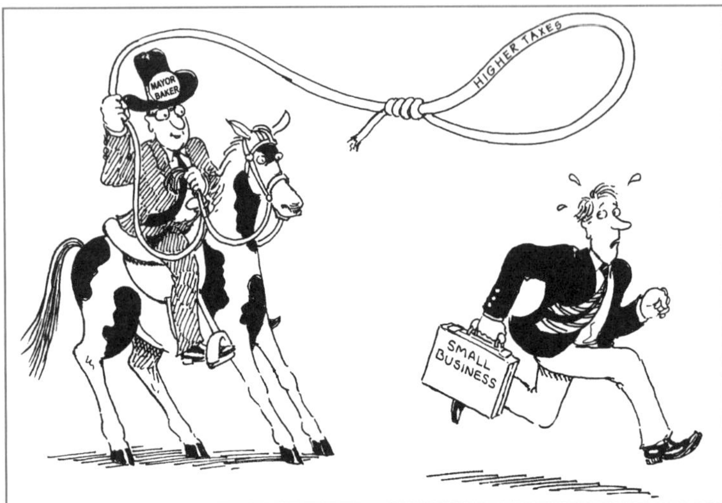

If Baker **raises** taxes, small businesses **will leave**.

CHECK POINT

Circle T (True) or F (False).

T F Baker is definitely going to raise taxes.

T F Small businesses are definitely going to leave.

CHART CHECK

Tick the correct answer.

Use the present simple in

❐ the *if* clause.

❐ the result clause.

Use a comma between the two clauses

❐ when the *if* clause comes first.

❐ when the result clause comes first.

AFFIRMATIVE STATEMENTS	
If Clause: Present	**Result Clause: Future**
If Baker **wins**,	he'**ll raise** taxes. he'**s going to fight** crime.

NEGATIVE STATEMENTS	
If Clause: Present	**Result Clause: Future**
If he **doesn't lower** taxes,	businesses **won't survive**.

YES/NO QUESTIONS	
Result Clause: Future	**If Clause: Present**
Will he **lower** taxes **Is** he **going to fight** crime	*if* he **wins the election**?

SHORT ANSWERS			
Affirmative		**Negative**	
Yes, he	**will**.	**No**, he	**won't**.
	is.		**isn't**.

***WH-* QUESTIONS**		
RESULT CLAUSE: FUTURE		***IF* CLAUSE: PRESENT**
What	**will** he **do** **is** he **going to do**	***if*** he **wins the election**?

EXPRESS CHECK

Unscramble these words to form a sentence. Add a comma if necessary.

fight • she • crime • she'll • If • wins

____

Grammar Explanations	Examples
1. Use **first conditional** sentences to talk about what will happen under certain conditions in the future. The *if* clause states the condition. The result clause states the result.	*if* clause / result clause ■ ***If*** Baker **wins**, he'**ll raise** taxes. *(It's a real possibility that Baker will win.)*
Use the **present simple** in the *if* clause. Use the **future** with ***will*** or ***be going to*** in the result clause.	■ ***If*** Dent **wins**, she'**ll improve** housing. ■ ***If*** Dent **wins**, she'**s going to improve** housing.
You can also use a **modal** in the result clause.	■ If you want to vote, you ***must*** **register**. ■ If you don't vote, you ***might*** **regret** it.
▶ **BE CAREFUL!** Even though the *if* clause refers to the future, use the present simple.	■ ***If*** she **wins**, she'll fight crime. NOT ~~If she will win . . .~~

2. You can **begin conditional sentences** with the *if* clause or the result clause. The meaning is the same.	■ **If you vote for Dent**, you won't regret it. OR ■ You won't regret it **if you vote for Dent**.
Use a **comma** between the two clauses only when the *if* clause comes first	

3. ***If*** and ***unless*** can both be used in conditional sentences but their meanings are very different.	■ ***If*** you vote, you'll have a say in the future of our country.
Use ***unless*** to state a negative condition.	■ ***Unless*** you vote, you won't have a say in the future of our country.
Unless often has the same meaning as ***if . . . not***.	OR ■ ***If*** you do**n't** vote, you won't have a say in the future of our country.

MATCH • *Each condition will have a result. Match the condition with the appropriate result.*

	Condition		Result
f	1. If Dent wins, she	a.	won't stay out of trouble.
______	2. If she lowers taxes, business people	b.	won't have a say in the government.
______	3. If the education system improves, we	c.	will have an educated work force.
______	4. Unless young people have hope for the future, they	d.	won't be able to vote.
______	5. If crime decreases, this	e.	will move their companies back to the city.
______	6. Unless you register, you	f.	will lower taxes.
______	7. If you don't vote, you	g.	will be a safer place to live.

2

COMPLETE • *Read this interview between* Politics Today (PT) *and MP Daniel Baker* (DB). *Complete it with the correct form of the verbs in brackets and* **if** *or* **unless**.

PT: What's the first thing you ___'ll do___ (1. do) ___if___ (2. if / unless) you ________ (3. get) elected?

DB: Well, it's been a long, hard campaign. ________ (4. If / Unless) I ________ (5. win), I ________ (6. take) a short break before I begin my new job.

PT: Sounds good. Where?

DB: Sorry, but I'd rather not say. ________ (7. If / Unless) I ________ (8. be) elected, I ________ (9. try) to keep my personal life private. Even politicians need privacy.

PT: I can understand that. Now, every election has a winner and a loser. What ________ you ________ (10. do) ________ (11. if / unless) you ________ (12. lose)?

DB: ________ (13. If / Unless) I ________ (14. lose) this election, I ________ (15. continue) to be active in politics. ________ (16. If / Unless) *all* parties ________ (17. cooperate), this country ________ (18. not be) as great as it can be. Finally, ________ (19. if / unless) the people ________ (20. not elect) me to office this time, I ________ (21. be) back next time to try again!

COMBINE • *Amy Chatsworth is trying to decide whether to go to law school. She made a decision tree to help her decide. In the tree, arrows connect the conditions and the results. Write sentences about her decisions. Use first conditional sentences.*

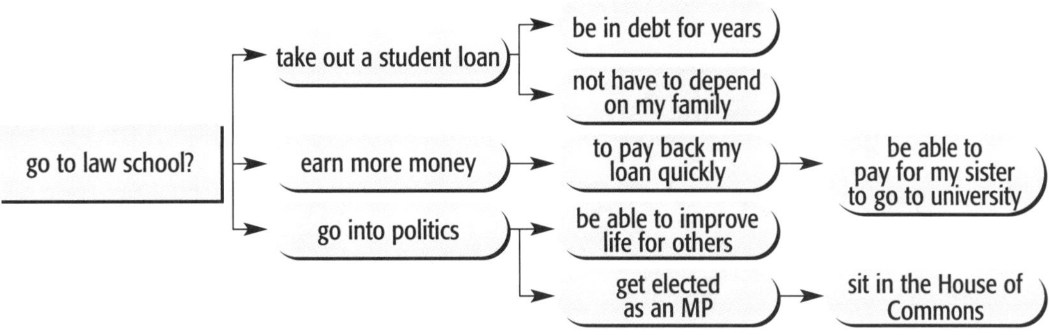

1. If I go to law school, I'll take out a student loan.
2. If I take out a student loan, I'll be in debt for years.
3. ______
4. ______
5. ______
6. ______
7. ______
8. ______
9. ______
10. ______

EDIT • *Read this diary entry. Find and correct six mistakes in the use of first conditionals. The first mistake has already been corrected. Don't forget to check punctuation!*

Should I campaign for student union president? I'll have to decide soon if I ~~wanted~~ want to run. If I'll be busy campaigning, I won't have much time to study. That's a problem, because I'm not going to get a good job if I get good marks this year. On the other hand, there's so much to do in this university and nothing is getting done if John Healy becomes president again. A lot of people know that. But will I know what to do if I'll get the job? Never mind. I'll deal with that problem, if I win.

Second Conditionals

CHECK POINT

Circle T (True) or F (False).

T F Schroeder, the piano player, wants to marry Lucy.

CHART CHECK

Circle T (True) or F (False).

T F Use the present simple in the ***if*** clause.

T F Use ***were*** for all subjects.

T F Use a comma between the two clauses when the result clause comes first.

AFFIRMATIVE STATEMENTS		
***If* Clause: Simple Past**		**Result Clause: *Would* + Base Form of Verb**
If	he **loved** her, he **were*** in love,	he **would get** married. he**'d get** married.

*Note that *were* is used for all subjects with *be*.

NEGATIVE STATEMENTS		
***If* Clause: Simple Past**		**Result Clause: *Would* + Base Form of Verb**
If	he **didn't love** her, he **weren't** in love,	he **would not get** married. he **wouldn't get** married.

YES/NO QUESTIONS		
Result Clause	***If* Clause**	
Would I **get** married	*if*	I **loved** her? I **were** in love?

SHORT ANSWERS	
Affirmative	**Negative**
Yes, I **would**.	No, I **wouldn't**.

WH- QUESTIONS		
Result Clause	***If* Clause**	
What **would** you **do**	*if*	you **loved** her? you **were** in love?

EXPRESS CHECK

Circle the correct words to complete this question.

What will / would he do if / when he was / were a millionaire?

Grammar Explanations	Examples
1. Use **second conditional** sentences to talk about unreal, untrue, imagined or impossible conditions and their results in the present. The *if* clause presents the unreal condition. The result clause presents the unreal result of that condition.	*if* clause — result clause ■ ***If*** I **loved** him, I **would marry** him. *(But I don't love him so I won't marry him.)* *if* clause — result clause ■ ***If*** I **had** more time, I **would travel**. *(But I haven't got time, so I don't travel.)*
2. Use the **past simple** in the *if* clause. Use ***would*** + **base form** of the verb in the result clause.	*If* clause — result clause ■ ***If*** they **had** money, they **wouldn't live** there.
► **BE CAREFUL!**	
a. The *if* clause uses the past simple form but the meaning is not past.	■ ***If*** I **had** more money ***now***, I would go on a trip round the world.
b. Don't use ***would*** in the *if* clause in present unreal conditional sentences.	■ ***If*** she **knew** the answer, she would tell you. NOT ~~If she would know the answer . . .~~
c. Use ***were*** for all subjects when the verb in the *if* clause is a form of ***be***. **USAGE NOTE:** You will sometimes hear native speakers use ***was*** in the *if* clause. However, many people think that this is not correct.	■ ***If*** I **were** rich, I would travel round the world. NOT ~~If I was rich . . .~~
3. You can also use a **modal** in the result clause.	■ If I had time, I ***could* read** more.
4. You can **begin conditional sentences** with the *if* clause or the result clause. The meaning is the same. Use a **comma** between the two clauses only when the *if* clause comes first.	■ **If I had more money**, I would move. OR ■ I would move **if I had more money**.
5. Statements beginning with ***If I were you, . . .*** are often used to give advice.	■ ***If I were you***, I'd read *Peanuts*. It's really funny.

TRUE OR FALSE • *Read each quotation from these* Peanuts *characters. Write T (True) or F (False) for the statement that follows.*

1. **SNOOPY:** If I were a human being, I wouldn't even *own* a dog!

   __F__ Snoopy is a human being.

2. **LUCY** to **SNOOPY:** You wouldn't be so happy if you knew what was going to happen.

   ______ Snoopy is happy.

3. **LUCY** to **LINUS:** If I were you, I'd sleep underneath that tree.

   ______ Lucy is giving Linus advice.

4. **SNOOPY** to **WOODSTOCK:** What would you do if you had forty dollars?

   ______ Woodstock has forty dollars.

5. **SNOOPY:** If I ate one more snowflake, I'd turn into a blizzard.

   ______ Snoopy plans to eat another snowflake.

6. **LUCY:** If we were married, Schroeder, I'd come in every morning and dust your piano.

   ______ Lucy dusts Schroeder's piano every morning.

2

COMPLETE • *Read part of an article about the comic strip* Peanuts. *Complete it with the correct form of the verbs in brackets.*

Peanuts

What makes *Peanuts* so popular? Of course, if it __weren't__ (1. not be) funny, people ______ (2. not like) it so much. But *Peanuts* provides more than just laughs. It addresses such universal themes as love, jealousy, loneliness and hope. If the characters ______ (3. not be) so real, we ______ (4. couldn't / identify) with them. Take Lucy, for example. In love with the piano-playing Schroeder, Lucy complains, 'If we ______ (5. be) married, and you ______ (6. love) golf, I ______ (7. hate) your golf clubs! If you ______ (8. drive) a sports car, I ______ (9. hate) your sports car! If you ______ (10. be) a bowler, I ______ (11. hate) your bowling ball.' Without looking up from his piano or missing a beat, Schroeder asks, 'So?' 'I hate your piano!' shouts Lucy as she kicks it out from under him. Recognisable behaviour? In *Peanuts* we see ourselves along with our weaknesses and hopes. But we don't have to analyse *Peanuts* to enjoy it.

If it ______ (12. not be) for comic strips like *Peanuts*, our lives ______ (13. might / be) a little less fun.

COMBINE • *Read about these* Peanuts *characters. What would happen if their situations were different? Combine the two sentences into one, using second conditional sentences.*

1. Schroeder ignores Lucy. She gets angry with him.

   If Schroeder didn't ignore Lucy, she wouldn't get angry with him.

2. Schroeder loves Beethoven. He plays his sonatas all the time.

   ____

3. Charlie Brown doesn't have enough friends. He feels lonely.

   ____

4. Sally doesn't know her teacher's name. She can't send her a card.

   ____

5. Linus is clever. He finds intelligent solutions to life's problems.

   ____

6. Woodstock and Snoopy have a close relationship. Woodstock confides in Snoopy.

   ____

7. Rerun's parents refuse to let him have a dog. He tries to borrow Charlie's dog.

   ____

8. Pigpen doesn't have enough baths. He's filthy.

   ____

4

EDIT • *Read this boy's diary entry. Find and correct six mistakes in the use of the second conditional. The first mistake has already been corrected.*

would

I've got to stop staying up late reading 'Peanuts'! If I weren't always so tired, I ~~will~~ be able to stay awake in class. Whenever the teacher asks me something, I don't know what to say. Then I get really embarrassed because of that nice red-haired girl that I like. I would talk to her if I wouldn't be so shy. My friend, Jason, says, 'If I was you, I'd ask her to a party.' but I'm too afraid that if I asked her, she would have said no. After school, I played football. Nobody wanted me in their team. If I play better, I would get chosen sometimes. Life is hard! I can really understand that Charlie Brown character in 'Peanuts' In fact, if I didn't laugh so hard while reading 'Peanuts', I would cried!

Unit 67 Third Conditionals

Section 5/ENTERTAINMENT 4A

Best Bets for Holiday Viewing

It's a Wonderful Life

Rating: ★★★★ out of ★★★★

What would have happened if you had never been born? George Bailey's guardian angel, Clarence, shows George that **life in Bedford Falls would have been very different if George hadn't been there**. In the process, Clarence teaches us all how our lives touch those of others. Highly recommended for the whole family.

George (seated) with his guardian angel

CHECK POINT

Circle T (True) or F (False).

T F George Bailey was never in Bedford Falls.

CHART CHECK

Tick the correct answers.

Use the past perfect in

❒ the *if* clause.

❒ the result clause.

Use a comma between the two clauses when

❒ the *if* clause comes first.

❒ the result clause comes first.

STATEMENTS	
***IF* CLAUSE: PAST PERFECT**	**RESULT CLAUSE: *WOULD (NOT) HAVE* + PAST PARTICIPLE**
If I **had (not) had** money,	I **would (not) have moved** away.

YES/NO QUESTIONS	
RESULT CLAUSE	***IF* CLAUSE**
Would you **have left**	*if* you **had had** money?

SHORT ANSWERS	
AFFIRMATIVE	**NEGATIVE**
Yes, I **would (have)**.	No, I **wouldn't (have)**.

WH- QUESTIONS	
RESULT CLAUSE	***IF* CLAUSE**
What **would** you **have done**	*if* you **had had** money?

CONTRACTIONS
would have = **would've** would not have = **wouldn't have**

EXPRESS CHECK

Complete this sentence with the correct form of the verb **study**. *Add a comma if necessary.*

I ______________________________ if I had known about the test today.

Grammar Explanations	Examples
1. Use **third conditional** sentences to talk about past conditions and results that never happened. The *if* clause presents the unreal condition. The result clause presents the imagined result of that condition.	*if* clause / result clause ■ ***If*** George **had died** young, he **wouldn't have had** children. *(But he didn't die young and he did have children.)* ■ ***If*** George **hadn't been born**, many people's lives **would have been** worse. *(But George was born so their lives were better.)*
2. Use the **past perfect** in the *if* clause. Use ***would have* + past participle** in the result clause.	*if* clause / result clause ■ ***If*** the film **had won** an Oscar, it **would have become** famous immediately.
3. You can also use **modals** in the result clause.	■ If George had gone to university, he ***might have* become** an architect. ■ If George had become an architect, he ***could have* designed** bridges.
4. You can **begin conditional sentences** with the *if* clause or the result clause. The meaning is the same. Use a **comma** between the two clauses only when the *if* clause comes first.	■ **If he had won a million dollars,** he would have travelled to China. OR ■ He would have travelled to China **if he had won a million dollars**.
5. Third conditionals are often used to express regret about what happened in the past.	■ ***If*** I **had known** Mary was back, I **would have invited** her to the party. *(I regret that I didn't invite her.)*

TRUE OR FALSE • *Read each numbered sentence. Write T (True) or F (False) for the statement that follows.*

1. If I had had time, I would have watched *It's a Wonderful Life*.

   __T__ I didn't have time to watch *It's a Wonderful Life*.

2. I would have recorded the film if my DVD hadn't broken.

   ______ I recorded the film.

3. If Clarence hadn't been there, George might have killed himself.

   ______ Clarence was there.

4. George wouldn't have met Mary if he hadn't gone to his brother's party.

   ______ George didn't go to the party.

5. George would have been happier if he had become an architect.

   ______ George became an architect.

6. The film wouldn't have been so good if James Stewart hadn't played the part of George Bailey.

   ______ James Stewart played the part of George Bailey.

2

COMPLETE • *George is thinking about the past. Complete his thoughts with the correct form of the words in brackets.*

1. I didn't go into business with my friend Pete. If I ___had gone___ (go) into business with him, I ___would have become___ (become) a success.
2. I couldn't go into the army because I was deaf in one ear. I __________ (go) into the army if I __________ (not lose) my hearing in that ear.
3. Mary and I weren't able to go on honeymoon. We __________ (can / go) away if my father __________ (not become) ill.
4. Clarence showed me how the world would look without me. I __________ (not know) that I was so important if Clarence __________ (not show) me.
5. My old boss once made a terrible mistake. If I __________ (not help) him, he __________ (can / go) to prison.
6. Mary __________ (may / not lead) a happy life if she __________ (not marry) me.
7. Life here __________ (be) really different if I __________ (not live).

REWRITE • *Read each true situation. Then write a third conditional sentence to express how things could have been different.*

1. Clarence wasn't a first-class angel so he didn't have much self-confidence.
   If Clarence had been a first-class angel, he would have had more self-confidence.
2. George was unhappy about his business. He shouted at his daughter on Christmas Eve.
   ____
3. Poor people could buy houses because George's business lent them money.
   ____
4. Mr Potter wasn't able to trick George so George didn't sell Potter the business.
   ____
5. George's Uncle Billy lost $8,000. George got into trouble with the law.
   ____
6. George's friends didn't know about his troubles. They didn't help him straightaway.
   ____
7. George's friends collected money for him so he didn't go to prison.
   ____

EDIT • *Read Clarence's diary entry. Find and correct six mistakes in the use of the third conditional. The first mistake has already been corrected. Remember to check punctuation!*

Dear Diary,

It's funny how things work out sometimes. If George ~~*hasn't*~~ hadn't *wanted to jump off that bridge on Christmas Eve, I might never have getting an important job like saving him. And if he hadn't been so stubborn, I would never had thought of the idea of showing him life in Bedford Falls without him. One of the saddest things was seeing all those people who didn't have homes. If George gave up and sold his business to Mr Potter, then Potter would have rented run-down flats to all those people. But because of George, they now have good homes. By the time we were finished, George realised he really had a wonderful life. In fact, he will have gone to prison happily, if his friends hadn't given him the money he needed. Well, luckily they helped him out and he didn't go to prison. And I got my wings and became a first-class angel!*

Wish: Present and Past

Tiny Fairy Tales THE THREE WISHES

The Three Wishes

One day, a poor woodcutter was given three wishes by a tree elf. When his hungry wife heard the news, she said, 'I **wish** I **had** some sausages.' At once five sausages appeared on a plate. The woodcutter was furious about wasting a wish. 'I **wish** those sausages **were hanging** from your nose,' he shouted. At once the sausages hung from her nose. The two struggled to get them loose but they could not. 'I **wish** I **hadn't made** that wish,' the woodcutter sighed. At once the sausages were on the plate again. The couple happily ate the sausages and wished for nothing more.

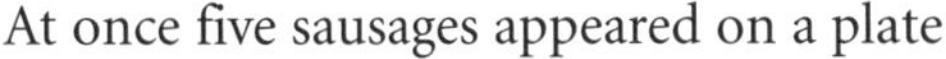

CHECK POINT

Tick the correct answer.

The woman wanted sausages

❒ that day.

❒ the day before.

CHART CHECK 1

Tick the correct answer.

In wishes about the present, what tense follows ***wish***?

❒ the present simple

❒ the past simple

WISHES ABOUT THE PRESENT			
Main Clause	**Wish Clause**		
She **wishes**	she	**had**	some food now.
		were*	rich.

*Note that *were* is used for all subjects with *be*.

CHART CHECK 2

Tick the correct answer.

In wishes about the past, what tense follows ***wish***?

❒ the past simple

❒ the past perfect

WISHES ABOUT THE PAST			
MAIN CLAUSE	**WISH CLAUSE**		
He **wishes**	he	**had had**	some food last night.
		had been	rich as a child.

EXPRESS CHECK

Complete these sentences with the correct forms of the verb **know**.

- I wish I ______________ a good story to tell my next class.
- I wish I ______________ more stories as a child.

Grammar Explanations	Examples
1. Use ***wish*** followed by a verb in the **past simple** to talk about things that you want to be true now but that are not true.	■ He **wishes** he ***had*** a yacht. *(He doesn't have a yacht but he wants one.)*
USAGE NOTE: After *wish*, you can use ***were*** instead of *was*.	■ Sometimes I **wish** I ***were*** a child again. OR ■ Sometimes I **wish** I ***was*** a child again.
2. Use ***wish*** followed by the **past perfect** to express regrets about events in the past.	■ They **wish** they ***had moved*** to the country. *(They didn't move to the country and now they think that was a mistake.)*
3. Use ***would*** after ***wish*** to express a desire for someone or something to act in a different way. This often communicates a complaint or a regret.	■ I **wish** you ***would* cook** breakfast. You've got more time than I have. ■ I **wish** she ***would* visit** more often. I really miss her.
Do not use *will* after *wish*.	NOT ~~I wish she will visit more often~~.
4. Use ***could*** or ***could have*** after ***wish*** to express ability.	■ He **wishes** he ***could* earn** more money. ■ He **wishes** he ***could have* found** a better job when he was younger.
Do not use *can* after *wish*.	NOT ~~He wishes he can earn more money~~.

TRUE OR FALSE • *Read each numbered sentence. Write T (True) or F (False) for the statement that follows.*

1. I wish I were a princess.

   __T__ I'm not a princess.

2. I hated living in a big house as a child.

   _____ I wish I had lived in a small house.

3. He wishes he could find a better job.

   _____ He likes his job.

4. They couldn't do computer classes at school so they are doing them now.

   _____ They wish they could do computer classes.

5. Jim's wife plays computer games a lot. He wants her to stop.

   _____ He wishes she wouldn't play computer games.

6. He wishes he had a lot of money.

   _____ He hasn't got a lot of money.

COMPLETE • *Read this article from a psychology magazine. Complete it with the correct form of the verbs in brackets.*

PSYCHOLOGY FOR YOU

WISHES AND SOLUTIONS

The old saying goes, 'If wishes were horses, then beggars would ride.' 'I wish it __were__ (1. be) that easy,' says therapist Joel Grimes. 'But we can't just wish problems __________ (2. will / go away). We have to find our own solutions.' According to him, complainers are really saying, 'I wish I __________ (3. have) a magical solution. I wish I __________ (4. not have to / deal) with this myself.' One client, for example, kept complaining, 'I wish I __________ (5. can / entertain) people but my flat is too small.' Grimes urged her to solve the problem. This year, she gave an open-house party, with people coming at different times. She still wishes she __________ (6. can / invite) her whole family last year but she learnt she could solve her own problems. 'At first clients get angry with me for not handing them solutions,' says Grimes. 'But when they experience their own power, they wish they __________ (7. know) about it sooner.'

REWRITE • *Joel Grimes's clients complain about things in the past and in the present. Rewrite their complaints as wishes.*

1. I didn't have time to read bedtime stories to my children.
   I wish I had had time to read bedtime stories to my children.
2. My husband won't ask for a pay rise.
   ______
3. We didn't save any money last month.
   ______
4. My boyfriend is unfit.
   ______
5. I'm too old to go back to school.
   ______
6. I can't stop smoking.
   ______
7. My son doesn't phone me.
   ______
8. My parents didn't understand me.
   ______

EDIT • *Read this diary entry. Find and correct five mistakes in the use of* **wish**. *The first mistake has already been corrected.*

Today, I said to Dr Grimes, 'I wish there ~~was~~ were a way to spend more time with my boyfriend but we're both too busy.' He just said, 'If wishes were horses, beggars would ride.' That's an easy thing to say but I wish I understand its meaning. Maybe it means that wishing won't solve problems. Well, that's why I went to see him!!! I wish he will tell me what to do right then and there but he refused. Speaking of wishful thinking, I wish Mark and I could have spent the weekend together next week. My exams are over but he's got to fly to Paris for his job. If wishes were horses, I'd ride one to Paris. Hey! Mark is always saying, 'I wish you would come with me sometimes.' I suppose I can go with him to Paris. Dr Grimes must have meant that I can solve my own problems. Now I wish I haven't been so rude to him.

SECTION ONE

Circle the letter of the correct answer to complete each sentence.

EXAMPLE:
Jennifer never ________ coffee. A (B) C D
(A) drink (C) is drinking
(B) drinks (D) was drinking

1. If you ________ a headache, you should take an aspirin. A B C D
   (A) 'll have got (C) have got
   (B) had got (D) are having
2. I wish we ________ a bigger house. This one is too small. A B C D
   (A) have (C) would have
   (B) had (D) had had
3. ________ it rains very hard, the streets flood. A B C D
   (A) If (C) During
   (B) Always (D) Unless
4. We'll be late unless we ________ now. A B C D
   (A) leave (C) had left
   (B) don't leave (D) have left
5. What would Tom do if he ________ the truth? A B C D
   (A) would know (C) knows
   (B) has known (D) knew
6. If I ________ you, I'd call and apologise. A B C D
   (A) am (C) were
   (B) would be (D) was
7. If I ________ you were ill, I would have called sooner. A B C D
   (A) have known (C) would have known
   (B) had known (D) know
8. If you want to go skiing, ________ to Les Arcs. A B C D
   (A) you go (C) go
   (B) you'll go (D) went
9. Jennifer has trouble with maths. She wishes she ________ more at school. A B C D
   (A) studies (C) had studied
   (B) has studied (D) studied

10. – If we invited you, would you come? A B C D
– Of course I ________.
(A) do (C) would have
(B) am (D) would

11. Thomas will win the election if he ________ harder. A B C D
(A) campaigns (C) will campaign
(B) would campaign (D) campaigned

12. If you ________ told us about the bad service, we would have eaten there. A B C D
(A) didn't (C) haven't
(B) wouldn't have (D) hadn't

SECTION TWO

Each sentence has four underlined words or phrases. The four underlined parts of the sentence are marked A, B, C and D. Circle the letter of the one underlined word or phrase that is NOT CORRECT.

EXAMPLE:
Mike usually (A) drives (B) to school but today (C) he walks (D). A B C (D)

13. If (A) you had been (B) here yesterday, you would have (C) see (D) Jean. A B C D

14. I wish (A) our family could of (B) taken (C) holidays when we were (D) younger. A B C D

15. Unless we (A) work harder, we will (B) finish (C) on time (D). A B C D

16. If (A) I will have (B) to make a difficult decision, (C) I always discuss (D) it with my friends. A B C D

17. If (A) Lara is (B) older, she would try (C) to get (D) a job in Edinburgh. A B C D

18. We could had (A) done (B) more if (C) we had had (D) more time. A B C D

19. We ate (A) outside tomorrow (B) unless (C) it rains (D). A B C D

20. I would (A) take (B) the job if (C) I am (D) you. A B C D

21. What would (A) you do (B) if you will (C) won (D) the lottery? A B C D

22. It's (A) hot, so you will feel (B) better, (C) if you drink (D) more water. A B C D

23. If I did (A) set (B) my alarm clock, I would (C) have (D) got up on time. A B C D

24. If (A) I have to fly (B), I would get (C) very nervous, so I usually drive (D). A B C D

25. Lynn wishes (A) she had (B) a bigger house and can (C) buy (D) a car. A B C D

Relative Clauses with Subject Relative Pronouns

Bill, come and meet the woman **who has** **changed my life.**

CHECK POINT

Circle T (True) or F (False).

T **F** The man is talking about the woman holding a report.

CHART CHECK

Tick the correct answers.

Relative clauses describe:

- ❐ nouns
- ❐ verbs

Relative clauses can go:

- ❐ before the main clause
- ❐ in the middle of the main clause
- ❐ after the main clause

RELATIVE CLAUSE AFTER THE MAIN CLAUSE

MAIN CLAUSE	RELATIVE CLAUSE		
	SUBJECT RELATIVE PRONOUN	VERB	
That's my friend	*who*	**lives**	**in Rome**.

RELATIVE CLAUSE INSIDE THE MAIN CLAUSE

MAIN CLAUSE	RELATIVE CLAUSE			MAIN CLAUSE (CONT.)
	SUBJECT RELATIVE PRONOUN	VERB		
My friend	*who*	**lives**	**in Rome**	is a dancer.

EXPRESS CHECK

Unscramble these words to form a sentence.

the man • works • who • in the cafeteria • That's

____

Grammar Explanations	Examples
1. Use **relative clauses** to identify or give additional information about nouns or indefinite pronouns such as ***someone***, ***somebody***, ***something***, ***another*** and ***other(s)***.	■ I know the woman **who lives there**. *(The relative clause identifies the woman we are talking about.)* ■ Rome is a city **which attracts tourists**. *(The relative clause gives additional information about the city.)*
The relative clause directly follows the noun (or pronoun) it is identifying or describing.	■ Someone **who has a lot of friends** is lucky. NOT ~~Someone is lucky who has a lot of friends~~.
2. Sentences with relative clauses can be seen as a combination of two sentences.	*I have a friend. + He loves to shop. =* ■ I have a friend **who loves to shop**. *My friend lives in Rome. + She paints. =* ■ My friend **who lives in Rome** paints.
3. Relative clauses are introduced by **relative pronouns**. **Subject relative pronouns** are:	
a. ***who*** or ***that*** for people **USAGE NOTE:** ***That*** is less formal than ***who***.	■ I have a **friend *who*** lives in Mexico. ■ I have a **friend *that*** lives in Mexico.
b. ***which*** or ***that*** for places or things **USAGE NOTE:** ***That*** is less formal than ***which***.	■ New York is the **city *which*** never sleeps. ■ New York is the **city *that*** never sleeps.
c. ***whose*** + **noun** for people's possessions	■ He's the **man *whose* dog** barks all day.
► **BE CAREFUL!** Do not use both a subject relative pronoun and a subject pronoun (*I, you, he, she, it, we, they*) in the same relative clause.	■ Scott is someone ***who* loves sports**. NOT ~~Scott is someone who he loves sports~~.
4. Subject relative pronouns have the **same form** whether they refer to singular or plural nouns or to masculine or feminine nouns.	■ That's the **man *who*** lives next door. ■ That's the **woman *who*** lives next door. ■ Those are the **people *who*** live next door.
5. The **verb in the relative clause** is singular if the subject relative pronoun refers to a singular noun. It is plural if it refers to a plural noun.	■ Ben is my **friend *who* lives** in Leeds. ■ Al and Ed are my **friends *who* live** in Nottingham.
► **BE CAREFUL!** When ***whose*** + **noun** is the subject of a relative clause, the verb agrees in number with the subject of the relative clause.	■ Meg is a person ***whose* friends depend** on her. NOT ~~Meg is a person whose friends depends on her~~.

IDENTIFY • *Read this paragraph about friendship. First circle the relative pronouns and underline the relative clauses. Then draw an arrow from the relative pronoun to the noun or pronoun it describes.*

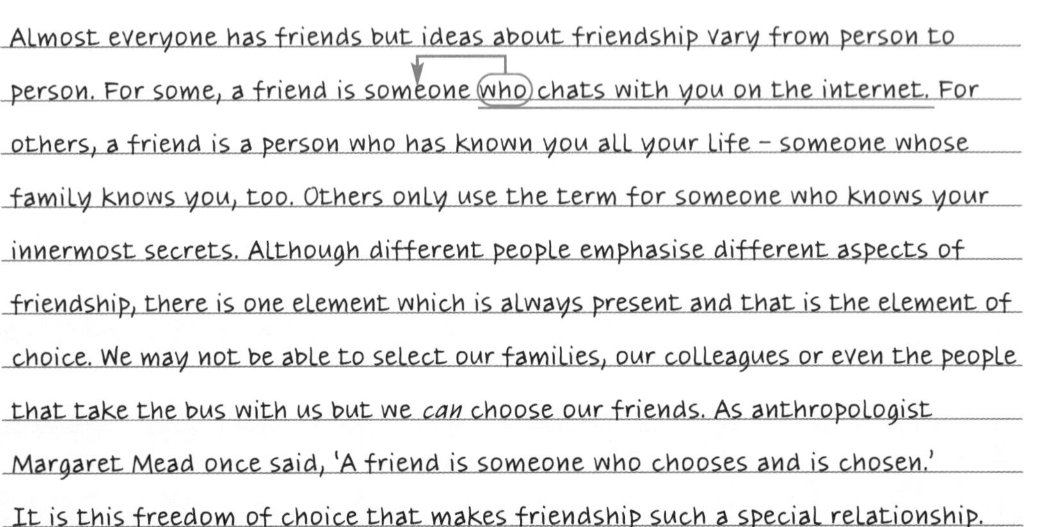

Almost everyone has friends but ideas about friendship vary from person to person. For some, a friend is someone who chats with you on the internet. For others, a friend is a person who has known you all your life – someone whose family knows you, too. Others only use the term for someone who knows your innermost secrets. Although different people emphasise different aspects of friendship, there is one element which is always present and that is the element of choice. We may not be able to select our families, our colleagues or even the people that take the bus with us but we *can* choose our friends. As anthropologist Margaret Mead once said, 'A friend is someone who chooses and is chosen.' It is this freedom of choice that makes friendship such a special relationship.

COMPLETE • *A magazine,* Psychology Today, *conducted a survey on friendship. Here are some of the results. Complete each sentence with an appropriate relative pronoun and the correct form of the verb in brackets.*

1. People __who__ __have__ (have) moved a lot have fewer friends.
2. People ________ ________ (have) lived in the same place have more friends.
3. The qualities ________ ________ (be) most important in a friend are loyalty, warmth and the ability to keep secrets.
4. Someone ________ ________ (face) a crisis turns to friends before family.
5. Betrayal is the cause ________ ________ (be) most often responsible for ending a friendship.
6. Many people have friends ________ social or religious backgrounds ________ (be) different from theirs.
7. Most people ________ friends ________ (include) members of the opposite sex say that these relationships are different from relationships with people of the same sex.
8. A survey ________ ________ (appear) in a magazine may not represent everyone.
9. Someone ________ ________ (not read) the magazine might have other ideas.

COMBINE • *Read each pair of sentences. Use a relative pronoun to combine them into one sentence.*

1. I have a friend. My friend lives in Mexico City.
   I have a friend who lives in Mexico City.
2. Mexico City is an exciting city. The city attracts a lot of tourists.
   ____
3. Steph has a brother. Her brother's name is Eric.
   ____
4. He works for a magazine. The magazine is very popular in Mexico.
   ____
5. Eric writes a column. The column deals with relationships.
   ____
6. An article won a prize. The article discussed friendships.
   ____
7. A person is lucky. That person has a lot of friends.
   ____

EDIT • *Read part of a student's essay. Find and correct six mistakes in the use of relative clauses. The first mistake has already been corrected.*

A writer once said that friends are born, not made. This means that we automatically become friends with people who ~~they~~ are compatible with us. I don't agree with this writer. Last summer, I made friends with some people who's completely different from me.

In July, I went to Barcelona to study Spanish for a month. In our group, there was a teacher which was much older than I am. We became really good friends. In my first week, I had a problem which was getting me down. Barcelona is a city who has a lot of distractions. As a result, I went out all the time and I stopped going to my classes. Bob helped me get back into my studies. After the trip, I kept writing to Bob. He always writes stories that is interesting and encouraging. Next summer, he's leading another trip what sounds interesting. I hope I can go.

Relative Clauses with Object Relative Pronouns or *When* and *Where*

Sophie,
Krakow is wonderful! Here's a picture of the main square with the café **where I spend all my time**. Can you find me with the new friend **that I made yesterday**? He's a writer, with gorgeous green eyes! I'm in love!
Lisa

CHECK POINT

Circle T (True) or F (False).

T F Lisa is pointing out her favourite café.

RELATIVE CLAUSE AFTER THE MAIN CLAUSE

MAIN CLAUSE	RELATIVE CLAUSE		
	Object Relative Pronoun	**Subject**	**Verb**
She reads all the books	*that*	**he**	**writes**.

RELATIVE CLAUSE INSIDE THE MAIN CLAUSE

MAIN CLAUSE	RELATIVE CLAUSE			MAIN CLAUSE (CONT.)
	Object Relative Pronoun	**Subject**	**Verb**	
The book	*that*	**they**	**borrowed**	seems very interesting.

CHART CHECK

Tick the correct answer.

The verb in the relative clause agrees with

❐ the noun in the main clause.

❐ the subject of the relative clause.

Circle T (True) or F (False).

T F The relative clause always follows the main clause.

EXPRESS CHECK

Unscramble these words to form a sentence.

I • the • films • all • he • directs • watch • that

____

Grammar Explanations	Examples
1. A **relative pronoun** can be the **object** of a relative clause. Notice that:	obj. *Eva is a writer. + I saw **her** on TV. =*
a. The **object relative pronoun** comes at the beginning of the relative clause.	obj. ■ Eva, ***who* I saw on TV**, is a writer.
b. Object relative pronouns have the **same form** whether they refer to singular or plural nouns or to masculine or feminine nouns.	■ That's the **man *who*** I met. ■ That's the **woman *who*** I met. ■ Those are the **people *who*** I met.
c. The **verb in the relative clause** agrees with the subject of the relative clause.	subj. verb ■ I like the columns ***which* he writes**. ■ I like the column ***which* they write**.
▶ **Be careful!** Do not use both an object relative pronoun and an object pronoun (*me, you, him, her, it, us, them*) in the same relative clause.	■ She is the writer ***who* I saw on TV**. Not ~~She is the writer who I saw her on TV.~~
Note: Object relative pronouns are often left out.	■ She is the writer **I saw on TV**.

2. Object relative pronouns are:	
a. ***who***, ***that*** or ***whom*** for people **Usage Note:** ***Whom*** is very formal and is rarely used in speech.	■ She's the writer ***who* I met**. ■ She's the writer ***that* I met**. ■ She's the writer **I met**. ■ She's the writer ***whom* I met**.
b. ***which*** or ***that*** for things	■ I read the book ***which* she wrote**. ■ I read the book ***that* she wrote**. ■ I read the book **she wrote**.
c. ***whose*** + **noun** for people's possessions	■ That's the author ***whose* book I read**.

3. A relative pronoun can be the **object of a preposition**.	
Usage Note: In **informal** speaking and writing, we put the preposition at the end of the clause and we often leave out the relative pronoun.	*He's the writer. + I work **for him**. =* ■ He's the writer ***that*** I work **for**. ■ He's the writer I work **for**.
In **formal** English, we put the preposition at the beginning of the clause. In this case, we use only ***whom*** and ***which*** (not *who* or *that*).	■ He's the writer **for *whom*** I work. ■ That's the book **about *which*** I told you.

4. ***Where*** and ***when*** can also be used to introduce relative clauses:	
a. ***Where*** refers to a place.	*That's the library. + She works **there**. =* ■ That's the library ***where* she works**.
b. ***When*** or ***that*** refers to a time.	*I remember the day. + I met him **then**. =* ■ I remember the day ***when* I met him**. ■ I remember the day ***that* I met him**.

IDENTIFY • *Read this part of a book review. Underline all the relative clauses with object relative pronouns. Circle the object relative pronouns and* **when** *or* **where**. *Then draw a line from the circled word to the noun it refers to.*

Section 4 **Books**

Lost in Translation: A Life in a New Language

At the age of nine, Eva Hoffman left Poland with her family. She was old enough to know what she was losing: Krakow, a city (that) she loved as one loves a person, the sun-baked villages where they had spent summer holidays and the conversations and escapades with her friends. Disconnected from a city where life was lived intensely, her father was overwhelmed by the transition to Canada. Eva lost the parent whom she had watched in lively conversation with friends in Krakow cafés. And nothing could replace her friendship with the boy whose home she visited daily and whom she assumed she would marry one day. Worst of all, however, she missed her language. For years, she felt no connection to the English name of anything that she felt was important. *Lost in Translation: A Life in a New Language* (Penguin, 1989) tells how Eva came to terms with her new identity and language. It's a story that readers will find fascinating and moving.

Eva Hoffman

COMPLETE • *A school newspaper, the* Chelsea Bugle (CB), *interviewed one of the school's international students, Maniya Suarez* (MS). *Complete the interview with relative pronouns,* **when** *or* **where** *and the correct form of the verbs in brackets.*

The Chelsea Bugle VOLUME IX, ISSUE 20

CB: Maniya Suarez is a student ___who___ (1.) many of you already ___know___ (2. know). Maniya, why did your family settle in London?

MS: The cousin ________ (3.) we ________ (4. stay) with at first lives here. That's the reason we chose London.

CB: What was the most difficult thing about going to school in the UK?

MS: The class in ________ (5.) I ________ (6. have) the biggest problems at first was English. It was hard to say the things ________ (7.) I ________ (8. want) to say.

CB: What is the biggest change ________ (9.) you ________ (10. experience) so far?

MS: We used to live in a house ________ (11.) there ________ (12. be) always a lot of people. Here I live with my parents and two younger sisters ________ (13.) I ________ (14. take care of) after school. I get a bit lonely sometimes.

Maniya Suarez

COMBINE • *Read each pair of sentences. Use a relative pronoun or* ***when*** *or* ***where****, to combine them into one sentence.*

1. That's the house. I grew up in the house with my sister Emily.
   That's the house that I grew up in with my sister Emiliy.
2. The house was beautiful. We lived in the house.
   ____
3. Emily and I shared a room. We spent a lot of time playing in it.
   ____
4. I had a good friend. I went to school with her.
   ____
5. I took piano lessons from a woman. I met her at my mum's office.
   ____
6. I remember one summer. The whole family went to the seaside then.
   ____
7. Those were good times. I'll always remember them.
   ____

EDIT • *Read this student's essay. Find and correct nine mistakes in the use of relative clauses with object relative pronouns. The first mistake has already been corrected.*

Tai Dong is the small city in southeastern Taiwan ~~which~~ [where OR in which] I grew up. My family moved there from Taipei the summer I was born. The house in which I grew up in is on a main street in Tai Dong. My father sold tea and my mother had a food stand in our front courtyard, where she sold omelettes early in the morning. A customer who I always chatted with him had a son my age. We were best friends. A cousin who his family I visited every summer lived with us. He was an apprentice which my father was teaching the tea business to. On the first floor of our house, we had a huge kitchen in where we all gathered for dinner. It was a noisy place. The bedrooms where the family slept was upstairs. My two brothers slept in one bedroom. I slept in one what I shared with my older sister. My younger sister shared a bedroom with another cousin which my family had adopted.

UNIT
71

Relative Clauses: Defining and Non-Defining

Oops!
This must be the picture file **he told me not to open**!

CHECK POINT

Circle T (True) or F (False).

T F There is only one picture file on the computer.

CHART CHECK

Tick the correct answer.

Which type of relative clause has commas around it?

❒ defining

❒ non-defining

Circle T (True) or F (False).

T F You can leave out a relative pronoun *only* when it is an object relative pronoun in a defining relative clause.

DEFINING RELATIVE CLAUSES

	Subject Relative Pronoun		
The computer	***which***	**is in the study**	is broken.

	(Object Relative Pronoun)		
The computer	***(which)***	**she bought last week**	is not working.

NON-DEFINING RELATIVE CLAUSES

	Subject Relative Pronoun		
The computer,	***which***	**is in the study,**	is broken.

	Object Relative Pronoun		
The computer,	***which***	**she bought last week,**	is not working.

EXPRESS CHECK

Cross out the relative pronouns where possible.

- I gave away my computer, which was only three years old.
- I bought a new one that had a lot more memory.
- It was the computer which we saw at E-Lectronics.

Grammar Explanations	Examples
1. Relative clauses can be **defining** or **non-defining**.	
a. Use a **defining relative clause** to identify which member of a group the sentence talks about.	■ I've got three phones. The phone **which is in the kitchen** is broken. *(The relative clause is necessary to identify which phone is meant.)*
b. Use a **non-defining relative clause** to give additional information about the noun it refers to. The information is not necessary to identify the noun.	■ I've got only one phone. The phone, **which is in the kitchen**, is broken. *(The relative clause gives additional information, but it isn't needed to identify the phone.)*
▶ **Be careful!** Do not use *that* to introduce a non-defining relative clause. Use ***who*** for people and ***which*** for places and things.	■ **Marie**, ***who*** introduced us at the party, rang me last night. Not ~~Marie, that introduced us at the party, . . .~~
2. A **non-defining relative clause** is separated from the rest of the sentence by **commas**.	■ The switch, **which is on the back**, is off. *(The machine has got only one switch. It's on the back.)*
Without commas, the clause is a **defining relative clause** and the sentence has a very different meaning.	■ The switch **which is on the back** is off. *(The machine has got more than one switch. This one is off.)*
Usage Note: Non-defining relative clauses are much more common in writing than they are in speech.	
3. You **can leave out**:	
a. **object relative pronouns** in defining relative clauses	■ That's the computer ***that* I bought**. ■ That's the computer **I bought**.
b. ***when***	■ I remember the day ***when* I met him**. ■ I remember the day **I met him**.
Usage Note: The most common spoken form is the one with no relative pronoun.	
4. You **cannot leave out**:	
a. **relative pronouns** in a non-defining relative clause	■ She remembers Mark, ***who* she visited often**. Not ~~She remembers Mark she visited often~~.
b. ***whose***	■ That's the author ***whose* book I read**. Not ~~That's the author book I read~~.
c. ***where***	■ That's the library ***where* I work**. Not ~~That's the library I work~~.

TRUE OR FALSE • *Read each numbered sentence. Write T (True) or F (False) for the statement that follows.*

1. Use the computer which is in the living room.

   __F__ There is only one computer.

2. Press the red button, which is on the right.

   ______ There is probably only one red button.

3. My sister who mends computers lives in Manchester.

   ______ I have more than one sister.

4. My stereo, which worked yesterday, doesn't work today.

   ______ It's likely that I have another stereo I can use.

5. A mobile phone which has voice activation is very convenient.

   ______ All mobile phones have voice activation.

6. My flatmate, who is afraid of computers, has never been on the internet.

   ______ I probably have more than one flatmate.

ADD & CROSS OUT • *Read this article about technophobia. Add commas where necessary. Cross out the relative pronouns that can be left out.*

ˌtech • no •ˈpho • bia *(noun)* a fear ~~that~~ some people have about using technology

If you have it, you're one of the 85 per cent of people that this new 'disease' has struck. Maybe you've bought a phone on which you can programme 99 numbers – but you can't turn it on. Or perhaps you have just read that your new CD player, which you have finally learnt to use, will soon be replaced by DVD which you have never even heard of.

Some experts say that things have just become too complex. William Staples who wrote a book on the electronic age tried to help a friend who had just bought a new stereo. The stereo which worked before wasn't working any more. 'On the front of the stereo, there were literally twenty buttons,' says Staples. Donald Norman who has written about the effects of technology on people blames the designers of these devices, not the people who use them. 'The best way to cure technophobia is to cure the reasons that cause it – that is, to design things that people can use and design things that won't break,' claims Norman. Michael Dyrenfurth who is a University lecturer believes we cause our own problems by buying technology that we just don't need. 'Do we really need electric toothbrushes?' he asks. According to Williams, important technology that we can't afford to run away from actually exists. To prosper, we need to overcome our technophobia and learn to use it.

COMBINE • *Read these pairs of sentences. Combine them by changing the second sentence into a relative clause. Use a relative pronoun only when necessary. Use commas for non-defining relative clauses.*

1. I bought a mobile. I can use it to send and receive email.
   I bought a mobile I can use to send and receive email.
2. My new mobile has become a necessary part of life. I bought it only a month ago.
   ____
3. I remember the day. I was afraid to use my new computer then.
   ____
4. Now, there are psychologists. They help technophobes use technology.
   ____
5. Dr Michelle Weil wrote a book about 'technostress'. She is a psychologist.
   ____
6. I work in an office. In my office, the software changes frequently.
   ____
7. A lot of people suffer from technostress. Those people work in my office.
   ____
8. Some people dream of a job. They can do the job without technology.
   ____

EDIT • *Read this student's book report. Find and correct six mistakes in the use of defining and non-defining relative clauses. The first mistake has already been corrected.*

I've just read a book called *Technostress*, which was written by Dr Michelle Weil. Her co-author was Dr Larry Rosen, that is her husband and also a psychologist. According to the authors, everybody feels stress about technology. Our mobiles and pagers, that we buy for emergencies, soon invade our privacy. Just because they can, people contact us at places, where we are relaxing. Another problem is having to learn too much, too fast. Technological changes, used to come one at a time, now overwhelm us. Dr Weil suggests dealing with technostress using tips from her latest book which can be purchased via her website.

SelfTest XIV

SECTION ONE

Circle the letter of the correct answer to complete each sentence. Choose Ø when no word is needed.

EXAMPLE:
Jennifer never ________ coffee. A (B) C D
(A) drink (C) is drinking
(B) drinks (D) was drinking

1. That's my friend ________ lives in Corby. **A B C D**
(A) which (C) whom
(B) who (D) where

2. The plants which ________ in the living room need a lot of water. **A B C D**
(A) are (C) is
(B) be (D) am

3. She's the woman ________ sister babysits for us. **A B C D**
(A) who (C) that's
(B) which (D) whose

4. That's the doctor for ________ Cliff works. **A B C D**
(A) that (C) whom
(B) which (D) whose

5. Marie, ________ I met at the party, called me last night. **A B C D**
(A) that (C) which
(B) who (D) whose

6. I remember Alan, ________ walked to school with. **A B C D**
(A) I (C) which I
(B) who I (D) who

7. I used to enjoy the summer, ________ we had a big family picnic. **A B C D**
(A) where (C) which
(B) when (D) that

8. Take in the roll of film ________ Uncle Pete took at the wedding. **A B C D**
(A) what (C) Ø
(B) with which (D) whom

9. Please pay all the bills ________ are due this week. **A B C D**
(A) Ø (C) when
(B) that (D) they

10. Let's try to agree on a time ________ we can all get together. **A B C D**
(A) which (C) Ø
(B) where (D) at

11. Tell me about the town ________ you grew up. A B C D
(A) that (C) which
(B) where (D) Ø

12. Annie found the souvenirs that ________ wanted at the gift shop. A B C D
(A) Ø (C) she
(B) where (D) which

SECTION TWO

Each sentence has four underlined words or phrases. The four underlined parts of the sentence are marked A, B, C and D. Circle the letter of the one underlined word or phrase that is NOT CORRECT.

EXAMPLE:
Mike usually (A) drives (B) to school but today (C) he walks (D). A B C (D)

13. After five hours, we (A) finally got to Glasgow (B), that (C) my aunt lives (D). A B C D

14. My favourite uncle, which (A) lives (B) in France, (C) arrived (D) last night. A B C D

15. Paul is someone (A) who (B) he (C) really loves (D) rugby. A B C D

16. One singer (A) who's (B) voice I (C) like a lot is (D) Madonna. A B C D

17. The stories (A) what (B) I've told (C) you are (D) all true. A B C D

18. I enjoyed (A) reading the article that (B) you told (C) me about it (D). A B C D

19. She's read some books (A) that (B) discusses (C) the time when (D) this area was undeveloped. A B C D

20. San Francisco (A), that (B) is (C) a beautiful city, has (D) a population of six million. A B C D

21. Do you know whom (A) wrote (B) the song that (C) Jo was (D) singing last night? A B C D

22. My aunt's new house (A) is (B) next to a beautiful beach in where (C) we go (D) swimming every day. A B C D

23. Ken, (A) who with (B) I went (C) to school, has become (D) a famous writer. A B C D

24. Do you remember the (A) night (B) which (C) we ate at the restaurant that (D) Bill owned? A B C D

25. Our neighbours, who their (A) daughter babysits (B) for us, (C) have (D) moved. A B C D

Direct and Indirect Speech: Imperatives

Sara! What are you doing?!
I've been having trouble sleeping. The doctor told me **not to eat a heavy meal before bed**, so I'm having it now.

CHECK POINT

Tick the doctor's exact words.

- ❐ 'Eat a heavy meal before bed.'
- ❐ 'Don't eat a heavy meal before bed.'
- ❐ 'Not to eat a heavy meal before bed.'

CHART CHECK

Tick the correct answer.

Which type of speech uses quotation marks?

- ❐ direct speech
- ❐ indirect speech

Circle T (True) or F (False).

T F Indirect imperatives always use the infinitive form of the verb (***to*** + base form).

DIRECT SPEECH		
Subject	**Reporting Verb**	**Direct Speech**
He	said,	'**Drink** milk.' '**Don't drink** coffee.'

INDIRECT SPEECH			
Subject	**Reporting Verb**	**Noun/ Pronoun**	**Indirect Speech**
He	told	her	**to drink** milk. **not to drink** coffee.
	said		

EXPRESS CHECK

Circle the correct words to complete these sentences.

- The doctor told me go / to go to bed at the same time every night.
- She said, 'Don't work / Not to work too hard.'

Grammar Explanations	Examples	
1. **Direct speech** is the exact words a speaker used. In writing, use quotation marks. **Indirect speech** reports what a speaker said without using the exact words. There are no quotation marks.	■ '**Come early and bring your National Health card**,' said the doctor. ■ The doctor told her **to come early and bring her National Health card**.	
2. The **reporting verb** (such as ***say*** or ***tell***) is usually in the past simple for both direct and indirect speech. ▶ **Be careful!** Put a personal direct object or someone's name after ***tell***. Do not put a personal direct object after ***say***.	Direct Speech ■ 'Drink warm milk,' he **said**. Indirect Speech ■ He **told** me to drink warm milk. ■ He **said** I should call him in the morning. Not ~~He told I should call him in the morning~~.	
3. Imperatives in direct speech use the base form of the verb. **Imperatives in indirect speech** use the **infinitive** to report:	Direct Speech	Indirect Speech
a. instructions	'**Come** early,' he said.	He said ***to come*** early.
b. commands	'**Wait**.'	He told me ***to wait***.
c. requests	'Could you please **arrive** by 8:00?'	She asked him ***to arrive*** by 8:00.
d. invitations	'Could you **join** us for lunch?'	She invited me ***to join*** them for lunch.
4. Use a **negative infinitive** (***not*** + infinitive) to report negative imperatives.	Direct Speech '**Don't go**.'	Indirect Speech He told her ***not to go***.
5. In **indirect speech**, make changes to keep the speaker's original meaning.		
a. Change **pronouns** and **possessives**.	■ He said to Ann, 'Tell **me your** problem.' ■ He told Ann to tell ***him her*** problem.	
b. Change **time phrases**.	■ 'Call me **tomorrow**.' ■ She said to call her ***the next day***.	
c. Change ***this*** and ***here***.	■ 'Sign **this** form **here**.' ■ She told him to sign ***that*** form ***there***.	

Check it out!

For punctuation rules for direct speech, see Appendix 25 on page 347.
For a list of common reporting verbs, see Appendix 13 on page 340.
For a list of common time word changes in indirect speech, see Appendix 14 on page 340.

IDENTIFY • *Read this article about sleep disorders. Circle all the reporting verbs. Underline all the direct imperatives once. Underline all the indirect imperatives twice.*

Tossing and Turning

BY CONNIE JAMES

Can't sleep? You're not alone. Millions of people are up tossing and turning instead of getting their beauty sleep. Dr Ray Thorpe, Director of the Sleep Disorders Clinic, (says), 'Don't think that loss of sleep is just a minor inconvenience.' During an interview he (told) me to think about what can happen if people drive when they're tired. Every year up to 200,000 car accidents are caused by drowsy drivers. Then he asked me to think about a recent industrial disaster. Chances are that it was caused at least in part by sleep deprivation.

Being an insomniac myself, I asked Dr Thorpe for some suggestions. He told me to stop drinking coffee. He said to have a warm glass of milk instead. 'A lot of old-fashioned remedies work. Have a high-carbohydrate snack like a banana before you go to bed,' he said. But he advises patients not to eat a heavy meal before turning in for the night. What about exercise? 'Regular exercise helps but don't exercise too close to bedtime,' he suggested. Finally, he told me not to despair. 'Don't worry about not sleeping. It's the worst thing to do,' he said. I don't know. After thinking about those industrial accidents, I doubt I'll be able to sleep at all!

CHOOSE • *Connie James visited Dr Thorpe's sleep clinic. Complete her notes with the correct words in brackets.*

Last week I visited the sleep clinic. Dr Thorpe rang and asked me ___to arrive___ (1. arrive / to arrive) at 8:30 __________ (2. tonight / that night). He __________ (3. said / told) me to bring __________ (4. my / your) nightshirt and toothbrush. I arrived on time. The nurse, Jean Blake, invited me __________ (5. watch / to watch) TV in the lounge. She __________ (6. said / told) to relax __________ (7. here / there) while they got my room ready. An hour later, Jean came back and got me ready for bed. She attached electrodes to my body and hooked me up to a machine. 'Could you please __________ (8. explain / to explain) what's going on?' I asked. The machine records brain activity. Jean told me __________ (9. don't / not to) leave the bed until __________ (10. tomorrow / the next) morning. To my surprise, I fell asleep at once. In the morning, Dr Thorpe told me that, apart from some leg movements during the night, I have healthy sleep patterns. He advised me __________ (11. get / to get) some more exercise.

REWRITE • *Read the advice that a TV reporter gave viewers about the common and very dangerous problem of feeling sleepy when driving. Rewrite his advice in indirect speech.*

1. 'Pull over and have a brief nap.' He told them to pull over and have a brief nap.
2. 'Don't have a long nap.' He said not to have a long nap.
3. 'Sing to yourselves.' ______________________________
4. 'Tune your radio to an annoying station.' ______________________________
5. 'Don't eat while driving.' ______________________________
6. 'Open your window.' ______________________________
7. 'Let cold air in.' ______________________________
8. 'Be careful when you stop your car.' ______________________________
9. 'Don't stop in a deserted place.' ______________________________
10. 'Don't drink and drive.' ______________________________

EDIT • *Read this student's diary entry. Find and correct fourteen mistakes in the use of indirect imperatives. The first mistake has already been corrected. Remember to check punctuation!*

In class today, John read one of his stories. It was wonderful. After the lesson, the teacher asked me ^to^ read a story in class next week. However, I begged her no to ask me next week because I'm having trouble getting ideas. She said me not to worry and she said to wait for two weeks. Then I talked to John and I asked him tell me the source of your ideas. He said that they came from his dreams and he told me keep a dream diary for ideas. He invited me 'to read some of his diary'. It was very interesting so I asked him to give me some tips on remembering dreams. He said getting a good night's sleep because the longer dreams come after a long period of sleep. He also tell me to keep my diary by the bed and to write as soon as I wake up. He said to no move from the sleeping position. He also told me to don't think about the day at first. (If you think about your day, you might forget your dreams.) Most important — every night he tells himself that to remember his dreams tomorrow morning.

UNIT
73

Indirect Speech: Statements (1)

It **looks** great on you!

He said it **looked** great on me. I'll take them all!

CHECK POINT

Tick the man's exact words.

❒ 'It looks great on you!' ❒ 'It looked great on me!'

CHART CHECK

Tick the correct answers.

What can change when you go from a direct to an indirect statement?

❒ the punctuation

❒ the word order in the statement

❒ the verb tense in the statement

❒ pronouns in the statement

DIRECT SPEECH		
SUBJECT	**REPORTING VERB**	**DIRECT STATEMENT**
She	said,	'I **like** the dress.' 'I **bought** it in the sale.' 'I'**ve worn** it twice.'

INDIRECT SPEECH				
SUBJECT	**REPORTING VERB**	**NOUN/ PRONOUN**	**INDIRECT STATEMENT**	
She	told	Jim me	*(that)*	she **liked** the dress. she **had bought** it in the sale. she **had worn** it twice.
	said			

EXPRESS CHECK

Circle the correct words to complete this sentence.

She <u>said / told</u> the salesperson that she <u>is / was</u> going to buy the dress.

Grammar Explanations	Examples
1. An **indirect speech statement** reports what a speaker said without using the exact words. The word ***that*** can introduce the indirect statement but you can also leave it out.	DIRECT SPEECH ■ **'It's a great dress,'** he said. INDIRECT SPEECH ■ He told her ***that*** **it was a great dress.** ■ He told her **it was a great dress.**
▶ **BE CAREFUL!** Use ***say*** as the reporting verb when the listener is not mentioned. Do not use ***tell***.	■ He **said** that it was a great dress. NOT ~~He told that it was a great dress~~.
2. When the **reporting verb** is in the **past simple**, the verb in the indirect speech statement is usually in a different tense from the verb in the direct speech statement.	

DIRECT SPEECH		INDIRECT SPEECH	DIRECT SPEECH	INDIRECT SPEECH
Present simple	→	**Past simple**	He said, 'It**'s** lovely.'	He said it ***was*** lovely.
Present continuous	→	**Past continuous**	'I**'m leaving**.'	She said she ***was leaving***.
Past simple	→	**Past perfect**	'I **did** it.'	He said that he ***had done*** it.
Present perfect	→	**Past perfect**	He said to her, 'I**'ve** never **lied**.'	He told her that he ***had*** never ***lied***.

Grammar Explanations	Examples
3. In indirect speech the **change of verb tense** is **optional** when reporting:	
a. something someone has **just said**	**A:** What did you just say? **B:** I said I**'m** tired. OR I said I **was** tired.
b. something that is **still true**	■ Rick said the bank ***wants*** a cheque. ■ Rick said the bank ***wanted*** a cheque.
c. a **general truth** or **scientific law**	■ She said that everyone ***lies*** sometime. ■ She said that everyone ***lied*** sometime.
4. When the **reporting verb** is in the **present simple**, do not change the verb tense in indirect speech.	■ 'I **run** a mile every day.' ■ She **says** that she ***runs*** a mile every day.
5. **REMEMBER!** Change pronouns, time expressions, ***this*** and ***here*** in indirect speech to keep the speaker's original meaning.	■ Ann told Rick, '**I** bought **this** dress **here**.' ■ Ann told Rick that ***she*** had bought ***that*** dress ***there***.

Check it out!

For a list of common reporting verbs, see Appendix 13 on page 340.
For a list of common time word changes in indirect speech, see Appendix 14 on page 340.

IDENTIFY • *Read this article about lying. Circle all the reporting verbs. Underline all the direct statements once. Underline all the indirect statements twice.*

THE TRUTH ABOUT LYING

BY JENNIFER MORGAN

At 9:00, Rick Thompson's bank phoned and said that his credit card payment was late. 'The cheque is in the post,' Rick replied quickly. At 11:45, Rick left for a 12:00 meeting. Arriving late, Rick told his client that traffic had been bad. That evening, Rick's fiancée wore a new dress. Rick hated it. 'It looks great on you,' he said.

Three lies in one day! Yet Rick is just an ordinary guy. Each time, he told himself that sometimes the truth causes too many problems. He told himself that his fiancée was happy with her purchase. Why should he hurt her feelings?

Is telling lies a new trend? The majority of people in a recent survey said that people were more honest ten years ago. Nevertheless, lying wasn't really born yesterday. In the eighteenth century, the French philosopher Vauvenargues was right about lying when he wrote, 'All men are born truthful and die liars.'

COMPLETE • *Read this magazine article. Complete it with the correct words in brackets.*

'Lying during a job interview is risky business,' ___said___ (1. said / told) Nikki Mason, director of a management consulting firm. 'The truth always ________ (2. has / had) a funny way of coming out.' Nikki tells the story of one woman applying for a job as an office manager. The woman ________ (3. said / told) the interviewer ________ (4. that / what) she ________ (5. has / had) a B.A. degree. Actually, she hadn't. She also said ________ (6. I / she) ________ (7. earnt / had earnt) £30,000 in her last job. The truth was £5,000 less. When the interviewer rang to check the information, the applicant's former boss told her that the applicant ________ (8. has lied / had lied). Another applicant, Gwen, reported that she ________ (9. is leaving / was leaving) her current job to advance her career. She got the new job. All went well until the company employed Pete, who had worked at Gwen's old company. Pete eventually told his boss that his old company ________ (10. fired / had fired) Gwen. The new company fired her too, proving, once again, that it doesn't pay to lie.

REPORT • *Lisa and Ben are talking about Ben's job hunt. Use the verbs in brackets to report their conversation. Make necessary changes in verbs and pronouns.*

1. **BEN:** I'm still looking for a job.
   (tell) He told her he was still looking for a job.
2. **LISA:** I've just heard about a job at a scientific research company.
   (say) ______________________________
3. **BEN:** I got a B.Sc. in Biochemistry from London.
   (say) ______________________________
4. **LISA:** They want someone with some experience as a programmer.
   (tell) ______________________________
5. **BEN:** I work as a programmer for Data Systems in Basingstoke.
   (tell) ______________________________
6. **LISA:** They don't want a recent graduate.
   (say) ______________________________
7. **BEN:** I got my degree four years ago.
   (tell) ______________________________
8. **LISA:** It sounds like the right job for you.
   (say) ______________________________

EDIT • *Read this student's essay. Find and correct ten mistakes in the use of indirect statements. The first mistake has already been corrected.*

Once, when I was a teenager, I went to my aunt's house. She collected pottery and when I got there, she ~~said~~ told me that she wants to show me a new bowl. She told she has just bought it. It was beautiful. When she went to answer the door, I picked up the bowl. It slipped out of my hands and smashed to pieces on the floor. When my aunt came back, I screamed and said what the cat had just broken your new bowl. My aunt looked at me in a funny way and told me that it isn't important. I couldn't sleep that night, and the next morning, I rang my aunt and confessed that I have broken her bowl. She said I had known that all along. I promised that I am going to buy her a new one. We still laugh about it now.

Unit 74 Indirect Speech: Statements (2)

They said **it would be windy** but this is ridiculous!

CHECK POINT

Tick the weather forecaster's exact words.

❒ 'It would be windy.'

❒ 'It will be windy.'

CHART CHECK

Tick the words that *__do not change__* *when you go from direct to indirect speech.*

❒ will

❒ ought to

❒ might

❒ must

❒ may

❒ should have

DIRECT SPEECH		
Subject	**Reporting Verb**	**Direct Statement**
He	said,	'I'**ll leave** now.' 'I'**m going to drive**.' 'The traffic **may be** bad.' 'She **might move**.' 'He **can help**.' 'They **have to stay**.' 'You **must be** careful.' 'They **ought to buy** batteries.' 'We **should have left** earlier.'

INDIRECT SPEECH				
Subject	**Reporting Verb**	**Noun/ Pronoun**	**Indirect Statement**	
He	told	Jim me them	*(that)*	he **would leave** then. he **was going to drive**. the traffic **might be** bad. she **might move**. he **could help**. they **had to stay**. I/we **had to be** careful. they **ought to buy** batteries. they **should have left** earlier.
	said			

EXPRESS CHECK

Read Jim's words. Tick the sentence that correctly reports what he said.

Jim: 'I may move soon.'

❐ Jim said that I may move soon. ❐ Jim said that he might move soon.

Grammar Explanations	Examples	
1. As you learned in Unit 73, when the **reporting verb** is in the **past simple**, the verb tense usually changes in the indirect speech statement.	Direct Speech She said, 'It's windy.'	Indirect Speech She said it ***was*** windy.
Modals often change in indirect speech, too. Direct Speech → Indirect Speech *will* → ***would***	Direct Speech I said, 'The wind **will be** strong.'	Indirect Speech I said the wind ***would be*** strong.
can → ***could***	They told us, 'You **can stay** with us.'	They told us we ***could stay*** with them.
may → ***might***	He said, 'The storm **may last** all night.'	He said that the storm ***might last*** all night.
must → ***had to***	She told us, 'You **must leave**.'	She told us we ***had to leave***.

Grammar Explanations	Examples	
2. Some verbs do not change in indirect speech. **a.** Do not change ***should***, ***could***, ***might*** and ***ought to*** in indirect speech.	Direct Speech 'You **should listen** to the weather report,' he told us.	Indirect Speech He told us that we ***should listen*** to the weather report.
b. Do not change the **past perfect** in indirect speech.	'I **had** just **moved** here a week before,' she said.	She said she ***had*** just ***moved*** there a week before.
c. Do not change verbs in the **second and third conditional** sentences in indirect speech.	'If I **knew**, I **would tell** you.' 'If I **had known**, I **would have told** you,' said Jim.	Jim said if he ***knew***, he ***would tell*** me. He said if he ***had known***, he ***would have told*** me.
d. Do not change **past modals** in indirect speech.	'I **should have left**.'	He said that he ***should have left***.

Grammar Explanations	Examples
3. Remember! Change pronouns, time phrases, ***here*** and ***this*** in indirect speech to keep the speaker's original meaning.	■ 'I got **here yesterday**.' ■ Sam told me ***he*** had got ***there the day before***.

CHOOSE • *Read what someone reported about the weather forecast. Then tick the sentence that shows the weather forecaster's exact words.*

1. She said it was going to be a terrible storm.
   - ☐ 'It was a terrible storm.'
   - ☑ 'It's going to be a terrible storm.'
2. She said the wind might reach 170 miles an hour.
   - ☐ 'The wind may reach 170 miles an hour.'
   - ☐ 'The wind would reach 170 miles an hour.'
3. She said there would be more rain the next day.
   - ☐ 'There will be more rain the next day.'
   - ☐ 'There will be more rain tomorrow.'
4. She told people that they should try to leave the area.
   - ☐ 'You should have tried to leave the area.'
   - ☐ 'You should try to leave the area.'
5. She said that they could expect a lot of damage.
   - ☐ 'We can expect a lot of damage.'
   - ☐ 'We could expect a lot of damage.'

2

REPORT • *You are on holiday in New York. Imagine you heard these rumours about a hurricane in Florida yesterday and you are reporting them today. Use* **They said** *to report the rumours.*

1. 'The hurricane will change direction tonight.'

   They said that the hurricane would change direction last night.
2. 'It's going to pass north of here.'

   ____
3. 'It may become a tropical storm when it lands here.'

   ____
4. 'They had to close some bridges yesterday because of high tides.'

   ____
5. 'They won't restore the electricity until tomorrow.'

   ____
6. 'The schools here may be closed for a while.'

   ____
7. 'We ought to use bottled water for a few days.'

   ____

REWRITE • *Read this interview with a meteorologist. Rewrite his answers as indirect speech. Change verb tenses when possible.*

1. **Q: A hurricane is just a bad storm, isn't it?**
   A: To be a hurricane, a storm must have winds of at least 74 miles an hour.
   He said that to be a hurricane, a storm must have winds of at least 74 miles an hour.

2. **Q: We seem to be having more of these big storms.**
   A: It's true, and they will probably become more frequent.
   ____

3. **Q: Why is that?**
   A: The planet may be getting warmer, and that can cause more severe storms.
   ____

4. **Q: What went wrong after the last storm?**
   A: The emergency services should have arrived much more quickly.
   ____

5. **Q: Is there a positive side to all this?**
   A: The new satellites will help. If we didn't have them, we wouldn't be able to warn people.
   ____

EDIT • *Read Rita's email to her friend Emily. Find and correct thirteen mistakes in the use of reported speech. The first mistake has already been corrected.*

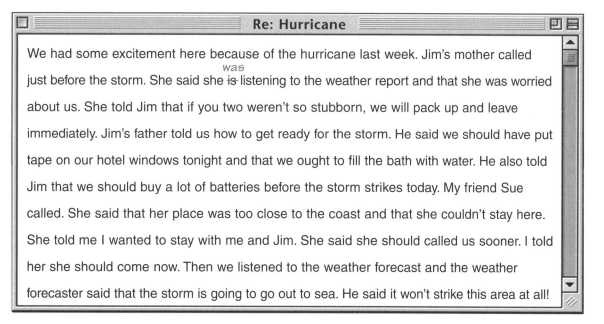

Re: Hurricane

We had some excitement here because of the hurricane last week. Jim's mother called just before the storm. She said she ~~is~~ was listening to the weather report and that she was worried about us. She told Jim that if you two weren't so stubborn, we will pack up and leave immediately. Jim's father told us how to get ready for the storm. He said we should have put tape on our hotel windows tonight and that we ought to fill the bath with water. He also told Jim that we should buy a lot of batteries before the storm strikes today. My friend Sue called. She said that her place was too close to the coast and that she couldn't stay here. She told me I wanted to stay with me and Jim. She said she should called us sooner. I told her she should come now. Then we listened to the weather forecast and the weather forecaster said that the storm is going to go out to sea. He said it won't strike this area at all!

Indirect Questions

?
Perhaps you didn't hear the question. Ms Bentley asked **why you were still single**.

The Stress Interview

CHECK POINT

Tick Ms Bentley's exact words.

❑ 'Why were you still single?'

❑ 'Why are you still single?'

CHART CHECK 1

Circle T (True) or F (False).

T F You can leave out ***if*** or ***whether*** in indirect *yes/no* questions.

T F You do not use ***do*** to form indirect *yes/no* questions.

DIRECT SPEECH: *YES/NO* QUESTIONS		
SUBJECT	**REPORTING VERB**	**DIRECT QUESTION**
He	asked,	'**Do you speak** French?' '**Can you use** a computer?'

INDIRECT SPEECH: *YES/NO* QUESTIONS				
SUBJECT	**REPORTING VERB**	**(NOUN/ PRONOUN)**	**INDIRECT QUESTION**	
He	asked	(Melissa) (her)	***if*** ***whether***	**she spoke** French. **she could use** a computer.

CHART CHECK 2

Circle T (True) or F (False).

T F An indirect question always ends in a question mark.

T F You do not use ***do*** to form indirect *wh-* questions.

DIRECT SPEECH: *WH-* QUESTIONS		
SUBJECT	**REPORTING VERB**	**DIRECT QUESTION**
He	asked,	'**Who told you** about the job?' '**When do you want** to start?'

INDIRECT SPEECH: *WH-* QUESTIONS			
SUBJECT	**REPORTING VERB**	**(NOUN/ PRONOUN)**	**INDIRECT QUESTION**
He	asked	(Melissa) (her)	***who* had told her** about the job. ***when* she wanted** to start.

EXPRESS CHECK

Unscramble these words to complete the indirect question.

why • he • job • his • left • had

He asked him ______________________________

Grammar Explanations	Examples
1. Use ***if***, ***whether*** or ***whether or not*** to form **indirect *yes/no* questions.**	DIRECT SPEECH ■ **'Can you type?'** she asked. INDIRECT SPEECH ■ She asked ***if*** **I could type.**
USAGE NOTE: ***Whether*** is more formal than ***if***.	■ She asked ***whether (or not)*** **I could type.**
2. In **indirect *yes/no* questions**, the subject comes before the verb, the same word order as in statements.	DIRECT SPEECH ■ **'Can I start** tomorrow?' INDIRECT SPEECH ■ He asked ***if*** **he could start** tomorrow. NOT ~~He asked could he start tomorrow.~~
Do not use ***do***, ***does*** or ***did*** to form indirect questions.	DIRECT SPEECH ■ **'Does the job provide** benefits?' INDIRECT SPEECH ■ He asked ***if*** **the job provided** benefits. NOT ~~He asked does the job provide benefits.~~
3. Use **question words** to form **indirect *wh-* questions.**	DIRECT SPEECH ■ **'Where is your office?'** I asked. INDIRECT SPEECH ■ I asked ***where*** **his office was.**
4. In **indirect *wh-* questions**, the subject also comes before the verb as in statements, and you do not use ***do***, ***does*** or ***did***.	DIRECT SPEECH **'Why did you leave** your job?' INDIRECT SPEECH ■ She asked me ***why*** **I had left** my job. NOT ~~She asked me why did I leave my job.~~
In **indirect *wh-* questions about the subject**, the question word is the subject and the verb follows as in statement word order.	DIRECT SPEECH ■ Bob asked, **'Who got** the job?' INDIRECT SPEECH ■ Bob asked ***who*** **had got** the job.
5. Indirect questions often end in a **full point**, not a question mark.	■ I asked ***why*** **I didn't get the job.** NOT ~~I asked why didn't I get the job?~~

Check it out! For a list of common verbs used to report questions, see Appendix 13 on page 340.

IDENTIFY • *Read this article about stress interviews. Underline all the indirect questions.*

The Stress Interview

A few weeks ago, Melissa Morrow had a stress interview, one which featured tough, tricky questions and negative evaluations. First, the interviewer asked why she couldn't work under pressure. Before she could answer, he asked who had written her application for her. Melissa was shocked but she handled herself very well. She asked the interviewer whether he was going to ask her any serious questions. Then she left.

Companies sometimes conduct stress interviews to see how candidates handle pressure. Suppose, for example, that there is an accident in a nuclear power plant. The plant's public relations officer must remain calm when reporters ask how the accident could have happened. Be aware, however, that in some countries, like the United States, certain questions are not allowed unless they are directly related to the job. If your interviewer asks how old you are, you can refuse to answer. The interviewer also should not ask whether you are married or how much money you owe. If you think a question is inappropriate, ask how it relates to the job. If it doesn't relate to it, you don't have to answer.

MATCH • *Tick the direct questions that match the indirect questions in the article.*

- ☐ 1. Can you work under pressure?
- ☑ 2. Who wrote your application for you?
- ☐ 3. Are you going to ask me any serious questions?
- ☐ 4. Was there an accident in a nuclear power plant?
- ☐ 5. How old are you?
- ☐ 6. When did you get married?
- ☐ 7. Is it an inappropriate question?

2

REPORT • *Claire's friend James wants to know all about her interview. Report his questions.*

1. 'What kind of job is it?' He asked what kind of job it was.
2. 'When is the interview?' ______
3. 'Where's the company?' ______
4. 'Do you need directions?' ______
5. 'How long does it take to get there?' ______
6. 'Are you going to drive?' ______
7. 'Who's going to interview you?' ______
8. 'When will they let you know?' ______

REWRITE • *These questions were asked at Claire's interview. Decide which ones Claire asked and which ones Pete, the manager, asked. Rewrite each question as indirect speech.*

1. 'What training is available for the job?'
   Claire asked what training was available for the job.
2. 'What experience do you have?'
   Pete asked what experience she had.
3. 'Are you going for interviews with other companies?'
   ____
4. 'What will my responsibilities be?'
   ____
5. 'How is job performance rewarded?'
   ____
6. 'What was your starting salary at your last job?'
   ____
7. 'Did you get on well with your last employer?'
   ____
8. 'Do you employ many women?'
   ____

EDIT • *Read part of a memo an interviewer wrote. Find and correct eight mistakes in the use of indirect questions. The first mistake has already been corrected. Check the punctuation!*

Memo

I did some stress questioning in my interview with Miles Denton this morning. I asked Mr Denton why ~~couldn't he~~ he couldn't work under pressure. I also asked him why did his supervisor dislike him. Finally, I enquired when he would leave our company? Mr Denton answered my questions calmly and he had some excellent questions of his own. He asked 'if we expected changes to the job.' He also wanted to know how often do we evaluate employees. I was impressed when he asked why did I decide to join this company. I think we should employ him.

UNIT 76 Embedded Questions

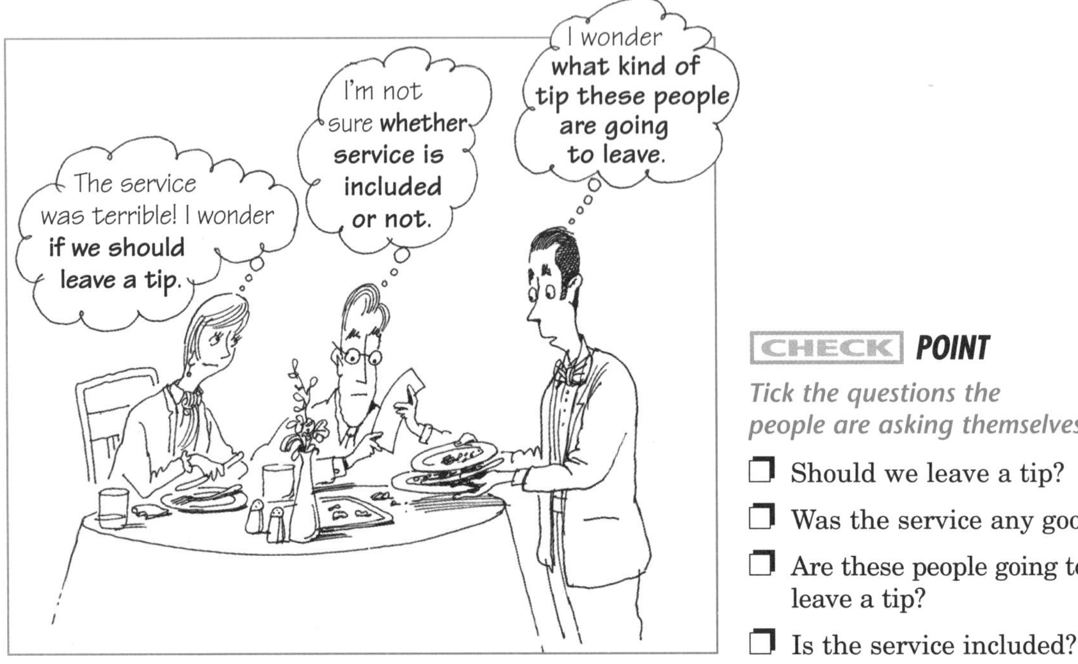

CHECK POINT

Tick the questions the people are asking themselves.

❐ Should we leave a tip?

❐ Was the service any good?

❐ Are these people going to leave a tip?

❐ Is the service included?

CHART CHECK

Circle T (True) or F (False).

T F Embedded questions always end with a full stop.

T F You can use the infinitive after ***whether*** or a question word.

MAIN CLAUSE	EMBEDDED QUESTION
I'm not sure	***if* I left** the right tip. ***whether* it was** enough.
Can you remember	***how much* it was?** ***where* we ate?**
I don't know	***whether* to tip.**
Do you know	***how much* to tip?** ***where* to leave** the tip?

EXPRESS CHECK

Punctuate these sentences.

A: Do you know how much to tip____

B: About 15%. But I'm not sure where to leave the tip____

Grammar Explanations	Examples
1. Unit 75 deals with **indirect questions** to report another person's words. Indirect questions are a kind of **embedded question** – one that is included in another sentence. This unit discusses embedded questions that do not report another person's words.	DIRECT QUESTION Should I tip? INDIRECT QUESTION He asked **if he should tip.** EMBEDDED QUESTION Do you know **whether I should tip?**
2. If the embedded question is **in a statement**, use a full stop at the end of the sentence. If the embedded question is **in a question**, use a question mark at the end of the sentence.	MAIN SENTENCE = STATEMENT ■ ***I don't know*** who our waiter is. MAIN SENTENCE = QUESTION ■ ***Do you know*** who our waiter is?
3. We often **use embedded questions** to **a.** express something we do not know. **b.** ask politely for information. **USAGE NOTE:** With strangers or in a formal situation, an embedded question is considered more polite than a direct question.	■ I wonder **why he didn't tip the waiter.** ■ Can you tell me **if the tip is included?** LESS FORMAL ■ Does the bill include the tip? MORE POLITE ■ Can you tell me **if the bill includes the tip?**
4. Introduce **embedded *yes/no* questions** with ***if***, ***whether*** or ***whether or not***. **USAGE NOTE:** ***Whether*** is more formal than ***if***. Introduce **embedded *wh-* questions** with a question word. You can also use the **infinitive** after a question word or ***whether***. ► **BE CAREFUL!** Do not use the infinitive after ***if*** or ***why***.	■ Do you know ***if* he tips?** ■ Do you know ***whether (or not)* he tips?** ■ Many tourists wonder ***how much* they should tip their waiter.** ■ Many tourists wonder ***how much* to tip.** ■ Some wonder ***whether* to tip** at all. ■ We wondered ***why* we should leave a tip.** NOT ~~We wondered why to leave a tip.~~
5. **BE CAREFUL!** Use **statement word order** in all embedded questions. Do not leave out ***if*** or ***whether*** in embedded *yes/no* questions. Do not use ***do***, ***does*** or ***did*** in embedded questions.	■ Could you tell me ***where* they are?** NOT ~~Could you tell me where are they~~? ■ Could you tell me ***if* it is** 6:00 yet? NOT ~~Could you tell me is it 6:00 yet~~? ■ I don't know ***when* the pizza came.** NOT ~~I don't know when did the pizza come.~~

Check it out!

For a list of common phrases introducing embedded questions, see Appendix 15 on page 340.

IDENTIFY • *Read this online advert for a book about tipping. Underline the embedded questions.*

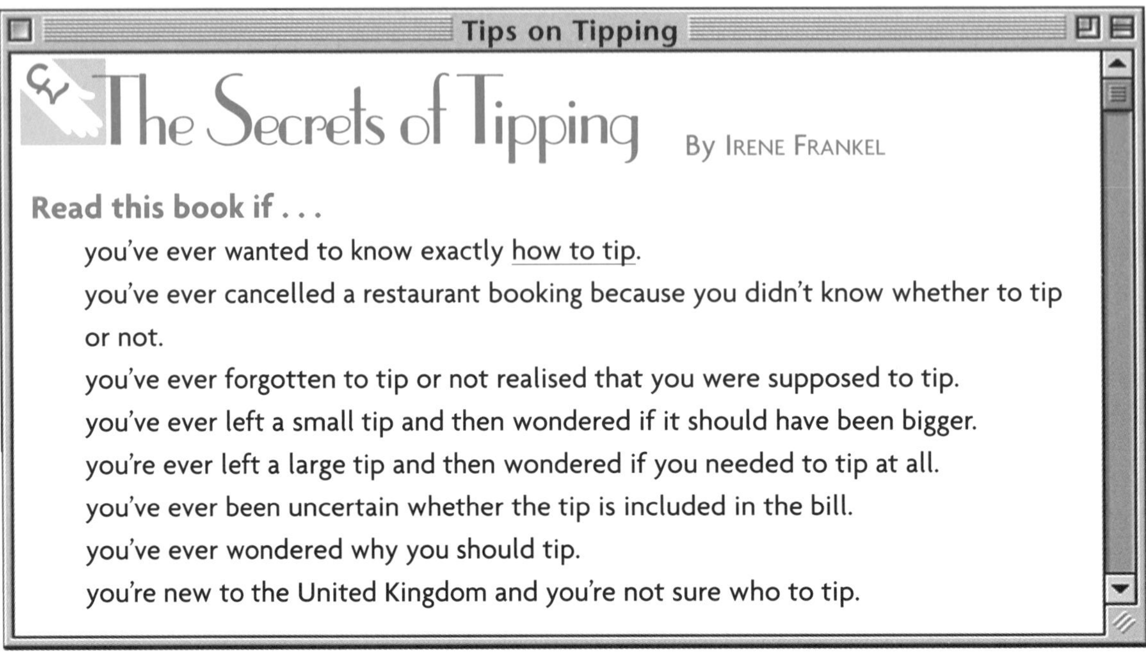

Tips on Tipping

The Secrets of Tipping

By IRENE FRANKEL

Read this book if . . .

you've ever wanted to know exactly how to tip.
you've ever cancelled a restaurant booking because you didn't know whether to tip or not.
you've ever forgotten to tip or not realised that you were supposed to tip.
you've ever left a small tip and then wondered if it should have been bigger.
you're ever left a large tip and then wondered if you needed to tip at all.
you've ever been uncertain whether the tip is included in the bill.
you've ever wondered why you should tip.
you're new to the United Kingdom and you're not sure who to tip.

REWRITE • *Complete these questions about tipping customs. Change the direct questions in brackets to embedded questions. Use the infinitive whenever possible. Use correct punctuation.*

1. Can you tell me whether *to tip in Canada?* ____________
   (Should I tip in Canada?)
2. I'm going to France. Please explain ____________
   (How can I tell if the tip is included in the bill?)
3. Can you tell me ____________
   (Why did waiters in Iceland refuse my tips?)
4. I'm moving to Japan. I'd like to know ____________
   (How much should I tip airport porters?)
5. We're visiting Australia. Please tell us ____________
   (Who expects a tip and who doesn't?)
6. I'm going on holiday to Norway. I'd like to know if ____________
   (Should I tip my ski instructor?)
7. I've got a new job in China. I need to know whether ____________
   (Is tipping still illegal there?)
8. In Germany the tip is included. I don't know whether ____________
   (Should I tip anyway?)

CHOOSE & REWRITE • *Two students from Newcastle are visiting Washington D.C. Complete their conversations. Choose the appropriate questions from the box and change them to embedded questions. Remember to punctuate the sentences correctly.*

How much should we tip the taxi driver?	**Where is the Smithsonian Museum?**
Could we rent a car and drive?	**What did they put in the sauce?**
Where can we buy metro tickets?	**~~Where is it?~~**

1. **Mary:** We're going to the Hotel Edison. Do you know where it is?
   Driver: Sure. Get in and I'll take you there.
2. **Mike:** *(whispering)* Do you know ________________
   Mary: According to the book, we're supposed to leave 10 to 15 per cent. I've got it.
3. **Mary:** Excuse me. Can you tell me ________________
   Officer: Just turn right at the corner. You'll see it.
4. **Mike:** I'd like to take the metro to the zoo, but I don't know ________________
   Mary: Probably at the station.
5. **Mary:** I want to visit Williamsburg. Do you think ________________
   Mike: Let's find out. That sounds fun.
6. **Mary:** This is delicious. Let's try to find out ________________
   Mike: It tastes like ginger and garlic to me.

EDIT • *Read this entry from a student's diary. Find and correct seven mistakes in the use of embedded questions. The first mistake has already been corrected. Remember to check the punctuation!*

When you live in a foreign country, even a small occasion can be an adventure! Before my date with James tonight, I didn't even know what ~~should I~~ I should wear! Jeans? A dress? John's Grill isn't a smart restaurant but it was James's birthday and I wanted to make it a big occasion. Alison was very helpful, as always. I knew how to get to John's Grill but I didn't know how long it was going to take to get there? I left at 6:00, which should have given me plenty of time, but when I got off the bus, I wasn't sure if to turn left or right. I asked a police officer where was John's and I was only a few minutes late. I had planned to take James out for a drink afterwards but I couldn't remember how I to find the place Alison had suggested and James has been here even less time than me. Anyway, when we got the bill, I was wondering whether to tip or no. I had to ask James did he know. Fortunately, he had read a great book called *Tips on Tipping* so he told me to leave about 15 per cent.

SECTION ONE

Circle the letter of the correct answer to complete each sentence.

EXAMPLE:

Jennifer never ________ coffee. **A (B) C D**

(A) drink (C) is drinking
(B) drinks (D) was drinking

1. 'You look beautiful in that dress.' **A B C D**
Last night she told me ________ beautiful in that dress.
(A) you look (C) I'll look
(B) you looked (D) I looked

2. We'd better find out ________ the train has left. **A B C D**
(A) if (C) has
(B) does (D) did

3. —Should we turn left or go straight on? **A B C D**
—Hmm. I'm not sure which way ________.
(A) do we turn (C) should we turn
(B) to turn (D) it turned

4. 'Why don't you join us for coffee, Don?' **A B C D**
After the film, we asked Don ________ us for coffee.
(A) would he join (C) to join
(B) why he didn't join (D) for joining

5. 'We must leave immediately!' **A B C D**
When the fire alarm rang, our teacher said ________ leave immediately.
(A) we had to (C) not to
(B) we have to (D) he must

6. 'Today is the happiest day of my life.' **A B C D**
At the reception last night, the groom said ________ the happiest day of his life.
(A) today was (C) yesterday was
(B) that day is (D) today is

7. I wonder who ________ **A B C D**
(A) our waiter is? (C) our waiter is.
(B) is our waiter. (D) is our waiter?

8. 'Please don't leave your boots in the hall.' **A B C D**
My mother is always telling me ________ boots in the hall.
(A) not to leave my (C) to not leave my
(B) not to leave your (D) don't leave my

9. 'Hi, Bob. Did you get the job?'
Bob's friend asked him ________ the job.
(A) did he get
(B) did you get
(C) if he had got
(D) had he got

A B C D

10. 'Weather patterns change.'
Experts now say that weather patterns ________.
(A) changed
(B) are changing
(C) had changed
(D) change

A B C D

SECTION TWO

Each sentence has four underlined words or phrases. The four underlined parts of the sentence are marked A, B, C and D. Circle the letter of the one underlined word or phrase that is NOT CORRECT.

EXAMPLE:
Mike usually (A) drives (B) to school but today (C) he walks (D). A B C (D)

11. The teacher said (A) the class that (B) hot air rises (C) and cold air sinks (D). A B C D

12. I asked (A) Sean how (B) to pronounce (C) his name? (D) A B C D

13. Gerry called (A) last week and said (B) that (C) he needed the report now (D). A B C D

14. Two days ago, the weather forecaster warned (A) us (B) that (C) a storm is coming (D). A B C D

15. Sandy called (A) from Miami and said (B) she (C) was swimming here (D). A B C D

16. Do you know (A) if or not (B) we (C) need (D) to bring our passports? A B C D

17. She didn't know if (A) to tip so she asked (B) me what (C) to do (D). A B C D

18. Ron said (A) that (B) he wasn't (C) sure but the rain might stop (D) already. A B C D

19. I'd like (A) lobster but the menu doesn't say (B) how much (C) does it cost (D). A B C D

20. Luke always (A) says that (B) he ran (C) a mile every day (D) these days. A B C D

21. Could you tell me when (A) the next train leaves (B) and where to buy (C) tickets. (D) A B C D

22. 'If (A) you can wait a few minutes, (B) I will give (C) you a lift. (D) Rhoda said. A B C D

23. Jim wants (A) to know could you (B) call him and tell (C) him where to meet (D) you. A B C D

24. The dentist said (A) to brush (B) three times a day and don't (C) eat (D) sweets. A B C D

25. At the interview they asked (A) me when can you (B) start (C) work. (D) A B C D

Appendices

 Irregular Verbs

Base Form	Past Simple	Past Participle
arise	arose	arisen
awake	awoke	awoken
be	was/were	been
beat	beat	beaten
become	became	become
begin	began	begun
bend	bent	bent
bet	bet	bet
bite	bit	bitten
bleed	bled	bled
blow	blew	blown
break	broke	broken
bring	brought	brought
build	built	built
burn	burnt	burnt
burst	burst	burst
buy	bought	bought
catch	caught	caught
choose	chose	chosen
cling	clung	clung
come	came	come
cost	cost	cost
creep	crept	crept
cut	cut	cut
deal	dealt	dealt
dig	dug	dug
do	did	done
draw	drew	drawn
dream	dreamt	dreamt
drink	drank	drunk
drive	drove	driven
earn	earnt	earnt
eat	ate	eaten
fall	fell	fallen
feed	fed	fed
feel	felt	felt
fight	fought	fought
find	found	found
fit	fit	fit
flee	fled	fled
fling	flung	flung
fly	flew	flown
forbid	forbade	forbidden
forget	forgot	forgotten
forgive	forgave	forgiven
freeze	froze	frozen
get	got	got
give	gave	given
go	went	gone

Base Form	Past Simple	Past Participle
grind	ground	ground
grow	grew	grown
hang	hung/hanged	hung/hanged
have	had	had
hear	heard	heard
hide	hid	hidden
hit	hit	hit
hold	held	held
hurt	hurt	hurt
keep	kept	kept
kneel	knelt	knelt
know	knew	known
lay	laid	laid
lead	led	led
leap	leapt	leapt
learn	learnt	learnt
leave	left	left
lend	lent	lent
let	let	let
lie (lie down)	lay	lain
light	lit	lit
lose	lost	lost
make	made	made
mean	meant	meant
meet	met	met
pay	paid	paid
prove	proved	proved/proven
put	put	put
quit	quit	quit
read /ri:d/	read /red/	read /red/
ride	rode	ridden
ring	rang	rung
rise	rose	risen
run	ran	run
say	said	said
see	saw	seen
seek	sought	sought
sell	sold	sold
send	sent	sent
set	set	set
sew	sewed	sewn
shake	shook	shaken
shine	shone	shone
shoot	shot	shot
show	showed	shown
shrink	shrank	shrunk
shut	shut	shut
sing	sang	sung

Base Form	Past Simple	Past Participle
sink	sank	sunk
sit	sat	sat
sleep	slept	slept
slide	slid	slid
smell	smelt	smelt
speak	spoke	spoken
speed	sped	sped
spell	spelt	spelt
spend	spent	spent
spill	spilt	spilt
spin	span/spun	spun
spit	spat	spat
split	split	split
spread	spread	spread
spring	sprang	sprung
stand	stood	stood
steal	stole	stolen
stick	stuck	stuck
sting	stung	stung
stink	stank	stunk
strike	struck	struck
swear	swore	sworn
sweep	swept	swept
swim	swam	swum
swing	swung	swung
take	took	taken
teach	taught	taught
tear	tore	torn
tell	told	told
think	thought	thought
throw	threw	thrown
understand	understood	understood
upset	upset	upset
wake	woke	woken
wear	wore	worn
weave	wove	woven
weep	wept	wept
win	won	won
wind	wound	wound
withdraw	withdrew	withdrawn
wring	wrung	wrung
write	wrote	written

2 Common Stative Verbs

Emotions
admire
adore
appreciate
care
detest
dislike
doubt
envy
fear
hate
like
love
regret
respect
trust

Mental States
agree
assume
believe
consider
disagree
disbelieve
estimate
expect
feel *(believe)*
find
guess
hesitate
imagine
know
mean
mind
presume
realise
recognise
remember
see *(understand)*
suppose
suspect
think *(believe)*
understand
wonder

Wants and Preferences
hope
need
prefer
want
wish

Perception and the Senses
feel
hear
notice
observe
perceive
see
smell
taste

Appearance and Value
appear
be
cost
equal
feel
look
matter
represent
resemble
seem
signify
smell
sound
taste
weigh

Possession and Relationship
belong
contain
have
own
possess

3 Common Verbs Followed by the Gerund (Base Form of Verb + *-ing*)

admit
advise
appreciate
avoid
can't help
celebrate
consider
delay
deny
detest
discontinue
discuss
dislike
endure
enjoy
feel like
finish
forgive
imagine
justify
keep *(continue)*
mention
mind *(object to)*
miss
postpone
practise
propose
recall
recommend
regret
report
resent
resist
risk
suggest
tolerate
understand

4 Common Verbs Followed by the Infinitive (*To* + Base Form of Verb)

afford
agree
appear
arrange
ask
attempt
choose
consent
decide
deserve
expect
fail
grow
help
hesitate
hope
hurry
intend
learn
manage
mean
need
neglect
offer
pay
plan
prepare
pretend
promise
refuse
request
seem
struggle
swear
volunteer
wait
want
wish
would like/love/hate
yearn

5 Verbs Followed by Objects and the Infinitive

advise
allow
ask*
cause
challenge
choose*
convince
enable
encourage
expect*
forbid
force
get
help*
hire
invite
need*
order
pay*
permit
persuade
promise*
remind
request*
require
teach
tell
urge
want*
warn
wish*
would like/love/hate*

*These verbs can also be followed by the infinitive without an object (example: *ask to leave* or *ask someone to leave*).

6 Common Verbs Followed by the Gerund or the Infinitive

begin
can't stand
continue
forget*
hate
like
love
prefer
remember*
start
stop*
try

*These verbs can be followed by either the gerund or the infinitive but there is a big difference in meaning.

7 Common Verb + Preposition Combinations

admit to
advise against
apologise for
approve of
believe in
choose between
complain about
count on
deal with
dream about/of
feel like/about
insist on
look forward to
object to
pay for
plan on
rely on
resort to
succeed in
talk about
think about
wonder about
worry about

8 Common Adjective + Preposition Combinations

accustomed to
afraid of
amazed at/by
angry with/about
ashamed of
aware of
awful at
bad at
bored with
capable of
careful of
concerned about
content with
curious about
different from
excited about
famous for
fed up with
fond of
glad about
good at
happy about
interested in
nervous about
opposed to
pleased about
ready for
responsible for
sad about
safe from
satisfied with
shocked at/by
sick of
slow at
sorry for/about
surprised at/about/by
terrible at
tired of
used to
worried about

9 Common Adjectives that Can Be Followed by the Infinitive*

afraid
alarmed
amazed
anxious
ashamed
curious
delighted
depressed
determined
disappointed
distressed
disturbed
eager
easy
embarrassed
encouraged
excited
fortunate
glad
happy
hesitant
likely
lucky
pleased
proud
ready
relieved
reluctant
sad
shocked
sorry
surprised
touched
upset
willing

*Example: *I'm happy to hear that.*

Irregular Comparisons of Adjectives, Adverbs and Quantifiers

ADJECTIVE	ADVERB	COMPARATIVE	SUPERLATIVE
bad	badly	worse	worst
far	far	further	furthest
good	well	better	best
little	little	less	least
many/a lot of	—	more	most
much*/a lot of	much*/a lot	more	most

**Much* is usually only used in questions and negative statements.

Common Participles used as Adjectives

-ed	*-ing*	*-ed*	*-ing*	*-ed*	*-ing*
alarmed	alarming	disturbed	disturbing	moved	moving
amazed	amazing	embarrassed	embarrassing	paralysed	paralysing
amused	amusing	entertained	entertaining	pleased	pleasing
annoyed	annoying	excited	exciting	relaxed	relaxing
astonished	astonishing	exhausted	exhausting	satisfied	satisfying
bored	boring	fascinated	fascinating	shocked	shocking
confused	confusing	frightened	frightening	surprised	surprising
depressed	depressing	horrified	horrifying	terrified	terrifying
disappointed	disappointing	inspired	inspiring	tired	tiring
disgusted	disgusting	interested	interesting	touched	touching
distressed	distressing	irritated	irritating	troubled	troubling

Some Adjectives that Form the Comparative and Superlative in Two Ways

ADJECTIVE	COMPARATIVE	SUPERLATIVE
common	commoner / more common	commonest / most common
deadly	deadlier / more deadly	deadliest / most deadly
friendly	friendlier / more friendly	friendliest / most friendly
happy	happier / more happy	happiest / most happy
lively	livelier / more lively	liveliest / most lively
lonely	lonelier / more lonely	loneliest / most lonely
lovely	lovelier / more lovely	loveliest / most lovely
narrow	narrower / more narrow	narrowest / most narrow
pleasant	pleasanter / more pleasant	pleasantest / most pleasant
polite	politer / more polite	politest / most polite
quiet	quieter / more quiet	quietest / most quiet
shallow	shallower / more shallow	shallowest / most shallow
true	truer / more true	truest / most true

13 Common Reporting Verbs

STATEMENTS

acknowledge	claim	indicate	reply
add	complain	maintain	report
admit	conclude	mean	say
announce	confess	note	state
answer	declare	observe	suggest
argue	deny	promise	tell
assert	exclaim	remark	warn
believe	explain	repeat	write

INSTRUCTIONS, COMMANDS, REQUESTS AND INVITATIONS

advise	invite
ask	order
caution	say
command	tell
demand	urge
instruct	warn

QUESTIONS

ask
inquire
question
want to know
wonder

Common Time Word Changes in Indirect Speech

DIRECT SPEECH		INDIRECT SPEECH
now	→	**then**
today	→	**that day**
tomorrow	→	**the next day** OR **the following day** OR **the day after**
yesterday	→	**the day before** OR **the previous day**
this week/month/year	→	**that week/month/year**
last week/month/year	→	**the week/month/year before**
next week/month/year	→	**the following week/month/year**

Common Phrases Introducing Embedded Questions

I don't know . . .
I don't understand . . .
I wonder . . .
I'm not sure . . .
I can't remember . . .
I can't imagine . . .
It doesn't say . . .

I'd like to know . . .
I want to understand . . .
I'd like to find out . . .
We need to find out . . .
Let's ask . . .

Do you know . . . ?
Do you understand . . . ?
Can you tell me . . . ?
Could you explain . . . ?
Can you remember . . . ?
Would you show me . . . ?
Who knows . . . ?

Verbs and Expressions Commonly Used Reflexively

amuse oneself	behave oneself	feel sorry for oneself	keep oneself	see oneself
ask oneself	believe in oneself	forgive oneself	kill oneself	take care of oneself
avail oneself of	blame oneself	give oneself	look after oneself	talk to oneself
be hard on oneself	cut oneself	help oneself	look at oneself	teach oneself
be oneself	deprive oneself of	hurt oneself	pride oneself on	tell oneself
be pleased with oneself	dry oneself	imagine oneself	push oneself	treat oneself
be proud of oneself	enjoy oneself	introduce oneself	remind oneself	wash oneself

Some Common Phrasal Verbs

(s.o. = someone s.t. = something)

Note 1: Inseparable phrasal verbs are shown with the object after the particle (***go after** s.t.*). **Separable phrasal verbs** are shown with the object between the verb and the particle (***call** s.o. **up***). Verbs which must be separated are shown with an asterisk (*) (***keep** s.t. **on***).

Note 2: Separable phrasal verbs can have the noun object either between the verb and the particle or after the particle (***call** Jan **up*** OR ***call up** Jan*). These verbs must, however, be separated when there is a pronoun object (***call** her **up*** NOT ~~*call up her*~~).

Phrasal Verb	Meaning
ask s.o. **round**	*invite to one's home*
block s.t. **out**	*stop from passing through (light, noise)*
blow s.t. **out**	*stop burning by blowing*
blow s.t. **up**	*fill something with air (a balloon, a water toy)*
blow (s.t.) **up**	*(make s.t.) explode*
break down	*stop functioning*
break out	*occur suddenly*
bring s.t. **about**	*make something happen*
bring s.o. or s.t. **back**	*return someone or something*
bring s.t. **out**	*introduce (a new product, a book)*
bring s.o. **up**	*raise (children)*
burn (s.t.) **down**	*burn completely*
call (s.o.) **back**	*return a phone call*
call s.t. **off**	*cancel*
call s.o. **up**	*telephone someone*
carry on s.t.	*continue*
carry s.t. **out**	*pursue a plan*
catch on	*become popular*
cheer (s.o.) **up**	*(make someone) feel happier*
clean (s.o. or s.t.) **up**	*clean completely*
clear (s.t.) **up**	*make clear*
come about	*happen*
come along	*accompany*
come back	*return*
come in	*enter*
come off s.t.	*become detached*
come out	*appear*
come up	*arise*
come up with s.t.	*invent*
cover s.t. **up**	*cover completely*
cross s.t. **out**	*draw a line through*
cut s.t. **down**	*bring down by cutting*
cut s.t. **off**	*1. stop the supply of something* *2. remove by cutting*
cut s.t. **out**	*remove by cutting*
dream s.t. **up**	*invent*
dress up	*put on special or formal clothes*
drink s.t. **up**	*drink completely*
drop by/in	*visit unexpectedly*
drop s.o. or s.t. **off**	*take someone/something to a place and leave them/it there*
drop out (**of** s.t.)	*leave*
eat out	*eat in a restaurant*
empty (s.t.) **out**	*empty completely*
end up	*1. do something unexpected or unintended* *2. reach a final place or condition*
fall off	*become detached*
figure s.o. or s.t. **out**	*understand (after thinking about)*
fill s.t. **in**	*complete with information (a form, an application)*
fill (s.t.) **up**	*fill completely*
find (s.t.) **out**	*learn information*
follow (s.t.) **through**	*complete*
fool around	*be playful*
get s.t. **across**	*get people to understand an idea*
get ahead	*make progress, succeed*
get along	*relate well*
get back	*return*
get by	*survive*
get out (**of** s.t.)	*leave (a car, a taxi)*
get s.t. **out of** s.t.*	*benefit from*
get together	*meet*
get up	*rise from bed*
give s.t. **away**	*give without charging money*
give s.t. **back**	*return something*
give s.t. **out**	*distribute*
give (s.t.) **up**	*stop, abandon*
go after s.o. or s.t.	*pursue*
go along with s.t.	*act in agreement with*
go back	*return*
go off	*explode (a gun, fireworks)*
go on	*continue*
go out	*leave*
go up	*be built*
grow up	*become an adult*
hand s.t. **in**	*give some work to a boss or teacher*
hand s.t. **out**	*distribute*
hang up	*put the phone down*
hang s.t. **up**	*put on a hook or hanger*

(continued on next page)

Phrasal Verb	**Meaning**
help (s.o.) **out**	*assist*
hold on	*wait, not hang up the phone*
keep (s.o. or s.t.) **away**	*(cause to) stay at a distance*
keep on	*continue*
keep s.t. **on***	*not remove (a piece of clothing or jewellery)*
keep up (with s.o. or s.t.)	*go as fast as*
lay s.o. **off**	*end someone's employment*
leave s.t. **on***	*1. not turn off (a light, a radio)* *2. not remove (a piece of clothing or jewellery)*
leave s.t. **out**	*omit*
let s.o. **down**	*disappoint*
let s.o. or s.t. **in**	*allow to enter*
let s.o. or s.t. **out**	*allow to leave*
lie down	*recline*
light (s.t.) **up**	*illuminate*
look out	*be careful*
look s.o. or s.t. **over**	*examine*
look s.t. **up**	*try to find in a book or on the internet*
make s.t. **up**	*create*
pass s.t. **round**	*distribute*
pay s.o. or s.t. **back**	*repay*
pay off	*be worthwhile*
pick s.o. or s.t. **out**	*1. select* *2. identify*
pick up	*improve*
pick s.o. or s.t. **up**	*1. lift* *2. get (an idea, a new book, an interest)*
play around	*have fun*
point s.o. or s.t. **out**	*indicate*
put s.t. **away**	*put something in an appropriate place*
put s.t. **back**	*return something to its original place*
put s.o. or s.t. **down**	*stop holding*
put s.t. **off**	*postpone*
put s.t. **on**	*cover the body with a piece of clothing or jewellery*
put s.t. **together**	*assemble*
put s.t. **up**	*erect*
run into s.o.	*meet accidentally*
run out (**of** s.t.)	*not have enough of a supply*
see s.t. **through***	*complete*
set s.t. **off**	*cause to explode*
set s.t. **up**	*1. establish (a business, an organisation)* *2. prepare for use*
show s.o. or s.t. **off**	*display the best qualities*
show up	*appear*
sign up	*register*
sit down	*take a seat*
stand up	*rise*
stay up	*remain awake*
stick with/to s.o. or s.t.	*not give up, not leave*
straighten (s.t.) **up**	*make neat*
switch s.t. **on**	*start a machine*
take s.t. **away/off**	*remove*
take s.t. **back**	*return*
take off	*depart (a plane)*
take s.o. **on**	*hire, employ*
take s.t. **out**	*borrow from a library*
talk s.o. **into***	*persuade*
talk s.t. **over**	*discuss*
team up with s.o.	*start to work with*
tear s.t. **down**	*destroy*
tear s.t. **up**	*tear into small pieces*
think s.t. **over**	*consider*
think s.t. **up**	*invent*
throw s.t. **away/out**	*discard*
touch s.t. **up**	*improve by making small changes*
try s.t. **on**	*put clothing on to see if it fits*
try s.t. **out**	*find out if something works*
turn s.o. or s.t. **down**	*1. reject* *2. decrease the volume (a radio, a TV)*
turn s.o. or s.t. **into**	*change from one form to another*
turn s.t. **off**	*stop a machine*
turn s.t. **on**	*start a machine*
turn out	*have a particular result*
turn up	*appear*
turn s.t. **up**	*increase the volume*
use s.t. **up**	*use completely, consume*
wake up	*arise after sleeping*
wake (s.o.) **up**	*awaken*
watch out	*be careful*
work s.t. **off**	*remove by work or activity*
work out	*1. be resolved* *2. exercise*
work s.t. **out**	*solve*
write s.t. **down**	*write on a piece of paper*
write s.t. **up**	*write in a finished form*

18 Some Common Irregular Plural Nouns

SINGULAR	PLURAL	SINGULAR	PLURAL	SINGULAR	PLURAL	SINGULAR	PLURAL
analysis	analyses	half	halves	child	children	mouse	mice
basis	bases	knife	knives	man	men		
crisis	crises	leaf	leaves	woman	women	deer	deer
hypothesis	hypotheses	life	lives			fish	fish
		loaf	loaves	foot	feet	sheep	sheep
		shelf	shelves	goose	geese		
		wife	wives	tooth	teeth	person	people

19 Spelling Rules for the Present Continuous

1. Add *-ing* to the base form of the verb.

   read   read*ing*
   stand   stand*ing*

2. If a verb ends in a silent *-e*, drop the final *-e* and add *-ing*.

   leave   leav*ing*
   take   tak*ing*

3. In a one-syllable word, if the last three letters are a consonant – vowel – consonant combination (CVC), double the last consonant before adding *-ing*.

   C V C
   ↓ ↓ ↓
   s i t   sit*ting*

   C V C
   ↓ ↓ ↓
   r u n   run*ning*

   However, do not double the last consonant in words that end in *w*, *x*, or *y*.

   sew   sew*ing*
   fix   fix*ing*
   enjoy   enjoy*ing*

4. In words of two or more syllables that end in a consonant – vowel – consonant combination, double the last consonant only if the last syllable is stressed.

   admít   admit*ting*   (The last syllable is stressed, so you double the *-t*.)
   whísper   whisper*ing*   (The last syllable is not stressed, so you don't double the *-r*.)

5. If a verb ends in *-ie*, change the *ie* to *y* before adding *-ing*.

   die   dy*ing*

20 Spelling Rules for the Present Simple: Third Person Singular *(he, she, it)*

1. Add *-s* for most verbs.

   work   work*s*
   buy   buy*s*
   ride   ride*s*
   return   return*s*

2. Add *-es* for words that end in *-ch*, *-s*, *-sh*, *-x*, or *-z*.

   watch   watch*es*
   pass   pass*es*
   rush   rush*es*
   relax   relax*es*
   buzz   buzz*es*

3. Change the *y* to *i* and add *-es* when the base form ends in a consonant + *y*.

   study   stud*ies*
   hurry   hurr*ies*
   dry   dr*ies*

   Do not change the *y* when the base form ends in a vowel + *y*. Add *-s*.

   play   play*s*
   enjoy   enjoy*s*

4. A few verbs have irregular forms.

   be   is
   do   does
   go   goes
   have   has

21 Spelling Rules for the Past Simple of Regular Verbs

1. If the verb ends in a consonant, add *-ed*.
   return returne*d*
   help help*ed*
2. If the verb ends in *-e*, add *-d*.
   live live*d*
   create create*d*
   die die*d*
3. In one-syllable words, if the verb ends in a consonant – vowel – consonant combination (CVC), double the final consonant and add *-ed*.
   C V C
   ↓↓↓
   h o p hop*ped*
   C V C
   ↓↓↓
   r u b rub*bed*

   However, do not double the last consonant in one-syllable words ending in *-w*, *-x*, or *-y*.
   bow bow*ed*
   mix mix*ed*
   play play*ed*
4. In words of two or more syllables that end in a consonant – vowel – consonant combination, double the last consonant only if the last syllable is stressed.
   prefér prefer*red* (The last syllable is stressed, so you double the *-r*.)
   vísit visit*ed* (The last syllable is not stressed, so you don't double the *t*.)
5. If the verb ends in a consonant + *y*, change the *y* to *i* and add *-ed*.
   worry worr*ied*
   carry carr*ied*
6. If the verb ends in a vowel + *y*, add *-ed*. (Do not change the *y* to *i*.)
   play play*ed*
   annoy annoy*ed*
   Exceptions: pay—paid, lay—laid, say—said

22 Spelling Rules for the Comparative *(-er)* and Superlative *(-est)* of Adjectives

1. Add *-er* to one-syllable adjectives to form the comparative. Add *-est* to one-syllable adjectives to form the superlative.
   cheap cheap*er* cheap*est*
   bright bright*er* bright*est*
2. If the adjective ends in *-e*, add *-r* or *-st*.
   nice nice*r* nice*st*
3. If the adjective ends in a consonant + *y*, change *y* to *i* before you add *-er* or *-est*.
   pretty prett*ier* prett*iest*
   Exception: shy shy*er* shy*est*
4. If the adjective ends in a consonant – vowel – consonant combination (CVC), double the final consonant before adding *-er* or *-est*.
   C V C
   ↓↓↓
   b i g big*ger* big*gest*

   However, do not double the final consonant in words ending in *-w* or *-y*.
   slow slow*er* slow*est*
   coy coy*er* coy*est*

23 Spelling Rules for Adverbs Ending in *-ly*

1. Add *-ly* to the corresponding adjective.
   nice nice*ly*
   quiet quiet*ly*
   beautiful beautiful*ly*
2. If the adjective ends in a consonant + *y*, change the *y* to *i* before adding *-ly*.
   easy eas*ily*
3. If the adjective ends in *-le*, drop the e and add *-y*.
   possible possib*ly*

   However, do not drop the e for other adjectives ending in -e.
   extreme extreme*ly*
   Exception: true tru*ly*
4. If the adjective ends in *-ic*, add *-ally*.
   basic basic*ally*
   fantastic fantastic*ally*

24 Contractions with Verb Forms

1. Present Simple, Present Continuous and Imperative

Contractions with *Be*

I am = **I'm**
you are = **you're**
he is = **he's**
she is = **she's**
it is = **it's**
we are = **we're**
you are = **you're**
they are = **they're**

Present Simple	Present Continuous
I'm a student. He's my teacher. We're from Canada.	I'm studying here. He's teaching verbs. We're living here.

I am not = **I'm not**
you are not = **you aren't** or **you're not**
he is not = **he isn't** or **he's not**
she is not = **she isn't** or **she's not**
it is not = **it isn't** or **it's not**
we are not = **we aren't** or **we're not**
you are not = **you aren't** or **you're not**
they are not = **they aren't** or **they're not**

Present Simple	Present Continuous
She's not ill. He isn't late. We aren't twins. They're not here.	She's not reading. He isn't coming. We aren't leaving. They're not playing.

Contractions with *Do*

do not = **don't**
does not = **doesn't**

Present Simple	Imperative
They don't live here. It doesn't snow much.	Don't run!

2. Past Simple and Past Continuous

Contractions with *Be*

was not = **wasn't**
were not = **weren't**

Contractions with *Do*

did not = **didn't**

Present Simple	Imperative
He wasn't a poet. They weren't twins. We didn't see her.	He wasn't singing. They weren't sleeping.

3. Future

Contractions with *Will*

I will = **I'll**
you will = **you'll**
he will = **he'll**
she will = **she'll**
it will = **it'll**
we will = **we'll**
you will = **you'll**
they will = **they'll**

will not = **won't**

Present Simple
I'll take the train. It'll be faster that way. We'll go together. He won't come with us. They won't miss the train.

(continued on next page)

Contractions with *Be going to*

I am going to	=	**I'm going to**
you are going to	=	**you're going to**
he is going to	=	**he's going to**
she is going to	=	**she's going to**
it is going to	=	**it's going to**
we are going to	=	**we're going to**
you are going to	=	**you're going to**
they are going to	=	**they're going to**

FUTURE WITH *BE GOING TO*

I'm going to buy tickets tomorrow.
She's going to call you.
It's going to rain soon.
We're going to drive to Leeds.
They're going to crash!

4. PRESENT PERFECT AND PRESENT PERFECT CONTINUOUS

Contractions with *Have*

I have	=	**I've**
you have	=	**you've**
he has	=	**he's**
she has	=	**she's**
it has	=	**it's**
we have	=	**we've**
you have	=	**you've**
they have	=	**they've**
have not	=	**haven't**
has not	=	**hasn't**

You've already read that page.
We've been writing for an hour.
She's been to Africa three times.
It's been raining since yesterday.
We haven't seen any elephants yet.
They haven't been living here long.
She hasn't taken any photos today.

5. MODALS AND MODAL-LIKE EXPRESSIONS

cannot	=	**can't**
could not	=	**couldn't**
should not	=	**shouldn't**
had better	=	**'d better**
would prefer	=	**'d prefer**
would not	=	**wouldn't**
would rather	=	**'d rather**

She can't dance.
We shouldn't go.
They'd better decide.
I'd prefer coffee.
She wouldn't.
I'd rather take the bus.

could have	=	**could've**
should have	=	**should've**
would have	=	**would've**
must have	=	**must've**
might have	=	**might've**

We could've walked.
We might've arrived late.

6. CONDITIONALS WITH *WOULD*

Contractions with *Would*

I would	=	**I'd**
you would	=	**you'd**
he would	=	**he'd**
she would	=	**she'd**
we would	=	**we'd**
you would	=	**you'd**
they would	=	**they'd**
would have	=	**would've**
would not	=	**wouldn't**

If I had time, I'd travel.
If you moved here, you'd be happy.
If she knew the answer, she'd tell you.
We'd buy a new car if we had the money.
If you invited them, they'd come.
If I had known, I would've told you.
I wouldn't do that if I were you.

25 Punctuation Rules for Direct Speech

Direct speech may either follow or come before the reporting verb. When direct speech follows the reporting verb,

a. Put a comma after the reporting verb.

b. Use opening quotation marks before the first word of the direct speech. Quotation marks can be single (') or double (") but note that single quotation marks are more common in British English.

c. Begin the quotation with a capital letter.

d. Use the appropriate end punctuation for the direct speech. It may be a full stop (.), a question mark (?) or an exclamation mark (!).

e. Put closing quotation marks (') or (") after the end punctuation of the quotation.

Examples: He said, 'I had a good time.'
She asked, 'Where's the party?'
They shouted, 'Be careful!'

f. For quotations inside quotations, use double quotation marks inside single quotation marks.

Example: 'I heard him shout "Come here!" but I ran away,' he said.

When direct speech comes before the reporting verb,

a. Begin the sentence with opening quotation marks.

b. Use the appropriate end punctuation for the direct speech.
If the direct speech is a statement, use a comma (,).
If the direct speech is a question, use a question mark (?).
If the direct speech is an exclamation, use an exclamation mark (!).

c. Use closing quotation marks after the end punctuation for the direct speech.

d. Begin the reporting clause with a lower-case letter.

e. Use a full stop at the end of the main sentence (.).

Examples: 'I had a good time,' he said.
'Where's the party?' she asked.
'Be careful!' they shouted.

26 Pronunciation Table

Vowels				**Consonants**			
Symbol	**Key Word**	**Symbol**	**Key Word**	**Symbol**	**Key Word**	**Symbol**	**Key Word**
iː	beat, feed	ə	banana, among	p	pack, happy	ʃ	ship, machine, station, special, discussion
ɪ	bit, did	aɪ	bite, cry, buy, eye	b	back, rubber	ʒ	measure, vision
eɪ	date, paid	aʊ	about, how	t	tie	h	hot, who
e	bet, bed	ɔɪ	voice, boy	d	die	m	men
æ	bat, bad	ɪə	beer	k	came, key, quick	n	sun, know, pneumonia
ɒ	box, odd,	eə	bare	g	game, guest	ŋ	sung, ringing
ɔː	bought, four, door	ɑː	bar, father	tʃ	church, nature, watch	w	wet, white
əʊ	boat, road	ʊə	tour	dʒ	judge, general, major	l	light, long
ʊ	book, good	ɜː	bird	f	fan, photograph	r	right, wrong
uː	boot, food,			v	van	y	yes, use, music
ʌ	but, mud, mother			θ	thing, breath		
				ð	then, breathe		
				s	sip, city, psychology		
				z	zip, please, goes		

Stress
ˈ shows main stress.

27 Pronunciation Rules for the Present Simple: Third Person Singular *(he, she, it)*

1. The third person singular in the present simple always ends in the letter *-s*. There are, however, three different ways of pronuncing the final sound of the third person singular.

/s/	/z/	/ɪz/
talks	loves	dances

2. The final sound is pronounced /s/ after the voiceless sounds /p/, /t/, /k/, and /f/.

top	tops
get	gets
take	takes
laugh	laughs

3. The final sound is pronounced /z/ after the voiced sounds /b/, /d/, /g/, /v/, /ð/, /m/, /n/, /ŋ/ and /l/.

describe	describes
spend	spends
hug	hugs
live	lives
breathe	breathes
seem	seems
remain	remains
sing	sings
tell	tells

4. The final sound is pronounced /z/ after *w*, *y* and all vowel sounds.

agree	agrees
try	tries
stay	stays
know	knows

5. The final sound is pronounced /ɪz/ after the sounds /s/, /z/, /ʃ/, /ʒ/, /ʧ/, and /ʤ/. /ɪz/ adds a syllable to the verb.

relax	relaxes
freeze	freezes
rush	rushes
massage	massages
watch	watches
judge	judges

6. *Do* and *say* have a change in vowel sound.

say	/seɪ/	says	/sez/
do	/du:/	does	/dʌz/

28 Pronunciation Rules for the Past Simple of Regular Verbs

1. The regular past simple always ends in the letter *-d*. There are, however, three different ways of pronuncing the final sound of the regular past simple.

/t/	/d/	/ɪd/
raced	lived	attended

2. The final sound is pronounced /t/ after the voiceless sounds /p/, /k/, /f/, /s/, /ʃ/, and /ʧ/.

hop	hopped
work	worked
laugh	laughed
address	addressed
publish	published
watch	watched

3. The final sound is pronounced /d/ after the voiced sounds /b/, /g/, /v/, /z/, /ʒ/, /ʤ/, /m/, /n/, /ŋ/, /l/, /r/, and /ð/.

rub	rubbed
hug	hugged
live	lived
surprise	surprised
massage	massaged
change	changed
rhyme	rhymed
return	returned
bang	banged
enrol	enrolled
appear	appeared
breathe	breathed

4. The final sound is pronounced /d/ after all vowel sounds.

agree	agreed
play	played
die	died
enjoy	enjoyed
row	rowed

5. The final sound is pronounced /ɪd/ after /t/ and /d/. /ɪd/ adds a syllable to the verb.

start	started
decide	decided

Used to or would?

1. Use *used to* and *didn't use to* + base form of the verb to talk about past habits and states.

   People used to live here.
   (But now they don't.)

   I didn't use to like coffee but now I love it.
   Did you use to have long hair when you were younger?

2. You can also use *would* + base form of the verb to describe repeated past actions.

   Be careful! You cannot use *would* to describe past states.

   As a child I would walk along the beach collecting shells.
   Some evenings, I would go down to the beach to watch the sunset.

   NOT ~~I would have long hair when I was younger.~~

Have or have got?

1. Use ***have*** or ***have got*** to talk about possessions. These two verbs mean the same thing. ***Have got*** is a present tense of ***have*** not the present perfect form of ***get***. ***Have got*** is more common than ***have*** in British English.

*I **have** a flat in Manchester.*	*I've got a flat in Manchester.*
The hotel has a swimming pool.	*The hotel's got a swimming pool.*

2. ***Have got*** is most common in the present and less common in the past.

   I had a bad headache yesterday.
   NOT ~~I had got a bad headache~~ . . .

3. Use ***have*** to talk about routines or regular activities.

   *I often **have** a salad for lunch.*
   NOT ~~I often have got a salad for lunch.~~
   The baby has a bath every night.
   NOT ~~The baby has got a bath every night~~.

4. Use ***have*** in many common expressions.

have lunch	have a bath	have a rest
have a chat	have a go	

Compound Nouns

1. Compound nouns are very common in English. Use two or three words together to make compound nouns.

   toothbrush = a brush you clean your teeth with
   bookshop = a shop where you buy books
   sister-in-law
   a letter box
   job centre

2. Most compounds are written as two separate words.

service station	bus stop	hot dog
credit card	head office	paper clip

3. Some short compounds are written as one word.

   bathroom
   postman
   hairbrush

4. A few have hyphens.

   mother-in-law
   T-shirt
   X-ray

British and American English

Grammar

British English	American English
The present perfect is used for recent past actions: *I've just seen Jim.*	The past simple or present perfect is used for recent past actions: *I just saw Jim.* OR *I've just seen Jim.*
The past participle *gotten* is not used: *Your French has got better since I last saw you.*	The past participle *gotten* is used: *Your French has gotten better since I last saw you.*
Have got and *have* are both used in negatives and questions: *Have you got my book?* OR *Do you have my book?* *I haven't got a car.* OR *I don't have a car.*	*Have* is more common in negatives and questions: *Do you have my book?* *I don't have a car.*
Collective nouns are more commonly used with a plural verb. Singular verbs are also possible: *The crew are/is on deck.* *The crowd are/is shouting.*	Collective nouns are more commonly used with a singular verb: *The crew is on deck.* *The crowd is shouting.*
Can't is used to say that something is not possible: *Sally can't be here. All the lights are out.*	*Can't* and *must not* are both used to say that something is not possible: *Sally can't/must not be here. All the lights are out.*
The definite article *the* is used with musical instruments: *I play the violin.*	The definite article *the* can be left out: *I play violin.* OR *I play the violin.*
And is usually used after the verb *go*: *Let's go and see Mike.*	*And* is often left out after the verb *go*: *Let's go see Mike.*

Spelling

British English	American English
centre, fibre, metre, theatre	center, fiber, meter, theater
colour, favourite, flavour, labour, honour	color, favorite, flavor, labor, honor
defence, licence	defense, license
practice (noun), practise (verb)	practice
programme	program
analyse, paralyse, realise	analyze, paralyze, realize
analogue, catalogue, dialogue	analog/analogue, catalog, dialog/dialogue

Vocabulary

British English	American English
aeroplane	airplane
angry	angry/mad
autumn	fall/autumn
barrister	lawyer/attorney
bill (in a restaurant)	check
biscuit	cookie
bonnet (of a car)	hood
boot (of a car)	trunk
car park	parking lot
chips	french fries/fries
crisps	potato chips
crossroads	intersection/crossroads
dustbin	trashcan
film	movie
first floor	second floor
flat	apartment
gear lever	gear shift/stick shift
ground floor	first floor
holiday	vacation
hooter	horn
jab	shot/injection
lift	elevator
lorry	truck
mad	crazy
main road	highway
motorway	freeway
nappy	diaper
pavement	sidewalk
petrol	gas
post	mail
public lavatory/toilet	rest room
queue (noun); queue (verb)	line; stand in line
rise	raise
rubber	eraser
rubbish	trash; garbage
shop	store
solicitor	lawyer/attorney
stupid	dumb/stupid
surgery	doctor's office
sweets	candy
tap	faucet/tap
timetable	schedule/timetable
torch	flashlight
trainers	sneakers
trousers	pants
underground	subway
windscreen	windshield
zebra crossing	crosswalk
zip	zipper

(continued on next page)

Other Differences

British English	American English
in Oxford Street	on Fifth Avenue
at the weekend	on the weekend
stay at home	stay home
in the team	on the team
different from/to	different than/from
outside the city	outside of the city/outside the city
11 June; the eleventh of June; June the eleventh; 11-06-95	June 11; June eleventh; 06-11-95
do something again	do something over/again
Monday to Friday	Monday through/to Friday
A to Z /ʒed/	A to Z /ʒiː/

Appendix Quiz

Read and answer the questions and tick the correct answers.

1 What is the past participle of the verb *light*?

2 *envy* is . . .
☐ an action verb. ☐ a stative verb.

3 If someone *lets you down*, are you . . .
☐ happy? ☐ sad?

4 What is the superlative form of the adjective *far*?
....

5 If something doesn't interest you, are you . . .
☐ boring? ☐ bored?

6 If you *used to* drink coffee, do you still drink coffee?
☐ Yes ☐ No

7 *tooth* has . . .
☐ a regular plural form. ☐ an irregular plural form.

8 If you *dress up*, do you wear jeans and trainers?
☐ Yes ☐ No

9 What are *chips* called in American English?
....

10 You form compound nouns with more than one word.
☐ True ☐ False

11 Which is correct?
☐ I've got a shower every morning.
☐ I have a shower every morning.

12 *would* can be used with both action and stative verbs.
☐ True ☐ False

13 The past participle and the base form of the verb *hit* are . . .
☐ the same. ☐ different.

14 The verb *weigh* can have a stative meaning.
☐ True ☐ False

15 If you *cheer someone up*, they feel . . .
☐ worse. ☐ better.

16 The plural form of *sheep* is . . .
☐ sheep. ☐ sheeps.

17 Which sentence is correct in British English?
☐ I didn't pack my suitcase yet.
☐ I haven't packed my suitcase yet.

18 The verb *want* is followed by the . . .
☐ *-ing* form. ☐ infinitive.

19 You *eat out* . . .
☐ at home. ☐ in a restaurant.

20 Your friend gives you a hot dog. Do you . . .
☐ stroke it? ☐ eat it?

21 Tick the correct sentence.
☐ I'm really annoying! Nothing is going right.
☐ I'm really annoyed! Nothing is going right.

22 There are two ways of forming the comparative and superlative of some adjectives.
☐ True ☐ False

23 Are you aware . . .
☐ of something? ☐ to something?

24 If you ask for the *check* at the end of your meal, you are in . . .
☐ a British restaurant. ☐ an American restaurant.

25 The verb *remember* cannot be followed by the *-ing* form.
☐ True ☐ False

Answer Key

1 lit **2** a stative verb **3** sad **4** furthest **5** bored **6** No **7** an irregular **8** No **9** french fries/fries **10** True **11** I have a shower every morning. **12** False **13** the same **14** True **15** better **16** sheep **17** I haven't packed my suitcase yet. **18** infinitive **19** in a restaurant **20** eat it **21** I'm really annoyed! Nothing is going right. **22** True **23** of something **24** an American restaurant **25** False

Answer Key

NOTE: In this answer key, where the contracted form is given, the full form is also correct, and where the full form is given, the contracted form is also correct.

Present Continuous

 **POINT**

It's happening now!

CHART CHECK 1

be + base form of verb + *-ing*
be

CHART CHECK 2

F

EXPRESS CHECK

are . . . leaving
are . . . performing OR 're . . . performing

I('m working) very hard these days, but I have some good news. Right now, I'm sitting at a desk in the Entertainment Section of the *Tribune*! Of course I('m) still (taking) journalism classes at night as well. The job is temporary – Joe Sims, the regular reporter, (is taking) this month off to write a book. This week we('re preparing) to interview your favourite group, the Airheads. In fact, at this very moment they're flying into town by helicopter. They('re performing) at the Theatre Royal all week. How (are) you (getting on)? (Are) you still (writing) music? Oops! The crew are calling me. We're leaving for the theatre now. Write soon!

2. are . . . going
3. 'm going
4. is waiting OR 's waiting
5. 'm working
6. aren't doing OR 're not doing
7. 're . . . sitting
8. 'm sitting
9. 'm . . . thinking
10. are staying

3. Why are you touring again?
4. What are you working on these days?
5. Who's singing now?
6. Is she replacing Tina?
7. No, she isn't. OR No, she's not.

I ~~write~~ 'm writing to you from my hotel room. Everyone else is ~~sleep~~ sleeping but I ~~sitting~~ 'm sitting here, looking at the sea. We're staying at the Plaza in Atlantic Beach and the view is beautiful. The tour is ~~goes~~ going well. The audience is crazy about the new songs but the fans ~~is~~ are always asking for you. How's the baby? Has she got a good voice? ~~Do~~ Are you teaching her to sing yet? Maybe both of you will come along for the next tour!

Present Simple

CHECK POINT

John's Typical Working Week

CHART CHECK

T, T, F

EXPRESS CHECK

Why does he work

In today's fast-paced world, we (never) escape stress. Stress (always) affects us psychologically but according to Dr Roads, author of the new bestseller, *Calm Down!*, it also affects us physically. For example, stress causes high blood pressure. Doctors (often) prescribe medication for stress-related illnesses. Medicine (usually) lowers a patient's blood pressure. But, Dr Roads claims, 'You don't (always) need pills. Relaxation exercises are (sometimes) as effective as pills. For example, breathing exercises relax you and lower your blood pressure at the same time – and it only takes a few minutes!'

3. go
4. rushes
5. isn't
6. is
7. doesn't finish
8. worries
9. hasn't got
10. hasn't got

3. Does he work on reports in the afternoon? No, he doesn't.
4. When does he see clients? He sees clients from 9:00 to 12:00.
5. Does he have a lunch break? Yes, he does.
6. What does he do from 12:30 to 5:00? He returns phone calls.
7. Where does he go at 5:30? He goes to evening classes.

I'm so tired. I ~~have never~~ never have time to relax. I work all day and ~~studies~~ study all night. My boss ~~tell~~ tells me that I need a holiday. I agree but ~~I~~ I'm afraid to take one. Does my boss ~~thinks~~ think that the office can function without me? I ~~dont~~ don't want them to think I'm not necessary. But my wife is unhappy, too. She ~~complain~~ complains that she never sees me any more. My schedule ~~are~~ is crazy. I don't think I can keep this up much longer. I don't ~~wants~~ want to give up evening classes, though. I ~~think often~~ often think that there has got to be a better way.

UNIT 3 Stative Verbs

CHECK POINT

has the flavour of chicken

CHART CHECK

T, T

EXPRESS CHECK

'm weighing, weighs

ANNA: This steak tastes delicious. Your salmon looks good, too.
BEN: Here, I'm putting some on your plate. I think you'll like it.
ANNA: Mmm. I do like it! Funny, I usually (don't like) fish.
BEN: Red (has) that effect on people.
ANNA: I have no idea what you're talking about. What do you mean?
BEN: Well, colours can change the way we (feel). For example, people often (feel) hungrier in a red room. I notice that you're looking at the red wallpaper.
ANNA: And I certainly feel hungry. I'm eating half your salmon.
BEN: That's OK. I'm tasting your steak. It's delicious!

2. is looking
3. cost
4. wants
5. hates
6. seems
7. likes
8. doesn't suspect
9. know
10. is thinking
11. hasn't got
12. is listening

3

2. 'm tasting
3. needs
4. Do . . . want
5. tastes
6. think
7. 'm thinking
8. isn't
9. sounds
10. 'm looking
11. don't know
12. is
13. 'm smelling
14. 'm not
15. love
16. smells
17. know
18. mean
19. feel

Not a good day! I feel depressed and I've got a headache. I~~'m needing~~ need to do something to change my mood and get rid of this pain. Last week, I~~'m reading~~ read an article about how smells can affect mood and even health, so at the moment I ~~smell~~ 'm smelling an orange (for the depression) and a green

(continued on next page)

apple (for the headache). They smell nice but I~~'m not thinking that~~ don't think I notice a difference in how I feel! I think I~~'m preferring~~ prefer to eat something when I feel down. But I worry that I~~'m weighing~~ weigh too much. So, at the moment I ~~have~~ 'm having a cup of peppermint tea with lemon. The article says that the peppermint smell helps you eat less. Well, I don't know about that! A chocolate ice cream sounds pretty good right now! It~~'s seeming~~ seems that there are no easy solutions.

Present Continuous and Present Simple

CHECK POINT

F, F

CHART CHECK

two parts
two forms

EXPRESS CHECK

PRESENT CONTINUOUS			
SUBJECT	BE	BASE FORM + -ING	
I	am	buying	flowers now.
You	are	buying	
He	is	buying	

PRESENT SIMPLE			
SUBJECT		VERB	
I	usually	buy	chocolates.
You		buy	
He		buys	

1

28 June: I'm sitting in a seat 3,000 metres above the earth en route to Argentina! I usually have dinner at this time but right now I've got a headache from the excitement. The person next to me is eating my food. She looks happy.

30 June: It's 7:30. My host's parents are still working. Carlos, the father, works at home. The youngest son, Ricardo, is sweet. He looks (and behaves) a lot like Bobby. Right now, he's looking over my shoulder and trying to read my diary.

4 July: The weather is cold now. I usually spend the first weekend of July at the beach but today I'm walking around in a heavy sweater.

6 August: I feel so tired tonight. Everyone else feels great in the evening because they have long naps in the afternoon.

2

1. **b.** 'm waiting
   c. look
   d. 'm working
   e. 's talking
   f. isn't looking OR 's not looking
   g. looks
   h. doesn't mean
2. **a.** 's talking
   b. 're doing
   c. 're standing
   d. Do . . . think
   e. 're going out
   f. don't think
   g. means
   h. come
   i. stand
3. **a.** is . . . walking
   b. doesn't start
   c. 's … got
   d. walks
   e. seem
4. **a.** are . . . shaking
   b. know
   c. shake
   d. meet

3 It's 12:30 and I ~~sit~~ *'m sitting* in the library. My classmates are eating lunch together but I'm not hungry yet. At home, we ~~eat never~~ *never eat* this early. Today our homework topic is 'culture shock'. It's a good topic for me right now because I'm ~~being~~ pretty homesick. I miss my old routine. At home we always ~~are having~~ *have* a big meal at 2:00 in the afternoon. Then we rest. But here in Toronto ~~I'm having~~ *I have* a conversation class at 3:00. Every day, I almost fall asleep in class, and my teacher ~~ask~~ *asks* me, 'Are you bored?' Of course I'm not bored. I just need my afternoon rest! This class ~~always is~~ *is always* fun. This term, we ~~work~~ *'re working* on a project with video cameras. My team is filming groups of people from different cultures. We are ~~analyse~~ *analysing* 'social distance'. That means how close to each other people stand. According to my new watch, it's 12:55, so I ~~leave~~ *'m leaving* now for my one o'clock class. Teachers here really ~~aren't liking~~ *don't like* it when you are late!

UNIT 5 Imperative

CHECK POINT

giving instructions on how to do an exercise

CHART CHECK

don't include a subject

EXPRESS CHECK

AFFIRMATIVE	
BASE FORM OF VERB	
Listen	to the music.
Touch	your toes.
Stand up	straight.

NEGATIVE		
DON'T	BASE FORM OF VERB	
Don't	listen	to the music.
Don't	touch	your toes.
Don't	stand up	straight.

1

2. c
3. b
4. e
5. d
6. a
7. f

2

2. Wash six strawberries.
3. Cut the strawberries in half.
4. Pour orange juice into the blender.
5. Add the fruit to the orange juice.
6. Blend the ingredients until smooth.

3

2. Learn
3. Reduce
4. Improve
5. Get
6. Don't miss
7. Take
8. Choose
9. Don't delay
10. Register

4 For the Black Belt essay, Master Gibbons gave us this assignment: ~~You write~~ *Write* about something important to you. My topic is *The Right Way*, the rules of life for the martial arts. First, ~~respects~~ *respect* other people – treat them the way you want them to treat you. Second, ~~helped~~ *help* people in need. In other words, use your strength for others, ~~not to~~ *don't* use it just for your own good. Third, ~~no~~ *don't* lie or steal. These are the most important rules to me.

SelfTest I

(Total = 100 points. Each item = 4 points.)

SECTION ONE

1. **B**
2. **D**
3. **A**
4. **A**
5. **D**
6. **A**
7. **B**
8. **B**
9. **C**
10. **B**
11. **A**
12. **A**
13. **D**
14. **D**
15. **B**

SECTION TWO

(Correct answers are in brackets.)

16. **A** (swims)
17. **C** (is raining)
18. **B** (are you)
19. **C** (don't)
20. **B** (seems)
21. **C** (hate)
22. **A** (usually arrives)
23. **B** (aren't OR are not)
24. **D** ('m always losing)
25. **B** (*delete* you)

UNIT 6 Past Simple: Affirmative Statements

CHECK POINT

1989
1999

CHART CHECK

two
-d or *-ed*

EXPRESS CHECK

was, were
came
saved

Matsuo Basho wrote more than 1,000 three-line poems or 'haiku.' He chose topics from nature, daily life and human emotions. He became one of Japan's most famous poets and his work established haiku as an important art form.

Matsuo Basho was born near Kyoto in 1644. His father wanted him to become a samurai (warrior). Instead, Matsuo moved to Edo (present-day Tokyo) and studied poetry. By 1681, he had many students and admirers.

Basho's home burnt down in 1682. Then, in 1683, his mother died. After these events, Basho felt restless. In 1684, he travelled on foot and on horseback all over Japan. Sometimes his friends joined him, and they wrote poetry together. Travel was difficult in the seventeenth century and Basho was often ill. He died in 1694, during a journey to Osaka. At that time he had 2,000 students.

2. wrote
3. were
4. led
5. became
6. left
7. saw
8. wore
9. wrote
10. addressed
11. appeared
12. happened
14. saw
15. bit
16. ate
17. drank
18. hopped

Today in class we read a poem by Robert Frost. I really ~~enjoy~~ enjoyed it. It was about a person who ~~choosed~~ chose between two roads in a forest. Before he made his decision, he ~~spents~~ spent a lot of time trying to decide which road to follow. Many people thought the person ~~were~~ was Frost. In the end, he ~~take~~ took the road that was less travelled on. He decided to be a poet. That decision ~~change~~ changed his life a lot.

Sometimes I feel a little like Frost. Two years ago I ~~decide~~ decided to come to this country. That ~~were~~ was the biggest decision of my life.

UNIT 7 Past Simple: Negative Statements and Questions

CHECK POINT

?, F, T

CHART CHECK 1

not
did not

CHART CHECK 2

was, were
did

EXPRESS CHECK

Did she have a navigator?
No, she didn't.

2. No
3. Yes
4. No
5. Yes
6. Yes
7. No

2. Where did she study? At Columbia University.
3. How long was she a social worker? For two years.
4. Where did her last flight leave from? From New Guinea.
5. How many books did she write? Three.
6. What was her nationality? American.
7. When did she disappear? In 1937.

3. Were
4. No . . . weren't
5. didn't want
6. Did . . . feel
7. Yes . . . did
8. didn't stop
9. Did . . . dream
10. didn't think
11. Were
12. No . . . wasn't
13. Was
14. No . . . wasn't

Hi! Did you ~~received~~ receive my last letter? I didn't ~~knew~~ know your new address so I sent it to your old one. When ~~you moved~~ did you move? Did your flatmate move with you? Right now I'm on board a plane flying to El Paso to visit Ana. Did you ~~met~~ meet her at the conference last year? I wanted to visit her in June but I ~~no had~~ didn't have the time. At first I was going to drive from Los Angeles but I decided to fly instead. This is only my third flight but I love flying! I ~~didnt~~ didn't know flying could be so much fun! Hope to hear from you.

UNIT 8 Used to

CHECK POINT

a habit he had in the past

CHART CHECK 1

T

CHART CHECK 2

did . . . use to

EXPRESS CHECK

used to
use to
say

In many ways, fashion used to be much simpler. Women didn't use to wear trousers to the office and men's clothes never used to come in bright colours. People also used to dress in special ways for different situations. They didn't use blue jeans as business clothes or wear tracksuits when they travelled. Today you can go to the opera and find some women in evening gowns while others are in blue jeans. Even buying jeans used to be easier – they only came in blue denim. I'm still not used to buying green jeans and wearing them to work!

2. used to have
3. used to dress
4. used to dance
5. used to wear
6. used to carry

(Answers may vary slightly.)

2. Trainers used to come in only two colours – black and white.
3. They didn't use to cost as much as they do these days. OR They used to cost less than they do these days.
4. Did people use to wear jeans fifty years ago?
5. Jeans and trainers didn't use to cost very much thirty years ago.
6. Did women use to wear jeans?

When I was younger, clothes didn't ~~used~~ use to be a problem. All the girls at my school used to ~~wore~~ wear the same uniform. I used to think that it took away from my freedom of choice. Now I can wear what I want but clothes cost

(continued on next page)

so much! Even blue jeans, today's 'uniform', used to be cheaper. My mum ~~uses~~ used to pay less than £30 for hers. I suppose they didn't ~~used~~ use to sell designer jeans back then. You know, I ~~was~~ used to be against school uniforms but now I'm not so sure!

UNIT 9 Past Continuous

CHECK POINT

what she was doing at the time of her accident

CHART CHECK 1

F

CHART CHECK 2

before the subject

EXPRESS CHECK

A: were . . . staying
B: was staying

2. F
3. T
4. ?
5. T
6. F

3. were sitting outside.
4. wasn't snowing.
5. were wearing sunglasses.
6. weren't wearing their gloves.
7. was serving drinks.
8. wasn't serving lunch.
9. wasn't smiling.
10. was using a mobile phone.

3. was recovering
4. wasn't performing
5. were . . . thinking
6. were waiting
7. wasn't thinking
8. were watching
9. Were . . . competing
10. was
11. was training
12. were . . . taking

This evening, Sheila and I ~~was~~ were looking at some photographs from my skiing trip with Fritz's family last year. By the end of the evening, we ^were laughing like crazy. That was my first experience on skis so the pictures were really embarrassing. In one shot, I was ~~came~~ coming down the slope on my back. In another one, my skis ~~was~~ were falling out of the ski lift while I was riding up the slope. Fritz ~~was taking~~ took that picture from the lift entrance. Good thing he ~~not~~ wasn't standing right under me! Where was I when Fritz was falling down the slope? Well, unfortunately I wasn't ~~carry~~ carrying my camera. That would have been a great picture! It was amazing how fast Fritz's girlfriend, Karyn, learned that weekend. She was doing jumps by the second day. By that time, I ~~spent~~ was spending a lot of time at the ski café.

UNIT 10 Past Continuous and Past Simple

CHECK POINT

2, 1

CHART CHECK

F, T

EXPRESS CHECK

When
was he driving

2. F
3. T
4. F
5. T

4. were waiting
5. noticed
6. Was . . . speeding
7. got
8. was
9. was going
10. reached
11. wasn't
12. were crossing
13. hit

14. Did . . . stop
15. saw
16. didn't
17. was talking
18. was driving
19. didn't stop
20. weren't paying
21. were crossing
22. Was . . . snowing
23. happened
24. was
25. wasn't
26. started
27. arrived

2. she was driving home, she listened to her car radio.
3. She pulled over to the side of the road . . . the visibility got very bad.
4. She heard about the accident . . . she was listening to the news.
5. She drove to the police station . . . it stopped snowing.
6. she was talking to the police, she was thinking about her article for the morning paper.

Yesterday, a man was talking on his mobile phone while he was ~~drive~~ *driving* his car. Maybe he ^*was* checking his diary while he was making his next appointment. He was certainly not concentrating on the road when the lights suddenly ~~was turning~~ *turned* red. The two men in the street ~~were trying~~ *tried* to jump out of the way when they saw him but it was too late. No one was badly hurt but that was just luck. Last year, the City Council ~~weren't passing~~ *didn't pass* the 'talking and driving' law. We need that law!

SelfTest 

(Total = 100 points. Each item = 4 points.)

SECTION ONE

1. **A**
2. **D**
3. **D**
4. **B**
5. **A**
6. **B**
7. **A**
8. **B**
9. **D**
10. **C**
11. **C**
12. **B**

SECTION TWO

(Correct answers are in parentheses.)

13. **C** (call)
14. **C** (was)
15. **A** (were)
16. **D** (were sleeping)
17. **B** (not)
18. **D** (dropped)
19. **A** (was)
20. **A** (did)
21. **D** (got)
22. **C** (got)
23. **B** (was driving)
24. **B** (*delete comma*)
25. **D** (saw)

 Present Perfect: *Since* and *For*

CHECK POINT

T

CHART CHECK 1

have + past participle
base form of verb + *-d* or *-ed*

CHART CHECK 2

a length of time

EXPRESS CHECK

driven: irregular
competed: regular
won: irregular
tried: regular

Martina Hingis picked up her first tennis racket at the age of two. (Since then), she <u>has become</u> one of the greatest tennis players in the world. Born in Slovakia, she <u>has lived</u> in Switzerland (for many years). She became the outdoor Swiss champion at the age of nine. (Since then) she <u>has won</u> many international competitions including Wimbledon, the US Open and the Australian Open.

For young stars like Martina, life has its difficulties. They are under constant pressure to win and they don't have time to just relax with friends. In fact, Martina <u>hasn't been to</u> school (since 1994) and she <u>has been</u> in the public spotlight (for years). But she seems to be handling her success well. (Since she turned professional), she <u>has played</u>

(continued on next page)

tennis all over the world and has earned millions of dollars. She sees her life as normal because tennis has been the most important thing to her (since she was a little girl).

3. 've been
4. for
5. For
6. has attended
7. hasn't done
8. Since
9. has taken
10. hasn't got
11. Since
12. has met
13. hasn't thought
14. 's known
15. since

2. How long has she lived in Switzerland?
(She has lived in Switzerland) for many years.
3. Has she won any competitions since the outdoor Swiss championship?
Yes, she has.
4. Has she been to school since 1994?
No, she hasn't.
5. How much money has she earned since her career began?
(She has earned) millions of dollars.
6. How long has tennis been important to her?
(Tennis has been important to her) since she was a little girl.

I ~~am~~ have been in Ms Clark's physical education class ~~since~~ for two months. I enjoy it a lot and have only ~~miss~~ missed two classes since the beginning of the term. I especially like tennis but since September we ~~don't play~~ haven't played because the weather ~~have~~ has been too cold. I also like volleyball and my team has ~~win~~ won two matches since we ~~have~~ started to compete with Lincoln School. I'm looking forward to the next match.

UNIT 12 Present Perfect: *Already, Just and Yet*

CHECK POINT

F

CHART CHECK 1

use *already* or *just*
use *not . . . yet*

CHART CHECK 2

T

EXPRESS CHECK

Have you had lunch yet?
Yes, I/we have. OR No, I/we haven't.

2. c
3. a
4. b
5. d

3. Has . . . disappeared already OR yet
4. Yes . . . has
5. have already developed
6. haven't been able . . . yet
7. Has . . . made . . . yet
8. No . . . haven't

3. Helmut has already baked the cake.
4. Gisela has already bought flowers.
5. Helmut hasn't put the turkey in the oven yet.
6. Gisela has already washed the windows.
7. Helmut has already mopped the floor.
8. Gisela has already hung the balloons.
9. Helmut hasn't washed the dishes yet.
10. Gisela hasn't wrapped the present yet.

4

I'm in a hurry. I haven't ~~went~~ been shopping ~~already~~ yet but I'll do it on the way home. Rita ~~have~~ has just had dinner and she's already had her bath. Have you ~~call~~ called Mr Jacobson yet? He's ~~called already~~ already called three times today. His daughter ~~has~~ hasn't had her flu shot yet.

Is it too late? See you later.

Present Perfect: Indefinite Past

CHECK POINT

now

CHART CHECK 1

T

CHART CHECK 2

before the past participle

CHART CHECK 3

F

EXPRESS CHECK

Have you ever watched 'The Simpsons'?
Yes, I/we have. OR No, I/we haven't.

2. F
3. T
4. F
5. F
6. F
7. T

2

2. 've had
3. 've . . . eaten
4. 've . . . been
5. have . . . wanted
6. 've . . . wanted
7. have . . . wanted
8. 've travelled
9. have . . . tried

2. I've never even been in a chat room.
3. How have you changed as an actor?
4. I've become more tolerant.
5. who has been your role model?
6. Charlie Chaplin has had great influence on me.
7. What has been your best moment on this show?
8. I've won the award.
9. what have you found most rewarding about the experience?
10. I've met some fantastic people.

I've never ~~laugh~~ laughed so much in my life! Did you see the blind date episode on 'Family'? Have you ~~never~~ ever seen anything so funny? I LOVE the show! It's the best show I have ever ~~saw~~ seen in my life. I 've really enjoyed it lately. By the way, have you ~~notice~~ noticed that Gary and Alison are beginning to get on? I think Gary ~~have~~ has started to fancy her. Last night, Alison ~~has~~ moved next door to Gary but he doesn't know yet! I can't wait to see what happens in the next episode. Does anyone know when Gary's book is coming out?

Present Perfect and Past Simple

CHECK POINT

T

CHART CHECK 1

the present perfect

CHART CHECK 2

have + past participle

EXPRESS CHECK

met, have been

Many modern marriages are finding interesting solutions to difficult problems. Joe and Maria, for example, have been married since 1995. After their wedding, the couple settled down in Ipswich, where Maria opened an accounting business. Then, in 1997, Joe lost his job. By that time, Maria's new business was booming, so they didn't consider moving. Joe never found a new job in Ipswich but in 1998, he got an exciting offer on the other side of the country – in Bristol. The couple have lived apart ever since. How have they handled this 'commuter marriage' up to now? Joe notes, 'It certainly hasn't been easy. We've been geographically separated for a few years but we've grown a lot closer emotionally. For that reason, it's been worth it.'

2. F
3. F
4. F
5. T

3. haven't stopped
4. has . . . been
5. slept
6. haven't had
7. saw
8. didn't do
9. didn't bother
10. Have . . . tried OR Did . . . try
11. Yes, I have. OR Yes, I did.
12. 've already drunk
13. drank

5. Did you start your business before your marriage?
6. No, I didn't.
7. How long have you owned your own business?
8. (I've owned my own business) since 1995/for *six* years.
9. When did you find your job in Bristol?
10. (I found my job in Bristol) in 1998/*three* years ago.
11. Has your commuter marriage been very difficult?
12. Yes, it has!

It's 8:00 P.M. It ~~was~~ 's been a hard week and it's not over yet! I still have to finish that report. I~~'ve started~~ started it last Monday but so far I've ~~wrote~~ written only five pages. And it's due next week! Work ~~was~~ has been so difficult lately. I've worked late every night this week. I'm tired and I ~~haven't got~~ didn't get much sleep last night. I miss Joe. I~~'ve seen~~ saw him last weekend but it seems like a long time ago.

Present Perfect Continuous

POINT

The girls are still collecting Beanie Babies.

CHART CHECK 1

T

CHART CHECK 2

been + base form + *-ing*

EXPRESS CHECK

A: has
B: For
A: been
B: collecting

2. b	4. b	6. b
3. a	5. a	

3. have been selling
4. has been living
5. has been sending
6. have been appearing
7. has . . . been attracting
8. has been buying
9. Have . . . been queueing
10. No, they haven't
11. haven't been asking

2. He hasn't been testing the rollerblades.
3. He hasn't been playing basketball.
4. He's been eating pizza.
5. He hasn't been drinking Coke.
6. He's been building a racing car.
7. He's been playing video games.
8. He hasn't been sending emails.

Thank you very much for the Pokémon cards. My friend and I have been ~~play~~ playing with them all day. So far, I ~~am~~ 've been winning. I really love Pokémon. My mum ^has been buying the toys for us because she thinks they're fun, too. All my friends ~~were~~ have been collecting the cards for months now. Tonya loves the computer game you sent, too. ~~She've~~ She's been asking me to play with her but I've been having too much fun with my cards.

I hope you are well. I've been ~~thought~~ thinking about you a lot. I hope you can come and visit us soon.

Love,

Patrick

UNIT 16 Present Perfect and Present Perfect Continuous

CHECK POINT

F, T

CHART CHECK

T

EXPRESS CHECK

A: eating
B: has . . . been
A: has OR 's
B: Has
A: No . . . hasn't

1

2. T
3. T
4. F
5. T
6. T

2

2. has published
3. have already died
4. has given
5. has spoken
6. have been waiting
7. has lived OR has been living
8. has worked OR has been working
9. has set up

3

2. 've . . . seen
3. has been living OR has lived
4. has experienced
5. has survived
6. have tested
7. have hunted
8. have saved
9. has been moving
10. has been eating
11. (has been) resting
12. has been raining OR has rained
13. have found OR have been finding

4

Elephants and their ancestors have been ~~live~~ living on this planet for 5 million years. Scientists have found their bones in many places, from Asia to North America. Present-day elephants ~~has~~ have also survived in different kinds of environments, including very dry areas in Niger, grasslands in East Africa and forests in West Africa.

Because of their great size and strength, elephants have always ~~fascinating~~ fascinated humans. Our fascination has almost caused African elephants to become extinct. Poachers (illegal hunters) have already ~~been killing~~ killed hundreds of thousands of elephants for the ivory of their tusks. After 1989, it became illegal to sell ivory. Since then, the elephant population has ~~been grown~~ grown OR been growing steadily. Recently, several countries have been protecting elephants in national parks and herds have ~~became~~ become larger and healthier.

UNIT 17 Past Perfect

CHECK POINT

Oprah decided on a career.

CHART CHECK 1

T

CHART CHECK 2

before the subject

EXPRESS CHECK

A: arrived
B: hadn't

1

2. T
3. T
4. F
5. F
6. T

2

2. hadn't yet got
3. had already got
4. hadn't yet got
5. hadn't yet got
6. had already been
7. hadn't yet built
8. had already starred

2. Had he reviewed . . .	No, he hadn't.
3. Had he reviewed . . .	Yes, he had.
4. Had he met . . .	No, he hadn't.
5. Had he recorded . . .	Yes, he had.
6. Had he worked out . . .	Yes, he had.

4 Oprah Winfrey is an amazing person! By the time she was twelve, she ~~has~~ had already decided on a career. Not long afterwards, she got her first radio job. Although she hadn't ~~have~~ had any experience, she became a news reporter. When she got her own TV chat show, she ~~has~~ had already acted in a major Hollywood film. By the late 1980s, 'Oprah Winfrey' had ~~became~~ become a household word. Then in 1994, she decided to improve the quality of chat show themes. She also made a personal change. She had always had a weight problem but in 1995, TV viewers saw a new Winfrey. She had ~~losed~~ lost almost 40 kilos as a result of dieting and working out. She had also ~~compete~~ competed in a marathon. She has really been an inspiration to many people.

UNIT 18 Past Perfect Continuous

CHECK POINT

T

CHART CHECK

been

EXPRESS CHECK

A: had . . . been practising
B: had been practising
A: Had . . . been practising
B: hadn't, had been practising

2. e
3. d
4. a
5. f
6. c

2. had been planning
3. had been laughing and joking
4. had been training
5. had been running
6. had been looking forward
7. had been waiting

3. had you been running
4. had you been going out
5. Had you been living
6. No, I OR we hadn't
7. Had you been expecting
8. No, I hadn't

I've just got back from the marathon! I'm tired but very happy. When I crossed the finishing line, I ~~have~~ had been running for four hours and twenty-five minutes. Jeremy was standing there. He had been ~~waited~~ waiting for me the whole time. We were both soaking wet – I, because I had been sweating; he, because it ~~has~~ had been raining just a little while before. I was so glad to see him. I had been ~~look~~ looking forward to this day for so long and hoping that I could finish the race in less than four and a half hours. When I got home, I called my parents. They had ^been watching the marathon on TV and had actually seen me cross the finishing line!

SelfTest

(Total = 100 points. Each item = 4 points.)

SECTION ONE

1. **C**
2. **D**
3. **C**
4. **A**
5. **B**
6. **C**
7. **B**
8. **B**
9. **C**
10. **A**
11. **B**
12. **A**
13. **D**
14. **A**

SECTION TWO

(Correct answers are in brackets.)

15. **C** (*delete* has)
16. **D** (yet)
17. **C** (seemed)
18. **A** ('ve been reading)
19. **A** (Have)
20. **D** (for)
21. **D** (taken)
22. **B** (has already been in business OR for fifty years already)
23. **C** (drink)
24. **C** (*delete* 've)
25. **C** (had)

UNIT 19 Future: *Be going to* and *Will*

CHECK POINT

The man is going to fall into the hole.

CHART CHECK 1

three

CHART CHECK 2

F

CHART CHECK 3

T

EXPRESS CHECK

It's going to rain.
I'll get an umbrella.

1 **Items ticked:** 2, 4, 5

2

2. He's going to go on a journey.
3. He's not going to drive. OR He isn't going to drive.
4. He's going to give a speech.
5. He's going to answer the phone.
6. He's not going to watch TV. OR He isn't going to watch TV.

3

3. 'll . . . use
4. Will . . . get
5. won't
6. will have
7. 'll repair
8. will . . . be
9. will have
10. will look
11. 'll open
12. 'll adjust
13. 'll . . . control
14. Will . . . prevent
15. will
16. will . . . cost
17. won't be

4

I'm sorry that we ~~will no~~ won't be able to get together in London. Martha will ~~misses~~ miss you, too. Perhaps we can get together sometime next month. Martha and I ~~am~~ are going to be in Birmingham until 15 July. After that, we are going ^to visit our son in Brighton. His wife is pregnant and ~~will~~ is going to have a baby in July. It's hard to believe that we ^are OR 're going to be grandparents!

How exciting that you ^are OR 're going to talk at the conference! I'm sure it ~~wills~~ will be great. I've got to run now. The sky is getting really dark and there~~'ll be~~ 's going to be a storm. I want to get out of this office before then. More later. Greg

UNIT 20 Future: Contrast

CHECK POINT

T, F

CHART CHECK

T, F

EXPRESS CHECK

I'm leaving in five minutes.
Are you going to the conference in May?

1

RUSS: Ellen! It's nice to see you. Are you presenting a paper this week?
GREEN: Hi, David. Yes. In fact, my talk starts at two o'clock.
RUSS: Oh, maybe I'll come. What are you going to talk about? Robots?
GREEN: Yes. I'm dealing with personal robots for household work.

(continued on next page)

RUSS: I'd like one of those! Where's your son, by the way? Is he here with you?

GREEN: No. Tony stays in Norfolk with his grandparents in the summer. I'm going to visit him after the conference. So, what are you working on these days?

RUSS: I'm still with the Mars Association. In fact, we're holding a news conference next month about the Mars shuttle launch.

GREEN: That's exciting. Maybe I'll see you there.

RUSS: Great. The conference begins at noon on the tenth.

2. it's going to rain
3. I'll see
4. I'll call
5. I'm going
6. I'm posting
7. I'm giving
8. will you be, lands, I'll see

1. 'll wait
2. 's going to rain, 'll check OR 'm going to check
3. **A:** do . . . board OR will . . . board OR are . . . going to board
   B: 're flying
4. 'll carry
5. **A:** do . . . land OR are . . . going to land OR will . . . land OR are . . . landing
   B: 're going to be OR 'll be
6. **A:** 're going to get OR get OR 're getting OR 'll get
   B: 'm having OR 'm going to have
7. 're going to start OR 'll start OR start

'Good evening, ladies and gentlemen. This ~~will be~~ is your captain speaking. We ~~be~~ are going to leave the Earth's field of gravity in about fifteen minutes. At that time, you ~~are~~ will be able to unbuckle your seat belts and float around the cabin. Host robots ^are going to OR will take orders for dinner soon. After these storm clouds, we ~~are having~~ 're going to have OR 'll have a smooth trip. The shuttle arrives on Mars tomorrow at 9:00. Tonight's temperature on the planet is a mild minus 20 degrees Celsius. By tomorrow morning the temperature ~~is~~ will be 18 degrees but it ~~is feeling~~ 's going to feel OR 'll feel more like 28 degrees. Enjoy your flight.'

UNIT 21 Future Time Clauses

CHECK POINT

The child is planning her future.

CHART CHECK

T, F

EXPRESS CHECK

What will she be when she grows up?
I think she'll be a scientist.

2. T
3. F
4. T
5. F
6. T

2. They are going to move to a larger house . . . Jeff gets a pay rise.
3. . . . they move to a larger house, they're going to have a baby.
4. Sarah will get a part-time job . . . they have their first child.
5. . . . Sarah goes back to work full-time, their child will be two.
6. Sarah will work full-time . . . Jeff goes to university OR Jeff will go to university . . . Sarah works full-time.
7. Jeff will find another job . . . he graduates.

I.
graduate

II.
1. get, 'll have OR 'm going to have
2. 've got, 'll buy OR 'm going to buy
3. 'll feel OR 'm going to feel, 've got

III.
1. get up, 'll buy OR 'm going to buy
2. speak, 'll ask OR 'm going to ask
3. 'll look OR 'm going to look, go
4. go, 'll improve OR 'm going to improve

4 Tomorrow is my first dance recital! By the time I ~~will~~ write my next diary entry, it will already be over! As soon as we finish the performance, there ~~are~~ is going to be a big party for us. Reporters will be there~~,~~ when we enter the room. While we ~~will~~ celebrate, the press will interview members of the dance group. As soon as I get up on Sunday morning, I'll buy the paper and read the interviews. We're going to perform this show for two weeks. As soon as it's finished, we ~~learned~~ 're going to learn OR 'll learn a new programme. I'm so excited. Ever since I was little, I've wanted to be a ballet dancer.

UNIT 22 Future Continuous

CHECK POINT

Before 12:00

CHART CHECK

T

EXPRESS CHECK

Will you be working tomorrow?
Yes, I will. OR No, I won't.
What will you be doing?
(Answers will vary.)

1 Today we find most robots working in factories around the world. But what will the robots of the future be doing? One designer predicts that in just a few years, small intelligent robots will be dealing with all the household chores. This is going to make life a lot easier. While one robot is cooking dinner, another one will be vacuuming the floor. But what about outside the home? Will robots be playing football or fighting wars? Scientists aren't sure. What is certain, however, is that robots will be playing a more and more significant role in our lives.

2
1. c. 'll be going
2. a. will . . . be leaving
   b. won't be getting
3. a. will . . . be coming
   b. 'll be taking
   c. Will . . . be having
   d. No, we won't.
4. a. 'll be visiting
   b. won't be buying

3
2. will be dusting OR is going to be dusting . . . is vacuuming OR vacuums the sitting room.
3. will be repainting OR is going to be repainting . . . is doing OR does the laundry.
4. is making OR makes . . . will be recycling OR is going to be recycling the rubbish.
5. will be giving OR is going to be giving Mr Gee . . . is shopping OR shops for food.
6. will be cooking OR is going to be cooking . . . is helping OR helps Tony with homework.
7. is playing OR plays . . . will be taking OR is going to be taking the dog for a walk.

4 In the future, robots will be ~~perform~~ performing more and more tasks for humans. This will ~~be having~~ have both positive and negative effects. On the one hand, while robots ~~will be doing~~ are doing OR do the boring and dangerous jobs, humans will be devoting more time to interesting pursuits. In this respect, robots will be making life a lot easier for humans. On the other hand, the widespread use of robots will be creating a lot of future unemployment. There is a risk that robots will be taking on jobs that humans need in order to earn a living. And some

(continued on next page)

robots could even become dangerous.

I'm afraid that in the not-too-distant future, robots will be operating nuclear power stations! And before too long, robots will ~~to~~ be fighting in wars. Although, on second thoughts, that will be better than humans killing each other!

UNIT 23 Future Perfect and Future Perfect Continuous

CHECK POINT

He hasn't been saving for three years yet.

CHART CHECK 1

F

CHART CHECK 2

T

EXPRESS CHECK

driving, driven

2. F
3. T
4. F
5. F
6. T

3. won't have graduated
4. will have studied OR will have been studying
5. won't have bought
6. 'll have been driving
7. won't have opened
8. 'll have been saving
9. will have accomplished

3. graduate
4. 'll have been thinking
5. is born
6. won't have graduated
7. will have already finished
8. celebrate
9. won't have started
10. 'll have already been getting
11. open
12. 'll have already become

By August I'll ~~be~~ [have been] a secretary for ten years. And I'll ~~earn~~ [have earned OR have been earning] almost the same salary for three years! That's why I've made a New Year's resolution to go back to college this year. First, I'm going to write for college magazines and start saving for tuition. By March, I'll have ~~work~~ [worked] out how much tuition will cost. Then I'll start applying. By summer, I ~~had~~ ['ll have] received acceptance letters. In August, I'll talk to my boss about working part-time and going to college part-time. By that time, I'll have ~~saved already~~ [already saved] enough to pay for a term's tuition. By next New Year's Day, I'll have been ~~study~~ [studying] for a whole term!

SelfTest IV

(Total = 100 points. Each item = 4 points.)

SECTION ONE

1. **C**
2. **A**
3. **A**
4. **B**
5. **B**
6. **B**
7. **A**
8. **B**
9. **C**
10. **A**
11. **B**
12. **C**
13. **C**
14. **B**

SECTION TWO

(Correct answers are in brackets.)

15. **B** (be)
16. **D** (will go)
17. **D** (finish)
18. **C** (driving)
19. **A** (be travelling)
20. **A** (will have finished OR will finish)
21. **B** (work OR be working)
22. **C** (already OR *delete* yet)
23. **A** (will you)
24. **D** (is)
25. **B** (have)

Wh- Questions: Subject and Predicate

CHECK POINT

the events on the night of 12 May
the names of people who saw the witness

CHART CHECK 1

T

CHART CHECK 2

F, T

EXPRESS CHECK

What happened last night?
What did you do next?

2. a
3. d
4. b
5. c
6. e

2. How did you get home?
3. Who gave you a lift?
4. What happened next?
5. Who(m) did you see?
6. Who is Deborah Collins?
7. What did you do?
8. How many people called you?

3. What time (OR When) does the court session begin?
4. How many witnesses testified?
5. Why did the jury find Adams guilty?
6. What happened?
7. How long (OR How many weeks) did the trial last?
8. Who spoke to the jury?
9. How much did Adams pay his barrister?
10. Who(m) did the prosecution question?

What time ^did^ the suspect return home?

Who ~~did see~~ saw him? Were there any witnesses?

~~Whom~~ Who was at home?

Why did he call A. Smith?

What ~~did happen~~ happened next?

Where ~~he did~~ did he go?

How much money ~~he took~~ did he take with him?

Question Tags

CHECK POINT

The man is commenting on the weather.

CHART CHECK

F, T, T

EXPRESS CHECK

You're an actor, aren't you?

KAY: Hi, Tom. It's a nice day, <u>isn't it?</u>
TOM: It certainly is. Not a cloud in the sky. How are you doing?
KAY: Fine, thanks. You don't know of any flats to rent, <u>do you?</u> My son is looking for one.
TOM: Is he? I thought he was staying with you.
KAY: Well, he really wants a place of his own. Do you know of anything?
TOM: As a matter of fact, I do. You know the Simpsons, <u>don't you?</u> Well, I've just found out that they're moving to Cheltenham next month.
KAY: They are? What kind of flat have they got?
TOM: It's a one-bedroom flat.
KAY: It's not furnished, <u>is it?</u>
TOM: No. Why? He doesn't need a furnished flat, <u>does he?</u>
KAY: Well, he hasn't got any furniture. But I suppose he can always buy some, <u>can't he?</u>
TOM: Why don't you give your son my number and I'll give him some more information?
KAY: Will you? Thanks, Tom.

2

2. j
3. h
4. f
5. b
6. g
7. a
8. c
9. e
10. d

3

2. did you
3. doesn't it
4. haven't they
5. aren't you
6. haven't you
7. isn't it

BEN: It's been a long time, Joe, ~~haven't~~ hasn't it?

JOE: That depends on what you mean by a long time, doesn't ~~that~~ it?

(continued on next page)

Ben: What are you doing round here, anyway? It's dangerous.

Joe: I can take care of myself. I'm still alive, ~~amn't~~ aren't I?

Ben: Yes, but you're still wanted by the police, ~~are~~ aren't you?

Joe: Look, I need a place to stay. You've got a place, haven't you? Just for one night.

Ben: I have to think of my wife and kids. You can find somewhere else, ~~can~~ can't you?

Joe: No. You've got to help me!

Ben:: I've already helped you enough. I went to prison for you, ~~haven't~~ didn't I?

Joe: Yeah, OK, Ben. You remember what happened last June, ~~do~~ don't* you?

Ben: OK, OK. I can make a phone call.

*OR: You ^don't remember what happened last June, do you?

Additions with *So, Too, Neither* and *Not either*

CHECK POINT

The men like the same things.

CHART CHECK

T, F, T

EXPRESS CHECK

and neither is Mark
and so does Gerald

2. F	4. T	6. T	8. T
3. T	5. F	7. F	9. T

2

2. too	4. did	6. So
3. neither	5. either	7. So

3

2. did I	4. do, too	6. do I	8. too
3. can I	5. do I	7. do I	

4 My brother is just a year older than I am. We have a lot of things in common.

First of all, we look alike. I am 1.8 m and so ~~he is~~ is he. I have straight black hair and dark brown eyes and so does he. We share many of the same interests, too. I love playing football and he ^does too. Both of us swim every day but I can't dive, and ~~either~~ neither can he.

Sometimes being so similar has its problems. For example, last night I wanted the last piece of chocolate cake and so ~~does~~ did he. Often I won't feel like doing the washing up and neither ~~won't~~ will he. Worst of all, sometimes I'm interested in a particular girl and so ~~he is~~ is he. However, most of the time I feel our similarities are really nice. So does my brother.

SelfTest

(Total = 100 points. Each item = 4 points.)

SECTION ONE

1. **A**	4. **A**	7. **D**	10. **A**
2. **C**	5. **D**	8. **D**	11. **B**
3. **A**	6. **D**	9. **B**	12. **A**

SECTION TWO

(Correct answers are in brackets.)

13. **C** (isn't)
14. **C** (didn't)
15. **D** (has his brother)
16. **D** (have)
17. **A** (did you work OR were you working)
18. **D** (it)
19. **D** (?)
20. **D** (I am, too OR so am I)
21. **D** (they)
22. **C** (aren't)
23. **D** (he)
24. **C** (go)
25. **A** (Why did you)

UNIT 27 Ability: *Can, Could, Be able to*

CHECK POINT

F

CHART CHECK 1

T

CHART CHECK 2

be

CHART CHECK 3

a form of *be*

EXPRESS CHECK

A: Is . . . to
B: is . . . can

1 An amazing number of teenagers have managed to set up highly successful internet businesses. Take John Davidson, for example. John could surf the net by the time he was six and by the age of eight, he could design web pages of his own. It wasn't long before he was able to persuade the bank to lend him enough money to start up his very own business. At the age of sixteen, he managed to persuade his parents to allow him to leave school, and his first business, 'Webmasters', was soon up and running.
Another teenager, Jim Leicester, very quickly realised he could make money doing what he enjoyed most: playing computer games. In 1999, he was able to sell five games he'd developed to a famous software company. Now Jim can earn up to £1000 a week by selling his programs.
Katy Fischer, an enterprising 18-year-old from Manchester, was also able to break into the dotcom world. Although she says she can't understand why she's been so successful, her parents certainly can. 'Katy was determined to prove she could start a business when she was just fourteen,' says her father, 'and through hard work, she's managed to do just that.'

2. John
3. Katy
4. John

2

1. can, 'll be able to
2. hasn't been able to, can
3. can't, 'll be able to
4. haven't been able to, can't, can't, 'll be able to

3

2. Were . . . able to communicate
3. can help
4. couldn't follow
5. couldn't decide
6. can manage
7. 'll be able to organise
8. be able to speak

4 Today in my 'Will B. Happy' teamwork course, I learnt about work styles – 'Drivers' and 'Enthusiasts'. I'm a Driver so I can make decisions but I'm not able ^to listen to other people's ideas. The Enthusiast in our group can ~~communicates~~ communicate well but you can't depend on her. Now I understand what was happening in my business class last year, when I couldn't ~~got~~ get on with my team. I thought that they all talked too much and ~~didn't~~ weren't able to work efficiently. I ~~could~~ was able to get an A for the course but it was hard. I can do a lot more on my own but some jobs are too big for that. Our instructor says that soon the Drivers will ^be able to listen and the Enthusiast ~~could~~ will be able to be more dependable.

UNIT 28 Permission: *May, Can, Could, Do you mind if . . .?*

CHECK POINT

The student is asking the teacher to allow him to take the test tomorrow.

CHART CHECK 1

could

CHART CHECK 2

F, T

EXPRESS CHECK

A: helps
B: Not at all, help

1

2. f	4. c	6. b
3. e	5. a	

3. Do you mind if he stays
4. I do (mind)
5. May I use
6. you may not OR you can't
7. you can't start
8. do you mind if I borrow
9. Not at all OR No, I don't OR Go ahead
10. you may open
11. Can I come
12. you can't OR I'm sorry

(Answers may vary slightly.)

2. Could I use your phone?
3. May I (OR we) park here?
4. Could we move up a few rows?
5. Can we (OR he) record (OR tape) the concert?
6. Do you mind if I (OR we) go home now (OR leave)?

2. B (can't)
3. B (swap)
4. B (can)
5. C (have)
6. A (may not OR can't)
7. D (plays)
8. A (No, I don't OR Not at all)
9. C (we)
10. A (Yes, of course)

Requests: *Will, Can, Would, Could, Would you mind . . .?*

 **POINT**

asking someone to do something

CHART CHECK 1

T

CHART CHECK 2

OK

EXPRESS CHECK

A: Would
B: No, not
A: would OR could
B: can't

1. **MARCIA:** Hi. You must be the new office assistant. I'm Marcia Jones. Let me know if you need anything.
   LORNA: Thanks, Marcia. Could you show me where the photocopier is?
   MARCIA: Certainly. It's over here.
2. **LORNA:** Marcia, would you show me how to use the fax machine?
   MARCIA: Yes, sure. Just put your fax in here and dial the number.
3. **MARCIA:** I'm going to lunch. Would you like to come?
   LORNA: Thanks, but I can't just now. I'm really busy.
   MARCIA: Do you want a sandwich from the coffee shop?
   LORNA: That would be great. Can you get me a tuna sandwich and a coffee, please?
   MARCIA: No problem. Will you answer my phone until I get back?
   LORNA: Of course.
4. **MARCIA:** Lorna, would you mind making some tea?
   LORNA: I'm sorry, but I can't do it now. I've got to finish this letter by 2:00.

2. a
3. a
4. b
5. a
6. b

2. you file these reports, please?
3. turning on the lights, please?
4. you buy some cereal, please?
5. you call back later, please?
6. you shut the door OR you mind shutting the door, please?

The meetings are going well but they have been extended by a day. Please ~~you could~~ could you call Doug Rogers to try to reschedule our sales meeting?

~~**Not at all**~~ Certainly OR Of course**. I'll do it straightaway.**

We'll need three extra copies of the monthly sales report. Would you ask Ann to see to that?

~~**Yes, I would**~~ Certainly OR Of course OR No problem**. (Ann—Could you do this?)**

I hate to ask but would you mind ~~to work~~ working on Saturday? We'll need the extra time to go over the new information I've got.

Sorry, but I ~~couldn't~~ can't. My in-laws are coming to stay. But Rob Dixon says he can come in to help out.

One last thing. I was going to pick up those new business cards but I won't be back in time. Would you mind doing that for me?

~~Yes, I would.~~ Not at all OR I'd be glad to. I'll stop at the printer's during my lunch break.

Advice: *Should, Ought to, Had better*

CHECK POINT

The interviewer is suggesting a type of job for the applicant.

CHART CHECK 1

T

CHART CHECK 2

should

EXPRESS CHECK

A: Should
B: No . . . shouldn't

 **Items checked:** 1, 5, 6

2. shouldn't
3. should
4. shouldn't
5. should
6. 'd better not
7. 'd better

2. You should (OR You ought to) look neat
3. What time should I arrive?
4. you shouldn't (OR you'd better not) arrive after 7:15
5. Should I take a gift?
6. You shouldn't (OR You'd better not) buy an expensive gift
7. What should I buy?
8. you should (OR ought to) get some flowers

 We are so happy to hear about your new job. Congratulations! Just remember – you shouldn't ~~to~~ work too hard. The most important thing just now is your studies. Maybe you ~~better~~ ought to work only two days a week instead of three. Also, we think you'd better ask your boss for time off during the exams. That way you'll have plenty of time to study. You ~~would~~ 'd better give this a lot of careful thought, OK? Please take good care of yourself. You'd ~~not better~~ better not start skipping meals and you definitely shouldn't ~~worked~~ work at night. At your age, you ~~shall~~ should always get plenty of sleep. Do you need anything from home? Should we send any of your books? Let us know.

Suggestions: *Could, Why don't?, Why not?, Let's, Shall we?, How about?*

 **POINT**

F

CHART CHECK 1

does not change for different subjects

CHART CHECK 2

F

EXPRESS CHECK

Let's take the train.
Maybe we could take the train.
Why not take the train?
How about the train?

1

EMILY: Why don't we go to the races? I hear they're really exciting.
MEGAN: I'd like to but I need to go shopping.
EMILY: Then let's go to the Temple Street Market tonight. We might even see some Chinese opera in the street while we're there.
MEGAN: That sounds like fun. If we do that, why not go to the races this afternoon?
EMILY: OK, but let's get something to eat first in one of those floating restaurants.
MEGAN: I don't think we'll have time. Maybe we could do that tomorrow. Shall we get *dim sum* at the Kau Kee Restaurant next door? Then we could take the Star Ferry to Hong Kong Island and the racecourse.
EMILY: Sounds good. For tomorrow, why not take one of those small boats – *kaido* – to Lantau Island? When we come back, we could have dinner at the Jumbo Palace.
MEGAN: Let's do that. It's a bit expensive but at least it floats!

2

2. Shall we
3. Why don't we
4. Maybe we could
5. Let's
6. Let's not

2. going to the beach?
3. buy another one.
4. we take a trip together?
5. try that new seafood place.

4

Emily 3:00

I'm going shopping. I'll be back at 5:00. Let's ~~eating~~ eat at 7:00. OK?

Megan

Megan 4:00

7:00 for dinner is fine.

Shall we ~~going~~ go to see a film afterwards?

See you later.

E.

Emily 5:00

I'm going to be too tired for a film. Maybe we could just ~~hanging~~ hang around the hostel after dinner. Let's talk about it later.

I'm going to have a nap.

M.

M— 6:00

Let's not eat at the same restaurant tonight.

Why don't we ~~trying~~ try a new place?

How about Broadway Seafood?

I'll meet you downstairs at 7:00.

E.

UNIT 32 Preferences: *Prefer, Would prefer, Would rather*

CHECK POINT

Teenagers like watching TV better than they like doing other things.

CHART CHECK 1

would prefer ('d prefer)

CHART CHECK 2

the gerund or the infinitive

EXPRESS CHECK

read, than, shopping

2. F
3. F
4. F
5. F
6. T
7. T

2. I'd rather not cook
3. Would . . . rather go
4. I'd rather not
5. I'd rather have
6. I'd rather not
7. I'd rather see

3

1. **A:** prefer . . . to
2. **A:** 'd rather . . . than
   B: prefer OR 'd prefer
3. **B:** 'd prefer
4. **A:** prefer . . . to
5. **B:** 'd rather . . . than
6. **A:** do . . . prefer . . .
   B: prefer . . . to

4

For my research, I interviewed fifty men and women. There was no difference in men's and women's TV preferences. I found that everyone prefers watching TV ~~than~~ to going to the cinema. Men and women both enjoy news programmes and documentaries. However, men would rather ~~watching~~ watch adventure programmes and science fiction, while women prefer soap operas. Men also like to watch all kinds of sport but women would rather see game shows ~~to~~ than sports. Reading preferences differ, too. Men prefer ~~to reading~~ to read OR reading newspapers, while women would rather read magazines and books. When men read books, they prefer ~~read~~ to read OR reading non-fiction and adventure stories. Women ~~are preferring~~ prefer novels.

SelfTest

(Total = 100 points. Each item = 4 points.)

SECTION ONE

1. **A**
2. **B**
3. **D**
4. **D**
5. **C**
6. **C**
7. **B**
8. **B**
9. **A**
10. **C**
11. **D**
12. **A**
13. **B**
14. **D**

SECTION TWO

(Correct answers are in brackets.)

15. **D** (able to dive)
16. **D** (?)
17. **C** (better not)
18. **A** (Would)
19. **B** (borrow)
20. **D** (ask)
21. **D** (give)
22. **C** (to)
23. **C** (was able to)
24. **C** (*delete* we)
25. **D** (than)

Necessity: *Have (got) to* and *Must*

CHECK POINT

a requirement

CHART CHECK 1

F

CHART CHECK 2

a form of *do*

EXPRESS CHECK

A: does . . . have to
B: must

DMV: Department of Motor Vehicles. May I help you?
BEN: I'm moving to the States soon. Will I have to get an American licence when I move?
DMV: Yes, you will. Residents must have an American licence.
BEN: When will I have to get my licence?
DMV: You have to replace your old licence ten days after you become a resident. So come in and apply for your licence when you get here.
BEN: Do I have to take any tests to exchange my British licence for an American one?
DMV: Since you already have a British licence, you won't have to take the full driving test. You will only have to take the written test.
BEN: How about an eye test?
DMV: Oh, everyone has got to take an eye test.
BEN: OK. Thanks a lot. You've been very helpful.

2. have to (OR have got to) pick up
3. Do . . . have to change
4. I don't
5. didn't have to do
6. have to (OR have got to) take
7. Does . . . have to pack
8. he doesn't
9. 's got to (OR has to) help
10. 've had to call

2. must not turn
3. must drive
4. must not drive
5. must ride
6. must not walk

How are you doing? We've been here about six weeks. It's strange living in the United States. There's no public transport, so you've ~~get~~ got to drive everywhere. I had to ~~signs~~ sign up for driving lessons so I can get my licence by the summer. It's the law here that everyone ~~musts~~ must wear a seat belt. I used to hate wearing a seat belt but with the traffic here, I have changed my mind. There are a lot of motorways and you've ~~got~~ got to know how to change lanes with a lot of fast traffic. Even my mum ~~have~~ has had to get used to it. Dad works from home, so he hasn't ~~has~~ had to do a lot of driving.

Have you beaten those computer games yet? 've I'm having a lot of trouble with 'Doom'. You got to write to me and tell me how to get past the fifth level!

UNIT 34 Choice: *Don't have to* No Choice: *Must not* and *Can't*

CHECK POINT

stop to ask for directions

CHART CHECK 1

do

CHART CHECK 2

F

EXPRESS CHECK

He doesn't have to stop here.
You must not drive too fast.

New drivers are usually excited about their new freedom: 'My mum doesn't have to drive me everywhere any more! I don't have to ask my friends for lifts to school!' When you haven't got your own car yet, any price seems worth paying. But once you buy a car, you can't forget your car payments and insurance premiums or you won't be a driver for very long. You can't leave petrol and servicing out of the budget, either. Car sharing offers an alternative to these problems, however. Members of car-sharing groups have a car when they need one for either short trips or holidays but they don't have the high expenses of ownership. They pay very little to use a shared car and they don't have to worry about servicing the car or paying the insurance. Fees for short trips are only about £5.00 an hour plus 50p per mile. Groups do not have strict requirements, either. Members must not have bad driving records or poor credit and they must not return the cars in bad condition or they will pay extra.

2

2. can't yell
3. can't turn
4. can't park
5. don't have to worry
6. don't have to get
7. haven't had to buy
8. can't bring
9. don't have to listen

2. don't have to bring
3. must not play
4. must not dive
5. don't have to be
6. don't have to leave

We got to the hotel late this evening because we got lost. But we were lucky – they kept our room so we ~~must not~~ didn't have to find another hotel.

Jimmy is really happy because he ~~don't~~ doesn't have to go to bed until after 10:00, when the swimming pool closes. We ~~mustn't~~ don't have to leave until 11:00 tomorrow (checkout time) so we can stay up later. Plymouth is only four hours away so we won't ~~had~~ have to drive the whole day tomorrow. It's going to be exciting. My parents say we absolutely must not ~~to~~ go to the beach by ourselves because there are sharks there. I'd love to see a shark (from a safe distance). I'll send a postcard of one.

UNIT 35 Expectations: *Be supposed to*

CHECK POINT

something he has forgotten to do

CHART CHECK

T

EXPRESS CHECK

A: were
B: was

It Wasn't Supposed to Be a Big Wedding

19 July – The Stricklands wanted a quiet wedding – that's why they went to the Isle of Skye, an island off the coast of Scotland. The island is quite small so the Stricklands packed their bikes for the ferry trip. The weather was supposed to be lovely and they had asked the Registrar to marry them on a hill overlooking the ocean.

'When we got there, we found a crowd of cyclists admiring the view,' laughed Beth.

When Bill kissed his bride, the cyclists burst into loud applause and rang their bicycle bells. 'We weren't supposed to have fifty wedding guests but we love cycling and we're not sorry,' Bill said.

While packing the next day, Beth left her wedding bouquet at the hotel. Minutes before the ferry was supposed to leave, Bill jumped on his bike, got the flowers and made it back to the ferry on time. 'Cyclists are supposed to stay fast and fit,' he said.

2. F **3.** F **4.** T **5.** T

2. a. Were . . . supposed to do
b. No, they weren't
c. were supposed to deliver
3. a. is supposed to start
b. are . . . supposed to stand
4. a. aren't (OR 're not) supposed to be
b. aren't (OR 're not) supposed to see
5. a. 'm supposed to wear
b. 's supposed to rain
6. a. 's supposed to be

I'm so sorry – I know I ~~am~~ was supposed to let you know about my plans to visit.

I've been awfully busy. My friend Nessie is getting married soon and she's asked me to be her chief bridesmaid. She and Gary want a big wedding. They're supposed to have about two hundred guests. I've got a lot of responsibilities. I ~~will be~~ am supposed to give Nessie a hen party before the wedding (that's a party where everyone brings presents for the bride). I am also ~~suppose~~ supposed to help her choose the bridesmaids' dresses. The best man's name is Jim. He's going to help Gary get ready. I haven't met him yet but he's ~~supposes~~ supposed to be very nice.

I'd better say goodbye now. I ^was supposed to be at the rehearsal five minutes ago.

P.S. About my visit – I'm ~~supposing~~ supposed to get some time off in July. Would that be convenient?

Future Possibility: *May, Might, Could*

POINT

F

CHART CHECK 1

T

CHART CHECK 2

in answers

EXPRESS CHECK

B: might
A: might
B: might not

ALICE: I've just heard that it <u>may snow</u> today. Are you going to drive to work?
BILL: No. I'll take the 7:30 train instead.
ALICE: I'll take the train with you. I've got some work to do in the library.
BILL: Great. Why don't you miss your afternoon class and have lunch with me, too?
ALICE: Oh, I <u>couldn't do</u> that. But let's meet at the station at 6:00 and go home together, OK?
BILL: I <u>might have to work</u> until 8:00 tonight. I'll call you and let you know.

1. Certain
2. Impossible
3. Possible

2. could
3. might
4. may not
5. 'm going to
6. may
7. might

3

3. She's going to a meeting with Mrs Humphrey at 11:00.
4. She may (OR might) have coffee with Sue after lectures.
5. She's going to go to work at 1:00.
6. She may (OR might) go shopping after work.
7. She may (OR might) take the 7:00 train.
8. She's going to pick up a pizza.

Every few years, the ocean near Peru becomes warmer. Called El Niño, this variation in temperature ~~maybe~~ may cause weather changes all over the world. The west coasts of North and South America might ~~to~~ have heavy rains. On the other side of the Pacific, New Guinea might ~~becomes~~ become very dry. Northern areas could have warmer, wetter winters and southern areas could become much colder. These weather changes affect plants and animals. Some fish ~~mayn't~~ may not survive in warmer waters. Droughts could ~~causing~~ cause crops to die and food may get very expensive. El Niño may happen every two years or it ~~could~~ may OR might not come for seven years. Will El Niños get worse in the future? They could ~~be~~ do. Pollution holds heat in the air and it ~~will~~ may OR might OR could increase the effects of El Niño but no one is sure yet.

Deduction: *May, Might, Could, Must, Have (got) to, Can't*

POINT

guessing

CHART CHECK 1

T

CHART CHECK 2

F

EXPRESS CHECK

A: could
B: can't, might

2. d
3. e
4. b
5. g
6. a
7. c

2. must
3. 's got to
4. could
5. Could
6. might be
7. can't
8. might not
9. may

2. I might (OR could) be
3. It could (OR might OR may) be the cat
4. You must eat a lot
5. Could it be
6. it can't (OR couldn't) be
7. It must come from your own pipe.
8. There can't (OR couldn't) be any other explanation.
9. there could (OR might OR may) be

The main character, Molly Smith, is a university professor. She is trying to find her dead grandparents' first home in Scotland. It may ~~being~~ be in a nearby town. The villagers there seem scared. They could ~~be~~ have a secret or they ~~must~~ might OR may OR could just hate strangers. Molly has some old letters that might lead her to the place. They are in Gaelic but one of her students ~~mights~~ might translate them for her. They ~~got to~~ have to/have got to be important because the author mentions them at the beginning of the novel. The letter must contain family secrets. Who is the bad guy? It couldn't be the student because he wants to help. It might ~~to~~ be the newspaper editor in the town.

UNIT 38 Expressing Regret about the Past

CHECK POINT

regrets things in his past

CHART CHECK 1

F

CHART CHECK 2

T

CHART CHECK 3

ought to have

EXPRESS CHECK

A: have
B: should have

2. T
3. T
4. F
5. T
6. T

2. shouldn't have done
3. should have studied
4. could have done
5. ought to have gone
6. shouldn't have stayed
7. could have prevented
8. might . . . have called
9. Should . . . have contacted
10. shouldn't have
11. could have saved

2. I shouldn't have eaten all the chocolate.
3. She might have called.
4. He could have offered to lend me some (money).
5. I shouldn't have jogged five miles yesterday.
6. They shouldn't have charged me (for the plastic bags).
7. I ought to have invited Cynthia (to the party).
8. He might have sent me a card.

About a week ago, Jennifer was late for work again and Doug, our boss, told me he wanted to get rid of her. I was really upset. Of course, Jennifer shouldn't ~~had~~ have been late so often but he might ~~has~~ have talked to her about the problem before he decided to let her go. Then he told me to make her job difficult for her so that she would resign. I just pretended I hadn't heard him. What a mistake! I ought ^to have confronted him right away. Or I could at least have warned Jennifer. Anyway, Jennifer is still here but now I'm worried about my own job. Should I ^have told Doug's boss? I wonder. Maybe I

(continued on next page)

should ~~handle~~ have handled things differently last week. The company should never ~~has~~ have employed this man.

Deduction in the Past

CHECK POINT

if it was possible that something happened

CHART CHECK 1

T

CHART CHECK 2

could

EXPRESS CHECK

have carved, might have

2. a	4. c	6. b
3. f	5. d	

2. They must have been
3. They may have
4. He might not have been
5. He must have

2. could not have built
3. had to have got
4. can't have known
5. could have carved
6. (could have) transported
7. might have been
8. may have lived
9. must have had

In 1927, Toribio Mexta Xesspe of Peru must ~~be~~ have been very surprised to see lines in the shapes of huge animals on the ground below his aeroplane. Created by the ancient Nazca culture, these forms are too big to recognise from the ground. However, from about 200 m in the air, the giant forms take shape. Without aeroplanes, how could an ancient culture ~~had~~ have made them? What purpose could they have had? Author Erich von Däniken believes that the drawings might have ~~mark~~ marked a landing strip for the spacecraft of astronauts from another planet. Archaeologists, however, now believe that the ancient Nazcan civilisation might ~~develop~~ have developed flight. They could ^have built hot-air balloons and ~~design~~ designed the pictures from the air.

SelfTest VII

(Total = 100 points. Each item = 4 points.)

SECTION ONE

1. **C**	5. **A**	8. **B**	11. **B**
2. **B**	6. **B**	9. **D**	12. **A**
3. **B**	7. **D**	10. **A**	13. **C**
4. **B**			

SECTION TWO

(Correct answers are in brackets.)

14. **C** (must not have known)
15. **D** (leave)
16. **C** (have)
17. **B** (looked)
18. **A** (have got to)
19. **C** (can't)
20. **A** (must not)
21. **B** (have)
22. **A** (may OR might OR could)
23. **A** (was OR is)
24. **C** (have to)
25. **A** (should have)

Adjectives and Adverbs

CHECK POINT

warm and cosy

CHART CHECK

F, F, T

***EXPRESS* CHECK**

A: slow, slowly
B: slow, slow

Students! Are you looking for a special place to live? Come to 140 Grant Street, Flat 4B. This flat is absolutely perfect for two serious students who are looking for a quiet neighbourhood, just 15 minutes from campus. This lovely flat is in a new building. It is a short walk to the bus stop. The bus goes directly into town. At night the bus hardly makes any stops at all. You can walk safely through the wonderful parks on your way home. The rent is very affordable. Call us on 020 551 6116. Don't delay! This flat will go fast.

2. terribly disappointed
3. surprisingly easy
4. extremely safe
5. incredibly fast
6. awfully slowly
7. very clearly
8. unusually loud
9. exceptionally pleasant

2. large
3. beautifully
4. happily
5. busy
6. nice
7. quiet
8. hardly
9. nice
10. shy
11. good

Some adverts for flats are so ~~funnily~~ funny! One advert described a place as '~~warmly~~ warm and cosy'. It was really hot and cramped but the owner insisted that it suited me ~~perfect~~ perfectly. I was trying very ~~hardly~~ hard not to laugh while he was describing it so I had to leave quickly. Another place I saw was supposed to be 'nice and ~~neatly~~ neat'. What a mess!! I left that place very ~~fastly~~ fast, too. I'm not asking for the moon! I only want a small place in a clean building with friendly neighbours. I'm looking at another place tomorrow. The advert says, 'Clean and bright. Small but convenient flat on lovely, ~~quietly~~ quiet street.' I wonder what that really means!

UNIT 41 Participles used as Adjectives

CHECK *POINT*

F

CHART CHECK

T

***EXPRESS* CHECK**

exciting	excited
interesting	interested
frightening	frightened
amusing	amused
tiring	tired

In some countries, people who are interested in meeting others turn for help to personal ads in newspapers and magazines, and online. A surprising number of busy people view these ads as a practical way of increasing their social circle. 'I've tried hard to meet people on my own,' said one satisfied customer. 'I was new to the town and wanted to make friends fast. The personals provided me with a quick way of meeting many interesting people in a short period of time.' Others are not so impressed. 'I think it's kind of depressing when people need to resort to placing ads to make friends,' observed one man. 'A friend of mine tried the ads several times and was really disappointed with the results. It's just not personal enough.'

2. puzzled
3. puzzling
4. interesting
5. interested
6. fascinating
7. fascinated
8. disappointed
9. surprising
10. surprised

3

2. boring
3. interested
4. fascinating
5. amused
6. horrifying
7. confusing
8. depressed
9. amazed
10. amusing
11. exhausted

Just got home. I'm ~~disappointing~~ disappointed with the evening. At first I thought Jake was an ~~interested~~ interesting guy but tonight I felt somewhat bored with his company. We saw a very ~~entertained~~ entertaining film but Jake didn't like it. In fact, it seems like we have completely different tastes in things. After the film, I tried to make conversation but all I really wanted was to go home. So, I told him I was ~~exhausting~~ exhausted and didn't want to get home late. If he asks me out again – I'm not ~~interesting~~ interested. Trying to meet people can be very ~~frustrated~~ frustrating.

UNIT 42 Adjectives and Adverbs: *As . . . as . . .*

CHECK POINT

cycling speed, control of bike

CHART CHECK

as, an adjective or an adverb

EXPRESS CHECK

A: as expensive as, as well as **B:** as good as

So you were riding the trails this weekend and you hit the dirt. Now your clothes look as bad as your bike. Never mind. They'll look as good as new next weekend. We checked out three major brands of powder and we can tell you which ones clean best and which ones don't remove trail stains as effectively as others.

Overall, Brite and Kleen aren't as expensive as Trend but they didn't perform as well, either. However, they were almost as good in particular categories. Trend removed both mud and grass stains effectively. Brite removed mud just as effectively as Trend but it didn't remove grass stains as well. Kleen was effective on grass stains but not on mud. Brite cleaned clothes as thoroughly as Kleen but again, Brite and Kleen weren't as good as Trend in this category. On the other hand, Brite came out on top in brightening. Colours washed in Kleen and Trend just didn't look as bright as the ones washed in Brite.

1. **b.** aren't as wide
   c. aren't as hard
2. **a.** cleans as effectively as
   b. isn't as unfriendly
   c. sounds as exciting as
   d. expresses . . . as clearly as
3. **a.** was as noisy as
   b. (will) pedal as quietly as

2. doesn't stop as slowly as
3. isn't as expensive as
4. doesn't feel as comfortable as
5. isn't as cheap
6. rides as comfortably as
7. handles as well as
8. don't handle as well as
9. are as easy to change as
10. (are) not as easy to change as

RE: Not as many bruises!

Inexperienced cyclists should try the South Trail at Deerstalker Park. The scenery is just as ~~beautifully~~ beautiful but its cycle track isn't as unfriendly ~~than~~ as the North Trail's. The slopes aren't as steep and you won't fall as ~~frequent~~ frequently because there aren't as many rocks. It isn't as short ~~like~~ [as] the North so you'll still get a good ride and you won't feel as discouraged at the end of the day.

Re: The (expensive) new Trax

Does anyone have any experience of this bike? I tested it in the shop car park and I'm not impressed. My old Trax changes gear ~~as just~~ [just as] easily and it handles as smoothly, too. Of course, it's not as ~~lightly~~ [light] but then it doesn't cost £999, either.

Unit 43 Adjectives: Comparatives

CHECK POINT

different from the old restaurant

CHART CHECK

F, T

EXPRESS CHECK

more . . . than

2. T 3. T 4. F 5. F

2. less expensive than OR isn't more expensive than
3. hotter . . . spicier than
4. more fattening than
5. healthier OR more healthy than

2. better . . . better, the better . . . the more expensive
3. the more popular . . . the slower
4. worse . . . worse, The smokier . . . the worse
5. The more crowded . . . the noisier
6. The bigger . . . the harder
7. more . . . more delicious, heavier . . . heavier

Pete's Place has just reopened under new management. The dining room looks bigger, ~~more bright~~ [brighter] and prettier ~~as~~ [than] the old one. Although the food isn't better, it *is* just as good. The menu is more varied and less ~~expensiver~~ [expensive]. Try one of their pasta dishes. You won't find a ~~more~~ fresher tomato sauce in town. And leave room for dessert. They just keep getting ~~good~~ [better] and better.

The waiters are friendly but not able to handle large numbers of people – the [more] crowded the restaurant, the slower the service. At dinnertime, the queues outside this popular eatery are getting longer and ~~more long~~ [longer]. Try lunchtime for a quieter and ~~relaxeder~~ [more relaxed] meal.

Unit 44 Adjectives: Superlatives

CHECK POINT

special

CHART CHECK

the, *-est*, *most* or *least*

EXPRESS CHECK

(the) nicest
(the) most beautiful
(the) warmest
(the) happiest

You are the best mother in the whole wide world. You are the cleverest, the brightest and the funniest of all mums I've ever known. You are the nicest mum I've ever had. You are the most wonderful and definitely the least impatient. No mum in the whole wide world is better than you. You are the greatest mother of all. I love you very very much! Happy Mother's Day!

2. the happiest . . . of my life
3. the best . . . in the school
4. the coldest . . . of the year
5. the nicest . . . in our family OR of all
6. the wisest . . . of all OR in our family

2. is the most unusual gift.
3. is the least practical gift.
4. is the smallest gift.
5. is the biggest gift.
6. is the most expensive gift.
7. is the funniest gift.

4 Ramadan is the ~~seriousest~~ most serious time in Muslim culture. During Ramadan, we do not eat from dawn to sunset. This is difficult for everyone but teenagers have the hardest time. Immediately after Ramadan is the Eid al-Fitr. This holiday lasts three days and it's the ~~most~~ happiest time of the year. On the morning of Eid, my family gets up early and goes to the mosque. After we've greeted our neighbours by saying 'Eid Mubarek' (Happy Eid), we go home. We eat the ~~big~~ biggest breakfast you have ever seen. Our parents give us presents, usually new clothes and money. One year, Eid came round the time I graduated from university. That year, I got the most beautiful clothes and the ~~fatter~~ fattest envelope of money of all the children in my family. Eid Mela is part of Eid al-Fitr. On that day, we all go to a big park. Last year at Eid Mela, I had the ~~better~~ best time of my life. I met my old friends and we all ate junk food and showed off our new clothes.

UNIT 45 Adverbs: Comparatives and Superlatives

CHECK POINT

T

CHART CHECK

more or *less*, *the*

EXPRESS CHECK

than, the best

In the first football game of the season, Norwich beat Stowe, 6 goals to 3. The Stowe team played a truly fantastic game but its defence is still weak. Norwich defended the ball much more aggressively than the Stowe team did. Of course, Joe Jackson helped win the game for Norwich. Norwich's star player was back on the field today, to the delight of his many fans. He was badly hurt at the end of last season but he has recovered quickly. Although he didn't play as well as people expected, he still handled the ball like the old Joe. He certainly handled it the most skilfully of anyone on the team. He controlled the ball the best, kicked the ball the furthest and ran the fastest of any of the players on either team. He played hard and helped the Norwich team look good. In fact, the harder he played, the better Norwich performed. Watch Joe this season.

And watch Stowe, too. They've got a new coach and they're training more seriously this year. I think we'll see them play better and better as the season progresses.

2. better
3. faster
4. less
5. more rapidly
6. harder
7. the most slowly OR the slowest
8. the most clearly
9. the longest
10. more quickly than
11. more thoroughly than

3. the most slowly OR the slowest
4. more slowly than OR slower than
5. the furthest
6. faster than
7. higher than
8. the best
9. the worst

Last night, I watched the Lakers and the Bulls. Both teams played more aggressively [than] I've ever seen them. In fact, they played the ~~better~~ best of any game I've watched this season. In the first half, Michael Jordan sprained his left ankle and Shaquille O'Neal was out of the game because of fouls. But they still didn't start the second half any slower ~~that~~ than the first. With Jordan out, Kukoc scored the most ~~frequenter~~ frequently of any player. He's been playing ~~more and more~~ better and better as the season goes on. In fact, [the] more he plays, the better he gets. The Bulls won by 97 to 88. The Lakers seemed to get tired at the end. They played ~~little~~ less and less consistently as the game went on.

SelfTest

(Total = 100 points. Each item = 4 points.)

SECTION ONE

1. C
2. A
3. A
4. B
5. C
6. A
7. B
8. C
9. D
10. B
11. A
12. C
13. D
14. B

SECTION TWO

(Correct answers are in brackets.)

15. C (the less)
16. C (of)
17. B (amazed)
18. C (sweet)
19. B (harder)
20. A (run as quickly)
21. B (*delete* more)
22. B (most)
23. C (more)
24. C (disgusting)
25. B (hot)

UNIT 46 Gerunds: Subject and Object

CHECK POINT

exercise

CHART CHECK

–ing, not

EXPRESS CHECK

A: Drinking
B: drinking
A: not drinking

Swimming is great exercise. It's healthy, fun and relaxing. Because swimming is a 'low-impact' sport, most people enjoy participating in this activity without fear of injury to their bones or muscles. Jogging, which is a 'high-impact' activity, can at times be harmful. I know this from personal experience. Last year while I was jogging, I injured my right knee. I don't go jogging any more. After a painful month of recovery, I stopped running and switched to water sports. I'm now considering joining a swimming team and competing in races.

2. Eating
3. Not drinking
4. increasing
5. doing
6. swimming
7. walking, running
8. not going

2. has stopped smoking
3. go swimming
4. denied OR denies smoking
5. admits being
6. is avoiding eating
7. is considering taking
8. can't stand being

Ways I Can Give Up ~~Smoke~~ Smoking Cigarettes

Pick an exact date to give up ~~smoke~~ smoking.

Stop smoking completely. (~~Cut~~ Cutting down is harder than stopping all at once.)

Avoid ~~to be~~ being around other smokers (at least at the beginning).

(continued on next page)

Start exercising daily. ~~To exercise~~ Exercising can reduce stress.

~~No~~ Not drinking coffee may help, too.

Imagine ~~been~~ being a non-smoker. Positive mental images can help.

Consider ~~to join~~ joining a support group.

Don't delay ~~to ask~~ asking for help. Call Dr Burns right away!

Keep trying and don't give up!

UNIT 47 Gerunds after Prepositions

CHECK POINT

F, T, F

CHART CHECK

a preposition, the gerund

EXPRESS CHECK

A: joining
B: joining

We, the members of the Student Council, would like to share with you the thoughts and concerns of the general student body. As you probably know, many students are complaining about life on campus. We are interested **in meeting** with you to discuss our ideas **for dealing** with these complaints.

We know that you are tired **of hearing** students complain and that you are not used **to working** with the Student Council. However, if you really believe **in giving** new ideas a try, we hope you will think **about speaking** to our representatives. We look forward **to hearing** from you soon.

2. in listening
3. about going, about driving
4. to staying, relaxing
5. for having
6. at learning
7. on coming
8. on reading, (on) going

2. We can make changes by telling the Dean about our concerns.
3. The Dean can help by listening to our concerns.
4. In some cases, students just complain instead of making suggestions for improvements.
5. Students get annoyed with some lecturers for coming late to class.
6. You can improve your work by studying regularly.

I have been attending Bedford College for a year. I'm very happy about ~~study~~ studying here. At first, it was quite hard getting used to ~~speak~~ speaking English all the time but now I feel very comfortable about ~~communicate~~ communicating in my second language.

I've just joined an international student group and I'm excited ~~with~~ about meeting new people. The summer break is coming and a few of us are planning on ~~do~~ doing some travelling together. Before ~~to join~~ joining this group, I used to spend holidays alone.

Please write. I look forward to ~~hear~~ hearing from you!

UNIT 48 Infinitives after Certain Verbs

CHECK POINT

Megan thinks 'Impatient' should consider his proposal more.

CHART CHECK

T, T, F

EXPRESS CHECK

I want to write to Annie.

1 Slow down! You appear to be in too much of a hurry. You've only known this person for a month and yet you've asked her to marry you! What's the big rush? *Why* can't you afford to wait? Are you afraid that if she gets to know you better, she may decide not to tie the knot? I agree with your girlfriend. You need to consider things more carefully. You can't expect her (or yourself) to make such an important decision so quickly. If you don't want to regret a hasty decision, I advise you both to get to know each other better before you hurry to the altar.

2. attempt to find
3. warns single people not to leave
4. urges them to use
5. fail to plan
6. plan to fail
7. wish to meet
8. Ask two friends to read
9. Choose to participate
10. advises people not to feel
11. wants to be

(Answers may vary slightly.)

2. would like Tom to call her at 10:00.
3. reminded Emily to buy petrol (today).
4. invited Mel to join them for coffee.
5. agreed to be home by 10:30.
6. forgot to go to the two o'clock staff meeting.
7. encouraged her to try again.
8. needs to use the car (tonight).

Annie advised me ~~joining~~ *to join* a club or take a class and I finally did it! I decided ^*to* become a member of the Outdoor Adventure Club and I went to my first meeting last night. I'm really excited about it. The club is planning a hiking trip next weekend. I definitely want to go rafting in the spring. At first I didn't want ~~signing~~ *to sign* up but the leader was so nice. He urged me ~~to not~~ *not to* miss this trip so I put my name on the list. After the meeting, a group of people asked me to go out with them. We went to a coffee shop and talked for hours. Well, I hoped ^*to* make some friends when I joined this club but I didn't expect everyone ~~being~~ *to be* so friendly. I'm glad Annie persuaded me ~~no~~ *not* to give up.

UNIT 49 Infinitives after Certain Adjectives and Nouns

CHECK POINT

Finding good chips is difficult.

CHART CHECK

to + base form of verb
certain nouns and adjectives

EXPRESS CHECK

It's convenient to eat fast food.
That's a low price to pay.

1 Please take a few (N) minutes to complete this questionnaire about fast-food restaurants. Tick (✓) all the answers that apply to you.

1. How often are you (A) likely to eat at a fast-food restaurant?
   - ❐ 1–3 times a week
   - ❐ 4–6 times a week
   - ❐ more than 6 times a week
   - ❐ never
2. In your opinion, fast food is:
   - ❐ (A) good to eat
   - ❐ a (N) way to save time
   - ❐ (A) fun to order occasionally
   - ❐ (A) unhealthy to have every day
3. Which statement best describes your feelings about the cost of fast food?
   - ❐ It's a high (N) price to pay for convenience.
   - ❐ You get a lot for not very much money.
4. Is it a good (N) idea to include healthy choices in fast-food menus?
   - ❐ Yes ❐ No

2. delighted to find
3. way to go
4. fun to eat
5. pleasure to eat
6. mistake to bring
7. outrageous to see
8. good to eat
9. essential to have
10. difficult to go

3

2. ready to cry
3. willing to work
4. hard to wake up
5. surprised to hear
6. eager to get
7. important to keep
8. time to decide
9. chance to show
10. easy to find

4

Tonight I made the decision ~~asked~~ to ask Chris to do the night shift. I really thought she was going to be glad ~~for getting~~ to get the offer. She has her own rent ^to pay and I know it's hard for ~~she~~ her to meet all her expenses. Looks like she was the wrong person ~~I asked~~ to ask! The problem was, she wasn't willing to ~~said~~ say Yes or No and I'm afraid I got a little impatient. It was wrong of me to threaten to ask Steve. I could tell that she was pretty upset to hear that. I'll think about giving her the promotion anyway. She deserves ~~getting~~ to get a break.

UNIT 50 Infinitives with *Too* and *Enough*

CHECK POINT

F, T

CHART CHECK

too

EXPRESS CHECK

She's too young to vote.
We're old enough to work.

2. b
3. a
4. b
5. a
6. b

2. It's too far for us to get home by ten. **G**
3. I'm mature enough to take care of myself. **G**
4. It's too dangerous to drive at night. **M**
5. I worry too much to give you permission. **M**
6. You aren't experienced enough to drive that far. **M**

2. cheap enough for us to afford
3. large enough to hold
4. too good for me to miss
5. big enough to share
6. too late to stop
7. old enough to stay
8. early enough to come
9. too slow to beat
10. safe enough to drive

4

The Phish concert was brilliant! Now I'm too excited ~~for sleeping~~ to sleep. That Mike Gordon really can sing. My voice isn't ~~enough good~~ good enough to sing in the shower! After the concert, we were really hungry but it was ~~to~~ too late to go for pizza. I HATE going home so early! It's too weird ^to understand. My friend Stan works and has to pay taxes but the law says he's too young ~~for staying~~ to stay out past 10:00! That's crazy enough to make me want to scream. That reminds me. I sure hope my mother changes her mind soon enough for ~~I~~ me to buy a ticket to the Hampton concert. They sell out very quickly. Why doesn't she think I'm mature ^enough to drive fifty miles? I'll have to do it sometime! Well, I'd better try to get some sleep or I'll be too tired ~~too~~ to get up in the morning.

Infinitives of Purpose

CHECK POINT

an address book, a dictionary, a note pad

CHART CHECK

T, F

EXPRESS CHECK

I use a PDA to store addresses.
I set my alarm clock in order not to oversleep.

JUDITH: It's 5:00. Aren't you going home?
LEE: No. I'm staying late to finish this report. What about you? Are you going straight home?
JUDITH: No. I'm going to stop at the bank to get some cash. Then I'm going to Lacy's to take advantage of the sale they're having.
LEE: Oh, what are you going to get?
JUDITH: One of those new PDAs they're advertising. I've been looking for something to help me with my work.
LEE: What's wrong with a normal organiser?
JUDITH: Nothing. But sometimes I need to surf the net.
LEE: What else are you going to use it for?
JUDITH: Oh, to store important names and phone numbers and to do my accounts.
LEE: What did we do before they invented all these electronic gadgets?
JUDITH: We made a lot of mistakes!

2. To withdraw £100.
3. To invite Rick and Tina to dinner.
4. To buy milk and eggs.
5. To buy batteries.
6. To check her tyres.

First Part:
3. f 4. a 5. d 6. e 7. c

Second Part:
3. She went to the shop (in order) to buy some pasta.
4. We disconnected our phone in order not to get any phone calls.
5. He turned on the radio (in order) to listen to the news.
6. He didn't tell me he was ill in order not to worry me.
7. She bought a PDA (in order) to store information.

I went to the dentist ~~for getting~~ to get my teeth cleaned today. While I was waiting, I used my PDA to study for the test. Then I used it to ~~helps~~ help me pronounce 'dental floss' for my appointment. After the dentist, I checked my calendar and saw 'Rick and Tina, dinner, 7:30'. I should use it in order ~~to not~~ not to forget appointments! Luckily, my recipes are already on the PDA so I used them ~~for making~~ to make a quick shopping list. When I got home, there was a note on my door – 'Call PLB'. I checked the PDA dictionary to find 'PLB'. The 'plumber' wanted to come in order ^to fix the taps! Rick, Tina and I played with the PDA all evening. You can programme it ~~for~~ to play computer games, too. I don't know how I lived without it!

Gerunds and Infinitives

CHECK POINT

F, T

CHART CHECK

T, F, T

EXPRESS CHECK

to go, Going, talking, to talk OR talking

2. T 3. F 4. T 5. F 6. F 7. T 8. T

2. to trust
3. to forget, to remember
4. going
5. to remember
6. to turn off
7. Playing, improving

(Answers may vary slightly.)

2. meeting Natalie last year (at Richard's party).
3. spilling juice (on the sofa).
4. listening to jazz OR listening to Richard play jazz (at his parties).
5. going dancing (some time), to go (dancing some time).
6. to give Joan a lift home, to stay a little longer.

What a great party! I usually avoid ~~to go~~ going to parties because it's such a problem for me to remember people's names. I'm so glad I read that book about ~~improve~~ improving your memory. The author suggested ~~to do~~ doing exercises and they really helped. I stopped ~~to worry~~ worrying about what people would think of me and I tried to pay attention to what people were saying. As a result, I had a great time! I'm even planning ~~going~~ to go OR on going dancing with this guy Leo next week.

I have an English test tomorrow so I should stop writing now and start studying. The book even had some good tips about ~~study~~ studying for an exam. I hope I remember ~~using~~ to use some of them tonight!

Make, Let, Help and Get

CHECK POINT

T

CHART CHECK

T, F, T

EXPRESS CHECK

A: to correct
B: to correct
A: stay
B: stay

2. F 3. T 4. F 5. T 6. F

2

2. made 3. let 4. help 5. got 6. made 7. got 8. let 9. let 10. help 11. made

3

2. made her work
3. didn't let them use
4. got him to clean
5. got him to pronounce
6. didn't let her speak
7. didn't make her leave

4

When I was a teenager, my parents never let me ~~to play~~ play until I had finished all my homework. They even made me ~~helping~~ help my brothers with their homework before I could have any fun. On the one hand, they certainly got me ^to learn a lot. On the other hand, they made me ~~became~~ become too serious. I wish they had let me ~~to~~ have a little more fun. When I become a parent, I want to get my child ~~learns~~ to learn about responsibility but also I would want to let ~~he or she~~ him or her have fun. As Ben Franklin said, 'All work and no play makes Jack a dull boy'. I want to avoid that mistake.

SelfTest IX

(Total = 100 points. Each item = 4 points.)

SECTION ONE

1. **C** 2. **A** 3. **A** 4. **B** 5. **D** 6. **C** 7. **A** 8. **C**

9. **A**
10. **D**
11. **B**
12. **C**
13. **B**
14. **A**

SECTION TWO

(Correct answers are in brackets.)

15. **B** (to change)
16. **C** (trying)
17. **B** (finding)
18. **A** (Getting)
19. **B** (not to)
20. **C** (old enough)
21. **D** (to seeing)
22. **A** (to buy)
23. **D** (not to fall)
24. **B** (watching)
25. **D** (to do)

UNIT 54 Phrasal Verbs: Inseparable

CHECK POINT

in a restaurant

CHART CHECK

before the direct object

EXPRESS CHECK

We ran into Bob.
He was eating out.

1 Ho Da-ming's new restaurant was failing. His customers rarely (came back). Why? Mr Ho contacted a feng shui consultant to (find out). Feng shui (meaning 'wind and water') is the ancient Chinese art of placing things in your surroundings. According to this art, the arrangement of furniture, doors and windows affects our health, wealth and happiness. Mr Ho was concerned about his business but he didn't (give up). Following the consultant's advice, he remodelled and redecorated his restaurant. His actions (paid off). Soon business (picked up) and Mr Ho became rich. 'It was the best decision I ever made,' he says happily. And he isn't alone in his enthusiasm. Feng shui (has caught on) with modern architects and homeowners everywhere.

1. has caught on
2. came back
3. paid off
4. find out
5. give up
6. picked up

2

2. back
3. up
4. up
5. up
6. out
7. up
8. out

3

2. turned out
3. come up with
4. went up
5. carried on
6. give up
7. paid off
8. go back

4

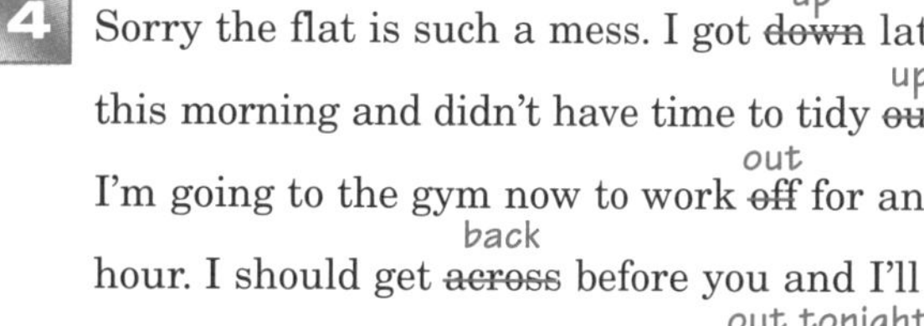

Sorry the flat is such a mess. I got ~~down~~ up late this morning and didn't have time to tidy ~~out~~ up. I'm going to the gym now to work ~~off~~ out for an hour. I should get ~~across~~ back before you and I'll clean up then. How about eating ~~tonight out~~ out tonight? Afterwards, we can get together with some of the guys and maybe see a film. Or maybe we'll come ~~over~~ up with a better idea.

P.S. I ran ~~Tom into~~ into Tom at the library. He'll drop ~~off~~ by to see you later.

UNIT 55 Phrasal Verbs: Separable

CHECK POINT

George is getting an idea for an invention.

CHART CHECK

Direct objects that are nouns can go before or after the particle.

EXPRESS CHECK

dreamt up that idea OR dreamt that idea up, dream it up

1 Did you know that two university dropouts thought up (the idea) of the first personal computer? What's more, they put (it) together in a garage. Inventions don't have to come out of fancy laboratories. Average people in classrooms, kitchens and home workshops often dream up (new and useful ideas).

The ability to think of something new seems like magic to many people but in fact anyone can develop the qualities of an inventor. First, inventors follow their curiosity. The Swiss inventor George de Mestral wanted to find out (the reason) it was so hard to remove burrs from his dog's coat. His answer led to the idea for Velcro®, now used to fasten everything from trainers to space suits. Second, inventors use imagination to put (things) together in new ways. Walter Morrison watched two men throwing a pan to each other and thought up (the Frisbee®), one of the most popular toys in the world. Perhaps most important, successful inventors don't give up. They continuously look up (information) about their ideas and try (new designs) out until they succeed.

2

2. set up
3. filled . . . up
4. keep . . . away
5. picked up
6. paid . . . back
7. carry out
8. brought about

3

2. figure it out
3. fill them in
4. handed it out
5. point it out
6. hand them in

4

3 May I dreamt ~~over~~ up a really good idea – a jar of paint with an applicator like the kind used for shoe polish. It can be used to touch ~~on~~ up spots on a wall when people don't want to paint a whole room. I know a manufacturer. I'll call ~~up him~~ him up and order several types so I can try them ~~in~~ out.

3 July I filled ~~down~~ in an application for a patent and posted it yesterday. I'll be able to set up a strong and convincing demonstration of the product ~~up~~ soon.

30 August I demonstrated the product at an exhibition for decorators. I wanted to point out that it's very clean to use so I put on white gloves for the demonstration. It went very well.

SelfTest X

(Total = 100 points. Each item = 4 points.)

SECTION ONE

1. **A**
2. **C**
3. **A**
4. **B**
5. **D**
6. **C**
7. **D**
8. **D**
9. **D**
10. **A**
11. **A**
12. **C**
13. **B**

SECTION TWO

(Correct answers are in brackets.)

14. **A** (it over)
15. **D** (up)
16. **D** (off the bus)
17. **D** (back)
18. **B** (get on the bus)
19. **D** (off)
20. **A** (up)
21. **B** (her up)
22. **D** (wake you up)
23. **D** (pick some stamps up for him . . . OR pick up some stamps for him . . .)
24. **D** (Meg into)
25. **B** (along / on)

UNIT 56 Nouns

CHECK POINT

Ra II

CHART CHECK 1

F

CHART CHECK 2

T, F

EXPRESS CHECK

were, was

Was Columbus really the first explorer to discover the Americas? Thor Heyerdahl didn't think so. He believed that ancient people were able to build boats that could cross oceans. To test his ideas, he decided to build a copy of the reed boats that were pictured in ancient paintings and sail across the Atlantic from North Africa to Barbados. Heyerdahl's team also copied ancient Middle Eastern pots and filled them with food for their journey – dried fish, honey, oil, eggs, nuts and fresh fruit. Ra, the expedition's boat, carried an international group including a Norwegian, an Egyptian, an Italian, a Mexican and a Chadian.

The first trip failed but everyone survived and wanted to try again. Departing on 17 May 1970, under the flag of the United Nations, Ra II crossed the Atlantic in 57 days. The expedition proved that ancient civilisations had the skill to reach the Americas long before Columbus.

3. Food
4. is
5. are
6. ideas
7. beans
8. rice
9. Potatoes
10. are
11. trips
12. vegetables
13. are
14. Is
15. equipment
16. batteries
17. news
18. stops
19. clothing
20. cold
21. bothers
22. bags

3

27 October I've been on the ~~canary~~ Canary Islands for three days now. I'll start back home when the ~~weathers are~~ weather is better. I was so surprised when I picked up my ~~posts~~ post today. My family sent me some birthday presents. My ~~Birthday~~ birthday is the 31st. I won't open the presents until then.

29 ~~october~~ October I think the weather is getting worse. I heard ~~thunders~~ thunder today but there wasn't any rain. I stayed in bed with my cat, Typhoon. Every time it thundered, ~~typhoon~~ Typhoon and I snuggled up closer under the covers. I started reading a ~~Novel~~ novel, 'Brave New World'.

30 October I left the Canary Islands today – just like ~~columbus~~ Columbus. There's a strong wind and plenty of sunshine now. I travelled 500 ~~Kilometres~~ kilometres.

31 October I'm 21 today! To celebrate, I drank some ~~coffees~~ coffee for breakfast and I opened my presents. I got some perfume and pretty silver ~~jewelleries~~ jewellery.

1 November The ~~electricities are~~ electricity is very low. I'd better not use much until I get near ~~plymouth~~ Plymouth. I'll need the radio then. It rained today so I collected ~~waters~~ water for cooking.

UNIT 57 Quantifiers

CHECK POINT

a good supply of chocolate

CHART CHECK

T, F, T, T

EXPRESS CHECK

A: many **B:** much

Are you ready? Many people don't realise that some natural disasters such as

(continued on next page)

earthquakes can strike with little warning. It may take several days for assistance to reach you. Prepare your disaster kit in advance! Here are a few tips.

- Water may be unsafe to drink. Store enough water for several days. Each person needs five litres per day for cooking and washing.
- You will also need food for several days. It's a good idea to store a lot of tinned meat, fruit, vegetables and milk. However, also include several kinds of high-energy food, such as peanut butter and raisins. And don't forget some 'comfort food' like biscuits and chocolate!
- If you haven't got any electricity, you might not have any heat, either. Keep some blankets, sleeping bags and extra clothes for everyone.
- Prepare a first aid kit with some pain killers, several sizes of plaster and an antiseptic.
- The cash machines might not be working. Have you got any cash? You shouldn't keep much money in the house but you should have a lot of small notes and a few larger notes, too.

2

2. any
3. Several
4. a great deal of
5. a lot of
6. Many
7. a few
8. many
9. few
10. Some
11. a little
12. a few

3

1. b. a few
   c. many
   d. much
   e. a few
   f. a little
2. a. a little
   b. few
   c. a few
   d. little
   e. a few

4

We had a big storm last week and we lost the electricity for ^a few days. Once I got over being scared, it was fun – a bit like camping. We've got an electric heater so we didn't have ~~some~~ any heat. We slept in our sleeping bags around the fireplace. We used up ~~many~~ a lot of wood! Mum baked some bread in a pan in the fireplace. She had to try several times but it was really good when it worked. We ate it with ^a little butter. The first night, we had ~~much~~ a lot of problems working out what to do. It got dark early and we only had a ~~little~~ few candles – and no TV! Jane is five and she was really frightened until we made hot chocolate over the fire. Finally, everybody took turns telling stories. I found out that Dad knows a lot ^of good stories.

UNIT 58 Articles: Indefinite and Definite

CHECK POINT

There is only one Earth.

CHART CHECK

F, T, T

EXPRESS CHECK

a, The

1

2. a
3. b
4. b
5. b
6. a

2

2. an
3. a
4. an
5. an
6. the
7. a
8. the
9. the
10. the
11. a
12. the
13. the

3

2. the
3. the
4. a
5. a
6. the
7. The
8. an, the
9. the

4 Once there was a plumber called Mario. ~~Plumber~~ The plumber had a beautiful girlfriend. One day, ~~a~~ an ape fell in love with the girlfriend and kidnapped her. The plumber chased the ape to rescue his girlfriend.

This simple tale became *Donkey Kong*, ~~a~~ the first video game with a story. It was invented by Sigeru Matsimoto, ~~a~~ an artist with Nintendo, Inc. Matsimoto loved ~~the~~ video games but he wanted to make them more interesting. He liked fairy tales so he invented a story similar to a famous fairy tale. ~~Story~~ The story was an immediate success and Nintendo followed it with *The Mario Brothers*. The rest is video game history.

UNIT 59 Ø (No Article) and *The*

CHECK POINT

the little girl

CHART CHECK

indefinite
plural

EXPRESS CHECK

A: the **B:** Ø **A:** the **B:** Ø

Do you enjoy theme parks? Tomorrow, Blare Gardens will open to the public for the first time. The park features a wide variety of rides and games that will appeal to both adults and children. And, of course, a theme park would not be complete without candy floss and hot dogs. The food at Blare Gardens promises to be very good. Come early, bring the whole family and be sure to stay for the firework display that takes place just after the sun sets. So check it out! You won't be disappointed.

2. Ø	10. Ø	18. the
3. Ø	11. Ø	19. Ø
4. Ø	12. Ø	20. the
5. the	13. the	21. Ø
6. Ø	14. the	22. Ø
7. Ø	15. the	23. Ø
8. Ø	16. Ø	24. the
9. Ø	17. the	25. the

2. the	7. Ø	11. The
3. the	8. Ø	12. the
4. Ø	9. Ø	13. the
5. the	10. Ø	14. the
6. Ø		

4 Hi! Blare Gardens is excellent! This is the best holiday we've ever been on! I love the rides here. I've been on ~~the~~ roller coasters before but nothing is like the one they've got here! And the food is great, too. I usually don't eat ~~the~~ hot dogs but the hot dogs here are great. So is the pizza. Do you like ~~the~~ theme parks? If so, you've got to get your family to come. The only problem is the crowds here. People have to queue to get into *everything* – even the toilets! See you soon.

UNIT 60 Reflexive Pronouns and Reciprocal Pronouns

CHECK POINT

F

CHART CHECK

F, T

EXPRESS CHECK

A: yourself
B: myself

1

Self-talk is the way we explain a problem to ourselves. It can affect the way we feel and the way we behave. Tom and Sara, for example, both lost their jobs when their company laid off a lot of people. Sara kept herself fit and spent time with friends. Tom gained ten pounds and spent all his time by himself. They were both unemployed so the situation itself can't explain why they acted so differently from each other. The main difference was the way Tom and Sara explained the problem to themselves. Sara believed that she herself could change her situation. Tom saw himself as helpless. Later, everyone got their jobs back. When they all talked to one another back at the office, Tom grumbled, 'They must have been desperate.' Sara replied, 'They finally realised they need us!'

2

1. yourselves
2. herself, ourselves
3. myself, yourself
4. each other, yourself
5. itself, ourselves
6. yourselves, one another

3

2. yourselves
3. themselves
4. himself
5. yourselves
6. each other OR one another
7. myself
8. myself
9. yourselves
10. myself

4

I forgot to call Sam on his birthday. I reminded ~~me~~ myself all day and I still forgot! I felt terrible. My sister, Anna, said, 'Don't be so hard on ~~yourselves~~ yourself,' but I didn't believe her. She prides ~~her~~ herself on remembering everything. Then I read an article on self-talk. It said that people can change the way they explain problems to ~~theirselves~~ themselves. I realised that the way I talk to ~~me~~ myself is insulting – like the way our maths teacher used to talk to us. I thought, Sam and I treat each other well. He forgave ~~myself~~ me for my mistake straightaway and I forgave him for forgetting our dinner date two weeks ago. Sam and I could forgive ~~themselves~~ each other so I suppose I can forgive ~~me~~ myself.

SelfTest XI

(Total = 100 points. Each item = 4 points.)

SECTION ONE

1. **C**
2. **B**
3. **D**
4. **C**
5. **A**
6. **A**
7. **C**
8. **C**
9. **C**
10. **C**
11. **C**
12. **A**

SECTION TWO

(Correct answers are in brackets.)

13. **A** (is)
14. **C** (Christmas)
15. **B** (is starting)
16. **B** (May)
17. **D** (the)
18. **A** (*delete* A *and capitalise* Money)
19. **D** (*delete* the)
20. **B** (much time)
21. **C** (few)
22. **B** (a little)
23. **B** (one another's)
24. **B** (a little)
25. **D** (the accountant)

UNIT 61 The Passive: Overview

CHECK POINT

the number of years the magazine has existed

CHART CHECK

T, T, F

EXPRESS CHECK

were printed

1

2. A
3. P
4. A
5. P
6. P
7. A
8. P
9. A
10. P

3. Tagalog is spoken
4. is spoken by 417 million people
5. Seventy-one million people speak
6. Arabic is spoken by
7. speak English
8. Swahili is spoken OR People speak Swahili

3. is published (~~the publisher~~)
4. is read (~~readers~~)
5. have been hired by our international offices
6. were purchased (~~the company~~)
7. are used (~~our writers~~)
8. is advertised (~~advertisers~~)
9. were (or was) interviewed by *Live at Ten TV*
10. was seen by millions of viewers

Two-thirds of Bolivia's five million people [are located] ~~locate~~ in the cool western highlands known as the Altiplano. For centuries, the grain quinoa has been [grown] ~~grew~~ in the mountains. Llamas [are] bred for fur, meat and transportation. And tin, Bolivia's richest natural resource, is [mined] ~~mining~~ ~~by miners~~ in the high Andes.

The Oriente, another name for the eastern lowlands, is mostly tropical. Rice is the major food crop and cows are raised for milk. Oil is also [found] ~~find~~ there.

Although Spanish is the official language, Native American languages are still spoken ~~by people~~. Traditional textiles are woven by hand and music [is] played on reed pipes whose tone resembles the sound of the wind blowing over high plains in the Andes.

UNIT 62 The Passive with Modals

CHECK POINT

somebody should do something about Ed's snoring

CHART CHECK 1

T, F

CHART CHECK 2

a modal or an auxiliary verb

EXPRESS CHECK

A: Will . . . be prepared
B: won't, will be prepared

Space Station *Unity* will be completed within the next decade and international teams of astronauts will then be sharing close quarters for long periods of time. What can be done to improve living conditions in space? Here's what former astronauts suggest:

- **Food** It doesn't taste as good in zero gravity. Food should be made spicier to overcome those effects. International tastes must also be considered.
- **Clothing** Layered clothing could help astronauts stay comfortable. The top layer could be removed or added as temperatures vary.
- **Sleeping** Because of weightlessness, sleep is often interrupted in space. Comfortable restraints must be provided to give a sense of stability.
- **Emotional Needs** People need rest time in space just as they do on Earth. Time ought to be provided for relaxation and privacy.

2. Is . . . going to be prepared
3. (is it going to be) squeezed
4. will be prepackaged
5. can be warmed up

(continued on next page)

6. should . . . be chosen
7. has to be offered
8. could be selected
9. Will . . . be used
10. had better be attached
11. ought to be made

2. should be kept
3. ought to be improved
4. could be designed
5. can be removed
6. ought to be given
7. are going to be delivered
8. will be done
9. will be stored

4 I used the sleeping restraints last night and slept a lot better. They ought to ~~make~~ be made more comfortable, though. I felt trapped. I've just looked in the mirror. My face is puffy and my eyes are red. I'd better ~~be got~~ get on the exercise bike right away. I can be ~~misunderstanding~~ misunderstood when I look like this. Last night, Max thought I was angry with him for turning on 'Star Trek'. Actually, I love that programme. I might be given early lunch shift today. I hope they have more chilli. It's nice and spicy and the sauce can actually ~~been~~ be tasted, even at zero gravity. Some of it had better be ~~fly~~ flown in on the shuttle pretty soon or there might be some unhappy astronauts! Speaking of unhappy, last night, Katy called and told me she was planning to leave school. I think she could be ~~talk~~ talked out of it but I'm afraid I'll get angry and shout if we discuss it. I might be overheard by others. We need some privacy here!

UNIT 63 The Causative

CHECK POINT

went to a hairdresser's

CHART CHECK

F, T, F

EXPRESS CHECK

A: done
B: done, do

2. T
3. T
4. T
5. F
6. T

3. Amy had the dog groomed.
4. They are going to get the windows cleaned.
5. They had the carpets shampooed.
6. Amy is going to have her ears pierced.
7. Jake got his hair cut.
8. They are going to have food and drinks delivered.

1. OR have it shortened
2. get (OR have) it dry cleaned
3. 're getting (OR having) them cleaned OR 're going to get (OR have) them cleaned
4. 'm getting (OR having) it cut OR 'm going to get (OR have) it cut
5. get (OR have) it coloured
6. Did . . . get (OR have) it painted

The party was last night. It went really well! The house looked great. Mum and Dad had the floors polished and all the windows ~~clean~~ cleaned professionally so everything sparkled. And of course we ~~had the whole house painted~~ painted the whole house ourselves last summer. (I'll never forget *that*. It took us two weeks!) I wore my new black dress that I ~~have~~ had shortened by Jill and I ~~got cut my hair~~ got my hair cut by Colin. He did a great job. There were a lot of guests at the party. We ~~had almost fifty people invited~~ had invited OR invited almost fifty people and they almost all turned up! The food was great too. Mum made most of the main dishes herself but she had the rest of the food ~~prepare~~ prepared by a caterer. Mum and Dad hired a professional photographer so at the end of the party we all ~~took our photos~~ had our photos taken. Dad's getting them back next week. I can't wait to see them!

SelfTest XII

(Total = 100 points. Each item = 4 points.)

SECTION ONE

1. **C**
2. **D**
3. **A**
4. **B**
5. **C**
6. **B**
7. **C**
8. **B**
9. **D**
10. **B**

SECTION TWO

(Correct answers are in parentheses.)

11. **C** (by)
12. **A** (*delete* were)
13. **C** (be corrected)
14. **D** (*delete* by the printer)
15. **A** (*delete* was)
16. **D** (return)
17. **C** (them done)
18. **C** (be discussed)
19. **A** (was painted)
20. **C** (couldn't OR wasn't able to)
21. **B** (grown)
22. **D** (was working)
23. **B** (have to be replaced)
24. **C** (cleaned)
25. **A** (be made)

UNIT 64 Zero Conditionals

CHECK POINT

T

CHART CHECK

T, F, F

EXPRESS CHECK

1. b
2. c
3. a

1 If you run into problems on your journey, remember your rights as a passenger. Often the airline company is required to compensate you for delays or damages. For example, the airline provides meals and hotel rooms if a flight is unduly delayed. However, the airline owes you a lot more if it caused the delay by overbooking. This can occur especially during holidays if airlines sell more tickets than there are seats. If all the passengers actually turn up, then the flight is overbooked. Airlines usually award upgrades or additional free travel to passengers who volunteer to take a later flight. However, if no one volunteers, your flight may be delayed. In that case, the airline must repay you 100 per cent of the cost of your ticket for a delay of up to four hours on an international flight. If the delay is more than four hours, you receive 200 per cent of the cost of your ticket.

2

1. OR The best time to go to Hong Kong is November or December if you hate hot weather.
2. If you're travelling with your children, take them to Lai Chi Kok Amusement Park in Kowloon. OR Take your children to Lai Chi Kok Amusement Park in Kowloon if you're travelling with them.
3. If you need a moderately priced hotel, I suggest the Harbour View International House. OR I suggest the Harbour View International House if you need a moderately priced hotel.
4. If you like seafood, there are wonderful seafood restaurants on Lamma Island. OR There are wonderful seafood restaurants on Lamma Island if you like seafood.
5. If you're fascinated by Chinese opera, you might like the street opera in the Shanghai Street Night Market. OR You might like the street opera in the

(continued on next page)

Shanghai Street Night Market if you're fascinated by Chinese opera.
6. If you'd like to get a good view of Hong Kong, you should take the funicular to the Peak. OR You should take the funicular to the Peak if you'd like to get a good view of Hong Kong.

2. I spend a lot of time at the pool if I stay at a hotel.
3. If I stay with friends, I spend time with them.
4. It's not so nice if I get a 'Dracula' flight.
5. It's very rewarding if you don't mind hard work.
6. If you have three flatmates, you don't have trouble finding dogwalkers.
7. If a flight has an empty seat, I travel free.

What a great weekend! If Lou and Tony aren't the best hosts in the world, I ~~won't~~ don't know who is. I've invited them to London but if you live in the Bahamas, you rarely want to leave. Tomorrow at midnight, I am doing a round trip from London to Singapore. There's always a price to pay. If I get a free weekend, I always get a 'Dracula' flight afterwards. Oh, well. If I ~~won't~~ don't fall asleep, I can usually get a lot of reading done. Pat and Ken both flew to London yesterday. I hope someone can walk Frisky for me. Usually, if I~~'ll be~~'m working, one of them is off. If Frisky is alone for a long time, he ~~barked~~ barks a lot. That disturbs the neighbours. Maybe I should just leave the TV on for him. He's always very calm if the TV is on. Or maybe I'd better call Pat and ask her about her timetable. If it ~~was~~'s 6:00 p.m. here in Singapore, it's 11:00 a.m. in London.

UNIT 65 First Conditionals

CHECK POINT

F, F

CHART CHECK

the *if* clause
when the *if* clause comes first

EXPRESS CHECK

If she wins, she'll fight crime.

2. e	4. a	6. d
3. c	5. g	7. b

3. get
4. If
5. win
6. 'll take OR 'm going to take
7. If
8. am
9. 'll try OR 'm going to try
10. will . . . do OR are . . . going to do
11. if
12. lose
13. If
14. lose
15. 'll continue OR 'm going to continue
16. Unless
17. cooperate
18. won't be OR isn't going to be
19. if
20. don't elect
21. 'll be OR 'm going to be

(possible answers)
3. If I take out a student loan, I won't have to depend on my family. OR I won't have to depend on my family if I take out a student loan.
4. If I go to law school, I'll earn more money. OR I'll earn more money if I go to law school.
5. If I earn more money, I'll be able to pay back my (student) loan quickly. OR I'll be able to pay back my (student) loan quickly if I earn more money.
6. If I pay back my loan quickly, I'll be able to pay for my sister to go to university. OR I'll be able to pay for my sister to go to university if I pay back my loan quickly.

7. If I go to law school, I'll go into politics. OR I'll go into politics if I go to law school.
8. If I go into politics, I'll be able to improve life for others. OR I'll be able to improve life for others if go into politics.
9. If I go into politics, I'll get elected as an MP. OR I'll get elected as an MP if I go into politics.
10. If I get elected as an MP, I'll sit in the House of Commons. OR I'll sit in the House of Commons if I get elected as an MP.

4

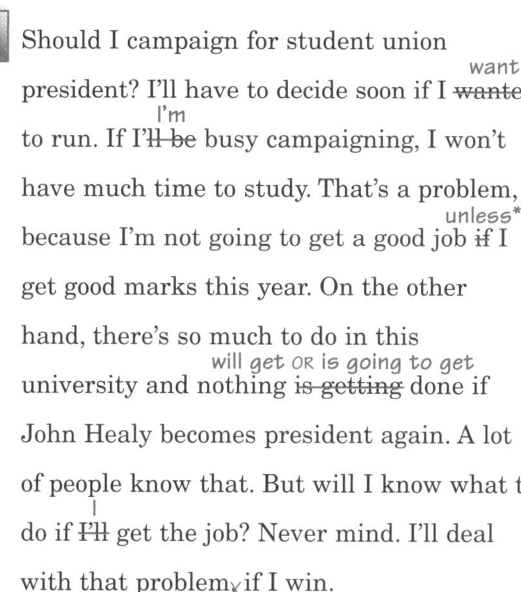
Should I campaign for student union president? I'll have to decide soon if I ~~wanted~~ want to run. If ~~I'll be~~ I'm busy campaigning, I won't have much time to study. That's a problem, because I'm not going to get a good job ~~if~~ unless* I get good marks this year. On the other hand, there's so much to do in this university and nothing ~~is getting~~ will get OR is going to get done if John Healy becomes president again. A lot of people know that. But will I know what to do if ~~I'll~~ I get the job? Never mind. I'll deal with that problem if I win.

*OR if I don't get

UNIT 66 Second Conditionals

CHECK POINT

F

CHART CHECK

F, T, F

EXPRESS CHECK

would, if, were

2. T
3. T
4. F
5. F
6. F

2. wouldn't like
3. weren't
4. couldn't identify
5. were
6. loved
7. 'd hate OR would hate
8. drove
9. 'd hate OR would hate
10. were
11. 'd hate OR would hate
12. weren't
13. might be

2. If Schroeder didn't love Beethoven, he wouldn't play his sonatas all the time.
3. If Charlie Brown had enough friends, he wouldn't feel lonely.
4. If Sally knew her teacher's name, she could send her a card.
5. If Linus weren't clever, he wouldn't find intelligent solutions to life's problems.
6. If Woodstock and Snoopy didn't have a close relationship, Woodstock wouldn't confide in Snoopy.
7. If Rerun's parents didn't refuse to let him have a dog, he wouldn't try to borrow Charlie's dog.
8. If Pigpen had enough baths, he wouldn't be filthy.

I've got to stop staying up late reading 'Peanuts'! If I weren't always so tired, I ~~will~~ would be able to stay awake in class. Whenever the teacher asks me something, I don't know what to say. Then I get really embarrassed because of that nice red-haired girl that I like. I would talk to her if I ~~wouldn't be~~ weren't so shy. My friend, Jason, says, 'If I ~~was~~ were you, I'd ask her to a party.' but I'm too afraid that if I asked her, she would ~~have said~~ say no. After school, I played football. Nobody wanted me in their team. If I ~~play~~ played better, I would get chosen sometimes. Life is hard! I can really understand that Charlie Brown character in 'Peanuts'. In fact, if I didn't laugh so hard while reading 'Peanuts', I would ~~cried~~ cry!

UNIT 67 Third Conditionals

CHECK POINT

F

CHART CHECK

the *if* clause
the *if* clause comes first

EXPRESS CHECK

would have studied

1

2. F
3. T
4. F
5. F
6. T

2

2. could (OR would) have gone OR would have been able to go, hadn't lost
3. could have gone, hadn't become
4. wouldn't have known, hadn't shown
5. hadn't helped, could have gone
6. might not have led, hadn't married
7. would have been, hadn't lived

3

(Answers may vary slightly)

1. OR Clarence would have had more self-confidence if he had been a first-class angel.
2. If George hadn't been unhappy about his business, he wouldn't have shouted at his daughter on Christmas Eve. OR George wouldn't have shouted at his daughter on Christmas Eve if he hadn't been unhappy about his business.
3. Poor people couldn't have bought (OR wouldn't have been able to buy) houses if George's business hadn't lent them money. OR If George's business hadn't lent them money, poor people couldn't have bought (OR wouldn't have been able to buy) houses.
4. If Mr Potter had been able to trick George, George would have sold Potter the business. OR George would have sold Mr Potter the business if Potter had been able to trick George.
5. If George's Uncle Billy hadn't lost £8,000, George wouldn't have got into trouble with the law. OR George wouldn't have got into trouble with the law if his Uncle Billy hadn't lost £8,000.
6. If George's friends had known about his troubles, they would have helped him straightaway. OR George's friends would have helped him straightaway if they had known about his troubles.
7. If George's friends hadn't collected money for him, he would have gone to prison. OR George would have gone to prison if his friends hadn't collected money for him.

4

It's funny how things work out sometimes. If George ~~hasn't~~ hadn't wanted to jump off that bridge on Christmas Eve, I might never have ~~getting~~ got an important job like saving him. And if he hadn't been so stubborn, I would never ~~had~~ have thought of the idea of showing him life in Bedford Falls without him. One of the saddest things was seeing all those people who didn't have homes. If George ~~gave up~~ had given up and sold his business to Mr Potter, then Potter would have rented run-down flats to all those people. But because of George, they now have good homes. By the time we were finished, George realised he really had a wonderful life. In fact, he ~~will~~ would have gone to prison happily, if his friends hadn't given him the money he needed. Well, luckily they helped him out and he didn't go to prison. And I got my wings and became a first-class angel!

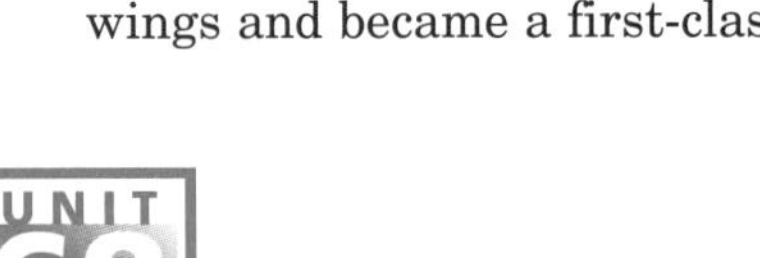

UNIT 68 *Wish:* Present and Past

CHECK POINT

that day

CHART CHECK 1

the past simple

CHART CHECK 2

the past perfect

EXPRESS CHECK

knew, had known

2. T
3. F
4. F
5. T
6. T

2. would go away
3. had
4. didn't have to deal
5. could entertain
6. could have invited OR had been able to invite
7. had known

2. I wish my husband would ask for a pay rise.
3. I wish we'd saved some money last month.
4. I wish my boyfriend weren't unfit OR were fit.
5. I wish I weren't too old to go back to school.
6. I wish I could stop (OR were able to stop) smoking.
7. I wish my son would phone me.
8. I wish my parents had understood me.

Today, I said to Dr Grimes, 'I wish there ~~was~~ were a way to spend more time with my boyfriend but we're both too busy.' He just said, 'If wishes were horses, beggars would ride.' That's an easy thing to say but I wish I ~~understand~~ understood its meaning. Maybe it means that wishing won't solve problems. Well, that's why I went to see him!!! I wish he ~~will tell~~ had told me what to do right then and there but he refused. Speaking of wishful thinking, I wish Mark and I could ~~have spent~~ spend the weekend together next week. My exams are over but he's got to fly to Paris for his job. If wishes were horses, I'd ride one to Paris. Hey! Mark is always saying, 'I wish you would come with me sometimes.' I suppose I can go with him to Paris. Dr Grimes must have meant that I can solve my own problems. Now I wish I ~~haven't~~ hadn't been so rude to him.

SelfTest XIII

(Total = 100 points. Each item = 4 points.)

SECTION ONE

1. **C**
2. **B**
3. **A**
4. **A**
5. **D**
6. **C**
7. **B**
8. **C**
9. **C**
10. **D**
11. **A**
12. **D**

SECTION TWO

(Correct answers are in brackets.)

13. **D** (seen)
14. **B** (could have)
15. **B** (won't)
16. **B** (have)
17. **B** (were)
18. **A** (could have)
19. **A** ('ll eat OR are going to eat)
20. **D** (were)
21. **C** (*delete* will)
22. **C** (*delete comma*)
23. **A** (had)
24. **C** (get)
25. **C** (could)

UNIT 69 Relative Clauses with Subject Relative Pronouns

CHECK POINT

F

CHART CHECK

nouns

in the middle of the main clause, after the main clause

EXPRESS CHECK

That's the man who works in the cafeteria.

1 Almost everyone has friends but ideas about friendship vary from person to person. For some, a friend is someone who chats with you on the internet. For others, a friend is a person who has known you all your life – someone whose family knows you, too. Others only use the term for someone who knows your innermost secrets. Although different people emphasise different aspects of friendship, there is one element which is always present and that is the element of choice. We may not be able to select our families, our colleagues or even the people that take the bus with us but we *can* choose our friends. As anthropologist Margaret Mead once said, 'A friend is someone who chooses and is chosen.' It is this freedom of choice that makes friendship such a special relationship.

1. OR that have
2. who (OR that) have
3. that (OR which) are
4. who (OR that) faces
5. that (OR which) is
6. whose . . . are
7. whose . . . include
8. that (OR which) appears OR appeared OR has appeared
9. who (OR that) doesn't read OR hasn't read

2. Mexico City is an exciting city that (OR which) attracts a lot of tourists.
3. Steph has a brother whose name is Eric.
4. He works for a magazine that (OR which) is very popular in Mexico.
5. Eric writes a column that (OR which) deals with relationships.
6. An article that (OR which) discussed friendships won a prize.
7. A person who (OR that) has a lot of friends is lucky.

A writer once said that friends are born, not made. This means that we automatically become friends with people who ~~they~~ are compatible with us. I don't agree with this writer. Last summer, I made friends with some people who~~'s~~ [were OR are] completely different from me.

In July, I went to Barcelona to study Spanish for a month. In our group, there was a teacher ~~which~~ [who OR that] was much older than I am. We became really good friends. In my first week, I had a problem which was getting me down. Barcelona is a city ~~who~~ [that OR which] has a lot of distractions. As a result, I went out all the time and I stopped going to my classes. Bob helped me get back into my studies. After the trip, I kept writing to Bob. He always writes stories that ~~is~~ [are] interesting and encouraging. Next summer, he's leading another trip ~~what~~ [that OR which] sounds interesting. I hope I can go.

UNIT 70 Adjective Clauses with Object Relative Pronouns or *When* and *Where*

CHECK POINT

T

CHART CHECK

the subject of the relative clause

F

EXPRESS CHECK

I watch all the films that he directs.

1 At the age of nine, Eva Hoffman left Poland with her family. She was old enough to know what she was losing: Krakow, a city (that) she loved as one loves a person, the sun-baked villages (where) they had spent summer holidays and the conversations and escapades with her friends. Disconnected from a city (where) life was lived intensely, her father was overwhelmed by the transition to Canada. Eva lost the parent (whom) she had watched in lively conversation with friends in Krakow cafés. And nothing could replace her friendship with the boy (whose) home she visited daily, and (whom) she assumed she would marry one day. Worst of all, however, she missed her language. For years, she felt no connection to the English name of anything (that) she felt was important. *Lost in Translation: A Life in a New Language* (Penguin, 1989) tells how Eva came to terms with her new identity and language. It's a story (that) readers will find fascinating and moving.

1. OR that
3. who OR whom OR that
4. stayed OR were staying
5. which
6. had
7. that OR which
8. wanted
9. that OR which
10. have experienced
11. where OR in which
12. were
13. who OR whom OR that
14. take care of

1. OR . . . in which I grew up . . .
2. The house that (OR which) we lived in was beautiful. OR The house in which we lived . . .
3. Emily and I shared a room where (OR in which) we spent a lot of time playing.
4. I had a good friend who (OR whom OR that) I went to school with. OR . . . with whom I went to school.
5. I took piano lessons from a woman who (OR whom OR that) I met at my mum's office.
6. I remember one summer when the whole family went to the seaside.
7. Those were good times that (OR which) I'll always remember.

Tai Dong is the small city in southeastern Taiwan ~~which~~ where OR in which OR that . . . in I grew up. My family moved there from Taipei the summer I was born. The house in which I grew up ~~in~~* is on a main street in Tai Dong. My father sold tea and my mother had a food stand in our front courtyard, where she sold omelettes early in the morning. A customer who I always chatted with ~~him~~ had a son my age. We were best friends. A cousin ~~who his~~ whose family I visited every summer lived with us. He was an apprentice ~~which~~ who OR whom OR that my father was teaching the tea business to. On the first floor of our house, we had a huge kitchen ~~in where~~ in which OR where we all gathered for dinner. It was a noisy place. The bedrooms where the family slept ~~was~~ were upstairs. My two brothers slept in one bedroom. I slept in one ~~what~~ that OR which I shared with my older sister. My younger sister shared a bedroom with another cousin ~~which~~ who OR whom OR that my family had adopted.

*OR the house which (OR that) I grew up in

Relative Clauses: Defining and Non-Defining

 **POINT**

F

CHART CHECK

non-defining
T

EXPRESS CHECK

It was the computer ~~which~~ we saw at E-Lectronics.

2. T
3. T
4. F
5. F
6. F

ˌtech • no • ˈpho • bia *(noun)* a fear ~~that~~ some people have about using technology

If you have it, you're one of the 85 per cent of people ~~that~~ this new 'disease' has struck. Maybe you've bought a phone on which you can programme 99 numbers – but you can't turn it on. Or perhaps you have just read that your new CD player**,** which you have finally learnt how to use**,** will soon be replaced by DVD**,** which you had never even heard of.

Some experts say that things have just become too complex. William Staples**,** who wrote a book on the electronic age**,** tried to help a friend who had just bought a new stereo. The stereo**,** which worked before**,** wasn't working any more. 'On the front of the stereo, there were literally twenty buttons,' says Staples. Donald Norman**,** who has written about the effects of technology on people**,** blames the designers of these devices, not the people who use them. 'The best way to cure technophobia is to cure the reasons that cause it – that is, to design things ~~that~~ people can use and design things that won't break,' claims Norman. Michael Dyrenfurth**,** who is a university lecturer**,** believes we cause our own problems by buying technology ~~that~~ we just don't need. 'Do we really need electric toothbrushes?' he asks. According to Williams, important technology ~~that~~ we can't afford to run away from actually exists. To prosper, we need to overcome our technophobia and learn to use it.

2. My new mobile, which I bought only a month ago, has become a necessary part of life.
3. I remember the day when I was afraid to use my new computer.
4. Now, there are psychologists who (OR that) help technophobes use technology.
5. Dr Michelle Weil, who is a psychologist, wrote a book about 'technostress'.
6. I work in an office where (OR in which) the software changes frequently.
7. A lot of people who work in my office suffer from technostress.
8. Some people dream of a job they can do without technology.

I've just read a book called *Technostress***,** which was written by Dr Michelle Weil. Her co-author was Dr Larry Rosen, ~~that~~ who is her husband and also a psychologist. According to the authors, everybody feels stress about technology. Our mobiles and pagers, ~~that~~ which we buy for emergencies, soon invade our privacy. Just because they can, people contact us at places where we are relaxing.

Another problem is having to learn too much, too fast. Technological changes, which used to come one at a time, now overwhelm us. Dr Weil suggests dealing with technostress using tips from her latest book, which can be purchased via her website.

SelfTest 

(Total = 100 points. Each item = 4 points.)

SECTION ONE

1. **B**	**4.** **C**	**7.** **B**	**10.** **C**
2. **A**	**5.** **B**	**8.** **C**	**11.** **B**
3. **D**	**6.** **B**	**9.** **B**	**12.** **C**

SECTION TWO

(Correct answers are in parentheses.)

13. **C** (where)
14. **A** (who)
15. **C** (*delete* he)
16. **B** (whose)
17. **B** (that OR which OR *delete* what)
18. **D** (*delete* it)
19. **C** (discuss)
20. **B** (which)
21. **A** (who)
22. **C** (in which OR where)
23. **B** (with whom)
24. **C** (when OR that OR *delete* which)
25. **A** (whose)

 Direct and Indirect Speech: Imperatives

CHECK POINT

'Don't eat a heavy meal before bed.'

CHART CHECK

direct speech
T

EXPRESS CHECK

to go, Don't work

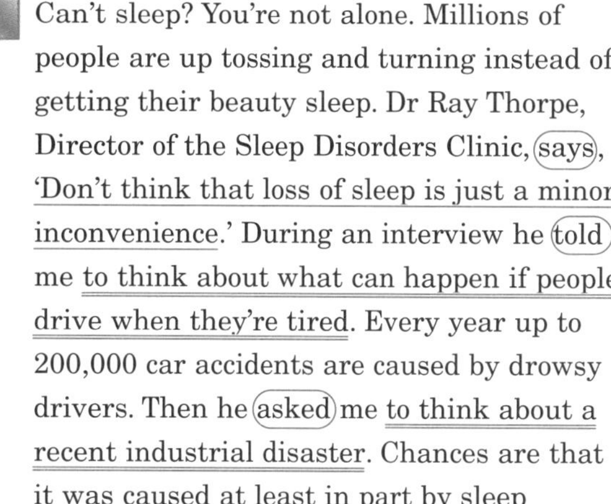

Can't sleep? You're not alone. Millions of people are up tossing and turning instead of getting their beauty sleep. Dr Ray Thorpe, Director of the Sleep Disorders Clinic, says, 'Don't think that loss of sleep is just a minor inconvenience.' During an interview he told me to think about what can happen if people drive when they're tired. Every year up to 200,000 car accidents are caused by drowsy drivers. Then he asked me to think about a recent industrial disaster. Chances are that it was caused at least in part by sleep deprivation.

Being an insomniac myself, I asked Dr Thorpe for some suggestions. He told me to stop drinking coffee. He said to have a warm glass of milk instead. 'A lot of old-fashioned remedies work. Have a high-carbohydrate snack like a banana before you go to bed,' he said. But he advises patients not to eat a heavy meal before turning in for the night. What about exercise? 'Regular wexercise helps but don't exercise too close to bedtime,' he suggested. Finally, he told me not to despair. 'Don't worry about not sleeping. It's the worst thing to do,' he said. I don't know. After thinking about those industrial accidents, I doubt I'll be able to sleep at all!

2. that night	**7.** there
3. told	**8.** explain
4. my	**9.** not to
5. to watch	**10.** the next
6. said	**11.** to get

1. OR He said to pull over and have a brief nap.
2. OR He told them not to have a long nap.
3. He told them (OR He said) to sing to themselves.
4. He told them (OR He said) to tune their radios to an annoying station.
5. He told them (OR He said) not to eat while driving.

(continued on next page)

6. He told them (OR He said) to open their windows.
7. He told them (OR He said) to let cold air in.
8. He told them (OR He said) to be careful when they stop their cars.
9. He told them (OR He said) not to stop in a deserted place.
10. He told them (OR He said) not to drink and drive.

In class today, John read one of his stories. It was wonderful. After the lesson, the teacher asked me *to* read a story in class next week. However, I begged her ~~no~~ *not* to ask me next week because I'm having trouble getting ideas. She ~~said~~ *told* me not to worry and she said to wait for two weeks. Then I talked to John and I asked him *to* tell me the source of ~~your~~ *his* ideas. He said that they came from his dreams and he told me *to* keep a dream diary for ideas. He invited me to read some of his diary. It was very interesting so I asked him to give me some tips on remembering dreams. He said ~~getting~~ *to get* a good night's sleep because the longer dreams come after a long period of sleep. He also ~~tell~~ *told* me to keep my diary by the bed and to write as soon as I wake up. He said ~~to no~~ *not to* move from the sleeping position. He also told me ~~to don't~~ *not to* think about the day at first. (If you think about your day, you might forget your dreams.) Most important – every night he tells himself ~~that~~ to remember his dreams ~~tomorrow~~ *the next* morning.

UNIT 73 Indirect Speech: Statements (1)

CHECK POINT

'It looks great on you!'

CHART CHECK

the punctuation
the verb tense in the statement
pronouns in the statement

EXPRESS CHECK

told, was

At 9:00, Rick Thompson's bank phoned and said that his credit card payment was late. 'The cheque is in the post,' Rick replied quickly. At 11:45, Rick left for a 12:00 meeting. Arriving late, Rick told his client that traffic had been bad. That evening, Rick's fiancée wore a new dress. Rick hated it. 'It looks great on you,' he said.

Three lies in one day! Yet Rick is just an ordinary guy. Each time, he told himself that sometimes the truth causes too many problems. He told himself that his fiancée was happy with her purchase. Why should he hurt her feelings?

Is telling lies a new trend? The majority of people in a recent survey said that people were more honest ten years ago. Nevertheless, lying wasn't really born yesterday. In the eighteenth century, the French philosopher Vauvenargues was right about lying when he wrote, 'All men are born truthful and die liars.'

2. has
3. told
4. that
5. had
6. she
7. had earned
8. had lied
9. was leaving
10. had fired

2. Lisa said (that) she had just heard about a job at a scientific research company.
3. Ben said (that) he had got a B. Sc. in Biochemistry from London.
4. Lisa told him (that) they wanted someone with some experience as a programmer.
5. Ben told her (that) he worked as a programmer for Data Systems in Basingstoke.
6. Lisa said (that) they didn't want a recent graduate.
7. Ben told her (that) he had got his degree four years ago OR before.
8. Lisa said (that) it sounded like the right job for him.

Once, when I was a teenager, I went to my aunt's house. She collected pottery and when I got there, she ~~said~~ told me that she ~~wants~~ wanted to show me a new bowl. She told ^me* she ~~has~~ had just bought it. It was beautiful. When she went to answer the door, I picked up the bowl. It slipped out of my hands and smashed to pieces on the floor. When my aunt came back, I screamed and said ~~what~~ that the cat had just broken ~~your~~ her new bowl. My aunt looked at me in a funny way and told me that it ~~isn't~~ wasn't important. I couldn't sleep that night, and the next morning, I rang my aunt and confessed that I ~~have~~ had broken her bowl. She said ~~I~~ she had known that all along. I promised that I ~~am~~ was going to buy her a new one. We still laugh about it now.

*OR She ~~told~~ said she . . .

UNIT 74 Indirect Speech: Statements (2)

CHECK POINT

'It will be windy.'

CHART CHECK

ought to, might, should have

EXPRESS CHECK

Jim said that he might move soon.

2. 'The wind may reach 170 miles per hour.'
3. 'There will be more rain tomorrow.'
4. 'You should try to leave the area.'
5. 'We can expect a lot of damage.'

2. They said (that) it was going to pass north of there.
3. They said (that) it might become a tropical storm when it landed there.
4. They said (that) they had had to close some bridges the day before because of high tides.
5. They said (that) they wouldn't restore the electricity until today.
6. They said (that) the schools there might be closed for a while.
7. They said (that) they ought to use bottled water for a few days.

2. He said (that) it was true, and (that) they would probably become more frequent.
3. He said (that) the planet might be getting warmer, and (that) that could cause more severe storms.
4. He said (that) the emergency services should have arrived much more quickly.
5. He said (that) the new satellites would help. He said (that) if we (OR they) didn't have them, we (OR they) wouldn't be able to warn people.

We had some excitement here because of the hurricane last week. Jim's mother called just before the storm. She said she ~~is~~ was listening to the weather report and that she was worried about us. She told Jim that if

(continued on next page)

~~you two~~ we weren't so stubborn, we ~~will~~ would pack up and leave immediately. Jim's father told us how to get ready for the storm. He said we should ~~have~~ put tape on our hotel windows ~~tonight~~ that night and that we ought to fill the bath with water. He also told Jim that we should buy a lot of batteries before the storm ~~strikes today.~~ struck that day. My friend Sue called. She said that her place was too close to the coast and that she couldn't stay ~~here~~ there. She told me ~~I~~ she wanted to stay with me and Jim. She said she should ^have called us sooner. I told her she should come ~~now~~ then. Then we listened to the weather forecast and the weather forecaster said that the storm ~~is~~ was going to go out to sea. He said it ~~won't~~ wouldn't strike this area at all!

UNIT 75 Indirect Questions

CHECK POINT

'Why are you still single?'

CHART CHECK 1

F, T

CHART CHECK 2

F, T

EXPRESS CHECK

why he had left his job.

1 A few weeks ago, Melissa Morrow had a stress interview, one which featured tough, tricky questions and negative evaluations. First, the interviewer asked why she couldn't work under pressure. Before she could answer, he asked who had written her application for her. Melissa was shocked but she handled herself very well. She asked the interviewer whether he was going to ask her any serious questions. Then she left.

Companies sometimes conduct stress interviews to see how candidates handle pressure. Suppose, for example, that there is an accident in a nuclear power plant. The plant's public relations officer must remain calm when reporters ask how the accident could have happened. Be aware, however, that in some countries, like the United States, certain questions are not allowed unless they are directly related to the job. If your interviewer asks how old you are, you can refuse to answer. The interviewer also should not ask whether you are married or how much money you owe. If you think a question is inappropriate, ask how it relates to the job. If it doesn't relate to it, you don't have to answer.

Items ticked: 2, 3, 5

2

2. He asked when the interview was.
3. He asked where the company was.
4. He asked if (OR whether) she needed directions.
5. He asked how long it took to get there.
6. He asked if (OR whether) she was going to drive.
7. He asked who was going to interview her.
8. He asked when they would let her know.

3

3. Pete asked if (OR whether) she was going for interviews with other companies.
4. Claire asked what her responsibilities would be.
5. Claire asked how job performance was rewarded.
6. Pete asked what her starting salary at her last job had been OR had been at her last job.
7. Pete asked if (OR whether) she had got on well with her last employer.
8. Claire asked if (OR whether) they (OR he) employed many women.

4 I did some stress questioning in my interview with Miles Denton this morning. I asked Mr Denton why ~~couldn't he~~ he couldn't work under pressure. I also asked him why ~~did~~ his supervisor ~~dislike~~ disliked him. Finally, I enquired when he would leave our company~~?~~. Mr Denton answered my questions calmly and he had some excellent questions of his own. He asked ~~,~~ if we expected changes to the job~~?~~. He also wanted to know how often ~~do~~* we evaluate employees. I was impressed when he asked why ~~did I decide~~ I had decided to join this company. I think we should employ him.

*OR how often we evaluated

UNIT 76 Embedded Questions

CHECK POINT

Should we leave a tip?
Is the service included?

CHART CHECK

F, T

EXPRESS CHECK

A: ? **B: .**

1 **Read this if . . .**

you've ever wanted to know exactly how to tip.
you've ever cancelled a restaurant booking because you didn't know whether to tip or not.
you've ever forgotten to tip or not realised that you were supposed to tip.
you've ever left a small tip and then wondered if it should have been bigger.
you've ever left a large tip and then wondered if you needed to tip at all.
you've ever been uncertain whether the tip is included in the bill.
you've ever wondered why you should tip.
you've new to the United Kingdom and you're not sure who to tip.

2

2. how to tell if the tip is included in the bill.
3. why waiters in Iceland refused my tips?
4. how much to tip airport porters.
5. who expects a tip and who doesn't.
6. I should tip my ski instructor.
7. tipping is still illegal there.
8. to tip anyway.

3

2. how much to tip (OR how much we should tip) the taxi driver?
3. where the Smithsonian Museum is?
4. where we can buy (OR where to buy) metro tickets.
5. we could rent a car and drive?
6. what they put in the sauce.

4 When you live in a foreign country, even a small occasion can be an adventure! Before my date with James tonight, I didn't even know what ~~should I~~ I should OR to wear! Jeans? A dress? John's Grill isn't a smart restaurant but it was James's birthday and I wanted to make it a big occasion. Alison was very helpful, as always. I knew how to get to John's Grill but I didn't know how long it was going to take to get there~~?~~. I left at 6:00, which should have given me plenty of time, but when I got off the bus, I wasn't sure ~~if~~ whether to

(continued on next page)

turn left or right. I asked a police officer where ~~was John's~~ John's was and I was only a few minutes late. I had planned to take James out for a drink afterwards but I couldn't remember how ~~I~~ to find the place Alison had suggested and James has been here even less time than me. Anyway, when we got the bill, I was wondering whether to tip or ~~no~~ not. I had to ask James ~~did he know~~ if he knew. Fortunately, he had read a great book called *Tips on Tipping* so he told me to leave about 15 per cent.

SelfTest 

(Total = 100 points. Each item = 4 points.)

SECTION ONE

1. **D**
2. **A**
3. **B**
4. **C**
5. **A**
6. **C**
7. **C**
8. **A**
9. **C**
10. **D**

SECTION TWO

(Correct answers are in brackets.)

11. **A** (told OR said to)
12. **D** (.)
13. **D** (then)
14. **D** (was coming)
15. **D** (there)
16. **B** (whether or not OR if)
17. **A** (whether)
18. **D** (might have stopped)
19. **D** (it costs)
20. **C** (runs)
21. **D** (?)
22. **D** (, ')
23. **B** (if you could)
24. **C** (not to)
25. **B** (I could)

Index

International Study Centre
Queen Margaret University College
Edinburgh EH12 8TS